D0076984

MARKETING APOCALYPSE

Is marketing in crisis? Some commentators have contended that marketing principles no longer appear relevant to the 'real world' of marketing managers. The foremost figures in the field are marketing's most outspoken critics rather than disseminators of the marketing message. Indeed, a number of noted academic authorities have announced nothing less than 'the end of marketing'.

While such apocalyptic sentiments are very much in keeping with our degraded, postmodern, pre-millennial times, the present volume of essays examines the extent to which the end of marketing *is* nigh. The authors explore the present state of marketing scholarship and put forward a variety of visions of marketing for the twenty-first century. Ranging from narratology to feminism, these prophesies are always enlightening, often provocative and occasionally outrageous. *Marketing Apocalypse* is required reading for anyone interested in the future of marketing.

Stephen Brown is Professor of Retailing at the University of Ulster, **Jim Bell** is Senior Lecturer in Marketing at the University of Ulster and **David Carson** is Professor of Marketing at the University of Ulster.

ROUTLEDGE ADVANCES IN MANAGEMENT AND BUSINESS STUDIES

1 MIDDLE MANAGERS IN EUROPE
Yves Frédéric Livian and John G. Burgoyne

2 MARKETING APOCALYPSE
Eschatology, Escapology and the Illusion of the End
Edited by Stephen Brown, Jim Bell and David Carson

Marc Chagall, *Isaiah Prophesying the Apocalypse* (1956)

MARKETING APOCALYPSE

Eschatology, escapology and the illusion of the end

Edited by Stephen Brown, Jim Bell and David Carson

London and New York

First published 1996
by Routledge
11 New Fetter Lane, London EC4P 4EE

Simultaneously published in the USA and Canada
by Routledge
28 West 35th Street, New York, NY 10001

Typeset in Garamond by
Datix International Limited, Bungay, Suffolk
Printed and bound in Great Britain by
Biddles Ltd, Guildford and Kings Lynn

British Library Cataloguing in Publication Data
A catalogue record for this book is available from the British Library

Library of Congress Cataloging in Publication Data
Marketing apocalypse: eschatology, escapology and the illusion of the end / edited by Stephen Brown, Jim Bell and David Carson.
p. cm.
Includes bibliographical references and index.
1. Marketing – Forecasting. 2. Twenty-first century – Forecasts.
I. Brown, Stephen, II. Bell, Jim, III. Carson, David
HF5415. 122.M393
658.8 – dc20 96–7572
CIP
ISBN 0–415–14822–7

THE SHALLOW MEN

This is the way marketing ends
This is the way marketing ends
This is the way marketing ends
Not with a bang but an olufsen
Not with a break but a kit-kat
Not with a coke but a smile

CONTENTS

FIGURES

TABLES

CONTRIBUTORS

Russell W. Belk is the N. Eldon Tanner Professor in the David Eccles School of Business at the University of Utah, USA. His research focus is on the meaning and importance of possessions in our lives. He is a Fellow and past president of the Association for Consumer Research and has published more than 200 papers, videos, and books about consumer research.

Jim Bell is a Senior Lecturer in International Marketing at the University of Ulster, Jordanstown, Northern Ireland. His research interests lie in the areas of small firm internationalisation and government export promotion policy.

Stephen Brown is Professor of Retailing at the University of Ulster, Coleraine, Northern Ireland. He has written widely on marketing theory and thought. His most recent book, *Postmodern Marketing*, was published by Routledge in 1995 and he is currently working on a sequel, imaginatively titled *Postmodern Marketing Two*.

Douglas Brownlie teaches and researches in marketing subjects in the Department of Marketing at the University of Stirling, Scotland. Before going there, he did much the same sort of thing at the University of Strathclyde, the University of Glasgow and University College, Cork. It is rumoured that he once had a background in engineering and marketing. He vaguely remembers working in the steel industry, but finds working in the education industry more challenging and fulfilling, if not as materially rewarding. In his current position, he hopes to practice his reading abilities, as well as having time to write.

Neil Buttimer was educated at University College, Cork, the Dublin Institute for Advanced Studies, and Harvard University, from which he holds a doctorate in Celtic Studies. His current research concentrates on literature and society in Early Ireland and on pre-famine Gaelic Ireland.

David Carson is Professor of Marketing at the University of Ulster, Jordanstown, Northern Ireland. His research interests lie in marketing for SMEs and marketing in service industries, particularly in travel and tourism. He has published widely in both of these areas. His recent research has focused on quality dimensions in marketing. He has extensive business experience both in consultancy and directorship roles. He is also Editor of the *European Journal of Marketing* and Chairman of the Marketing Education Group, UK.

Miriam Catterall is a Lecturer in Marketing at the University of Ulster, Jordanstown, Northern Ireland. Her research interests lie in qualitative marketing research and research methods. She has considerable business experience in the market research industry.

John Desmond is a Lecturer at Heriot-Watt University, Scotland. He holds a degree in psychology and a postgraduate diploma in marketing. While at Manchester Business School, he was responsible for a team of researchers under the banner of the Centre for Business Research. The main focus of his doctoral thesis was on the way in which the institutional context shapes the development of corporate identity. His research interests are in seeking to develop theory in the area of corporate communications and in helping to develop more reflexive and critical approaches to marketing.

Benoît Heilbrunn teaches marketing and consumer behaviour at the Groupe ESC Lyon and at Université Paris III-Sorbonne. His areas of interest include philosophy, semiology, aesthetics, and their possible infusion in marketing thought. He is an editor of *European Perspectives in Consumer Behaviour*, to be published in 1996 by Prentice Hall.

Patrick Hetzel is an Associate Professor of Marketing at the Institut d'Administration des Enterprises of the University Jean Moulin Lyon 3. He received his MBA from the University of Strasbourg and his PhD in management science from the University of Lyon. He has taught marketing in twelve different countries. His research focuses on design management, consumer behaviour, postmodernity and fashion. He has published in numerous journals, books and conference proceedings (over 50 papers). He is also a board member of the French Marketing Association (AFM). In 1996, he will be a visiting professor at the Calson School of Management at the University of Minnesota in Minneapolis (USA).

Morris B. Holbrook is the W. T. Dillard Professor of Marketing in the Graduate School of Business at Columbia University, New York. His research has appeared in many different journals and has covered a wide variety of topics in marketing and consumer behaviour with a special focus on issues related to communication in general and to aesthetics, semiotics, hermeneutics, advertising, the media, art, and entertainment in particular. Recent books include *Consumer Research: Introspective Essays on the Study of Consumption*; *Daytime Television Game Shows and the Celebration of Merchandise*; *The Semiotics of Consumption* (with Elizabeth C. Hirschman); and *Postmodern Consumer Research: The Study of Consumption as Text* (also with Elizabeth C. Hirschman). The author's hobbies involve playing the piano, attending jazz and classical concerts, watching movies, going to the theatre, collecting musical recordings, taking stereographic photos, and being very kind to cats.

Donncha Kavanagh studied engineering at University College, Dublin and at the University of Missouri. He worked in construction, software development, project management and sales before joining the Department of Management and Marketing at University College, Cork. He is currently completing doctoral studies in Lancaster University under Luis Araujo and Geoff Easton. His research concentrates on industrial markets, socio-technical systems and organisation theory.

Ray Kent is a Senior Lecturer in Marketing in the Department of Marketing, University of Stirling. He has published books on the history of empirical sociology in Britain, marketing research methods and the measurement of media audiences. He is currently undertaking research on the problems of marketing communications for non-profit, voluntary organisations that offer services to sensitive groups.

Pierre McDonagh is currently a Lecturer in Marketing at the University of Stirling. Previously he was a Lecturer in Marketing at the Cardiff Business School, University of Wales, and in the School of Finance and Information at The Queen's University of Belfast. He has industrial experience in the manufacture of textiles and the newspaper industry and his main research interests lie in the study of the impact of environmental issues upon marketing communication, the professionalisation of marketing education and the enlightenment of the myth of geo-matria.

Pauline Maclaran is a Lecturer in Marketing and Business Studies at The Queen's University of Belfast, Northern Ireland. Her research interests are in small business marketing and in the development of marketing theory.

Stephanie O'Donohoe is a Lecturer in Marketing at the University of Edinburgh. She is a graduate of the College of Marketing and Design and of Trinity College, Dublin, and completed her PhD at the University of Edinburgh. Her research focuses on consumers' experiences of advertising, and the limitations of traditional advertising theory in accounting for these.

Andrea Prothero is a Lecturer in Marketing at the University of Stirling, Scotland. Prior to this, she was a Lecturer in Marketing at the Cardiff Business School, University of Wales. She is currently writing up a PhD thesis on ecological issues in marketing.

Lorna Stevens is a Research Assistant at the University of Ulster, Jordanstown, Northern Ireland. Her research interests include marketing cultures and feminist issues in marketing and consumer behaviour.

Michael J. Thomas is Professor of Marketing at Strathclyde University. During 1995 he was Chairman of the Chartered Institute of Marketing. He has published a number of books and journal articles. He is editor of *Marketing Intelligence and Planning*, and is on the editorial board of the *Journal of Marketing Management*, *Journal of the Market Research Society*, *Journal of International Marketing*, *Journal of East West Business*, *Journal of Brand Management*, *International Marketing Review*, and *Journal of Marketing Practice*. He travels abroad regularly as a visiting professor (Indiana University Graduate Business School, Georgetown University Business School, University of Tennessee, Rochester Institute of Technology, University of Malta, University of Karlstad). He believes only in the efficacy of ornithology as a means to saving souls.

PREFACE

There's an old academic parlour game, which I've just invented, where points are awarded for players' ability to identify the disciplinary source of certain distinctive words and phrases. As you might expect, most participants associate 'taboo', 'fetish' and 'totem' with social anthropology; consider 'hegemony', 'praxis' and 'agency' to be characteristically sociological; and deem 'utility', 'equilibrium' and, it goes without saying, '*ceteris paribus*', the undoubted mark of an egotist (sorry, economist). However, on all the occasions I've played this game – which is approximately never – I have yet to encounter anyone who automatically connects 'apocalypse' with marketing. Whereas words like 'new', 'improved', 'free', 'everything must go' and, disconcertingly, 'don't ask for credit as a refusal often offends', are almost always associated with Marketing, the term 'apocalypse' is usually taken to pertain to Theology, Philology, Numerology or some other disciplinary denizen of the academic netherworld.

Obscure as the relationship between 'apocalypse' and 'marketing' seems to be, at least initially, the origins of this book reside in an even more enigmatic expression. I first encountered *eschatology* (a theological term meaning the study of endings) in the late 1980s, when I was wrestling with the wheel of retailing theory, but the word did not really impinge upon my personal research agenda until a memorable day in March 1990. My colleague, Jim Bell, and I were in Germany with a group of postgraduate students, who were conducting international marketing research on behalf of several Northern Ireland companies. One morning, on our befuddled descent to breakfast – after a heavy night imbibing Jägermeister (for medicinal purposes only, you understand) – Jim looked at the breakfast buffet display, which contained numerous eco-conscious products, and said, 'You know, Stephen, I'm beginning to think that we have reached the end of marketing.'

'Marketing eschatology, Jim,' I replied and, after the resonance of what I'd said finally registered, added a rider to the effect, 'Now, *that's* got a ring to it!'

Later that morning, we took the train to Frankfurt-on-Main and, as was our wont on residentials, decided to partake of some cultural nourishment. It transpired that a Chagall retrospective had just opened at the local art gallery, which we eventually tracked down after numerous wrong turns and pit-stops to soothe our still unsettled systems. The exhibition comprised a collection of the artist's works that had been inspired by scenes and stories from The Bible (the series commenced in 1930 when Chagall was commissioned to illustrate an edition of the good book, but he returned to the theme throughout his long working life), though the small gallery was so full of people that it was difficult to enjoy the experience. After a quick circuit, we were about to leave when one particular painting literally stopped us in our tracks. Until that day, I had never really subscribed to the idea that works of art possessed overwhelming power – albeit I had often felt a tingling of the spine in the presence of great art – but when I looked at Jim and he looked at me, we both knew that something special was happening. We checked the catalogue for the name of the painting and, translating roughly from the German, discovered that it was entitled 'Isaiah Prophesying the Apocalypse'. We had received a message from God.

Our Pauline conversion, our fleeting moment of rapture, our epiphany in a hot and crowded art gallery, concluded with an agreement that somehow, somewhere, someday, we would try to do something together on marketing eschatology. Prompted by the rising tide of concern about the parlous state of marketing scholarship and thanks, in no small part, to the enthusiastic exhortations of our distinguished colleague, Professor David Carson, the idea of the Marketing Eschatology Retreat finally crystallised in mid-1994. A *call for papers*, addressed to 'marketing heretics, evangelists, supplicants, flagellants, dissenters, revivalists, charismatics, doubters, adepts, bigots – in fact anyone bar marketing Trappists' was widely circulated and, by all accounts, caused quite a stir. Interestingly, the initial reactions to the call fell into two main categories, both of which were singularly, if inadvertently, appropriate to the overall theme. On the one hand, many people responded to the call for papers with an abrupt rejoinder: 'what the hell is marketing eschatology?'. Given that the term pertains specifically to the end of the world – the Last Judgement, Doomsday, Heaven and Hell, etc. – this remark could not have been more apt. Better still was the reaction of a second group of respondents, all of whom made a witty comment about, or allusion to, 'escapology' ('sorry, but I'm tied up at the moment', 'if I could just get out of these chains, I'd love to join you', 'sure, you'll only end up tying yourselves in knots', etc. etc.). As the introductory chapter makes clear, however, one of the principal attractions of eschatology, apocalypse, millenarianism and so on is the very fact that they appear to offer a means of escape, albeit invariably chimerical. Eschatology, in effect, is a form of escapology.

Apart from the comedians and cynics, a third constituency – apostates one and all – responded creatively to our call for papers and, of these, the chosen few were invited to break bread at the Marketing Eschatology Retreat. The event was held at St Clement's, a retreat house in the hills overlooking Belfast, and over a three-day period all manner of dissident, revisionist and schismatic marketing thoughts were fomented, floated, fellated and, occasionally, fought over. In keeping with the 'we have come to bury Caesar not to praise him' tradition, the gathering concluded that while the end of marketing was not yet nigh, a new beginning was badly, indeed urgently, needed. The end of marketing may thus be illusory, at least for the time being, but this book represents a record of some of the questions asked, ideas imbibed and prophesies articulated during that remarkable weekend in late September.

In light of the illusion of the end, it is fitting that this preface should be written in the month named after Janus, the Roman god of beginnings and endings. Before you begin reading about the manifold ends of marketing, however, let me just take this opportunity to extend my heartfelt thanks to Jim Bell and David Carson, without whose heroic efforts this volume would not have come to fruition. Anne Marie Doherty, the conference administrator, was unstinting in her endeavours to make the Retreat a success, for which I am eternally grateful (well, I would be but everlasting life is unlikely in my particular case). On behalf of the co-editors, I would like to thank our respective Heads of School, Terry Cradden and Bill Clarke, for underwriting, attending and generally beating the Retreat. Acknowledgements are also due to Pat Ibbotson and Sharon Dornan, who assisted with the difficult task of assembling the final manuscript, and to everyone at Routledge, especially Alan Jarvis, Sally Close and Ceri McNicol, for their encouragement and support. Finally, I would like to express my personal debt of gratitude to the contributors, who revised and returned their chapters at very short notice, though I reckon the receipt of my threatening Christmas card helped expedite the process (well, it was the season of peace and goodwill, after all). And, last but not least, an enormous vote of thanks is in order for all the staff at St Clement's, Father Robert McGoran and Sister Claire Oligo in particular, for making our weekend so memorable.

Stephen Brown
Coleraine
January 1996

1

APOCAHOLICS ANONYMOUS

Looking back on the end of marketing

Stephen Brown, Jim Bell and David Carson

APOCALYPSE THEN

It is no exaggeration to state that the end of the world goes back to the beginning of time, or the dawn of civilisation at least. As the copious histories of the End make clear, humankind is, and always has been, addicted to the apocalypse (e.g. Rubinsky and Wiseman 1982; Friedrich 1982; Reiche 1985; Kamper and Wulf 1989; Bull 1995a). Whether it be the second coming of Christ, the ancient Norse myth of Ragnarök, the Hindu doctrine of *Kali Yuga*, the final blast of Israfil's trumpet anticipated by Islam, the well-publicised predictions of the Mayan and Aztec calenders (which disconcertingly converge on the year 2012 A.D.), or the multiplicity of secular apocalypses expounded by contemporary Jeremiahs, the idea of impending doom looms large in the human psyche. We are, so it seems, transfixed by terminal visions, mesmerised by the millennium, entranced by eschatological expectations, consumed by chiliastic conjecture and, thanks to the protection afforded by the well-lubricated prophylactic of prophesy, ever eager to embrace and fructify the end of time (McGinn 1979; Wagar 1982; Ward 1993; Campion 1994; O'Leary 1994). According to Kermode (1967: 12), indeed, the second coming was confidently expected in A.D. 195, 948, 1000, 1033, 1236, 1260, 1367, 1420, 1588 and 1666, to name but a few. The Jehovah's Witnesses *alone* have rescheduled the end of the world on nine separate occasions (1874, 1878, 1881, 1910, 1914, 1918, 1925, 1975, 1984). And Mann's (1992) recent compilation of projected terminations stretch from 1998 to 6300 A.D., though his inventory is by no means exhaustive.

Just as this seemingly insatiable human desire for *Dies Irae* has made itself felt at many different times, so too it is made manifest in many different forms (Chandler 1993; Wainwright 1993; Skinner 1994; Kumar 1995a). These range from the rivers of molten metal awaited by the followers of Zoroaster, the Stoic prophesy of universal conflagration and the ancient Egyptian god Amun's determination to return the world to its original watery state (as recorded in the *Book of the Dead* c. 2000 B.C.), to some Native Americans' belief in the Great White Beaver of the North, which is slowly gnawing its way through the tree-trunk that supports the Earth precariously above a bottomless pit. A bottomless pit also features in the principal Judeo-Christian version of the End, that recounted in the book of Revelation (Figure 1.1), alongside the appearance of the Antichrist, the Parousia (second coming), the cosmic battle of Armageddon, the one-thousand-year earthly reign of Christ, the loosing of Satan, the Last Judgement, the descent of New Jerusalem and the onset of everlasting life (or, for the contributors to this volume at least, eternal damnation).

Although comparatively few people now consider this Biblical schema to be the literal truth – the growth of Christian fundamentalism notwithstanding (Cotton 1995; Weiss 1995; *Economist* 1995) – the modern, desacralised world is not exactly short of apocalyptic surrogates. Granted, the prospect of a large-scale thermo-nuclear conflict has receded in the aftermath of the collapse of the Soviet empire, but a more than adequate substitute for the position of Public Eschatology Number One has been found in the shape of imminent ecological catastrophe – greenhouse effect, global warming, ozone layer depletion, melting ice-caps *et alia.* There are, moreover, any number of alternative end-times scenarios including overpopulation, resource depletion, famine and pestilence (AIDS in particular), earthquakes, tidal waves, incoming meteorites, alien invasions and, depending upon which scientific theory one subscribes to, the sudden implosion, or gradual running down, of the universe (Frankel 1987; Chandler 1993; Quinby 1994; Lorie 1995).

This multiplicity of imagined endings is paralleled in certain respects by terminological profusion, some would say *con*fusion. As a glance at almost any work of prophetic literature makes clear, there is a rich and resonant vocabulary associated with the End – Gog, Magog, Armageddon, Abbadon, etc. Although for most people, and the sub-editors of tabloid newspapers, the contents of this apocalexical lucky-bag are all-but interchangeable, it is necessary to stress that end-times terms are not synonymous. True, the precise definitions of words like eschatology, teleology, chiliasm, millenarianism and apocalypse are mutable, prone to disputation and, in practice, inclined to shade into each other, but they are by no means one and the same. *Eschatology*, for example, is the study of endings, the end of the world in particular, whereas *teleology* presumes that history has an 'end', in the sense of destination, culmination or purpose. Thus, it is perfectly possible to conceive of an historical destination, such as a communist or utopian state, which does not necessarily involve the end of the world. *Millenarianism* and *chiliasm*, likewise, pertain to the scriptural contention that Christ will rule for a thousand years (the millennium) prior to the final battle with Satan and the commencement of the Kingdom of God. In practice, however, the former term is often used to describe any religious or secular movement that seeks to establish an earthly paradise, or suffers from calendrically induced anxieties, and the latter is usually reserved for believers in Biblical-style millennial milieux (Friedländer 1985; Campion 1994; O'Collins 1994; Bull 1995b).

More importantly perhaps for the purposes of the present discussion, the word 'apocalypse' is widely associated with death, destruction, chaos and

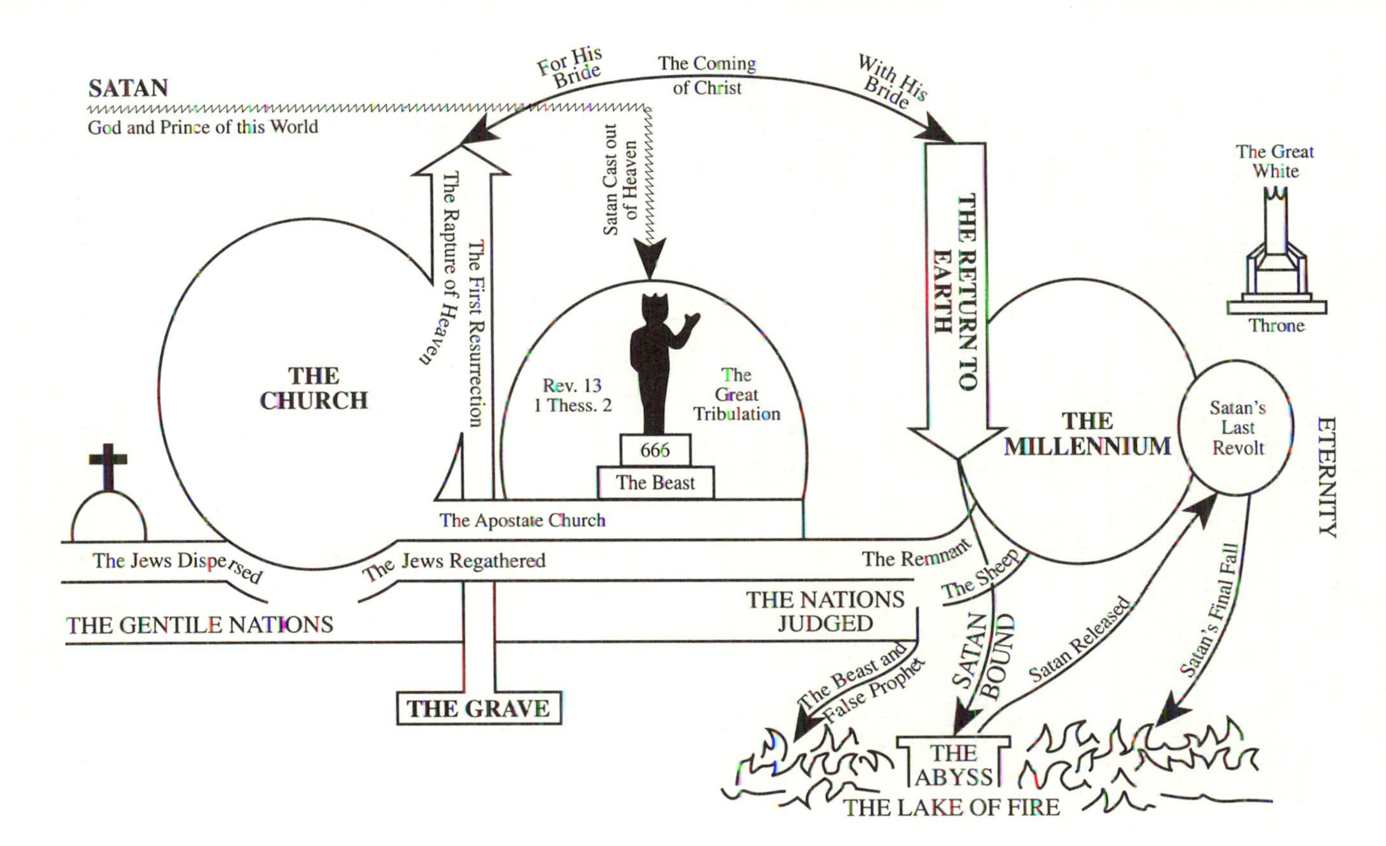

Figure 1.1 Visualising the End
Source: adapted from Boyer (1992)

carnage. It is, in effect, an umbrella or colloquial term for the signs and wonders, the murder and mayhem, the weeping, wailing and gnashing of teeth that purportedly presage the end of the world. Strictly speaking, however, apocalypse means 'revelation', the unveiling of that which is hidden, albeit in the Judeo-Christian tradition this unveiling *involves* end-times scenes of total disaster and utter devastation (Boyer 1992; Rowland 1995). More strictly still, the word apocalypse refers to a distinctive literary form which flourished in the period 100 B.C. to 200 A.D. (at least sixteen and possibly as many as seventy Judaic apocalypses have been identified). According to Collins (1984: 4), in fact, apocalypse is 'a genre of revelatory literature with a narrative framework, in which a revelation is mediated by an otherworldly being to a human recipient, disclosing a transcendent reality which is both temporal, insofar as it envisages eschatological salvation and spatial, insofar as it envisages another, supernatural world'. As a rule, furthermore, most apocalypses consist of a three-stage plot sequence variously described as 'crisis, judgement and vindication' (McGinn 1995), 'destruction, judgement and regeneration' (Fortunati 1993), and, 'decadence, end and renovation' (Kermode 1995). They also tend to be pseudonymous, in that the works are almost invariably attributed to a revered sage or leader from the past – Ezra, Enoch, Daniel and so on. In a very real sense, then, the apocalyptic author is positioned at a point beyond time and proceeds to look back, so to speak, on the end of the world (Zamora 1989; Noakes 1993; O'Leary 1994; Boyarin 1996).

Although some Biblical scholars have manned the definitional barricades, arguing that 'apocalypticism in the full sense of the word . . . existed only for about 200 years, and formed a unique mentality' (Funkenstein 1985: 57), it is generally accepted that several major variants on the eschatological theme can be discerned. Quinby (1994), for example, distinguishes between *divine*, *technological* and *ironic* apocalypses; Kermode (1985) identifies what he terms the apocalyptic *set*, *canon* and *interpretations*; and, Bull (1995b) notes *sacred* and *secular* strains of apocalypse, though the former is sub-divided into *spiritual* and *historical* varieties. Such schemata tend to differ in their taxonomic detail, but they do suggest three main types of apocalypse, the first of which is the traditional scriptural model espoused by religious fundamentalists, who anticipate the End in accordance with God's plan and foresee a heavenly home for the chosen few. The second is a desacralised version of the same, in that it expects earthly destruction by the hand of humankind itself, whether it be thermo-nuclear-induced immolation, environmental catastrophe, contagious illness or whatever. The third category, by contrast, comprises an anti-nomian, rebellious, nihilistic, essentially apocalyptic worldview that is apparent in many strands of late-twentieth-century popular culture. Described in lurid, often grotesque, detail in Parfrey's (1990) notorious compendium, *Apocalypse Culture*, this contemporary mindset is made manifest in films (*The Rapture*, *Terminator 2: Judgement Day*), books (Stephen King's *The Stand*, J.G. Ballard's *Billennium*), rock music (van Halen's *The Seventh Seal*, Def Leppard's *Armageddon It*), and, not least, the dyspeptic ruminations of the postmodern intelligentsia (see Greisman 1974; Wagar 1982; Friedländer 1985; Boyer 1992; Dellamora 1996a; Pask 1996).

APOCALYPSE WHY

If, for want of a better word, we are apocaholics, it seems reasonable to inquire into the causes of our addiction to the End. According to the celebrated literary critic, Frank Kermode (1967, 1985, 1995), it is nothing less than a fundamental correlate of the human condition. Human beings require consonance, they need things to make sense and are predisposed to impose structure on the existential flux, chaos and fragmentation of our daily lives. The idea that we live within a sequence of events between which there is no relation, pattern or progression is simply unthinkable. Hence, he argues, humankind is inclined to foist a beginning, middle and end upon time, whether it be the changing of the seasons, the mundane ticking of a clock (tick-tock being a complete narrative, as opposed to the unending succession that is tick-tick-tick), or, indeed, the entire western literary canon with its predilection for once-upon-a-times and happily-ever-afters (Abrams 1971; White 1980; Zamora 1989). Just as our individual lives have a clearly discernible plot structure, so too we 'project our existential anxieties on to history' (Campion 1994: 346), 'we hunger for ends and for crises' (Kermode 1967: 55), we can't avoid 'a certain metaphysical valorisation of human existence' (Eliade 1989: vii).

Another, closely related, interpretation of apocalypse is that it is primarily a form of *escape*. For Eliade (1989), humanity's seemingly insatiable desire for endings is actually an indication of optimism and hope, in so far as the prospect of redemption and renewal enables people to cope with the trials, tribulations and torments of their quotidian existence (see also Cohen and Taylor 1992; Rojek 1993). The fact that things seem to be getting worse provides a curious form of comfort, since it indicates that the end is at hand, that justice will be done. The hour, after all, is reputed to be darkest just before dawn (Reiche 1985; McGinn 1995). It is surely no accident, moreover, that the proponents of apocalypse invariably assume that *they* will be among the survivors, that *they* comprise the elect, that, despite the dreadful, short-term sufferings soon to be endured, rewards await *them* in the world to come (Rowland 1995; Shaffer 1995). In this respect, it is noteworthy that very few religious eschatologies assume that the end of the world is total, final or absolute (Eliade 1991). On the contrary, there is always something after the end, usually a qualitatively different – eternal, perfect, immeasurably superior – environment where, as one of the most lyrical and moving passages in the Bible makes abundantly clear, 'God shall wipe away all tears from their eyes; and there shall be no more death, neither sorrow, nor crying, neither shall there be any more pain: for the former things are passed away' (*Revelation* 21: 4).

While many may accept McGinn's (1995: 76) declaration that declarations of the end are, in the end, expressions of 'hope for a better time to come', or appreciate Kumar's (1995a: 202) assertion that, 'the apocalyptic myth holds in an uneasy but dynamic tension the elements of both terror and hope', the very idea of wishing for the end is undeniably difficult to comprehend. Indeed, as the recent case of the Solar Temple cult amply illustrates, the active pursuit of Doomsday – the desire, as it were, to accelerate Armageddon – strikes most non-initiates as completely wrongheaded, utterly bizarre and, if events involving the Branch Davidians in Waco, Texas, are at all representative, nothing less than sheer lunacy.[1] Lifton (1985), however, maintains that these ostensibly eccentric behaviours are actually a manifestation of a primordial thanatic impulse, a universal urge towards the void. Certainly, there is no denying the orgiastic excitement associated with the unleashing of wild forces, the innate thrill of total devastation, the will to self-obliteration, the all-too-human 'desire for deep pain' (Ronell 1994: 74). It is only by letting slip the dogs of war, by destroying everything, by, in effect, 'pressing the plunger and watching the indestructible edifice slide majestically to its doom' (Brown 1995a: 304), that we come to know what it *really* feels like to be alive (Hill 1994; Dellamora 1996b). More importantly perhaps, it is only by imagining the end that we are inspired to prevent or circumvent it (Gebauer 1989). The very act of staring into the apocalyptic abyss, be it secular or sacred, ultimately serves to renew our faith since it persuades us of the importance of avoiding the drop. If nothing else, then, the threat of impending doom concentrates the mind wonderfully and acts as a powerful incentive to get our house in order before the fateful day. So much so, that almost everything from the discovery of America and the Scientific Revolution to the modern, progressivist, western worldview has been attributed to the eschatological propellant of the Judeo-Christian tradition (Nisbet 1980; Campion 1994; Reeves 1995).

Although the above attempts to make sense of our 'sense of an ending' go some way towards explaining the pervasiveness of terminal visions, they do not shed light on the reasons why some periods, and indeed peoples, are more prone to millenarianism than others (Zamora 1989). For many commentators, these apocalyptic fits are essentially a manifestation of calendrical symbolism, what Focillon (1969) terms 'centurial mysticism'. In other words, the fact that certain key dates, most notably the ends of centuries and millennia (but also years like 1984, or, on a more human scale, the dreaded 40th birthday)[2], are imbued with social, political, cultural and – dare one say it – *zeitgeistian* significance, and thereby carry eschatological connotations (Showalter 1982; Schwartz 1990; Meštrović 1991; Docker 1994). To some extent, admittedly, such expectations are simply self-fulfilling prophesies. Thanks partly to the celebrated and much recycled predictions of Nostradamus, Edward Cayce, etc., everyone already 'knows' that the apocalypse is due to occur in or around the year 2000 (Mann 1992; Lorie 1993; Skinner 1994). This provides a convenient 'peg' for films, television programmes, magazine articles and, er, books, which are then cited as evidence of acute PMT (pre-millennial tension).[3] The whole process is thereby perpetuated, accelerated and whipped into a frenzy of excitement until the fateful day passes without incident, when eschatological hopes are attached to the next available end-times totem (in this respect, apocalypses are akin to pre-deregulation buses – you wait for years and years and then several come at once).

APOCALYPSE (N)EVER

Terminal visions may proliferate at *fins de siècle*, but the dramatic history of millenarian cults, sects and movements reveals that, thanks to the virtually unlimited date-setting opportunities spawned by countless works of secular and sacred prophesy, it is possible to make predictions of the end for almost any conceivable time – or place (Cohn 1970; Thomas 1971; Rubinsky and Wiseman 1982; Hamilton 1995). Sudden, short-lived and irrational though such radical attempts to overthrow the existing order undoubtedly are, millenarianism is usually associated with times of economic distress, political turmoil and social dislocation, and tends to involve marginalised, disadvantaged or persecuted groups within the host society. As demonstrated by the Ghost Dance phenomenon of late-nineteenth-century Native Americans, the Cargo Cults of mid-twentieth-century Melanesians, the periodic revival of the Inkarri myth in South America, Thomas Müntzer's disastrous seventeenth-century attempt to build an Anabaptist utopia in Munster, or, indeed, the emergence of Christianity itself, which commenced in the aftermath of the Roman invasion of Palestine as an extreme fundamentalist sect on the lunatic fringe of Judaism, apocalypticism is often a sign of despair, of desperation, of an escape into anti-authoritarian otherworldliness by the disaffected, the downtrodden, the dispossessed, the disinherited, the defeated.

It is easy to dismiss eschatological expectations as irrational, psychosomatically induced symptoms of social disquiet – very real and meaningful though they are for the individuals concerned – but there is no shortage of apocalyptic play-dough with which contemporary millenarians can mould their preferred end-times scenario (war, pestilence, population pressure, environmental catastrophe, etc., etc., etc.). Although analogous catalogues of impending horror have been compiled on numerous occasions in the past 2000-plus years, Kumar (1995a) contends that there is one crucial difference between apocalypses past and present. In the past, as noted earlier, the portents of the end were always accompanied by millennial expectations of a new beginning, by the belief that better times were around the corner, by the assumption that temporary trials and tribulations presage a period of recrudescence and renovation. Today, however, the current crops of would-be terminators are characterised, above all, by their indifference, their melancholy, their complete lack of faith in the post-apocalyptic future. According to Kumar, indeed, this disillusion with doomsday is particularly clearly inscribed in the principal intellectual development of the late twentieth century: postmodernism. Its exponents, he asserts, have been happy to announce all manner of 'endings' – history, economics, philosophy, ideology, truth, man, reason, nature, art, psychoanalysis, modernity, grand narratives, to name but the most prominent – without any concomitant commitment to the cerebral equivalent of a New Jerusalem (Brown 1995b; Norris 1995). In intellectual circles at least, it seems that our degenerate, postmodern world really is ending with a whimper rather than a bang, with Jacques Derrida's (1982) 'end without an end', with, to transpose the famous aphorism of one of the giants of *modern* science, eighteenth-century geologist Charles Hutton, 'no vestige of an end, no prospect of a beginning' (see Gould 1987).

In fairness to Kumar (1995b), few would demur from his attempted encapsulation of the postmodern condition. As its manifold adepts are at pains to point out, postmodernity represents the 'last gasp of the past' (Adair 1992: 15); it is characterised by an 'all-pervasive air of exhaustion' (Brown 1995b: 99); its explicants are 'suspended between belief and doubt waiting for the end of the millennium' (Latour 1993: 9). That said, it is arguable that Kumar has overlooked a significant aspect of postmodern eschatology: namely, its apostles' refusal to take apocalypse seriously. Many of the leading lights of postmodernism have written about end-times (e.g. Eco 1994; Jameson 1994; Huyssen 1995), but they do so in the foreknowledge that apocalypse is perpetually postponed – always has been, always will be – and, hence, consider themselves free to play with the conventions of the genre (Dellamora 1996b). Thus, Derrida (1984) contends that the concept of crisis is in crisis, Foucauldian feminists have (apocalyptically) announced the end of apocalypse (Zamora 1989; Quinby 1994), Kroker *et al.* (1989) maintain that we are already living in an era of post-millennial consciousness on the other side of the year 2000, and Hewitt (1996: 18) asks us to ponder how we can possibly, 'posit an apocalyptic rupture when it is, in fact, the concept of historical rupture itself that has been ruptured'.

Postmodernism, as Meštrović (1994: 1) rightly points out, is a 'fun version of the apocalypse' and it almost goes without saying that the high priest of postmodernity, Jean Baudrillard, has commented at length on what he considers to be 'the illusion of the end'. In a tour-de-force of tongue-in-cheek theorising, Baudrillard (1988, 1989, 1994) demonstrates that the traditional concepts or models of time are no longer applicable to our *fin de millennium.* The modern idea that time *has* a shape – be it linear, cyclical or indeed shapeless[4] – has been superseded by the simple but startling postmodern notion that time *can* be shaped. In other words, the postmodern Plasticine that is time, can be bent, broken, twisted, turned, plotted, plaited, extruded, entangled, distorted, discarded, compressed, contorted, replayed, recycled and much more besides. The end, he contends, *cannot* take place because history has, variously, run out of energy as it nears its culmination; accelerated beyond escape velocity only to orbit like a satellite; slowed down, cryogenised and is living in suspended animation until the year 2000; and, above all, that it has been thrown into reverse, into rewind, into a process of systematic erasure.[5] The real end, in fact, occurred some time ago and we are now involved in a desperate exercise of retrospection – a rummage through the pseudo-events and hyperreal happenings in history's dustbin – in an attempt to identify the point when the great consummation actually took place, took us unawares whilst we were otherwise occupied, when our attention was somehow distracted.

APOCALYPSE WHEN

For many mainstream marketers, the foregoing discussion may have proved somewhat interesting but basically irrelevant. What, they may well ask, has the Apocalypse got to do with the theory and practice of modern marketing? Why, moreover, waste time on metaphysical speculation when there are so many idolaters, apostates and barbarians who remain to be converted to the gospel of marketing orientation? Some readers, admittedly, may appreciate that marketing is widely regarded (by non-marketers) as the apotheosis of postmodernity and it follows that the eschatological concerns of certain postmodern theorists are likely to have some relevance, albeit tangential, to the marketing condition. Others may recognise that, like it or not, marketing activities are part and parcel of millennium-mongering, whether it be the creation of products like *666 Jellybeans*, the sublime advertising slogan for Pizza Hut, 'Beware of 666, it's the Anti-Pizza', or companies like End-Time Foods, which specialises in producing consumables for the afterlife (perishables presumably, though one can't help wondering about their 'best before' datestamping policy). Yet other readers may intuit that the leaders of millenarian movements – e.g. Montanus, Jan Matthys, Thomas Venner, Tanchelm, Ian de Stella, Peter the Hermit, Shabbetai Tsvi – were endowed with what many would today consider to be innate marketing skills. Indeed, one only has to examine the operations of the present generation of apocalyptics, such as Jack Van Impe, Pat Robertson, Jerry Falwell, Morris Cerullo or Salem Kirban, to appreciate that their marketing activities are of the highest order, especially given the intangibility – to put it mildly – of the product they purvey (Brown 1995c).

Be that as it may, the purpose of this volume is not the marketing of the Apocalypse, interesting though such an exercise would prove in these degraded pre-millennial times. Nor is it an elaborate attempt to smuggle the contraband of postmodernism past the customs and excise officers of the marketing academy, much-needed though such illicit intellectual indulgences undoubtedly are. The objective of the present text, rather, is to reflect on marketing's growing crisis of representation, the seemingly widespread belief that marketing is in a state of terminal decline, that the marketing discipline is hell-bent on a process of chiliastic self-destruction. As a glance through recent back-issues of the principal journals clearly demonstrates, many leading academics and practitioners are experiencing crises of faith, thinking heretical thoughts, casting doubt on the wisdom of their intellectual calling and, in some extreme cases, openly suggesting that the end of marketing is nigh (e.g. Lynch 1994; Wensley 1995; Thomas 1994, 1995). None other than the founding-father of the marketing concept, Peter Drucker (1994: 95), maintains that 'The assumptions on which the organisation has been built and is being run no longer fit reality.' Professor Peter Doyle (1995: 23, 34), an internationally renowned academic authority, attributes marketing's latter-day 'decline . . . failure . . . demise' to a combination of changing business conditions and the arrogance of marketing practitioners. And, after summarising the parlous state of marketing scholarship, Brownlie *et al.* (1994: 8) conclude that, 'marketing as a domain of knowledge and practice is itself becoming as myopic, complacent and inward looking as all the once great but now defunct myopic companies. Is the end of marketing as we once knew it in sight?'

Such expressions of disquiet are by no means novel – intermittent declarations of 'crisis' are just as old and almost as predictable as the periodic paroxysms of 'rediscovery' (Fisk 1971; Bennett and Cooper 1982; Mueller-Heumann 1986) – but announcements of the 'end' of marketing have been decidedly thin on the ground hitherto. More to the point perhaps, these premonitions of Doomsday come at a time when there is considerable evidence of marketing's out-and-out triumph in the marketplace of ideas. According to Hooley and Saunders (1993: 3), marketing is 'on the lips of many managers'; it is generally considered to be the key to long-term business success (Baker and Hart 1989); it is in the ascendant as an academic subject-area (Saunders 1993); it is being enthusiastically embraced in fields as diverse as health care, public administration and not-for-profit (Butler and Collins 1995), not to mention the erstwhile command economies of eastern Europe (Hooley 1993); and, as Huczynski (1993) makes clear, the diverse writings of the current crop of management gurus – Peters, Porter, Handy, Blanchard, etc. – concur on the overwhelming importance of a marketing orientation. Indeed, after decades of disdain, not only is marketing being treated with, admittedly grudging, respect by adjacent academic specialisms, but none other than the hardest of hard sciences increasingly complain that the best and brightest students are tending to gravitate towards the likes of marketing and advertising (Carey 1995; Brockman 1995). So much so, that the scientific establishment now acknowledges its need to become more marketing orientated, an admission which has led one cynic to conclude that 'science needs marketing more than marketing needs science' (Brown 1996: 262).

The accumulating evidence of marketing's simultaneous success and failure, triumph and disaster, advance and retreat could simply be dismissed as the perennial antithetical perspectives of optimists and pessimists – one sees the proverbial half-full glass while the other is already wondering how to avoid buying the next round of drinks. Alternatively, and in keeping with the ethos of the present volume, the apparent contradiction could be passed off as an instantiation of pre-millennial tension, as one of the manifold paradoxes of our paradoxical postmodern times. While both the apocryphal and zeitgeistian arguments have merit, the apocalyptic literature may help shed some light on the seemingly schizophrenic state of contemporary marketing scholarship. As McGinn (1995) points out, it is invariably at the very moment of a concept's, precept's, culture's, institution's or idea's greatest triumph that doubts start to accumulate, that premonitions of decline transpire, that terminal visions proliferate. What is more, it is only *after* this eschatological sense of an ending emerges that it becomes apparent that the teleological end has *already* been attained. Since it can't be discerned at the time, the apogee of a concept, culture or whatever, only becomes clear in retrospect. In the words of that great illusionist of the end, Jean Baudrillard (1994: 103–5):

> Ideas proliferate like polyps or seaweed and perish by suffocating in their own luxuriant vegetation . . . Every idea and culture becomes universalised before it disappears. As with stars, their maximum expansion comes at the point of death, their transformation into red giants and then black dwarfs . . . This ending of cultures is not perceptible from within. From within, a culture is immortal; it seems to approach its end only in an asymptotic curve. It has, in fact, already disappeared. The elevation of a value to universality is a prelude to its becoming transparent, which itself is a prelude to its disappearance.

Just as Baudrillard maintains that the fulfilment of an illusion, dream, metaphor or utopia effectively comprises its sentence of death, so too the latter-day triumph of marketing is the underlying cause of its terminal illness. Indeed, it is arguable that the end of marketing actually occurred some time ago. The precise moment, naturally, is moot, but a strong case can surely be made for Shelby Hunt's (1976) decisive intervention in the 'broadening' debate of the 1970s, when he unilaterally – not to mention presumptuously – declared victory for Kotler and like-minded marketing imperialists and hubristicly announced that, as of then, the overwhelming priority was to go forth and multiply by 'marketing marketing to non-marketers'. The fate of marketing was sealed at that moment, though it took twenty years of uncontrolled expansion before people fully realised the fact of marketing's demise. Coming to terms with its passing will doubtless take almost as long, since the corpse continues to swell – and expansion, remember, is taken as an indicator of success in the western tradition – but few seriously doubt that the vast bulk of contemporary marketing scholarship comprises little more than intellectual necrophilia. As exemplified by the current enthusiasm for 'relationship marketing' – a stiff in sheep's clothing if ever there was one – all of the discipline's long-dead ideas, decomposing concepts and mouldering metaphors are being recuperated, resuscitated, reanimated and recycled in a frantic, forlorn and utterly futile attempt to demonstrate that there is life after Kotler.

Or are they?

APOCALYPSE HOW

The present book represents an attempt to address some of these questions concerning the supposed 'end of marketing'. Its twelve chapters, plus introduction and conclusion, comprise revised versions of papers presented at the Marketing Eschatology Retreat, described in the preface. The contributions are a mixture of the general and the specific, the academic and managerial in orientation, and, what someone with a weakness for dreadful puns might describe as the contrasting perspectives of 'prophet' and 'not-for-prophet' marketing. The chapters also demonstrate different levels of engagement with the apocalyptic metaphor and/or deal with different aspects of eschatological doctrine.[6] However, in keeping with the traditional tripartite structure of the apocalyptic literary genre, the book is divided into three major sections: 'crisis', 'judgement' and 'renovation'. Each individual chapter, moreover, exhibits elements of this overarching schema, albeit with differing degrees of emphasis and approach. All of the contributors, in other words, address the degenerate state of the marketing discipline, contend that things cannot go on as before, and conclude with a revelation concerning their recommended way or ways forward. Lest there is any misunderstanding, it must be stressed that this framework was not imposed upon, nor suggested to, the contributors. Its emergence, rather, seems to reflect what Dickey (1995: 184) describes as 'infiguration', Kermode's (1967) celebrated thesis that most works of literature in the western tradition are predicated upon the tripartite apocalyptic schema (boy meets girl, boy loses girl, boy gets girl, etc.).

Appropriately, therefore, the first chapter deals specifically with this trinitarian inclination, which is very strongly marked in marketing thought, and relates it to the work of a celebrated twelfth-century prophet, Abbot Joachim de Fiore. Brown goes on to argue that the venerable production-sales-marketing eras periodisation should be replaced with a parodic postmodern version of the same and contends that the three eras schema has itself evolved through three eras – the three eras production era, the three eras sales era and the three eras marketing era. Another long-established trichotomous construct, the marketing concept, is the subject of the second chapter by McDonagh and Prothero. Presented in the form of a three-act play, their exposition maintains that the marketing concept is not only increasingly inappropriate at a time of growing ecological concern, but its perpetuation serves to stifle innovative or unorthodox approaches to marketing scholarship. Equally innovative in its mode of explication, the third chapter comprises a cyber-platonic dialogue which examines the relationship between cosmological belief systems, like religion and science, and everyday questions of belief, such as whether to believe what someone tells us or, indeed, what we tell them. Brownlie and Desmond invite us to take them seriously if we dare, though this doesn't necessarily mean that they are in fact serious. The final chapter in the first section is less unorthodox in its form, but the content of Belk's exegesis on Las Vegas – as an exemplar of today's hyperreal world, which was created by marketing but cannot be explained by its traditional tools and techniques – succeeds in offering some post-apocalyptic hope for the consumption-saturated future.

The second section deals specifically with the end of marketing, or, to be more precise, seeks to pass judgement on the idea of the end. Heilbrunn offers a deconstruction of the eschatological paradigm, explores the interstices between teleology and eschatology, and closes with the suggestion that narratology, as practised by Propp and Greimas, provides the basis upon which marketing scholarship can be pursued in the new millennium. Kent, likewise, makes a case for the end of the end of marketing, intimating that the intrinsic spirit of marketing will survive attacks by eschatologists, postmodernists and fellow members of the lunatic fringe, especially if a more phenomenologically informed worldview is adopted. The lunatic fringe, by contrast, is posited as a site of potential resistance to the eschatological perspective by Buttimer and Kavanagh. Drawing upon the literature on deviance, transgression, disruption and the carnivalesque, they recommend inversion rather than abandonment, seek to substitute perversion for progression and champion marketing madness instead of moderation. Hetzel is equally critical of the idea of the end and, by means of a detailed case study of *Nature et Decouvertes*, an ecologically orientated retailing organisation, maintains that marketing is set to continue, even if it progressively mutates into a form of anti-marketing marketing.

The third and final section comprises four chapters, each of which articulates an alternative vision for the future of marketing. The first, by Thomas, suggests that the current crisis of confidence is largely attributable to the growing divide – the yawning gulf – between academics and practitioners. It is only by abandoning our delusions of intellectual grandeur and admitting that we have much to learn from the new generation of marketing managers, that the discipline can shake off its present state of self-obsessed lethargy, iniquitous lassitude and unpardonable élitism. The academic–industry interface also features in the next chapter, though O'Donohoe concentrates on an essentially methodological solution to the ills that beset advertising research. She argues that the traditional positivistic approach is incapable of uncovering advertising's deeper meanings and, as an alternative, proposes an ethnographically informed perspective. An even more radical methodological possibility is postulated in the penultimate chapter, where Catterall, Maclaran and Stevens indicate that marketing research has been inhibited – indeed profaned – by its innate phallocentrism. Until such times as these underpinning androcentric premises are extirpated and a more feminist inflected worldview is adopted, the marketing patriarchs will continue on their disastrous journey down the highway to Hell. In the final chapter of the third section, however, Holbrook prefers to rely on cat's eyes to see the road ahead. His catalogical vision, scatological wordplay and catalytic catechism for the cataclysm combine to collapse eschatology, apocalypse and the rest into post-structuralist undecidables of language. This DerriDada, as it were, is singularly appropriate since none other than Jacques Derrida, the great post-structuralist philosopher, contends that the play of linguistic signification does have an ultimate limit and that limit is *apocalypse* (Derrida 1984, 1994). In the end, as in the beginning, was the Word.

APOCALYPSE NOW

At a time, then, when many commentators are contending that the high church of marketing is facing its final days; when doubts are increasingly being cast on eternal marketing verities; when the four commandments of analysis, planning, implementation and control are routinely ignored; when false conceptual idols, such as relationship marketing, are widely and indiscriminately worshipped; when schismatic tendencies are clearly discernible; when the high priests of marketing scholarship are losing faith; when it would appear that, if the unbelievers are to be believed, the end of marketing is nigh, this book attempts to address and answer some fundamental, not to say fundamentalist, questions. Have we precipitated a marketing Armageddon? Are we doomed to disciplinary damnation? Has marketing become doctrinaire and dogmatic? When and how did we stray from the path of academic righteousness? Is it finally time to say Amen to the marketing concept? Or, as the concluding chapter will seek to examine, is the land of marketing milk and honey – Marcadia – just around the corner, almost within our grasp, attainable with one last superhuman effort? Time, and the reviewers of this volume, will no doubt tell.

Regardless of its reception in the marketplace of ideas – where the book will doubtless be dismissed as the ravings of the Branch Derrideans – the fact of the matter is that down the decades and centuries, the apocalyptic spirit has inspired, and continues to inspire, an enormous amount of artistic, literary, spiritual and intellectual endeavour. According to Ronell (1994: xiv), it is nothing less that the 'legacy of the western logos, promising finite transcendence, but also a new, infinitising start . . . offering the narcissistic comfort that goes along with closure'. In keeping with the precise meaning of 'apocalypse', the contributors to this book attempt to reveal the hidden truth about the state of modern marketing. They seek to separate the wheat from the chaff, the sheep from the goats and the saints from the sinners. Interestingly, however, just as the very act of considering the ultimate limit only serves to reveal its limits (i.e. in thinking about the end, we can't avoid reflecting on what happens *after* the end or, conversely, what happened *before* the beginning), so too the ensuing discussions of marketing eschatology inevitably gravitate towards and settle on the manner of marketing's continuation, on marketing escapology, on the very illusion of the end. Paradoxical though this appears, it is very much in keeping with contemporary postmodern sentiment, with what Derrida (1984) terms 'apocalypse without apocalypse' – that is end-time without revelation (though in the case of *Marketing Apocalypse*, it is revelation without end-time). If, of course, after reading this book, you conclude that the apocalyptic metaphor is irrelevant to today's *fin de siècle* marketing milieu; well, what the hell, it's not the end of the world . . .

NOTES

1 Under the leadership of Joseph di Mambro, the Order of the Solar Temple held that its adepts would be reincarnated – not so much after death as *through* death – on the star Sirius. Fifty-three members of the sect committed suicide in October 1994 and a further dozen followed suit fourteen months later. On 19 April 1993, eighty-two members of the Branch Davidian sect, including its charismatic leader, David Koresh, died in a firestorm in Waco, Texas. The siege commenced on 28 February when one hundred agents from the Bureau of Alcohol, Tobacco and Firearms moved in on Koresh's heavily armed compound and it ended fifty days later, after a disastrous final assault by the FBI.

2 In this respect, it is interesting to note Kermode's (1995) contention that *every* generation has its crop of intellectuals who seek to disseminate terminal visions. Isn't it remarkable, he wryly concludes, that ends, crises, transitions and the like, seem to occur 'at the very moment when Foucault, or whoever, happened to be around to witness and explain it' (Kermode 1995: 261). In keeping, moreover, with Kermode's (1967) thesis that we project our existential anxieties on to history, it is surely no accident that crisis-mongers of marketing – be it George Fisk in the 1970s, Russell Belk in the 1980s or Douglas Brownlie in the 1990s – are invariably (c. 40-year-old) men facing the uncertainties of middle life.

3 For example, *The Observer Life Magazine* ran a three-week series on millenarian-style movements in May 1995. The contributions ranged from an 'A to Z of Cults' to Self's suggestion that the most pernicious sect of the late-twentieth century was, in fact, untrammelled *consumption*.

4 At the risk of oversimplifying a complex issue, three basic models of time have traditionally been identified: *cyclical*, where events repeat themselves again and again; *linear*, where time unfolds like an arrow shot from a bow; and *shapeless*, the assumption, beloved by historians, that there is no pattern to time (or, rather, that the pattern of time is patternless). Unlike many early tribal societies, which tended to subscribe to the cyclical view, Judaism – and, thereafter, the entire western tradition – adopted a linear model of time, assuming that it possessed a beginning, middle and end. Granted, this cliché concerning Judeo-Christian linearity has been challenged by a number of commentators, who highlight copious examples of 'time's cycle' in the Biblical canon (e.g. Campion 1994). Nevertheless, the *predominance* of 'time's arrow' is highly significant from an apocalyptic perspective. As Wagar (1982: 43) makes clear, 'In the linear model, the end acquires a gravity that it cannot have in the cyclical. The end is once-only, facilitating a once-only judgement of all creaturely being. Justice is done.'

5 Outlandish perhaps, and readily dismissed as pretentious intellectualising of the most extravagant kind, Baudrillard's flights of fancy are never less than dazzling in their brilliance. Consider the following, far from atypical, example:

> We are in the process of wiping out the entire twentieth century, effacing all the signs of the Cold War one by one, perhaps even all trace of the Second World War and all of the political or ideological revolutions of the twentieth century . . . At the rate we are going we shall soon be back at the Holy Roman Empire. And perhaps this is the illumination this *fin de siècle* offers and the true meaning of that controversial formula "the end of history". The fact is that, in a sort of enthusiastic work of mourning, we are in the process of retracting all the significant events of this century, of *whitewashing* it, as if everything that had taken place (revolutions, the division of the world, exterminations, the violent transnationality of states, nuclear cliffhanging) – in short, history in its modern phase – were merely a hopeless imbroglio, and everyone had set about undoing that history with the same enthusiasm that had gone into making it.

> Restoration, regression, rehabilitation, revival of the old frontiers, of the old differences, of particularities, of religions – and even resipiscence in the sphere of morals. It seems that all the signs of liberation achieved over a century are fading and will in the end perhaps be snuffed out one by one: we are engaged in a gigantic process of *revisionism* – not an ideological revisionism but a revisionism of history itself, and we seem to be in a hurry to finish it before the end of the century, secretly hoping perhaps to be able to start again from scratch in the new millennium.
>
> (Baudrillard 1994: 32–3)

6 A distinction, for example, is often made between personal and communal eschatologies, though these are not clear-cut in practice. Millennial doctrine is equally fragmented, as the contrast between pre- and post-millennialism amply testifies. Subscribers to the former believe that Christ will return *before* the one-thousand-year period of earthly bliss, whereas those who cleave to the latter assume that the second coming occurs *after* the millennium (see for example Enzensberger 1978; Boyer 1992; Gavin 1994).

REFERENCES

Abrams, M.H. (1971), *Natural Supernaturalism: Tradition and Revolution in Romantic Literature*, Norton, New York.

Adair, G. (1992), *The Postmodernist Always Rings Twice*, Fourth Estate, London.

Baker, M.J. and Hart, S.J. (1989), *Marketing and Competitive Success*, Philip Allan, Hemel Hempstead.

Baudrillard, J. (1988), 'The year 2000 has already happened', in A. Kroker and M. Kroker (eds), *Body Invaders: Panic Sex in America*, The New World Perspectives: Montreal, pp. 35–44.

Baudrillard, J. (1989), 'The anorexic ruins', in D. Kamper and C. Wulf (eds), *Looking Back on the End of the World*, Semiotext(e), New York, pp. 29–45.

Baudrillard, J. (1994), *The Illusion of the End*, trans. C. Turner, Polity, Cambridge.

Bennett, R.C. and Cooper, R.G. (1981), 'The misuse of marketing: an American tragedy', *Business Horizons*, 24 (6), pp. 51–61.

Boyarin, J. (1996), 'At last, all the *Goyim*: notes on a Greek word applied to Jews', in R. Dellamora (ed.), *Postmodern Apocalypse: Theory and Cultural Practice at the End*, University of Pennsylvania Press, Philadelphia, pp. 41–58.

Boyer, P. (1992), *When Time Shall Be No More*, Belknap, Cambridge, Mass.

Brockman, J. (1995), *The Third Culture: Beyond the Scientific Revolution*, Simon and Schuster, New York.

Brown, S. (1995a), 'Postmodern marketing research: no representation without taxation', *Journal of the Market Research Society*, 37 (3), pp. 287–310.

Brown, S. (1995b), *Postmodern Marketing*, Routledge, London.

Brown, S. (1995c), 'Six sixty-six and all that (or, what the hell is marketing eschatology?)', in S. Brown *et al.* (eds), *Proceedings of the Marketing Eschatology Retreat*, University of Ulster, Belfast, pp. 1–13.

Brown, S. (1996), 'Art or science?: fifty years of marketing debate', *Journal of Marketing Management*, 12 (4), pp. 243–67.

Brownlie, D. *et al* (1994), 'The new marketing myopia: critical perspectives on theory and research in marketing – introduction', *European Journal of Marketing*, 28 (3), pp. 6–12.

Bull, M. (1995a), *Apocalypse Theory and the Ends of the World*, Blackwell, Oxford.

Bull, M. (1995b), 'On making ends meet', in M. Bull (ed.), *Apocalypse Theory and the Ends of the World*, Blackwell, Oxford, pp. 1–17.

Butler, P. and Collins, N. (1995), 'Marketing public sector services: concepts and characteristics', *Journal of Marketing Management*, 11 (1–3), pp. 83–96.
Campion, N. (1994), *The Great Year: Astrology, Millenarianism and History in the Western Tradition*, Arkana, Harmondsworth.
Carey, J. (1995), *The Faber Book of Science*, Faber and Faber, London.
Chandler, R. (1993), *Doomsday*, Word Publishing, Milton Keynes.
Cohen, S. and Taylor, L. (1992), *Escape Attempts: The Theory and Practice of Resistance to Everyday Life*, Routledge, London.
Cohn, N. (1970), *The Pursuit of the Millennium*, Pimlico, London.
Collins, J.J. (1984), *The Apocalyptic Imagination: An Introduction to the Jewish Matrix of Christianity*, Crossroads, New York.
Cotton, I. (1995), *The Hallelujah Revolution: The Rise of the New Christians*, Little Brown, London.
Dellamora, R. (1996a), 'Queer apocalypse: framing William Burroughs', in R. Dellamora (ed.). *Postmodern Apocalypse: Theory and Cultural Practice at the End*, University of Pennsylvania Press, Philadelphia, pp. 136–67.
Dellamora, R. (1996b), 'Introduction', in R. Dellamora (ed.), *Postmodern Apocalypse: Theory and Cultural Practice at the End*, University of Pennsylvania Press, Philadelphia, pp. 1–14.
Derrida, J. (1982), 'The ends of man', in *Margins of Philosophy*, Harvester Wheatsheaf, Hemel Hempstead, pp. 109–36, trans. A. Bass.
Derrida, J. (1984), 'Of an apocalyptic tone recently adopted in philosophy', *Oxford Literary Review*, 6 (2), pp. 3–37, trans. J.P. Leavey.
Derrida, J. (1994), *Specters of Marx:The State of the Debt, the Work of Mourning and the New International*, Routledge, New York, trans. P. Kamuf.
Dickey, L. (1995), 'Saint-Simonian industrialism as the end of history: August Cieszkowski on the teleology of universal history', in M. Bull (ed.), *Apocalypse Theory and the Ends of the World*, Blackwell, Oxford, pp. 159–99.
Docker, J. (1994), *Postmodernism and Popular Culture: A Cultural History*, Cambridge University Press, Cambridge.
Doyle, P. (1995), 'Marketing in the new millennium', *European Journal of Marketing*, 29 (13), pp. 23–41.
Drucker, P.F. (1994), 'The theory of the business', *Harvard Business Review*, 72 (September–October), pp. 95–104.
Eco, U. (1994), *Apocalypse Postponed*, Indiana University Press, Bloomington.
Economist, (1995), 'America and religion – the counter-attack of God', *The Economist*, 336 (7922), pp. 19–21.
Eliade, M. (1989 [1954]), *The Myth of the Eternal Return: Cosmos and History*, Arkana, Harmondsworth.
Eliade, M. (1991 [1952]), *Images and Symbols: Studies in Religious Symbolism*, Princeton University Press, Princeton.
Enzensberger, H.M. (1978), 'Two notes on the end of the world', *New Left Review*, 110 (July–August), pp. 74–80.
Fisk, G. (1971), 'The role of marketing theory', in G. Fisk (ed.), *New Essays in Marketing Theory*, Allyn and Bacon, Boston, pp. 1–5.
Focillon, H. (1969 [1951]), *The Year 1000*, Ungar, New York, trans. F.D. Weick.
Fortunati, V. (1993), 'The metamorphosis of the apocalyptic myth: from utopia to science fiction', in K. Kumar and S. Bann (eds), *Utopias and the Millennium*, Reaktion, London, pp. 81–9.
Frankel, B. (1987), *The Post-industrial Utopians*, Polity, Cambridge.
Friedländer, S. (1985), 'Themes of decline and end in the nineteenth-century western imagination', in S. Friedländer *et al.* (eds), *Visions of Apocalypse: End or Rebirth?*, Holmes and Meier, London, pp. 61–83.

Friedrich, O. (1982), *The End of the World: A History*, Fromm International, New York.
Funkenstein, A. (1985), 'A schedule for the end of the world: the origins and persistence of the apocalyptic mentality', in S. Friedländer *et al.* (eds), *Visions of Apocalypse: End or Rebirth?*, Holmes and Meier, New York, pp. 44–60.
Gavin, J. (1994), *Faith and the Future: Studies in Christian Eschatology*, Paulist Press, New York.
Gebauer, G. (1989), 'The place of beginning and end: caves and their systems of symbols', in D. Kamper and C. Wulf (eds), *Looking Back on the End of the World*, Semiotext(e), New York, pp. 19–28.
Gould, S.J. (1987), *Time's Arrow, Time's Cycle: Myth and Metaphor in the Discovery of Geological Time*, Penguin, Harmondsworth.
Greisman, H.C. (1974), 'Marketing the millennium: ideology, mass culture and industrial society', *Politics and Society*, 4 (4), pp. 511–24.
Hamilton, M.B. (1995), *The Sociology of Religion*, Routledge, London.
Hewitt, J. (1996), 'Coitus Interruptus: fascism and the deaths of history', in R. Dellamora (ed.), *Postmodern Apocalypse: Theory and Cultural Practice at the End*, University of Pennsylvania Press, Philadelphia, pp. 17–40.
Hill, M.O. (1994), *Dreaming the End of the World: Apocalypse as a Rite of Passage*, Spring Publications, Dallas.
Hooley, G.J. (1993), 'Raising the Iron Curtain: marketing in a period of transition', *European Journal of Marketing*, 27 (11/12), pp. 6–20.
Hooley, G.J. and Saunders, J. (1993), *Competitive Positioning: The Key to Market Success*, Prentice Hall, Hemel Hempstead.
Huczynski, A.A. (1993), *Management Gurus: What Makes Them and How to Become One*, Routledge, London.
Hunt, S.D. (1976), 'The nature and scope of marketing', *Journal of Marketing*, 40 (July), pp. 17–28.
Huyssen, A. (1995), *Twilight Memories: Marking Time in a Culture of Amnesia*, Routledge, New York.
Jameson, F. (1994), *The Seeds of Time*, Columbia University Press, New York.
Kamper, D. and Wulf, C. (1989), *Looking Back on the End of the World*, Semiotext(e), New York.
Kermode, F. (1967), *The Sense of an Ending: Studies in the Theory of Fiction*, Oxford University Press, New York.
Kermode, F. (1985), 'Apocalypse and the modern', in S. Friedländer *et al.* (eds), *Visions of Apocalypse: End or Rebirth?*, Holmes and Meier, New York, pp. 84–106.
Kermode, F. (1995), 'Waiting for the End', in M. Bull (ed.), *Apocalypse Theory and the Ends of the World*, Blackwell, Oxford, pp. 250–63.
Kroker, A., Kroker, M. and Cook, D. (1989), *Panic Encyclopedia: The Definitive Guide to the Postmodern Scene*, Macmillan, Basingstoke.
Kumar, K. (1995a), 'Apocalypse, millennium and utopia today', in M. Bull (ed.), *Apocalypse Theory and the Ends of the World*, Blackwell, Oxford, pp. 200–24.
Kumar, K. (1995b), *From Post-industrial to Post-modern Society: New Theories of the Contemporary World*, Blackwell, Oxford.
Latour, B. (1993), *We Have Never Been Modern*, Harvester Wheatsheaf, Hemel Hempstead, trans. C. Porter.
Lifton, R.J. (1985), 'The image of the "end of the world": a psychohistorical view', in S. Friedländer *et al.* (eds), *Visions of Apocalypse: End or Rebirth?*, Holmes and Meier, New York, pp. 151–67.
Lorie, P. (1993), *Nostradamus, The Millennium and Beyond: The Prophesies to 2016*, Bloomsbury, London.
Lorie, P. (1995), *Revelation: Prophesies for the Apocalypse and Beyond*, Boxtree, London.

Lynch, J.E. (1994), 'The end of marketing?', in O. Westall (ed.), *British Academy of Management Annual Conference Proceedings*, Lancaster University, Lancaster, pp. 322–4.

Mann, A.T. (1992), *Millennium Prophecies: Predictions for the Year 2000*, Element, Shaftesbury.

McGinn, B. (1979), *Visions of the End: Apocalyptic Traditions in the Middle Ages*, Columbia University Press, New York.

McGinn, B. (1995), 'The end of the world and the beginning of Christendom', in M. Bull (ed.), *Apocalypse Theory and the Ends of the World*, Blackwell, Oxford, pp. 58–89.

Meštrović, S.G. (1991), *The Coming Fin de Siècle*, Routledge, London.

Meštrović, S.G. (1994), *The Balkanization of the West*, Routledge, London.

Mueller-Heumann, G. (1986), 'Toward a professional concept for marketing', *Journal of Marketing Management*, 1 (3), pp. 303–13.

Nisbet, R. (1980), *History of the Idea of Progress*, Heinemann, London.

Noakes, S. (1993), 'Gracious words: Luke's Jesus and the reading of sacred poetry at the beginning of the sacred era', in J. Boyarin (ed.), *The Ethnography of Reading*, University of California Press, Berkeley, pp. 38–57.

Norris, C. (1995), 'Versions of apocalypse: Kant, Derrida, Foucault', in M. Bull (ed.), *Apocalypse Theory and the Ends of the World*, Blackwell, Oxford, pp. 227–49.

O'Collins, G.S.J. (1994), 'In the end, love', in J. Gavin (ed.), *Faith and the Future: Studies in Christian Eschatology*, Paulist Press, New York, pp. 25–42.

O'Leary, S.D. (1994), *Arguing the Apocalypse: A Theory of Millennial Rhetoric*, Oxford University Press, Oxford.

Parfrey, A. (1990), *Apocalypse Culture*, Feral House, Portland.

Pask, K. (1996), 'Cyborg economies: desire and labour in the *Terminator* films', in R. Dellamora (ed.), *Postmodern Apocalypse: Theory and Cultural Practice at the End*, University of Pennsylvania Press, Philadelphia, pp. 182–98.

Quinby, L. (1994), *Anti-apocalypse: Exercises in Genealogical Criticism*, University of Minnesota Press, Minneapolis.

Reeves, M. (1995), 'Pattern and purpose in history in the later medieval and renaissance periods', in M. Bull (ed.), *Apocalypse Theory and the Ends of the World*, Blackwell, Oxford, pp. 90–111.

Reiche, H.A.T. (1985), 'The archaic heritage: myths of decline and end in antiquity', in S. Friedländer *et al.* (eds), *Visions of Apocalypse: End or Rebirth?*, Holmes and Meier, New York, pp. 21–43.

Rojek, C. (1993), *Ways of Escape: Modern Transformations in Leisure and Travel*, Routledge, London.

Ronell, A. (1994), *Finitude's Score: Essays for the End of the Millennium*, University of Nebraska Press, Lincoln.

Rowland, C. (1995), '"Upon whom the ends of the ages have come": apocalyptic and the interpretation of the New Testament', in M. Bull (ed.), *Apocalypse Theory and the Ends of the World*, Blackwell, Oxford, pp. 38–57.

Rubinsky, Y. and Wiseman, I. (1982), *A History of the End of the World*, William Morrow, New York.

Saunders, J. (1993), 'Marketing Education Group conference 1993', in M. Davies *et al.* (eds), *Emerging Issues in Marketing*, University of Loughborough, Loughborough, pp. ii–iv.

Schwartz, H. (1990), *Century's End: A Cultural History of the Fin de Siècle from the 990s Through the 1990s*, Doubleday, New York.

Shaffer, E. (1995), 'Secular apocalypse: prophets and apocalyptics at the end of the eighteenth century', in M. Bull (ed.), *Apocalypse Theory and the Ends of the World*, Blackwell, Oxford, pp. 137–58.

Showalter, E. (1982), *Sexual Anarchy: Gender and Culture at the Fin de Siècle*, Bloomsbury, London.

Skinner, S. (1994), *Millennium Prophesies: Predictions for the Year 2000 and Beyond from the World's Greatest Seers and Mystics*, Virgin, London.

Thomas, K. (1971), *Religion and the Decline of Magic*, Penguin, Harmondsworth.

Thomas, M.J. (1994), 'Marketing – in chaos or transition?', *European Journal of Marketing*, 28 (3), pp. 55–62.

Thomas, M.J. (1995), 'Preface', in M.J. Thomas (ed.), *Gower Handbook of Marketing, Fourth Edition*, Gower, Aldershot, pp. xxv–xxvi.

Wagar, W.W. (1982), *Terminal Visions: The Literature of Last Things*, Indiana University Press, Bloomington.

Wainwright, A.W. (1993), *Mysterious Apocalypse: Interpreting the Book of Revelation*, Abingdon Press, Nashville.

Ward, K. (1993), *Images of Eternity*, Oneworld, Oxford.

Weiss, P. (1995), 'Outcasts digging in for the Apocalypse', *Time*, 145 (17), pp. 34–5.

Wensley, R. (1995), 'A critical review of research in marketing', *British Journal of Management* 6 (December), pp. S63–S82.

White, H. (1980), 'The value of narrativity in the representation of reality', *Critical Inquiry*, 7 (1), pp. 5–27.

Zamora, L.P. (1989), *Writing the Apocalypse: Historical Vision in Contemporary U.S. and Latin American Fiction*, Cambridge University Press, Cambridge.

Part I

CRISIS

2

TRINITARIANISM, THE ETERNAL EVANGEL AND THE THREE ERAS SCHEMA

Stephen Brown

INTRODUCTION

Father, Son and Holy Spirit. Sex, drugs and rock 'n' roll. Past, present and future. Tall, dark and handsome. Wine, women and song. Eat, drink and be merry. Earth, sea and sky. Lights, camera, action. Beginning, middle and end. The good, the bad and the ugly. Small, medium, large. Faith, hope and charity. Hook, line and sinker. Lock, stock and barrel. Guitar, bass and drums. Burger, fries and coke. Food, gas, lodging. Liberty, equality, fraternity. Ku, Klux Klan. Vidi, vini, vici. Friends, Romans, countrymen. Tom, Dick and Harry. Jesus, Mary and Joseph. Red, white and blue. Green, white and gold. Peace, love and understanding. Truth, justice and the American way. Blood, sweat and tears. Rum, sodomy and the lash. Front, back and side. Ready, steady, go. Gold, silver and bronze. Game, set and match. Hip, hip, hooray. Bell, book and candle. Bewitched, bothered and bewildered. Rag, Tag and Bobtail. Tick, tack, toe. Left, right and centre. Here, there and everywhere. Morning, noon and night. Nine, nine, nine. Pounds, shillings and pence. Length, breadth and depth. Ready, willing and able. Sick, sore and tired. Deaf, dumb and blind. Ear, nose and throat. Birth, life and death. Gold, frankincense and myrrh.

As the above, by no means exhaustive, list of examples illustrates, thinking in threes is a very common occurrence. A moment's reflection, indeed, indicates that this trinitarian inclination is made manifest in many ways, shapes and forms, whether it be the Three Wise Men, three course meals, the Three Musketeers, the Three Stooges, the Three Degrees, three piece suites, three wishes, three dimensions, three little pigs, three blind mice, Three Men in a Boat, three card trick, three points for a win, the three Rs of reading, writing and 'rithmatic, three coins in a fountain, three times a lady, three strikes and you're out, three steps to heaven or, on a more elevated plane, trichotomous concepts like Freud's id, ego and superego, Hegel's thesis, antithesis, synthesis, Popper's three worlds theory, Newton's three laws of motion, Peirce's sign, designatum and interpretant, Chomsky's three models of language and Aristotle's tripartite classification of literary genres. True, thinking in twos and fours –

and their derivatives, most notably five, seven, ten and twelve – are also deeply embedded in the human psyche, but there is no doubt that the trinity remains of very great significance (see Butler 1970; Sebeok 1988; Campion 1994). As the good book itself makes clear, 'a threefold cord is not quickly broken' (*Eccles.* 4:12).

Regardless of the extent of one's agreement or disagreement with commentators, such as Adair (1994) and Reeves and Gould (1987), who consider thinking in threes to be imbued with deep symbolic-cum-cabbalistic power – and doubtless bad luck, which also runs in threes, attaches itself to anyone who scoffs at such mysticism – it is undeniable that trinitarianism is widespread in the theory and practice of marketing. The latter is exemplified by the copious advertising slogans predicated on trichotomies: Beanz, Meanz, Heinz; Work, Rest and Play; Anytime, Anyplace, Anywhere; Snap, Crackle and Pop; Finger Lickin' Good; We Try Harder; Master the Moment; Kills Bugs Dead!; Just Do It; Vorsprung durch Technik; Where's The Beef?; Tense, Nervous Headache?; Prolongs Active Life; Soft, Strong and (very, very) Long (Twitchell 1996). The former, as a glance through any textbook amply demonstrates, includes such redoubtable conceptual constructs as STP (segmentation, targeting, positioning), intensive/extensive/exclusive distribution, convenience, comparison and speciality goods, core/actual/augmented products, discount, congruent and premium prices, cognition, affect and conation, limited decision taking, extended decision taking and routinised response behaviour, Porter's generic strategies (cost, differentiation, focus), Kotler's typology of publics, products and organisations, Hunt's three dichotomies model, Calder and Tybout's triadic classification of knowledge, Bristor and Fischer's three schools of feminist consumer research, Bagozzi's three types of exchange and, not least, the marketing concept itself with its tripartite emphasis on profit, co-ordination and customer orientation. Granted, dichotomous and, especially, quadripartite thinking are also a commonplace in marketing (industrial/consumer, quantitative/qualitative, product/service, above/below the line, 4Ps, SWOT, four utilities, Ansoff Matrix, PLC stages and so on), but the trinity appears to possess what can only be described as unerring, undying and universal appeal.

Undoubtedly the most prevalent, and perhaps the most execrated, expression of trinitarianism in marketing thought is the familiar 'production era, sales era, marketing era' schema. Recycled in the opening chapters of almost every introductory text, the three eras framework is also one of the finest examples of eschatological thinking in marketing. As this chapter will seek to demonstrate, the construct is on a clear line of descent from the apocalyptic vision of an enormously influential twelfth-century theologian, the Eternal Evangel, Abbot Joachim de Fiore. In appropriately trichotomous fashion, therefore, the chapter commences with a consideration of the three eras periodisation schema; turns to a discussion of the characteristics, context and communication of Joachimism; and concludes with an exposition of what I modestly consider to be the 'mother of all marketing models'.

THE THREE ERAS SCHEMA

Thirty-something years ago, a momentous paper entitled 'The Marketing Revolution' was published in the *Journal of Marketing*. Written by Robert J. Keith, then Executive Vice President and consumer products director of The Pillsbury Company, it intimated that his organisation was in the throes of a marketing equivalent of the Copernican revolution in science. According to Keith, from its foundation in 1869 to the 1930s, Pillsbury was 'product oriented', in that it was preoccupied with the manufacturing process, with new products being launched to dispose of manufacturing by-products rather than serve a market need. From the 1930s to the 1950s, the company was characterised by a 'sales orientation', where a sophisticated sales organisation, backed up with advertising and market analysis, was assembled to help purvey its many and varied product lines. The ensuing era, however, was 'marketing oriented', in so far as the purpose of Pillsbury was no longer to mill flour, nor to manufacture and sell a wide range of products, but to satisfy the needs and desires – both latent and actual – of its customers. Just as the celebrated sixteenth-century Polish scientist had demonstrated that the earth was not the centre of the solar system, so too The Pillsbury Company was no longer at the centre of the business universe. 'Today,' Keith (1960: 35) portentously announced, 'the customer is at the centre.'

Although the article is only four pages long, contains not a single citation and, to be perfectly frank, now reads like a hackneyed after-dinner speech or carefully air-brushed Pillsbury press release, Keith's paper is widely considered to be the marketing analogue of St Augustine's *City of God* or Martin Luther's ninety-five theses. Along with Levitt's (1960) contemporaneous classic, 'Marketing Myopia', it is one of the most frequently anthologised papers in the entire marketing canon. Its fame, admittedly, is partly attributable to the fact that it is one of the earliest – and most cogent – articulations of the modern marketing concept. However, the Copernican analogy, the 'scientific' overtones, the suggestion that his organisation's experience was typical of most major American businesses, the hints of a heroic internal struggle to have the marketing concept accepted within Pillsbury, the intimation that the glorious marketing revolution had only just begun and, above all, the production–sales–marketing eras schema itself, combined to ensure that Keith's rhetorical *tour de force* quickly earned its place in the pantheon of marketing 'classics'.

Seminal statement though it was, 'The Marketing Revolution' has not been without its critics. Apart from the seemingly perpetual debate over the precise nature of the modern marketing concept, which comprises an implicit critique of Keith's paper, a recent textual deconstruction by Marion (1993) concludes that it was essentially a politically motivated document, designed to promote a palace revolution *within* Pillsbury, and which eventually propelled Keith into the position of Chief Executive Officer. Be that as it may, the principal bone of academic contention concerning this much-reprinted contribution is its tripartite model of historic periodisation.[1] After undertaking a detailed content analysis of twenty-five introductory and advanced marketing textbooks, which revealed that the three eras schema was included in all but four, Hollander (1986) posited that Keith's periodising framework was hopelessly flawed. It completely ignored the fact that many companies were 'marketing oriented' by the mid-nineteenth century, that marketing degree programmes, professional associations and research organisations were established long before the so-called 'marketing era', and, as illustrated by his arrestingly titled monograph, *Was there a Pepsi Generation Before Pepsi Discovered it?*, that youth-based market segmentation was widespread prior to the 1940s (Hollander and Germain 1992). While the periodising schema undoubtedly served a purpose, primarily the ease with which it could be adapted for machine-gradable examination papers, it also impeded the serious study of marketing history and reinforced marketing's traditional preoccupation with managerial perspectives, rather than (say) broader societal concerns (see Hollander 1986).

Alongside and reinforcing Hollander's critique of the three eras schema, another devastating attack on the framework was published in the premier marketing journal. Concentrating on the 'myth' of the production era, Fullerton (1988) argued that the supposed characteristics of the 1870–1930 period – demand exceeded supply, limited competition, firms concentrated on production rather than marketing, which was unnecessary since products sold themselves – simply did not accord with the historical facts. Indeed, as Fullerton's exhaustive list of examples convincingly demonstrated, received wisdom concerning the period did not correspond with the evidence in any of the three most advanced economies of the time, Britain, Germany and the United States. By thus highlighting that 'modern' marketing institutions and practices were commonplace during the so-called 'production era' – and, moreover, throughout the subsequent 'sales era' – the entire periodising schema was shown to be totally inadequate and in sore need of replacement. To this end, Fullerton proposed a 'complex flux' model of marketing evolution, which comprised four separate but interpenetrating eras: the era of antecedents (c. 1500–1750); the era of origins (1750–1870); the era of institutional development (1850–1929); and the era of refinement and formalisation (1930–present). Despite appearances to the contrary, however, the model was not simply a substitution of four eras for three and the judicious manipulation of key dates. On the contrary, Fullerton's framework sought to combine elements of continuity and incremental development, whilst allowing for the possibility of sudden, catastrophic change.

Although it provides a more nuanced and historically informed picture of the evolution of modern marketing in the western world, the 'complex flux' model has not been universally acclaimed. Besides Fullerton's (1988: 121) spurious attempt to legitimise his sub-Annales School schema by claiming that it represents 'mainstream historical research' (history is as riven with intellectual faction-fighting as marketing and the Annales School has long passed its best-before date), the model has been attacked by Gilbert and Bailey (1990) for concentrating on marketing practice and its caricature of the established framework. However, perhaps the most damning critique of the complex flux model is the simple fact that it has not succeeded in supplanting the production-sales-marketing era schema. It is ten years now since Fullerton (1985) first articulated his position (according to Gummesson (1993), the period necessary for cutting-edge academic thinking to make its way into mainstream textbooks) and, notwithstanding the imprimatur of marketing's most prestigious journal, the fact of the matter is that the three eras framework is still featured in many best-selling textbooks (Pride and Ferrell, McCarthy and Perrault, etc.). True, an analysis of fifteen recent introductory volumes by the author, revealed that the traditional periodising schema, albeit very common, is no longer ubiquitous, but it has most certainly *not* been replaced by the complex flux model.[2] If anything, there is some evidence to suggest that texts have become slightly *less* historical than hitherto, in that the traditional 'evolution of marketing' sub-section has occasionally been excised completely or transmuted into the contention that, at any given time, organisations may be 'production oriented', 'sales oriented' or 'marketing oriented'. Clearly, it would be unfair to regard this apparent anti-historical tendency as a profoundly paradoxical outcome of the evangelical endeavours of distinguished marketing historians like Ron Fullerton or Stanley Hollander. Nevertheless, it is legitimate to ask why 'historically minded' textbook writers continue to opt for the three eras schema when superior alternatives are readily available or, more to the point, why extensive criticism of the periodising concept 'has not changed the general academic outlook' (Hollander 1995: 100). In this respect, it may be worthwhile attempting to examine the roots of the production–sales–marketing schema since, as one of Hollander's acolytes aptly put it, looking back helps us see ahead (Savitt 1989).

THE ETERNAL EVANGEL

By any reckoning, Abbot Joachim de Fiore (c. 1135–1202) must rank as one of the most remarkable figures in the history of western thought. Variously described as 'a twelfth-century prophet-genius' (Nisbet 1980: x), 'massively overestimated' (Campion 1994: 601) and 'the most influential European until Karl Marx' (Rubinsky and Wiseman 1982: 77), his works and attributed works have impinged directly or indirectly upon the consciousness of countless generations of intellectuals. Even today, some eight hundred years after his death, Joachimite prophesies continue to generate considerable academic debate among theologians and philosophers of history, as does the hypothesis that de Fiore was the original source of the 'progressive' western worldview (e.g. Reeves 1995; Kumar 1995; Kermode 1995; Bull 1995).

The son of a court notary, Joachim was born in Celica, a small town in Sicily, and, after a deeply affecting pilgrimage to the Holy Land, he first became a hermit on Mount Etna, then a Benedictine monk, and eventually founded a new order at San Giovanni da Fiore, high in the Calabrian mountains. In 1183, primed by decades of biblical study, exegesis and contemplation of works of prophesy (Johnnite revelations and Sybilline oracles in the main), Joachim experienced the first of several visions concerning the nature of the Trinity, the future of the church and the end of the world. Encouraged by Pope Lucius III, the abbot recorded his speculations in a series of works, principally the *Liber Concordie*, the *Exposito in Apocalypism* and the *Psalterium decem chordarum*. His reputation as a *magnus propheta* thereby established, Joachim was consulted – in his inaccessible mountaintop retreat! – by a procession of popes, princes and kings, including Richard the Lion-Heart, and was once uniquely honoured with an invitation to expound his theories in front of the papal court.

History, according to this much-vaunted Calabrian abbot, had a clearly discernible shape or pattern. The shape comprised three great, slightly overlapping ages (*status*), each of which was associated with one of the elements of the Trinity, and between which lay degraded periods of transition (*transitus*). The first *status*, which ran from Adam to Jesus Christ, was the Age of the Father; the second, which commenced with Jesus and was due to end in 1260, was the Age of the Son; and the third, final and soon to be consummated dispensation was the Age of the Holy Spirit. Each of these three great phases was qualitatively different from, in most respects an *improvement* on, its predecessor, though as a consequence of concordance between the eras (i.e. direct parallels), it proved possible to identify and predict the distinctive features of the impending Age of the Spirit. Indeed, in a virtuoso display of trinitarian thinking, Joachim associated a distinctive array of plants, animals, images and symbols with each of the individual stages. Thus, for example, whereas the first *status* was symbolised by Winter and the second by Spring, the third was the equivalent of high Summer. The Age of the Father, likewise, was associated with infancy, nettles and the light of the stars; the Age of the Son with youth, roses and the light of the Moon; and the forthcoming Age of the Spirit with maturity, lilies and the light of the Sun. Most importantly for the subsequent secularisation of his meliorative schema, however, the first era's emphasis on labour, slavery and the rule of law, having given way to a second phase concerned with discipline, service and the pursuit of truth, was about to be superseded by an Elysium of contemplation, praise and, not least, liberty (Manuel 1965; Campion 1994).

As a loyal servant of the church, with no discernible heretical or schismatic inclinations, Joachim de Fiore was held in very high regard by his spiritual and lay contemporaries. Yet it is clear that his schema contained very serious implications for religious orthodoxy. By creating, in effect, a pecking order among the elements of the Trinity and intimating that the established church – which was associated with the Second Age – was soon to be replaced by two new ascetic orders of 'spiritual men', Joachim's three age framework possessed revolutionary potential. Within a few years of his death, pseudo-Joachite tracts, containing sub-Sibylline prophesies and teachings, were in widespread circulation. Thanks, moreover, to the proselytising endeavours of a breakaway monastic order, the Franciscan Spirituals, his revelations had been elevated to quasi-canonical status. This eventually led, in 1254, to one of the most notorious incidents in medieval Christendom, when an over-enthusiastic Joachite, Gerardo de Burgos, declared that the contents of the Old and New Testaments – associated with the first and second *status* respectively – had been utterly abrogated (McGinn 1979, 1985). Henceforth, all scriptural authority resided in the Third Testament – the so-called Eternal Evangel (or everlasting gospel) – made up of the teachings of Joachim de Fiore. Although Gerardo had selflessly assembled, edited and glossed a selection of the master's thoughts, the appearance of his book, *Introductorius in Evangelum Aeternum*, provoked an enormous outcry. A list of thirty-one errors in de Burgos' argument was forwarded to Pope Alexander IV, who duly set up a papal commission, which declared Joachim a heretic, ordered the burning of *Introductorius* and imprisoned Gerardo for good measure. The controversy, however, only served to further publicise the prophesies of Joachim, not least his calculation that the Second Age was due to end in 1260. Thus, by fanning the flames of Joachite-induced apocalyptic expectation, which were further stoked by famine in 1258, plague in 1259 and the first recorded procession of flagellants in 1260, the Eternal Evangel episode prompted one of the most serious outbreaks of millenarianism in the entire pre-Reformation period (Cohn 1970).

While the all-embracing catholicism of Joachim de Fiore's tripartite paradigm has induced raptures of ecstasy among many subsequent commentators (e.g. McGinn 1980; Gruner 1985; Kermode 1985; Reeves and Gould 1987), it is necessary to stress that his periodising framework was not created *ex nihilo*. On the contrary, the notion of three great historical ages, associated with the father, son and holy spirit respectively, had been employed by a host of earlier theological thinkers including Hildegard of Bingen, Robert of Deutz and the ninth-century Irish philosopher, John Scotus Erigena (McGinn 1985). The historical schema, what is more, and Joachim's evident fondness for threesomes were a commonplace of the Classical world – Platonism in particular – and have been traced back to the proto-literate civilisations of the ancient Near East (Trompf 1979). In fact, some sceptics have gone so far as to suggest that Joachimite thought contains nothing original and that his reputation rests entirely on being in the right place at the right time (Campion 1994).

It is, of course, undeniable that Joachim de Fiore was blessed with a formidable publicity machine in the shape of the Spiritual Franciscans and the hapless Gerardo de Burgos. He was writing, moreover, at a time of great social, economic and spiritual dislocation, when millennial tensions were widespread and the established church was believed to be irredeemably corrupt. Human nature being what it is, Joachim's reputation as both a renowned prophet and a notorious heretic, whose books and teachings were officially proscribed, undoubtedly added considerably to the Calabrian abbot's innate attraction.

Nevertheless, by succeeding in, first, positioning the (then) present in a degenerate and tumultuous transition zone at the end of the Second Age; second, suggesting that a qualitatively superior era was at hand and due to be realised here on earth; and, third, that the appearance of the Age of the Spirit could be accelerated by human intervention, Joachim's tripartite schema was ripe for adoption, adaptation and application by ensuing generations of visionaries, utopians and exponents of 'progressive' historical teleologies (Manuel and Manuel 1979; Nisbet 1980; Kumar 1991).

As the minutely detailed bibliographic analyses of Reeves (1969), McGinn (1985) and Reeves and Gould (1987) clearly demonstrate, Joachim de Fiore's tripartite model of history has proved enormously influential in the centuries since his death. Apart from its *direct* effects on the intellectual endeavours of pivotal theological thinkers like St Thomas Aquinas, Bonaventure, Thomas Muntzer and Martin Luther, and non-theological notables such as Columbus, Cortes and Nostradamus, the gradual secularisation of Joachim's periodising schema by Petrarch, Postel, Le Roy and Campenella amongst others, ensured that it continued to underpin manifold post-Enlightenment models of historical development (Manuel 1965; Gruner 1985). The three-age theories of Lessing, Schelling, Fichte and Vico were all directly indebted to the work of Joachim de Fiore, as was Hegel's dialectic of thesis, antithesis and synthesis. Henri Saint-Simon and Auguste Comte, the founding fathers of modern sociology, openly acknowledged the influence of the Calabrian abbot (Comte, for example, arranged history in three great ages – the theological, the metaphysical and the positive – and his entire system of positivism was predicated on threesomes). Marx's three stages of primitive society, class society and communism were also deeply Joachite in tenor and, indeed, it has been suggested that trinitarian schemata as diverse as Stone Age–Bronze Age–Iron Age, Ancient/ Medieval/ Modern, the Third Reich, the Third International, the Third Rome and even the contemporaneous division into first, second and third worlds are latter-day instantiations of Joachimism (Campion 1994).

In addition to the monumental periodising frameworks of Comte, Marx and analogous historicists, a host of creative writers and artists have drawn heavily upon the teachings of Joachim. Building upon a tradition that stretches back to Donne, Dante and beyond, literary luminaries as diverse as George Sand, George Eliot, Matthew Arnold, Walter Pater, W.B. Yeats, James Joyce, D.H. Lawrence, Max Jacob, Isak Dinesen (Karen Blixen), Muriel Spark and, most recently, Umberto Eco, have all been inspired by the visions of the great twelfth-century prophet. There is, admittedly, an on-going debate in scholarly circles about the *precise* limits of Joachim's influence. Some analysts of the history of thought argue that almost any tripartite model of historical development owes a debt to the Calabrian abbot (Nietzsche's, Jung's, Foucault's and Baudrillard's spring immediately to mind), whereas others contend that de Fiore's influence can only be inferred when his works, or clearly identifiable aspects of his corpus, are *specifically* referred to (see Campion 1994; Reeves

1995; Kermode 1985, 1995). Regardless of whether one subscribes to the former or latter position, the fact remains that Joachim de Fiore's periodising schema is deeply embedded in the intellectual unconscious of the western world and ever ready to manifest itself in many, varied and, as often as not, mutated forms.

THE MOTHER OF ALL MARKETING MODELS

In a recent overview of his life's work, Stanley C. Hollander (1995) has returned to the emergence of the modern 'marketing era', contending that this issue represents one of the most thorny topics on the research agenda of marketing historians. Restating his earlier position that the supposed postwar 'revolution' in marketing practice and thought was not particularly revolutionary (though it may have seemed revolutionary with the resumption of marketing normality in the aftermath of the hostilities), he suggests that the perpetuation of the production–sales–marketing eras myth is little more than a self-serving conspiracy on the part of marketing executives and academics, who like to think that they are somehow better or more sophisticated than their predecessors. While there is more than a little merit in Hollander's belief that the three eras schema is mad, bad and dangerous to know, the prevalence of trinitarian thinking in the western intellectual tradition, coupled with the long and influential arm of the Calabrian abbot, suggests that the traditional tripartite framework will not be readily dislodged. On the contrary, it is arguable that the postulation of more sophisticated and historically precise models simply cannot compete with the elementalism – some would say archetypal power – of the established schema. Indeed, as the deconstructionists rightly point out, the very act of engaging critically with the original only serves to ensure its continuation (Brown 1995a).

Rather than seeking to censure the three eras schema, it may be more appropriate to fight fire with fire by proposing an alternative but equally debatable three stage framework: for example, the Pre-modern Marketing Era (up to approx. 1900), the Modern Marketing Era (1900–99) and the soon to be consummated Post-modern Marketing Era (2000 plus). Marketing historians, of course, are likely to be aghast at such recidivism and postmodernists outraged since it implies an underpinning meta-narrative. However, since when has historical accuracy or academic apoplexy ever inhibited the dissemination of a provocative or outlandish suggestion? In truth, by sidestepping the discredited production era/sales era elements of the established schema, whilst retaining its inherent trichotomous appeal, and implying, in time-honoured Joachite fashion, that a whole new, qualitatively superior age is impending, such a model could be the answer to textbook writers' prayers. What is more, by failing to specify precise dates for the various eras, it offers enormous scope for further academic debate and publication opportunities, thereby ensuring its successful propagation.

Amusing as it is to contemplate the replacement of the original three eras schema with a parodic postmodern version of the same, the very longevity of the production–sales–marketing era paradigm means that it is unlikely to be superseded by a framework that offers little more than a triadic interpretation of historical events. After all, there are any number of tripartite models of marketing periodisation which have failed to set academic imaginations alight (Kotler's three stages of marketing consciousness, Kelly's three ages of marketing ethics, Tedlow's three eras of mass marketing and so on). It is clear, therefore, that for a model to make a serious impact on the academic marketing mindset, it must be as primordial as the three eras schema, *only more so.* Ideally, such a conceptualisation should not only employ the established trinitarian division, but it should also seek to embrace several other symbolically significant numerics, such as twosomes and foursomes. With this objective in mind, it is possible to assemble a 'mother of all marketing models' which postulates a three eras schema concerning a dichotomous debate (e.g. art versus science) using a fourfold taxonomic typology (such as the 4Ps).

The pro-science era (1945–83)

Fifty-odd years ago, a pivotal event occurred in the history of marketing scholarship, when Paul D. Converse (1945: 14) alluded to the 'science or art of marketing . . . the classified body of knowledge which we call the science of marketing'. Although these were little more than throw-away remarks in a paper primarily devoted to the results of a questionnaire survey of sixty-four marketing researchers, they started a debate which still periodically erupts in the marketing literature and the changing course of which can be divided into three broad eras. The first of these commenced in 1945 with Converse's passing comments, but despite the early sallies of Brown (1948), Alderson and Cox (1948) and Vaile (1949), it didn't really get started until the following decade. In a substantive, closely argued paper, Bartels (1951) assessed the current state of marketing scholarship and the nature of scientific endeavour. He surmised that while there was some evidence of the use of the scientific method in marketing, the discipline's manifest lack of theories, principles and laws meant that it did not yet qualify as a science. With continued, systematic effort, however, marketing could well become a science in the fullness of time.

Bartels' suggestion, coupled with the growing preparedness to speak openly of 'marketing science' (e.g. Cox and Alderson 1950), prompted Hutchinson (1952) into penning a tart rejoinder.

> In appraising the progress which has been made in developing a science of marketing one is tempted to make allowances for the relatively short period of time in which the issues have been under discussion. But whatever allowances are called for, one is likely to be somewhat disappointed over the lack of progress to date . . . There seems to be little

> evidence to support the claim that all that is needed is time and patience until there will emerge the new and shining science of marketing . . . There is a real reason, however, why the field of marketing has been slow to develop a unique body of theory. It is a simple one: marketing is not a science. It is rather an art or a practice, and as such more closely resembles engineering, medicine and architecture than it does physics, chemistry or biology. It is the drollest travesty to relate the scientist's search for knowledge to the market research man's seeking after customers. In actual practice . . . many and probably most of the decisions in the field resemble the scientific method hardly any more closely that what is involved in reading a road map or a time table.
>
> (Hutchinson 1952: 287–91)

Notwithstanding Hutchinson's heroic attempt to emasculate marketing's seemingly insatiable 'physics envy', it is fair to say that by the early 1960s the battle had been decisively won by the scientific wannabes. In an era informed by the Ford and Carnegie Reports and the celebrated Two Cultures controversy, the establishment of the Marketing Science Institute in 1962, combined with the AMA's stated aim of advancing the science of marketing and the publication of Buzzell's (1963: 32) famous paean to the scientific worldview ('to be against science is as heretical as to be against motherhood'), ensured that no-one seriously questioned the appropriateness of marketing's aspiration to scientific status. Granted, there was a great deal of discussion about whether the discipline had or had not attained its ultimate objective. For some commentators marketing was already a science or proto-science (Mills 1961; Lee 1965; Robin 1970; Kotler 1972; Ramond 1974). For others, it had either a considerable way to go or was pursuing a pleasant if somewhat utopian day-dream (Borden 1965; Halbert 1965; Kernan 1973; Levy 1976). Nonetheless, as Schwartz (1965: 1) stressed at the time, 'the various expressions of opinion have not revealed anyone who is opposed to the development of a science of marketing'. Indeed, the culmination of the 'debate' occurred in 1976, when Shelby Hunt, in a much-cited, award winning article, evaluated the state of marketing scholarship against the three – naturally! – characteristic features of science (distinct subject matter, underlying uniformities and intersubjectively certifiable research procedures) and found that it passed, or certain aspects of it passed, on all counts. 'The study of the positive dimensions of marketing', he concluded, 'can be appropriately referred to as marketing science.'

In retrospect, therefore, it is apparent that the first phase of the 'art versus science' controversy was characterised by the 4Ps of *positivism*, *penitence*, *pubescence* and *positioning*. *Positivism* does not simply refer to the fact that the model of science being pursued by marketers was characterised by universal laws and objective knowledge, but also to the overwhelmingly positive, progressive, optimistic, forward-looking attitudes of the individuals concerned. The attainment of 'scientific' status was generally considered to be A Good Thing, a worthwhile pursuit, a noble endeavour and, indeed, one that could be attained if it were not for the bad old intuitive, seat-of-the-pants, unscientific attitudes that still too often prevailed and about which prospective marketing scientists were suitably *penitent* and self-critical. In fact, Newman (1965: 20) went so far as to threaten recalcitrant revolutionaries with 'the pains of hastened obsolescence'. Set against this, it was generally acknowledged that marketing's continuing preoccupation with piecemeal data gathering, rather than theory construction, was attributable to *pubescence*, the comparative youth of the subject area, the fact that it was only fifty years old and, unlike analogous applied sciences like engineering and medicine, had not progressed beyond the artistic or craftsman stage of disciplinary development. Yet despite its academic immaturity and predilection for improper procedures, many maintained that marketing was moving in the right direction, had achieved a great deal in a short period of time and, for some enthusiasts at least, already warranted the 'scientific' appellation. Such assertions – and diverse counter-claims – ensured that much time and effort was devoted to *positioning*, to defining the nature, scope and characteristics of both 'marketing' and 'science' and placing the perceived state of marketing thought against these putative measures of 'scientific' attainment.

The anti-science era (1983–99)

If the first great age of the art–science debate began with a whimper, it ended – and the second era commenced – with an almighty bang. In the fall of 1983, Paul Anderson challenged the fundamental philosophical premises of marketing 'science'. The received view, variously described as 'positivist', 'positivistic' or 'logical empiricist' rested on the assumption that a single, external world existed, that this social reality could be empirically measured by independent observers using objective methods, and that it could be explained and predicted through the identification of universal laws or law-like generalisations. Aided and abetted by like-minded revolutionaries, Anderson sought to highlight the shortcomings of this scientific worldview, principally its reliance upon the flawed 'verification theory of meaning', the inadequacies of its falsificationist procedure, the difficulties presented by the inherent theory-ladenness of observation and, not least, the fact that innumerable attempts to demarcate 'science' from 'non-science' had signally failed to do so (see Peter and Olson 1983; Deshpande 1983; Hirschman 1986).

In these circumstances, Anderson (1983, 1986, 1989) concluded that marketing was ill-served by the traditional positivistic perspective – what he termed *science*[1] – and that a relativist approach – dubbed *science*[2] – had much more to offer. This maintained that, although an external world may well exist 'out there', it was impossible to access this world independently of human sensations, perceptions and interpretations. Hence, reality was not objective and external to the observer but socially constructed and given meaning by human actors. What counted as knowledge about this world was *relative* to different times, contexts and research communities. Relativism held that there were no universal standards for judging knowledge claims, that different research communities constructed different worldviews and that science was a social process where consensus prevailed about the status of knowledge claims, scientific standards and the like, though these were not immutable. Science was *so* social, in fact, that Peter and Olson (1983), in their ringing endorsement of the relativist position, concluded that science was actually a special case of marketing, that successful scientific theories were those which performed well in the marketplace of ideas thanks to the marketing skills of their proponents.

It almost goes without saying that this eschewal of the orthodox idea of marketing science – as objectively proven knowledge – and its attempted replacement with the notion of science as societal consensus, provoked a ferocious reaction. The foremost defender of the faith, Shelby D. Hunt (1984, 1990, 1992) was particularly scathing about relativism, arguing that its pursuit would not only lead inexorably to nihilism, irrationalism, incoherence and irrelevance, but it also threatened to subvert the past four hundred years of scientific and technological progress (Western Civilisation in Peril – Shock!). Battle was thus joined, and over the next decade or thereabouts the heavyweights of marketing scholarship slugged it out, though it is apparent in retrospect that the revolutionaries triumphed (in so far as marketing scholarship is much less epistemologically and methodologically monolithic than before). At the same time, however, the controversy opened the door for contemporary, postmodern critiques of the western scientific worldview, which are often couched in virulent, not to say apocalyptic, phraseology (Firat *et al.* 1994; Venkatesh *et al.* 1993). While postmodernists recognise that western science has provided enormous material benefits, they contend that its promise of perpetual plenitude has been achieved at a very heavy social, environmental and political price. The mass of society may be better off than before, but the division of wealth is as unequal as ever, arguably more unequal. The rise of the west, they argue, has been at the expense of the subjugation, exploitation, usurpation and coca-colonisation of 'the rest'. And, while progress may have been made by some people (white, male, heterosexual, university professors, for instance), and in certain economic-technocratic spheres of activity, the same is not necessarily true for other groups of people – coloured, female, homosexual, the unemployed, etc. – and in non-scientific areas of human endeavour, such as morality or spirituality (Brown 1995b).

Just as the first great era of the art or science debate could be encapsulated in a 4Ps framework, so too the second can be summarised in terms of the 4Ps of *philosophy*, *polemic*, *partition* and *perplexity*. Regardless of one's assessment of the outcome of the Hunt–Anderson contest, there is no question that it was conducted at a high level of *philosophical* sophistication and that the associated skirmishes on terrain as diverse as 'truth', 'reification', 'realism', 'incommensurability', 'objectivity', 'method' and more besides, forced mainstream marketing academics to consider issues that go to the very heart of scientific understanding. The caricature – the cartoon version – of science that characterised much of the first phase of the great debate was well and truly buried. No less comprehensively interred, as marketing scholarship descended into extremely acrimonious and highly personalised *polemic*, was the hitherto prevailing sense of collegiality, of community, of collective endeavour. True, the participants in first era exchanges were quite prepared to disagree over the precise placement of marketing on the art–science continuum, but there was a general consensus about the desirability of the ultimate aim of attaining scientific status. The demise of this sense of overall purpose in the second era resulted in the effective *partition* of the marketing discipline into embittered and mutually antagonistic factions, variously, often pejoratively, labelled as positivists/post-positivists, realists/relativists, modernists/post-modernists and, not least, practitioners/academics (cf. O'Shaughnessy and Holbrook 1988; Calder and Tybout 1989; Hunt 1994). Hence, the ultimate legacy of this period of internecine warfare appears to be a widespread sense of *perplexity* and bemusement. By almost any measure, marketing is more 'successful' now than it has ever been, but mounting challenges to its hitherto unimpeachable 'scientific' mission have created an all-pervasive air of uncertainty and a growing preparedness to explore alternative, 'post-scientific' possibilities (Kavanagh 1994).

The non-science era (2000–)

In appropriately Joachite fashion, the present phase of the great 'marketing – art or science?' debate lies in a degraded transition zone between dispensations two and three. It is characterised by schism, cynicism, ennui and, dare one suggest, pre-millennial unease. The overwhelming optimism of the first great age of marketing science – the sense of progress, of forward movement – has been supplanted by a profoundly pessimistic, some would say nihilistic, world-view where achievements are few, crises many and science no longer offers the prospect of salvation. When we re-read the publications of first generation scientific aspirants, we are not only appalled by their preparedness to hold up the Atom Bomb as an exemplar of scientific achievement (Brown 1948; Mills 1961), but cannot fail to be amused by the naïve assumption that, irrespective of its ultimate attainability, western science was an appropriate, unproblematic role model for marketing. By contrast, Anderson's (1994: 14) recent contention that 'the dogged pursuit of the mantle of sciencehood has severely damaged marketing's credibility', is much more in tune with contemporary sentiment – sentiments shared by many academic specialisms (Appleyard 1992; Midgeley 1992). Indeed, even the proponents of marketing science have attempted to step back from their earlier, extravagant expectations or expressed serious doubts about the present, parlous state of affairs (Buzzell 1984; Hunt 1984, 1994).

Although it is impossible to predict the precise nature of the impending third *status*, Joachimite teachings emphasise three important facts: (1) that the eras are qualitatively different and in most respects an improvement on one another; (2) that the essential character of each succeeding stage is already apparent within its immediate predecessor; and (3) that there is always an element of concordance between the various dispensations. Certainly, when the first two phases of the great art–science debate are examined, these historical lessons appear to hold good. As we have seen, the first age, with its optimistic unilateralism and emphasis on positioning, was superseded by a second era of pessimistic pluralism and sophisticated philosophical argument. Similarly, the characteristic feature of the Second Age – a concern with the *type* of science considered appropriate for marketing – was alluded to by several first phase commentators some time prior to Hunt's official pronouncement and Anderson's subsequent heresy (Taylor 1965; Robin 1970; Dawson 1971; O'Shaughnessy and Ryan 1979). Both dispensations, moreover, were distinguished by a dialectical tendency, in so far as the emergent ethos was quickly challenged and, as often as not, the challengers succeeded in mustering and articulating the most coherent arguments, even though they failed to carry the day (e.g. Hutchinson in Age One and Hunt in Age Two).

If we accept that Joachite tendencies are discernible in the art versus science controversy, then the following possibilities suggest themselves for the forthcoming Non-science Era (a.k.a. the Age of the Marketing Spirit). First and foremost, marketers will recognise that the time spent pursuing 'scientific' status is time wasted and that marketing should seek to be designated an 'art'. It seems astonishing that in the entire history of the debate almost no one attempted to make the case *for* marketing as art. Many people, most notably Hutchinson, maintained that marketing was an art and destined to remain an art, but they did not suggest that marketing should *aspire* to artistic status. In fact, most discussions of the art of marketing focused on art, as in artisan (i.e. the craft or technology of marketing), rather than art as in aesthetics, art as the very pinnacle of human achievement, art as a quasi-spiritual endeavour.

Second, it is clear that this qualitatively different – and arguably superior – status of marketing scholarship is *already* discernible within the present Second Age. Thus, several prominent marketing intellectuals have advocated the study of artistic artefacts – books, films, plays, poetry, etc. – and itemised the benefits to be obtained from the liberal arts (humanities) end of the academic spectrum (Belk 1986; Holbrook and Grayson 1986; Holbrook *et al.* 1989). Other prescient thinkers have espoused an increasingly aesthetic-cum-spiritual orientation (Kavanagh 1994) and, indeed, certain creative individuals have demonstrated, through the use of new literary forms (NLF), that marketing scholarship can be an artistic achievement *in itself* (Sherry 1993; Holbrook 1995; McDonagh 1995; Smithee 1996).

Third, and most significantly, the impending aesthetic turn in marketing is likely to inspire a dialectical reaction, where the proponents of marketing science will seek to articulate a cogent defence of their position, or, more likely, move to an increasingly postmodern conception of science (chaos theory, fuzzy logic, GAIA, etc.). However, whereas the second age was characterised by schismatic tendencies, a seemingly irrevocable split into multifarious warring factions, the non-science Age of the Marketing Spirit will revert to the first great era of mutual tolerance, collegiality, magnanimity and co-operation, and prompt the realisation that there are many forms of marketing knowledge, numerous routes to marketing understanding, both 'artistic' and 'scientific', and that marketing always has been and always will be a very broad church.

Doubtless for some died-in-the-wool marketing fundamentalists, this vision seems less like a non-science era than a nonsense era. If, however, it does come to pass, it can be tentatively prophesied that the following 4Ps will obtain: *poetics*, an increased concern with aesthetics and spirituality; *plenitude*, where there will be a smorgasbord of intellectual choice; *peace*, in so far as the divisions of the past are successfully transcended; and, *purpose*, wherein a whole new sense of direction is apparent. Marketing paradise, in short, is just around the corner, almost within our grasp, but only if we pray hard enough, pardon our enemies and, last but not least, the lion of marketing science is prepared to lie down with the artistic marketing lamb.

CONCLUSION

A complete generation has now passed since Keith (1960) sketched out his celebrated production–sales–marketing eras schema and, while the construct has been criticised on numerous occasions, it remains a permanent fixture in many if not most best-selling marketing textbooks. For some marketing scholars, this is a comparatively trivial matter – a minor introductory-level irritation – even though it can be convincingly argued that textbooks comprise the repository, the shop window, the very epitome of marketing knowledge (see Bartels 1951; Peter and Olson 1983; Gummesson 1993). For others, the mindless recycling of Keith's model is indicative of the innate slothfulness of slapdash textbook writers or, worse, a maleficent attempt to inculcate an entirely false sense of marketing progress (Hollander 1986, 1995). It is equally arguable, of course, that invoking the customary periodising framework performs a simple 'ritual' function, in that it provides an obligatory and easily assimilable nod to the past by proponents of an essentially ahistorical worldview. More to the point perhaps, the three eras schema is predicated upon a primordial, possibly archetypal, human tendency to think in threes. This trinitarian inclination is made manifest in many ways, shapes and forms, but it is exemplified by copious tripartite models of historical development, of which Joachim de Fiore's has proved profoundly influential. While it is a gross exaggeration to suggest that Keith was *directly* influenced by the Eternal Evangel, his framework unquestionably lies on a clear line of descent from the work of the great twelfth-century apocalyptic.

Given the primeval power of trinitarian thinking, this chapter has contended that the discredited production–sales–marketing eras schema will only be deleted from the disciplinary record when it is trumped by a typology that succeeds, in effect, in upping the archetypal ante. To illustrate the point, a 'mother of all marketing models', comprising a three stage explication of a dichotomous debate employing a quadripartite taxonomy, was postulated. The model deliberately contravenes almost every precept of acceptable marketing scholarship – it is crude, it is speculative, it is historicist, it is factually inaccurate, it is pre-postmodern – but it is premised on the presuppositions that twosomes, threesomes and foursomes possess primordial appeal, that truth is less important than rhetorical dexterity and (Lyotardian) performativity, that in these degenerate times the suckers of marketing scholarship can be duped into accepting anything with vaguely utopian overtones, and, above all, that by offending so egregiously against convention, the schema might be condemned out of hand by apoplectic marketing academics, thereby ensuring that it is widely discussed, developed and disseminated.

Irrespective of its future demonisation, the mother of all marketing models demonstrates an important point about the Three Eras schema; namely, that this periodising framework has an intellectual history of its own. Indeed, when the trajectory of the conceptualisation is examined, it is clear that the three eras saga can *itself* be divided into three eras – the Three Eras Production Era, the Three Eras Sales Era and the Three Eras Marketing Era. The Three Eras Production Era commenced with Keith's paper and first generation textbook writers' propagation of the construct to an undiscriminating yet eager marketing audience, one which considered itself in the commercial vanguard but lacked a sophisticated sense of its past. Keith's model, in other words, was the intellectual equivalent of 'you can have any schema you want, as long as it's the three eras schema'. The Three Eras Sales Era involved attempts by marketing historians, like Hollander and Fullerton, to persuade marketing academics of the error of their historicist ways, to highlight the scholarly shortcomings of stage-type models of development and, most importantly of all, to sell their own more historically informed alternatives. Unfortunately, the upshot of these high-pressure sales tactics has been largely negative, in so far as many textbooks appear to have abandoned historical perspectives completely (or, alternatively, added several more stages to the original model). By contrast, the impending Three Eras Marketing Era is premised on a recognition of the fact that people *need* and *want* simple, easily remembered, progressivist models of historical development, especially ones predicated on a trinitarian framework with all its archetypal-cum-cabbalistic power. After all, if we don't believe that we know more than our marketing predecessors, that we have advanced and are going to continue to advance, why do we bother to go on? The production–sales–marketing eras schema may be a complete myth, but, as the above exercise in instant myth-making seeks to show, myths are necessary, myths are important, myths have their place, myths help foster our sense of ourselves, myths are the mother tongue of humankind (Reiche 1985).

NOTES

1 Although the three eras schema is usually attributed to Keith, his paper also mentioned a fourth era of 'marketing control', albeit in passing. This element of the model has been conveniently forgotten in the ensuing decades of indiscriminate recycling by textbook writers. It would be an interesting philological task to uncover who was responsible for dropping Keith's fourth era and when it occurred. Certainly, the 'classic' schema was in circulation by the mid-sixties (e.g. King 1965).

2 This exercise was deeply unscientific, since it involved examining all the basic marketing and marketing management texts on display at the 1995 AMA Summer Educators' Conference. Only one drew upon Fullerton's framework, though the 'complex flux' model was not mentioned by name.

REFERENCES

Adair, G. (1994), 'In praise of the threesome', *The Sunday Times*, 5 June, 10, p. 9.

Alderson, W. and Cox, R. (1948), 'Towards a theory of marketing', *Journal of Marketing*, 13 (October), pp. 137–52.

Anderson, L.McT. (1994), 'Marketing science: where's the beef?', *Business Horizons*, 37 (1), pp. 8–16.

Anderson, P.F. (1983), 'Marketing, scientific progress and scientific method', *Journal of Marketing*, 47 (Fall), pp. 18–31.

Anderson, P.F. (1986), 'On method in consumer research: a critical relativist perspective', *Journal of Consumer Research*, 13 (September), pp. 155–73.

Anderson, P.F. (1989), 'On relativism and interpretivism – with a prolegomenon to the 'why' question', in E.C. Hirschman (ed.), *Interpretive Consumer Research*, Association for Consumer Research, Provo, pp. 10–23.

Appleyard, B. (1992), *Understanding the Present: Science and the Soul of Modern Man*, Picador, London.

Bartels, R. (1951), 'Can marketing be a science?', *Journal of Marketing*, 16 (January), pp. 319–28.

Belk, R.W. (1986), 'Art versus science as ways of generating knowledge about materialism', in D. Brinberg and R.J. Lutz (eds), *Perspectives on Methodology in Consumer Research*, Springer-Verlag, New York, pp. 3–36.

Borden, N.H. (1965), 'The concept of the marketing mix', in G. Schwartz (ed.), *Science in Marketing*, Wiley, New York, pp. 386–97.

Brown, L.O. (1948), 'Toward a profession of marketing', *Journal of Marketing*, 13 (July), pp. 27–31.

Brown, S. (1995a), 'Postmodernism, the wheel of retailing and will to power', *International Review of Retail, Distribution and Consumer Research*, 5 (3), pp. 387–414.

Brown, S. (1995b), *Postmodern Marketing*, Routledge, London.

Bull, M. (1995), 'On making ends meet', in M. Bull (ed.), *Apocalypse Theory and the Ends of the World*, Blackwell, Oxford, pp. 1–17.

Butler, C. (1970), *Number Symbolism*, Barnes and Noble, New York.

Buzzell, R.D. (1963), 'Is marketing a science?', *Harvard Business Review*, 41 (1), pp. 32–40, 166–70.

Buzzell, R.D. (1984), 'Preface to – is marketing a science?', in S.W. Brown and R.P. Fisk (eds), *Marketing Theory: Distinguished Contributions*, John Wiley, New York, p. 66.

Calder, B.J. and Tybout, A.M. (1989), 'Interpretive, qualitative and traditional scientific empirical consumer behaviour', in E.C. Hirschman (ed.), *Interpretive Consumer Research*, Association for Consumer Research, Provo, pp. 199–208.

Campion, N. (1994), *The Great Year: Astrology, Millenarianism and History in the Western Tradition*, Arkana, Harmondsworth.
Cohn, N. (1970), *The Pursuit of the Millennium: Revolutionary Millenarians and Mystical Anarchists of the Middle Ages*, Pimlico, London.
Converse, P.D. (1945), 'The development of the science of marketing – an exploratory survey', *Journal of Marketing*, 10 (July), pp. 14–23.
Cox, R. and Alderson, W. (1950), *Theory in Marketing*, Richard D. Irwin, Chicago.
Dawson, L.M. (1971), 'Marketing science in the Age of Aquarius', *Journal of Marketing*, 35 (July), pp. 66–72.
Deshpande, R. (1983), '"Paradigms lost": on theory and method in research in marketing', *Journal of Marketing*, 47 (Fall), pp. 101–10.
Firat, A.F., Sherry, J.F. and Venkatesh, A. (1994), 'Postmodernism, marketing and the consumer', *International Journal of Research in Marketing*, 11 (4), pp. 311–16.
Fullerton, R. (1985), 'Was there a "production era" in marketing history? A multinational study', in S.C. Hollander and T. Nevett (eds), *Marketing in the Long Run*, Michigan State University, East Lansing, pp. 388–400.
Fullerton, R.A. (1988), 'How modern is modern marketing? Marketing's evolution and the myth of the "production era"', *Journal of Marketing*, 52 (January), pp. 108–25.
Gilbert, D. and Bailey, N. (1990), 'The development of marketing – a compendium of historical approaches', *Quarterly Review of Marketing*, 15 (2), pp. 6–13.
Gruner, R. (1985), *Philosophies of History: A Critical Essay*, Gower, Aldershot.
Gummesson, E. (1993), 'Marketing according to textbooks: six objections', in D. Brownlie *et al.* (eds), *Rethinking Marketing: New Perspectives on the Discipline and Profession*, Warwick Business School, Coventry, pp. 248–58.
Halbert, M. (1965), *The Meaning and Sources of Marketing Theory*, McGraw-Hill, New York.
Hirschman, E.C. (1986), 'Humanistic inquiry in marketing research: philosophy, method and criteria', *Journal of Marketing Research*, 23 (August), pp. 237–49.
Holbrook, M.B. (1995), *Consumer Research: Introspective Essays on the Study of Consumption*, Sage, Thousand Oaks.
Holbrook, M.B., Bell, S. and Grayson, M.W. (1989), 'The role of the humanities in consumer research: close encounters and costal disturbances', in E.C. Hirschman (ed.), *Interpretive Consumer Research*, Association for Consumer Research, Provo, pp. 29–47.
Holbrook, M.B. and Grayson, M.W. (1986), 'Cinematic consumption: symbolic consumer behaviour in *Out of Africa*', *Journal of Consumer Research*, 13 (December), pp. 374–81.
Hollander, S.C. (1986), 'The marketing concept: a déjà vu', in G. Fisk (ed.), *Marketing Management Technology as a Social Process*, Praeger, New York, pp. 3–29.
Hollander, S.C. (1995), 'My life on Mt. Olympus', *Journal of Macromarketing*, 15 (1), pp. 86–106.
Hollander, S.C. and Germain, R. (1992), *Was There a Pepsi Generation Before Pepsi Discovered It? An Historical Approach to Youth-based Segmentation in Marketing*, NTC Business Books, Lincolnwood.
Hunt, S.D. (1976), 'The nature and scope of marketing', *Journal of Marketing*, 40 (July), pp. 17–28.
Hunt, S.D. (1984), 'Should marketing adopt relativism?', in P.F. Anderson and M.J. Ryan (eds), *Scientific Method in Marketing*, American Marketing Association, Chicago, pp. 30–4.
Hunt, S.D. (1990), 'Truth in marketing theory and research', *Journal of Marketing*, 54 (July), pp. 1–15.
Hunt, S.D. (1992), 'For reason and realism in marketing', *Journal of Marketing*, 56 (April), pp. 89–102.
Hunt, S.D. (1994), 'On rethinking marketing: our discipline, our practice, our methods', *European Journal of Marketing*, 28 (3), pp. 13–25.

Hutchinson, K.D. (1952), 'Marketing as a science: an appraisal', *Journal of Marketing*, 16 (January), pp. 286–93.
Kavanagh, D. (1994), 'Hunt versus Anderson: round 16', *European Journal of Marketing*, 28 (3), pp. 26–41.
Keith, R.J. (1960), 'The marketing revolution', *Journal of Marketing*, 24 (January), pp. 35–8.
Kermode, F. (1985), 'Apocalypse and the modern', in S. Friedländer *et al.* (eds), *Visions of Apocalypse: End or Rebirth?*, Holmes and Meier, New York, pp. 84–106.
Kermode, F. (1995), 'Waiting for the End', in M. Bull (ed.), *Apocalypse Theory and the Ends of the World*, Blackwell, Oxford, pp. 250–63.
Kernan, J.B. (1973), 'Marketing's coming of age', *Journal of Marketing*, 37 (October), pp. 34–41.
King, R.L. (1965), 'The marketing concept', in G. Schwartz (ed.), *Science in Marketing*, John Wiley, New York, pp. 70–97.
Kotler, P. (1972), 'A generic concept of marketing', *Journal of Marketing*, 36 (April), pp. 46–54.
Kumar, K. (1991), *Utopianism*, Open University Press, Milton Keynes.
Kumar, K. (1995), 'Apocalypse, millennium and utopia today', in M. Bull (ed.), *Apocalypse Theory and the Ends of the World*, Blackwell, Oxford, pp. 200–24.
Lee, C.E. (1965) 'Measurement and the development of science and marketing', *Journal of Marketing Research*, 2 (February), pp. 20–5.
Levitt, T. (1960), 'Marketing myopia', *Harvard Business Review*, 38 (July–August), pp. 45–56.
Levy, S.J. (1976), 'Marcology 101 or the domain of marketing', in K.L. Bernhardt (ed.), *Marketing: 1776–1976 and Beyond*, American Marketing Association, Chicago, pp. 577–81.
Manuel, F.E. (1965), *Shapes of Philosophical History: The Ways in Which Philosophical Historians Over the Past Twenty Centuries Have Looked at the Nature of Man and the Shape of Human History*, Allen and Unwin, London.
Manuel, F.E. and Manuel, F.P. (1979), *Utopian Thought in the Western World*, Belknap, Cambridge.
Marion, G. (1993), 'The marketing management discourse: what's new since the 1960s', in M.J. Baker (ed.), *Perspectives on Marketing Management Volume Three*, Wiley, Chichester, pp. 143–68.
McDonagh, P. (1995), 'Q: is marketing dying of consumption? A: yes, and the answer is consumption!', in Brown *et al.* (eds) *Proceedings of the Marketing Eschatology Retreat*, University of Ulster, Belfast, pp. 48–59.
McGinn, B. (1979), *Visions of the End: Apocalyptic Traditions in the Middle Ages*, Columbia University Press, New York.
McGinn, B. (1980), 'Symbolism in the thought of Joachim of Fiore: a reinterpretation', in A. Williams (ed.), *Prophecy and Millenarianism: Essays in Honour of Marjorie Reeves*, Longman, Harlow, pp. 143–64.
McGinn, B. (1985), *The Calabrian Abbot: Joachim of Fiore in the History of Western Thought*, Macmillan, New York.
Midgeley, M. (1992), *Science as Salvation: A Modern Myth and its Meaning*, Routledge, London.
Mills, H.D. (1961), 'Marketing as a science', *Harvard Business Review*, 39 (September–October), pp. 137–42.
Newman, J.W. (1965), 'Marketing science: significance to the professor of marketing', in G. Schwartz (ed.), *Science in Marketing*, John Wiley, New York, pp. 20–32.
Nisbet, R. (1980), *History of the Idea of Progress*, Heinemann, London.
O'Shaughnessy, J. and Holbrook, M.B. (1988), 'Understanding consumer behaviour: the linguistic turn in marketing research', *Journal of the Market Research Society*, 30 (2), pp. 197–223.

O'Shaughnessy, J. and Ryan, M.J. (1979), 'Marketing, science and technology', in O.C. Ferrell, S.W. Brown and C.W. Lamb (eds), *Conceptual and Theoretical Developments in Marketing*, American Marketing Association, Chicago, pp. 557–89.

Peter, J. P. and Olson, J. C. (1983), 'Is science marketing?', *Journal of Marketing*, 47 (Fall), pp. 111–25.

Ramond, C. (1974), *The Art of Using Science in Marketing*, Harper and Row, New York.

Reeves, M. (1969), *The Influence of Prophecy in the Later Middle Ages: A Study in Joachimism*, Clarendon Press, Oxford.

Reeves, M. (1995), 'Pattern and purpose in history in the later medieval and renaissance periods', in M. Bull (ed.), *Apocalypse Theory and the Ends of the World*, Blackwell, Oxford, pp. 90–111.

Reeves, M. and Gould, W. (1987), *Joachim of Fiore and the Myth of the Eternal Evangel in the Nineteenth Century*, Clarendon, Oxford.

Reiche, H.A.T. (1985), 'The archaic heritage: myths of decline and end in antiquity', in S. Friedländer *et al.* (eds), *Visions of Apocalypse: End or Rebirth?*, Holmes and Meier, New York, pp. 21–43.

Robin, D.P. (1970), 'Toward a normative science in marketing', *Journal of Marketing*, 24 (October), pp. 73–6.

Rubinsky, Y. and Wiseman, I. (1982), *A History of the End of the World*, William Morrow, New York.

Savitt, R. (1989), 'Looking back to see ahead: writing the history of American retailing', *Journal of Retailing*, 65 (3), pp. 326–55.

Schwartz, G. (1965), 'Nature and goals of marketing science', in G. Schwartz (ed.), *Science in Marketing*, John Wiley, New York, pp. 1–19.

Sebeok, T.A. (1988), 'One, two, three spells UBERTY', in U. Eco and T.A. Sebeok (eds), *The Sign of Three: Dupin, Holmes, Pierce*, Indiana University Press, Bloomington, pp. 1–10.

Smithee, A. (1996), 'Kotler is dead!', *European Journal of Marketing*, in press.

Taylor, W.J. (1965), '"Is marketing a science?" revisited', *Journal of Marketing*, 29 (July), pp. 49–53.

Trompf, G.W. (1979), *The Idea of Historical Recurrence in Western Thought: From Antiquity to the Reformation*, University of California Press, Berkeley.

Twitchell, J.B. (1996), *AdcultUSA: The Triumph of Advertising in American Culture*, Columbia University Press, New York.

Vaile, R.S. (1949), 'Towards a theory of marketing – a comment', *Journal of Marketing*, 14 (April), 520–2.

Venkatesh, A., Sherry, J.F. and Firat, A.F. (1993), 'Postmodernism and the marketing imaginary', *International Journal of Research in Marketing*, 10 (3), pp. 215–23.

3

MAKING A DRAMA OUT OF A CRISIS

The final curtain for the marketing concept

Pierre McDonagh and Andrea Prothero

INTRODUCTION

This chapter begins with a short play depicting, amongst other things, the demise of the marketing academy, and its subsequent, more eclectic revival. The play's main message is further explored by examining the academy's forerunner of marketing knowledge development, the marketing concept. A play was chosen as the main means of communicating our message first, and foremost, as a result of the authors' (the first author in particular) boredom with conventional academic marketing papers. Secondly, and perhaps more importantly as an attempt to move away from yet another 'scientific' paper in marketing. The literature already shows the reliance upon the scientific method in marketing (Brown 1995b, Wright and Pickton 1995, Anderson 1994, etc.), and as this work considers issues, for example marcomarketing, which cannot be examined scientifically (Tamilia 1992), then a scientific treatment was obviously not the way forward for us. This said the authors are not aiming to partake in the Hunt versus Anderson debate (see Kavanagh 1994) but simply see their artistic New Literary Form (Brown 1995b) as the most suitable for this chapter. Thus this work should be judged 'on the basis of its literary and aesthetic value rather than on its functional utility or methodological rigour' (Kavanagh 1994). As Brown (1995b) stresses,

> Marketing paradise, in short, is just around the corner, almost within our grasp, but only if we pray hard enough, pardon our enemies and, last but not least, the lion of marketing science is prepared to lie down with the artistic marketing lamb.
>
> (p. 310)

The second aim of this work is to highlight why we believe it is finally time for the marketing academy to allow the final curtain for the marketing concept to be ceremoniously drawn and permit the academy to move forward in its research efforts. As this chapter highlights there are too many addons and extensions to the marketing concept, and we do not wish to contribute yet another addition. More meaningful concepts are called for.

PROLOGUE TO THE PLAY

This short play is written in the tradition of a Greek Tragedy. It revolves around the day-to-day happenings in a night-club called The Metropolis, based in a small village called Banbridge, located somewhere in the Northern hemisphere of the marketing academy. Clearly, in reverence of tradition, it has to be inferred that the characters are fictitious and any resemblance to persons alive or dead is coincidental. Suffice it to say that, in reality, one of the authors grew up some twenty-two miles away from a town with the same name and a very well-known night-club.

The Metropolis is analogous to the present day fortress marketing of our academy, based in a dilapidated building, in need of internal renovation and externally of a new coat of paint. Its bar, stage area and dance floor, the *disco inferno*, were once the hub of Northern youth activity but many of the locals have now stopped 'strutting their stuff' on a Friday and Saturday night down at The Metropolis in favour of new haunts. The 1970s neon sign still flashes sporadically over the main hacienda-like entrance of white marble pillars, headed by crafted golden eagles, weathered by the unkind lashings from the north westerly wind common in the region.

The Oracle, or BIG O as the locals call him, is the owner of The Metropolis and the fount of all knowledge about entertainment in the area. Many say he *is* entertainment, the maestro, certainly his sidekick and resident DJ, LISRELLI reveres this man's view of the business world, not to mention his religious choice of the nightly Top 40 records to be played. These people are representative of the guardians of the marketing faith, our professorial literati.

The PRINCESS, an American born in Nashville of European extract, is Big O's star attraction, known for her purist renditions of classic songs. She is a close personification to marketing knowledge which is currently referred to as muzak. Her stage name, given by Big O, is MOTHER F and she has a backing group called the UCKERS who have been chosen for their similarity of appearance, albeit deliberately flawed, to the Princess. At the time of writing the Princess is being held very much against her will in The Metropolis. Bored and forced to sing songs that she is tired of, she is declining into ill health and is very, very irritable.

The bouncers STOCKY, ACHING and WATERY patrol the entrance to The Metropolis with the prowess of Welsh scrum halves, who have seen better glory days. They are akin to the majority of the reviewers of marketing knowledge creation. Elsewhere, a well-travelled FROG roams the Northern hemisphere, previously a glamorous PRINCE fallen on hard times. P can be whoever or whatever you want him to be.

ACT 1

SCENE 1: The Metropolis

[*Stage Left,* {*Sfx* (*sound effects*)} the PRINCESS *warbles the last verse of Sinatra's My Way, splutters to a stop while* BIG O *and* LISRELLI *are at the bar drinking pints of Carling, while* THE UCKERS *continue twisting some more gooey Wrigleys around their Ratnered fingers*].

MOTHER F/THE PRINCESS: Fuck it, why do I always have to sing this ole shite muzak! Don't you think people are fed up listening to *My Way*!! I want to make my own songs, be remembered, and cut a vinyl record which is really different and . . . [*interrupted mid sentence*].

BIG O: Princess baby, baby baby! . . . I've been in this business since before you christened Pampers and believe me this is what people want to hear, I know, and besides it would have to be a CD **not** vinyl, now do it just the way I like it eh, come on!

LISRELLI [*aside to* BIG O]: What about that VH-1 offer of a video shoot here, I could groove on down and Mother F and The Uckers could do '*That's the way I like it.*'

BIG O: Sweetie, okay I'm going to arrange an MTV shoot for you and everyone can see just how good you are. Now isn't that better?

PRINCESS/MOTHER F: Wow, really that would sure be neat. {*Sfx And through it all I did it myyyy waay*}

LISRELLI: But, O are you sure?

BIG O: Lis, trust me on this one. Now blast out 'you're the one that I want' to get these punters charged up.

MEANWHILE

[*In a queue outside The Metropolis,* FROG *hops into the pocket of one of the more together looking persons. As a lover of music, it was one of his treats to hear what people were listening to nowadays. Just as he was approaching the neon sign the person's coat was grabbed and he overheard:*]

ACHING: No winkle pickers. [*As he pointed at the person's shiny leather boots*].

STOCKY: And certainly no toads!!

[FROG *feels himself being grabbed by his legs and receives the full force of* WATERY'S *boot after* STOCKY *threw him high in the air. After he hurtled along the alley* FROG *smacked off the stage door just as one of the* UCKERS *was making her way out for a Marlboro. Miss* UCKER *lifts dazed* FROG *onto the wall and gives him a peck on the cheek. As she disappears up the heavily littered alley* FROG *transforms into* P, *the person formerly known as Prince, he grins at the person in whose pocket he had originally been. The person faints muttering 'That's no normal toad boy!'* P *carefully sneaks out of the alley passing a group of grungers who are busy graffiti-spraying the side-wall with 'Kurt Lives You (*BIG O*) Die'. As he looks over his shoulder he laughs to himself, decides to get away from this place and heads out the main road. He starts hitch-hiking. On the back of an old soggy box of Tatyo crisps he writes 'Somewhere better fun than here' and waits patiently.*]

SCENE 2: Back in The Metropolis

PRINCESS/MOTHER F: These people are from VH-1 not MTV Lis, I think O is being taken for a ride.

LISRELLI: No, no sure it's all the same company anyway, but it's interesting that they want you to sing the old classics, O really does have his finger on the pulse, doesn't he?

PRINCESS/MOTHER F: Sure thing [*Facial expression saying you jerk, what a loser!*].

VH-1 SUIT: Okay the Uckers are ready, so can you give this one your best. {*Sfx 'Come on do the Locomotion'*}.

[*Two hours later on the outskirts of Banbridge, P has managed to walk four miles but can only get a lift heading back to Banbridge from a pig farmer named* JOSEPH. *As the weather is taking a turn for the worse, he is in no position to argue and accepts. He embarks on an educational trip on the problems of dumping pig slurry without being caught out by the authorities. As they approach the town once again the protest monologue is interrupted*].

DRIVER/JOSEPH: Okay son this is as far as I'm going! Check out the bars in this place. If you fancy a bop The Metropolis used to pull in the crowds last time I stayed here.

P: Great thanks a lot [*facial expression saying thank fuck for that!* 'the most boring man in the world award' *goes to you mate*] see you around, I'll check out this Metropolis place and see what the vibe's like [*in your dreams, I've just experienced how good it is, and I'm not welcome!*].

[{*Sfx Truck driving away off a side road*} P *enters the first bar and orders a Jack*

Daniel's. In the corner there's a wall-mounted Sony with evening news blasting out. Some underage drinker shouts to the barman].

UNDERAGE DRINKER: Oy Sammy! Stick VH-1 on, cos we want a good laugh. No one's interested in the news around here anyway.

[P *notes the comment and thinks maybe this place has got some good points after all. He turns to watch the TV and falls instantly in a dream-like stare thinking wow! But she looks so Barbie-dolled and pissed off*].

UNDERAGE DRINKER: There's Big O's old doll, sure she wouldn't know a good song if it jumped up and bit her on the nose! Talk about boring.

BARMAN: Less of that or you'll be outa here pronto! Sure you know that wee woman is cooped up in The Metropolis all the time, it's no wonder she's out of touch.

P [*convinced he could rescue that vision from her sad muzak, addresses the underage drinker*]: Do you go to that disco much in The Metropolis?

UNDERAGE DRINKER: Disco at The Metropolis, is your head cut? My Granny used to go to discos I go to [*with emphasis*] raves and I wouldn't be seen dead in there in a month of Sundays. Yer man O's a loonie – he asks you to fill in questionnaires predicting next week's favourite classic!

P: Well what if we both went for a laugh and switched the records for one of my more recent tapes? [P *was careful here as he liked some of the older stuff by Hendrix, The Sex Pistols, Dylan, Prince and even TRex; he didn't want to give his lust game away too soon*].

UNDERAGE DRINKER: Aye alright I know a couple of old Quomen who might be interested in causing a bit of aggro with the sheep-shaggers, so we can sneak in.

P: Well that's that settled then, have a drink.

ACT 2

SCENE 1: ENTRANCE TO THE METROPOLIS

QUOMAN [*to* STOCKY]: Oy mister! I'm on the guest list, can I have me backstage pass?

STOCKY, ACHING and WATERY [*in unison*]: Don't even think about it sunshine.

We don't want the likes of you in here, no ripped denims.

QUOMAN 2: Your head's up your arse! They're not ordinary denims they're Wranglers! I'll do yee! you stupid Welsh bastards!

[*A skirmish follows with the inevitable outcome of the ejected* QUOMEN *cursing the Welsh but in the meantime both* P *and his companion sneak into the disco inferno and are met by a few interested gazes from the ageing stilettoed gold-diggers ceremonially camped around the dance floor*].

LISRELLI [*over the Tannoy*]: Here's one to get you going. Love your body how about a dance? {*Sfx 'I should be so lucky'*}

P and UNDERAGE DRINKER: Jaysus Christ, let's get a drink!

P: What do you want?

UNDERAGE DRINKER: That's easy, they only serve Carling [*laughs*].

[*After a couple of pints the underage drinker is excited by the prospect of switching* LISRELLI*'s muzak tape with an edited compilation that* P *has made earlier. Once the time is right, that is the* PRINCESS *is almost ready to come on stage, seated at a table near the dance floor* P *will signal to his drinking buddy*].

P [*nods and then grabs the* PRINCESS*'s attention*]: Why haven't you sung these songs before? [*whisks her up to the dance floor. After a quick switch-over,* LISRELLI *is involved in a temper tantrum with the underage drinker and exits the DJ booth. The disco inferno is filled with the sounds from a compilation tape* P *has made for the occasion*].

{*Sfx,* Fresh Prince, *Boom Shake the Room*; Snap, *Do you see the Light*; Joe Public, *Live and Learn*; James Brown, *Sex Machine*; Sex Pistols, *Anarchy and My Way*; Urban Cookie Collective, *The Key, The Secret*; Terrorvision, *Alice;* Prince, *Sign 'o' the Times;* Dylan, *Subterranean Homesick Blues*; Digable Planets, *Cool Like That*; Neneh Cherry, *Sassy*; Nirvana, *Should of been a Son*; Beck, *Loser*, The 4 Of US, *Sensual Thing*, Massive Attack, *Protection*; U2, *Mysterious Ways*; Nine Inch Nails, *Heresy*; and Cypress Hill; *Insane on the Brain*}.

[*After an invigorating spell on the dance floor* P *and the* PRINCESS *are observed deep in conversation*].

PRINCESS: I've never heard music like this!! I don't know why they're not in my record collection.

P: Maybe some people were afraid of the fact you might like them! Who knows you might even change your style. You know you have a great voice but why do you choose to sing lousy songs? Why don't we make some new songs together?

PRINCESS: That would be really . . .

[*Before he can hear her response,* P *feels the fury of* STOCKY, ACHING *and* WATERY *who have been programmed, by an infuriated* BIG O *and whinging* LIS, *to get rid of this interloper. Lifted by the scruff of his neck he greets his underage buddy mid air. They are propelled head first out of the entrance*].

P: Dickheads, don't they know good music when they hear it, what's their problem anyway?

UNDERAGE DRINKER: I told you so, they're past their sell-by date in there, sad losers!

P: Anyway paraphrasing Marx, I wouldn't want to belong to any club that would have me as a member!

UNDERAGE DRINKER: I didn't realise you were a commy!

P: Christ, you're as bad as they are! It's a joke, a bit like this place. Who do they think they're kidding? Themselves!

[*A group of rockers on the street corner observe the scene and all join in a crass version of* {*Sfx 'Don't rock the boat baby!'*}].

SCENE 2: INSIDE THE DISCO INFERNO

BIG O: Now where do you think you're going [*as he grabs* PRINCESS *round the waist*], you're on honey.

LISRELLI: And now Ladies and Gentleman, the moment you've all been waiting for, Mother F and the Uckers!!

[*Spontaneous applause*].

[*The Uckers look worriedly at Mother f as she rasps into a screaming version of* My Way *and, after thirty seconds of high pitched screaming, spontaneously combusts leaving a mysteriously ashened M on the stage floor*].

BIG O: What the fuck's going on tonight? Has the whole place gone mad?

Where is she ?

LISRELLI: Shite! Better call the doc.

BIG O: Just stick *your* bloody tape in again. Yes, yes she's fine. [*He smiles to one of the horrified onlookers and a horrible feeling of nausea seizes hold of him*].

[*Suddenly screams of terror are heard as one of the* UCKERS *notices a fireball, started side stage in the rubbish, and before long* LIS and BIG O *are on the street watching the local fire brigade trying to salvage a burning Metropolis*].

ONE OF THE FIREMEN: Well it's gutted, but I think we've saved the dressing room.

BIG O [*turning to a tearful* LISRELLI]: Where did it all go wrong?

LISRELLI: I don't know boss, I didn't see anything until it was too late.

ACT 3

Three days later: Outside a blackened Metropolis

[*Gazing at the numerous wreaths of flowers left for* MOTHER F *against the collapsed entrance to The Metropolis* BIG O *and* LISRELLI *are in despondent mood*].

BIG O [*Spotting* P *on the other side of the road*]: Isn't that the person who caused all this hassle for us?

LIS: Yeah, let's kick his head in now!

[*As they get closer to* P *they can see tears on his cheeks and notice he is visibly upset and look at each other puzzled.* P *turns*].

P: She could have been somebody you know, she had the potential but you just couldn't let her be herself and grow up, just too protective and scared of losing control, it's all your fault you sad bastards!

[BIG O *and* LISRELLI *are moved by this display of emotion and in unison*],

BIG O and LISRELLI: What exactly do you mean, our fault?

[*Seeing that they still were unaware of their impact on the* PRINCESS P *launches into a diatribe of insulting insights on their behaviour towards* PRINCESS. *Finally, in an attempt to waken them to their isolated views, he asks them when was the last time they'd been to a* rave. *As* BIG O *and* LIS *ruminate over the concept of a* rave *they all have arrived outside the dressing room door*].

LIS and BIG O [*blubbering*]: If only our baby would open the door so we could talk to her and apologise.

P [*looking at them*]: Maybe she will.

[*After a few moments, when all three are in silent reflection, the dressing room door creaks open.* PRINCESS *miraculously appears, tears running down her face but with a look of defiance in her eyes and sporting a freshly shaved mohican hairstyle*].

BIG O [*stupefied*]: Ooh my God, what's happened? Don't worry [*which he quickly follows by*], I'll buy you the best blonde wig money can buy.

[LISRELLI *faints to the floor*].

PRINCESS: No. It's over. I'm never singing that muzak again! I want to make new sounds with P and other folks as well.

P [*smiling at the* PRINCESS]: Rave on, rave on.

Forty days later

There are signs of revival in Banbridge after the insurance money arrived to rebuild The Metropolis. With P, as a new entertainments adviser, BIG O has now renamed the place The Academy. To relaunch the club so that it appeals to everyone in the community The Academy, firstly, runs a series of weekly theme nights, for rockers, grungers, ravers, etcetera. Then The Academy introduces an all-comers night entitled '*Rave on Lis*', with no restrictions on the entrance. There are plans for a relaunch of the PRINCESS, with an MTV unplugged special, where she sings both the old classics and new songs to an even greater audience. BIG O has also been heard in conversation with a tour management company for a live tour including the Point, RDS, Wembley. It seems that, after a period in the musical and entertainments wilderness, The Academy is beginning to emerge with a new vitality and get the reputation of the night-spot to be seen at, once again.

EPILOGUE

Why a play?

This short play is an attempt to broaden our minds by trying to take a step back and reflect in consideration of 'what it is exactly that the small world of marketing academics does'. By use of the simple musical analogy, the authors compare much of the marketing academy's knowledge creation to a formulaic type of muzak, thus named because of the authors' belief that it is one-dimensional (Saren and Brownlie 1995) and blinkered. This is typified by the style of Stock, Aitken and Waterman music with which we are all too familiar in contemporary UK society. Most of us have been (over) exposed to the early works of Kylie Minogue, Jason Donovan, Rick Astley and Sonia, to name but a few.

Why joint names of Mother F and the Princess?

Mother F represents the frustrated existence of a being. The frustration has been caused by the continued myopic focus on a sheltered creation, of marketing knowledge. Because of this the person is self-consuming and destined to cause her own destruction. The Princess is her other side, her potential, if you like the range of voice that is currently untapped.

Why muzak?

It is important to realise that this analogy is not just due to the authors' own abhorrence and intolerance of what they believe to be naff sounds, but also to highlight that muzak has a role to play in society. Conversely, the writers believe, *music* has a more varied and interesting role to play! Furthermore one is unlikely to dismiss a friend as meaningless and worthless, simply due to their taste in music. Musical pluralism is much more easily tolerated than epistemological and methodological pluralism in academic marketing circles. But yes, the authors are aware that in purist music circles difficulties have existed in the past with Mozart's music being dismissed for having too many notes. We have moved on slightly and in most western democracies people are entitled to listen to whatever they like musically. Why then is this not the case in the marketing academy? In the past few years there have been several attempts at diagnosing the malaise of marketing, notably Brownlie and Saren (1992), Brown (1993), Kavanagh (1994). These people seek to gather and produce knowledge in ways that previously were deemed unsuitable and indeed downright unacceptable. However, it seems that whilst the mainstream marketing academy is willing to listen and publish, albeit in a limited way, such prognoses, these in-house physicians are still regarded as heretics whose prophesies are suitably unheeded. In the preceding play they probably would have complained about the choice of records being played every night only to have their complaints go overlooked. Nowhere is this more apparent than in the development of the marketing academy's favourite friend, the marketing concept.

IN THE BEGINNING – THE MARKETING ACADEMY CREATED THE MARKETING CONCEPT

The marketing concept was first discussed in the 1940s and 1950s (Barksdale and Darden 1971; Bell and Emory 1971; Converse and Hugey 1946). According to Barksdale and Darden (1971), the first business to adopt its core principles was the American corporation General Electric. It was developed (Bell and Emory 1971: 38) in order to 'operationalise a basic philosophy of marketing held by economists and marketing theorists', stemming from the eighteenth century (Dixon 1992). Over time it has been affirmed as the 'optimal marketing management philosophy' (Houston 1986: 81), and one of the most accepted general paradigms of the discipline (Day and Wensley 1983) where,

> The marketing concept has not only provided the foundation for the methodology and organization of marketing it is also the *raison d'être* in the Western world.
>
> (Arndt 1977, in Elliott 1990: 20)

Thus the development of marketing theory within the marketing academy has:

> tended to focus on operational problems relating to customer decision making within the confines of the marketing concept.
>
> (Day and Wensley 1983: 88)

Whilst the concept itself has been defined in different ways (Lichtenthal and Wilson 1992) its basic elements centre on three broad principles (Barksdale and Darden 1971; Bell and Emory 1971; Hollander 1986): first, the concept sees an orientation to the needs and wants of the consumer as the core element of business activity; second, profit is the main evaluation criterion; and, third the successful use of the concept requires an integrated effort within the organisation.

THE DEMISE OF THE MOVING STATUE

Despite the profound glorification which the concept has enjoyed in the marketing literature in the past fifty or so years, it has been subject to criticism from various quarters, from as long ago as 1971 (Bell and Emory 1971). Indeed, criticisms have tended to focus on the same issues (Brown 1995a). As Dixon (1992) reminds us, the ideas addressed are old ones and discussed at the expense of more important issues. Table 3.1 provides a summary of relevant areas which help explain the slow, painful but necessary demise of the concept. This act has occurred in broad daylight, albeit unnoticed by many modern marketing academics and writers of basic/introductory marketing textbooks. The following quotations from the recent edition of *The Marketing Book* illustrate this,

> Market segmentation is at the very heart of the marketing concept.
>
> (Evans 1994: 329)

Table 3.1 The demise of the moving statue

Shortcomings	*Authors*
Death by ideology	
1 Confusion between meaning of original concept and its built up ideology	Brownlie and Saren 1992
2 Theoretical foundations seriously flawed	Brown 1995; Alvesson 1994
3 Based on neo-classical economic theory: 'is this an appropriate theory of the firm?'	Day and Wensley 1983
And on the Sixth Day God created man. And on the eighth day marketers created wants.	
Consumer issues:	
1 Satisfying needs and wants is descriptive – but description does not describe reality	Dixon 1992
a Wants not always individual (family)	
b Consumer wants cannot be separated from human wants	
c No consideration for conflict	
d Wants also influenced by marketing efforts	Brownlie and Saren 1992; Dickinson *et al.* 1986
2 What about needs that are not satisfied?	Brownlie and Saren 1992
3 What if there's no available technology and/or costs to satisfy demand?	Dixon 1992
4 Ethical/legal issues	Dixon 1992
5 What if consumers do not know their needs?	Dickinson *et al.* 1986; Houston 1986
6 How can consumers know their future needs?	Houston 1986
Marketplace issues	
1 Customers' needs met by intermediaries who may have inconsistent interests	Dixon 1992
2 Focus on individual wants at expense of long-term consumer interests	Abratt and Sacks 1988
3 What about affected consumers (e.g. passive smokers)?	Dixon and Diehn 1992
4 What about dissatisfaction in the unserved market?	Dixon and Diehn 1922
5 What about other company needs (e.g. profits, efficiency)?	Brownlie and Saren 1992; Takas 1974; Dixon 1992
Consumer sovereignty – give me a break?	
1 Economic term, limits recognised fifty years ago	Dixon 1992
2 Marketing concept more concerned with legitimising existence of large organisation	Smith 1987
3 Companies more concerned with satisfying profit demands	Bell and Emory 1971
4 Why is there consumerist movement?	Arndt 1977; Bell and Emory 1971
5 Do we want consumer sovereignty and democracy?	Dixon 1992

Shortcomings	*Authors*
'The mythical identity of the marketing concept, consumer sovereignty and social welfare arises from a complete misunderstanding of the conceptual foundations of a free market economy' (Dixon 1992: 124).	
Competition – a disciple left in the wilderness	
1 No original emphasis on competition	Elliott 1990; Brown 1995
2 Not just satisfying consumers' needs but doing so better than the competition	Sachs and Benson 1978; Zeithaml and Zeithaml 1984
3 Adopting marketing concept may actually make companies less competitive	Hirschman 1983
We have the technology (not included with adoption of the marketing concept)	
1 What about technological/production, R&D capabilities of companies?	Kaldor 1971; Kerby 1972; Tauber 1974; Hayes and Abernathy 1980
2 Companies do not only satisfy consumer needs. What about technological expertise, R&D resources, labour and production capacity, strategic objectives and existing product/market experience?	Brownlie and Saren 1992
3 Role of consumer is product improvement, not product development: '. . . few if any of the really significant product innovations which have been placed on the market to date were developed because the inventor sensed that a latent pool of needs was yearning to be satisfied' (Kerby 1972: 31).	Dixon and Diehn 1992
Welcome to the real world	
1 Reality of marketplace is different to that suggested by marketing concept	Brownlie and Saren 1992; Dixon 1992; Dixon and Diehn 1992; Piercy 1992
2 Marketing concept irrelevant because of changes in organisational environment	Elliott 1990
3 Few companies take on board the concept	Trustrum 1989
And the problem is . . . implementation	
1 Main problem not the concept but its implementation	Houston 1986; Kohli and Jaworski 1990; Piercy 1992; Webster 1981; Webster 1988; Whittington and Whipp 1992
2 Suggestions for improvement: a Internal marketing b Development of a market orientation	Piercy and Morgan 1991; Narver and Slater 1990; Lichtenthal and Wilson 1992; Ruekert 1992

Shortcomings	*Authors*
3 Concept may never have been 'properly tried' within companies	Brownlie and Saren 1992
4 Concept focuses on the marketplace at expense of internal HRD	Dixon and Diehn 1992
The extension on the extension	
1 Extension rather than elimination is preferred response of the marketing academy	
a Inclusion of innovation, competition and society	Brown 1995
b Strategic marketing concept which considers the external environment	Eliott 1990
c A professional concept which considers the needs of marketing practitioners	Mueller-Heumann 1986
d Compromise between satisfying consumers' and company's other needs	Trustrum 1989; Brownlie and Saren 1992
e A customer value driven concept	Webster 1994a, 1994b
f A repositioned concept which considers 'affected' and other customers	Dixon and Diehn 1992
'The upshot is that if the marketing concept does not encompass the needs of business and social organisations today, a new discipline will emerge. Issue by issue, other disciplines will teach what marketing overlooks' (Dixon and Diehn 1992: 439).	
Macromarketing/societal marketing – a new sacred cow?	
1 The welfare of consumers, society at large	Bell and Emory 1971; Feldman 1971
2 MC considers individuals, business, economics, profitability but not society as a whole	Abratt and Sacks 1988; Lazer 1969; Schwartz 1971; Takas 1974
3 What about the consequences of materialism for society?	Dawson 1969; Feldman 1971; Kotler and Levy 1969; Lavidge 1970; Shuptrine and Osmanski 1975
4 What about consequences for the natural environment?	Lavidge 1970; Prothero 1990
Macromarketing . . . and the problem is implementation	
1 What's in society's best interests should not be determined by marketers because:	Gaski 1985
a this is undemocratic	
b Marketers do not have the qualification to determine what is in the best interests of society	

a business can be successful only if its offer matches the wants of buyers at least as effectively as its best competitors. Marketing management is the task of planning this match. It is based upon the analysis of distributors,

> the selection of target market segments and the design of marketing mixes which will provide the firm with a differential advantage.
>
> (Doyle 1994: 420)

It is the concept which has helped lead to the development of a definition of marketing. The AMA definition developed in 1988, however, is micro in nature and takes, for example, no account of macromarketing, this is despite the fact that

> A lack of understanding about macromarketing is really a lack of understanding about marketing itself and its rich intellectual history . . . To say that the tumultuous 1960s or 1970s gave birth to macromarketing gives the impression that it was then that marketing's broader impact on society was first noticed and needed to be studied. It presumes that past marketing scholars had been impervious to marketing's societal perspective. Nothing could be further from the truth given that early economists turned marketers qua macromarketers focused most of their attention on macro issues . . . It is somewhat ironic to think that the very nature of macromarketing as a general understanding about marketing is now relegated as a sub-field or niche within the marketing domain.
>
> (Tamilia 1992: 90)

Some writers have however witnessed the act and said of the marketing concept it is 'limited and unrealistic' (Elliott 1990: 20) and is 'deeply, perhaps irredeemably flawed' (Brown 1995a: 8).

Table 3.1 shows fundamental difficulties with the concept's development, ideological problems and theoretical foundations. One must therefore ask what this means if much of the research, as suggested above, conducted within the marketing academy stems from a flawed concept. What is interesting to ask is not only what the problems of this are (as indicated in Table 3.1), but perhaps more importantly why this has happened. In the opinions of the authors, this scenario has resulted because of the biased nature of the marketing academy, in its one-sided generation of marketing knowledge. Despite numerous criticisms, the marketing academy still uses the concept as one of the frontrunners in the pursuit of marketing knowledge (one only has to look at the recent market orientation literature to highlight this). Returning to the analogy of the preceding play, Muzak in this case is the marketing concept. The developers of that muzak, the mainstream members of the marketing academy, can therefore be blamed for the lack of alternative paradigms and epistemological and methodological pluralism within our discipline.

Many attempts at suggesting more pluralistic research methods within the marketing discipline are quickly dismissed. Those who have attempted to look at the marketing concept from a macromarketing perspective, for instance, face a two-pronged attack: first on the relevance of the subject to marketing; and, second, questions on the reliability, validity and generalisability of their chosen research method. All of this seems ironic when one considers the suggestion by Austen (1983) that the marketing concept (upon which so much mainstream marketing knowledge is based) is dogmatic rather than scientific.

A discussion of the marketing concept is just one example of the development of marketing knowledge within the marketing academy. Whilst the debate surrounding the pursuit of more pluralistic means of developing marketing knowledge continues, the marketing academy is still publishing biased journals and continuing to develop one-sided marketing knowledge. Those who attack this remain on the outskirts of The Metropolis and are not welcome to participate in the future development of mainstream marketing knowledge [muzak]. This is because the heads of the discipline [*Big O and his merry friends*] do not believe in the pursuit of eclectic marketing knowledge [*music*]. Wise up guys or you may find those on the fringes get pissed off at waiting to have their knowledge base accepted and publish their work in other, more pluralistic disciplines, which, by the way, just happen to be more credible in the social sciences than marketing! Worse yet (from the point of view of the current mainstream) the fringe may become so big it eventually becomes the mainstream. Even worse, when this happens, the new mainstream may decide to also become biased and one-sided and pursue the same goals of exclusivity currently pursued by the mainstay of today's marketing academy. A Metropolis, part two? Watch this space.

It therefore seems safe to suggest that the marketing concept's life has come to an end. Indeed, there is more to life than the marketing concept. Thus, the time has come to announce publicly that the concept is dead. As Descombes (1993) argues, certain projects fail because they try to account for the culture of a period by linking it to a metaphysics or a particular form of rationality. Presently the marketing academy is moving on to more meaningful ways of understanding our world. Thus, in order to avoid a marketing apocalypse we need a new beginning where one can build upon constructive criticism (Alvesson 1994; Geuss 1981; O'Connor 1994; O'Neill 1989) and emerge, perhaps via some postmodern catharsis, into our period of reflexive modernisation (Beck 1992; Lash and Wynne 1992). It is the opinion of these authors that this new beginning should not entail yet another extension on the marketing concept, as illustrated in Table 3.1. At the end of the day the concept itself is seriously flawed, and extending it, or improving its implementation is not the best way forward. This key player in our discipline has outlived its usefulness (if it ever had any uses in the first place). What we need are new, more creative ways of moving the discipline forward.

SOME SUGGESTIONS FOR THE FUTURE (WE ARE NOT ALONE)

Whilst there is not enough space in this work to go into great detail as to what this new beginning may entail, such discussion is found elsewhere (McDonagh 1995a, 1995b; Prothero 1995), we feel some ideas for further thought should be introduced. One main factor is how we study consumption in the future. Now we have abolished the notion of 'satisfying needs and wants at a profit', what are we going to put in its place? The first issue of consideration is perhaps allowing ourselves to learn from our extended family of social science in seeking the common ground and adopting the rhetoric associated with the study of the manufacture of consumption. Recently there have been a number of excellent general texts on the subject of consumption (Bocock 1993; Miller 1995) and this must surely be a strong contender as the beginning of our new way forward. We have a lot to learn from our colleagues in other social sciences who have been studying consumption for many years (Beck 1992; Campbell 1995; Goldman 1992; Leff 1995; Veblen 1912, 1953; Williamson 1978). As marketing academics we should be prepared to acknowledge this fact.

We feel this process has thankfully already begun; unfortunately, but not surprisingly, going unnoticed within the mainstream marketing academy. One of the aims of this chapter is to highlight the process to all realms of the marketing academy. There is a danger of remaining incestuous in the academy so that those outside its domain will offer society a more meaningful and acceptable interpretation of what marketing has become (Brownlie and Saren 1995; Whittington and Whipp 1992).

One could argue that marketing can be viewed in a richer vein as the symbolic manufacture of consumption (Baudrillard 1993 and 1995) and not the satisfaction of needs and wants in what has been called marketique (McDonagh 1995b). Thus, rather than extend the marketing concept as previous marketing academics have tended, we must bury it and celebrate a new life with the study of this manufacture of what Leiss *et al.* (1990) call the 'theatre of consumption' in contemporary society. In this scenario the academic community in contemporary society form an eclectic group of social scientists offering a rich analysis of consumption. Indeed there are already, within the marketing academy, pioneers of this new beginning (O'Donohoe 1992, 1994; Lannon 1994; Ritson and Elliott 1995, Brown 1995b), we must commend their stance and learn from their chosen research topics, methods and views of the world. This may well permit a new eclectic beginning to the study of consumption within the marketing academy of the future and this may help eliminate the potential problem recently discussed by Baker (1995: 631)

> In losing sight of the origins of our subject and the principles upon which it was founded, there seems to be a distinct threat that we will seek to erect a new temple of knowledge without any adequate foundations.

This temple of knowledge however must not only be built on the foundations of the marketing academy, but also on those of other disciplines in the social sciences.

It is refreshing to note that we have some friends in the wilderness experiencing the same dilemmas as ourselves (Godard 1993) – but we have the exciting prospects of investigating the various cultures of marketing (Griswold

1994) that exist in today's rationalised society (Ritzer 1993) or taking a holistic ecological perspective following Bookchin (1980). But at a time when the academy and social science generally seem to be undergoing some critical analysis it could do worse than to consider the wisdom of Frost during 1916.

> Two roads diverged in a yellow wood, and I –
> I took the one less travelled by,
> And that has made all the difference.
>
> p. 410

ACKNOWLEDGEMENTS

The authors would like to thank Rick Delbridge, Tom Keenoy, Lisa O'Malley and Maurice Patterson for comments on earlier versions of this chapter.

REFERENCES

Abratt, R. and Sacks, D. (1988), 'The Marketing Challenge: Towards Being Profitable and Socially Responsible', *Journal of Business Ethics*, vol. 7, no. 7, pp. 497–507.
Alvesson, M. (1994), 'Critical Theory and Consumer Marketing', *Scandinavian Journal of Management*, vol. 10, no. 3, pp. 291–313.
Anderson, L.McT. (1994) 'Marketing Science: Where's the Beef?', *Business Horizons*, 37 (1), pp. 8–16.
Arndt, J. (1977), 'A Critique of Marketing Concepts', in White P.D. and Slater C. (eds), *Macromarketing*, University of Colorado.
Austen, A. (1983), 'The Marketing Concept: Is It Obsolete?', *Quarterly Review of Marketing*, 9 (1), pp. 6–8.
Baker, M.J. (1995), 'A Comment on: "The Commodification of Marketing Knowledge"', *Journal of Marketing Management*, 11 (7), pp. 634–9.
Barksdale, H.C. and Darden, B. (1971), 'Marketers' Attitudes Toward the Marketing Concept', *Journal of Marketing*, vol. 35, October, pp. 29–36.
Baudrillard, J. (1993), *Symbolic Exchange and Death*, Sage, London.
Baudrillard, J. (1995), *Le crime parfait*, Editions Galilee, Paris.
Beck, U. (1992), *Risk Society: Towards a New Modernity*, Sage, London.
Bell, M.L. and Emory, C.W. (1971), 'The Faltering Marketing Concept', *Journal of Marketing*, vol. 35, October, pp. 37–42.
Bennett, R.C. and Cooper, R.G. (1981), 'The Misuse of Marketing: An American Tragedy', *Business Horizons*, vol. 24, no. 6, pp. 51–61.
Bocock, R. (1993), *Consumption*, Routledge.
Bookchin, M. (1980), *Toward an Ecological Society*, Black Rose Books, Montreal.
Brown, S. (1993), 'Postmodern Marketing?' *European Journal of Marketing*, vol. 27, no. 4, pp. 19–34.
Brown, S. (1995), *Postmodern Marketing*, Routledge.
Brown, S. (1995a), 'Life Begins at 40? Further Thoughts on Marketing's "Mid-Life Crisis"', *Marketing Intelligence and Planning*, vol. 13, no. 1, pp. 4–17.
Brown, S. (1995b), 'Trinitarianism, the Eternal Evangel and the Three Eras Schema', in Brown, S. *et al.* (eds), *Proceedings of the Marketing Eschatology Retreat*, University of Ulster, Belfast, pp. 298–314.
Brownlie, D. and Saren, M. (1992), 'Developing the Marketing Concept as an Ideological

Resource', Sixth Annual Conference of the British Academy of Management, University of Bradford, pp. 147–8.

Brownlie, D. and Saren, M. (1992), 'The Four Ps of the Marketing Concept: Prescriptive, Polemical, Permanent and Problematic', *European Journal of Marketing*, vol. 26, no. 4, pp. 34–47.

Brownlie, D., Saren, M., Whittington, R. and Wensley, R. (1994) 'The New Marketing Myopia: Critical Perspectives on Theory and Research in Marketing – Introduction', *European Journal of Marketing*, vol. 28, no. 3, pp. 6–12.

Cahill, D.J. and Warshawsky, R.M. (1993), 'The Marketing Concept: A Forgotten Aid for Marketing High-Technology Products', *Journal of Consumer Marketing*, vol. 10, no. 1, pp. 17–22.

Campbell, C. (1995), 'The sociology of consumption', in Miller, D. (ed.), *Acknowledging Consumption*, Routledge, London, pp. 96–126.

Converse, P.D. and Hugey, H.W. (1946), *The Elements of Marketing*, Prentice Hall, New York.

Dawson, L.M. (1969), 'The Human Concept: New Philosophy for Business', *Business Horizons*, vol. 12, pp. 29–38.

Day, G.S. and Wensley, R. (1983), 'Marketing Theory with a Strategic Orientation', *Journal of Marketing*, vol. 47, Fall, pp. 79–89.

Descombes, V. (1993), *The Barometer of Modern Reason: On the philosophies of current events*, Oxford University Press.

Dholakia, N. (1988), 'Interpreting Monieson: Creative and Destructive Tensions', *Journal of Macromarketing*, vol. 8, Fall, pp. 11–14.

Dickinson, R.A., Herbst, A. and O'Shaughnessy, J. (1986), 'Marketing Concept and Customer Orientation', *Journal of Marketing*, vol. 20, no. 10, pp. 18–23.

Dixon, D.F. (1992), 'Consumer Sovereignty, Democracy and The Marketing Concept: A Macromarketing Perspective', *Canadian Journal of Administrative Sciences*, vol. 9, no. 2, pp. 116–25.

Dixon, L.M. and Diehn, D. (1992), 'The Challenged Marketing Concept: A Repositioning Strategy for a Concept in the Decline Stage' AMA Conference, pp. 432–40.

Doyle, P. (1994), 'Managing the Marketing Mix', in Baker, M. (ed.), *The Marketing Book*, Butterworth-Heinemann Ltd, Oxford, pp. 227–37.

El Ansary, A.I. (1974), 'Societal Marketing: A Strategic View of the Marketing Mix in the 1970s', *Journal of the Academy of Marketing Science*, vol. 2, pp. 553–66.

Elliott, G. (1990), 'The Marketing Concept – Necessary, But Sufficient?', *European Journal of Marketing*, vol. 24, no. 9, pp. 20–30.

Evans, M. (1994), 'Market Segmentation', in Baker, M. (ed.), *The Marketing Book*, Butterworth-Heinemann Ltd.

Feldman, L. (1971), 'Societal Adaption: A New Challenge for Marketing', *Journal of Marketing*, vol. 37, no. 3, pp. 54–60.

Firat, A.F., Venkatesh, A. and Sherry, J.F. Jr. (eds) (1993), Special issue on post modernism, marketing and the consumer, *International Journal of Research in Marketing*, vol. 10, no. 3, pp. 215–341.

Frost, R. (1951), *1874–1963 Complete Poems of Robert Frost*, Jonathon Cape, London.

Gaski, J.F. (1985), 'Dangerous Territory: The Societal Marketing Concept Revisited', *Business Horizons*, vol. 28, pp. 42–7.

Geuss, R. (1981), *The Idea of a Critical Theory*, Cambridge University Press.

Godard, J. (1993), 'Theory and Method in Industrial Relations: Modernist and Postmodernist Alternatives', in Adams, R. and Meltz, N. (eds), *IR Theory: its Nature, Scope and Pedagogy*, IMLR/Rutgers Univ. Press and Scarecrow Press, Mefuchan, NJ and London, pp. 283–306.

Goldman, R. (1992), *Reading Ads Socially*, Routledge.

Griswold, W. (1994), *Cultures and Societies in a Changing World*, Sage.

Hayes, R.H. and Abernathy, W.J. (1980), 'Managing Our Way to Economic Decline', *Harvard Business Review*, vol. 58, July–August, pp. 67–77.
Hirschman, E. (1983), 'Aesthetics, Ideologies and the Limits of the Marketing Concept', *Journal of Marketing*, vol. 47, Summer, pp. 45–55.
Hollander, S.C. (1986), 'The Marketing Concept: *A Déjà Vu*', in Fisk, G. (ed.), *Marketing Management Technology as a Social Process*, Praeger, New York, pp. 3–29.
Houston, F.S. (1986), 'The Marketing Concept: What It Is and What It Is Not', *Journal of Marketing*, vol. 50, April, pp. 81–7.
Hunt, S.D. (1983), 'General Theories and the Fundamental Explanada of Marketing', *Journal of Marketing*, vol. 47, Fall, pp. 9–17.
Kaldor, A.G. (1971), 'Imbricative Marketing', *Journal of Marketing*, vol. 35, April, pp. 19–25.
Kavanagh, D. (1994), 'Hunt Versus Anderson: Round 16', *European Journal of Marketing*, vol. 28, no. 3, pp. 26–41.
Kerby, J.K. (1972), 'The Marketing Concept: Suitable Guide to Product Strategy', *Business Quarterly*, vol. 37, Summer, pp. 31–5.
Kohli, A.K. and Jaworski, B.J. (1990), 'Market Orientation: The Construct, Research Propositions, and Managerial Implications', *Journal of Marketing*, vol. 54, no. 2, pp. 1–18.
Kotler, P. (1972), 'A Generic Concept of Marketing', *Journal of Marketing*, vol. 36, April, pp. 46–54.
Kotler, P. and Levy, S. (1969), 'Broadening the Concept of Marketing', *Journal of Marketing*, vol. 31, no. 1, pp. 10–15.
Kotler, P. and Zaltman, G. (1971), 'Social Marketing: An Approach to Planned Social Change', *Journal of Marketing*, vol. 35, July, pp. 3–12.
Lannon, J. (1994), 'Mosaics of Meaning: Anthropology and Marketing', *The Journal of Brand Management*, vol. 2, no. 3 pp. 155–68.
Lash, S. and Wynne, B. (1992) 'Introduction', in Beck, U. (1992), *Risk Society: Towards a New Modernity*, Sage, London.
Lavidge, R. (1970), 'The Growing Responsibilities of Marketing', *Journal of Marketing*, vol. 34, no. 1, pp. 25–8.
Lazer, W. (1969), 'Marketing's Changing Social Relationships', *Journal of Marketing*, vol. 33, no. 1, pp. 3–9.
Leff, E. (1995), *Green Production: Toward an Environmental Rationality*, The Guilford Press, New York.
Leiss, W., Kline, S. and Jhally, S. (1990), *Social Communication in Advertising, Persons, Products and Images of Well-Being*, Routledge, London.
Lichtenthal, J.D. and Wilson, D.T. (1992), 'Becoming Market Oriented', *Journal of Business Research*, vol. 24, pp. 191–207.
McDonagh, P. (1995a), 'Sustainable Communication: Pipe Dream for Green Advertisers or the New Way Forward for Business to Communicate?', in Bergadaa, M. (ed.), *Marketing Today and for the 21st Century*, Proceedings of the 24th Annual Conference of the European Marketing Academy, vol. I, pp. 731–51, Essec, Cergy-Pontoise, France.
McDonagh, P. (1995b) 'Q. Is Marketing dying of Consumption? A. Yes, and the answer is Consumption!', Proceedings of Marketing Eschatology Retreat, 23–24 September 1995, University of Ulster, pp. 48–59.
Miller, D. (ed.) (1995), *Acknowledging Consumption*, Routledge.
Monieson, D. (1988), 'Intellectualization in Macromarketing: A World Disenchanted', *Journal of Macromarketing*, vol. 8, Fall, pp. 7–14.
Mueller-Heuman, G. (1986), 'Toward a Professional Concept for Marketing', *Journal of Marketing Management*, vol. 1, no. 3, pp. 301–13.
Narver, J.C. and Slater, S.F. (1990), 'The Effect of a Market Orientation on Business Profitability', *Journal of Marketing*, vol. 54, no. 4, pp. 20–35.

O'Connor, M. (ed.) (1994), *Is Capitalism Sustainable? Political Economy and the Politics of Ecology*, The Guilford Press, New York.
O'Donohoe, S. (1992), 'Towards an Understanding of Advertising Involvement?', in Grunet, K.G. and Fuglede, D. (eds), *Marketing for Europe – Marketing for the Future*, Proceedings of the 21st Annual Conference of the European Marketing Academy, vol. II, pp. 905–24, Aarhus School of Business, Denmark.
O'Donohoe, S. (1994), 'Advertising uses and gratifications', *European Journal of Marketing*, 28 (8/9), pp. 52–75.
O'Neill, J. (ed.) (1989), *On Critical Theory*, University Press of America, Lanham, New York and London.
Piercy, N. (1992), *Market-Led Strategic Change*, Butterworth-Heinemann, Oxford.
Piercy, N. and Morgan, N. (1991), 'Internal Marketing: The Missing Half of the Marketing Programme', *Long Range Planning*, 24 (2), pp. 82–93.
Prothero, A. (1990), 'Green Consumerism and the Societal Marketing Concept: Marketing Strategies for the 1990s', *Journal of Marketing Management*, vol. 6, no. 2, pp. 87–103.
Prothero, A. (1995), 'The Marketing Concept–the End of Life as we know it?', in Brown, S. *et al.* (eds), Proceedings of the Marketing Eschatology Retreat, University of Ulster, Belfast, pp. 177–88.
Ritson, M. and Elliott, R. (1995), 'A Model of Advertising Literacy: The Praxiology and Co-creation of Advertising Meaning', in Bergadaa, M. (ed.), *Marketing Today and for the 21st Century*, Proceedings of the 24th Annual Conference of the European Marketing Academy, vol. I, pp. 1035–54, Essec, Cergy-Pontoise, France.
Ritzer, G. (1993), *The McDonaldization of Society*, Sage, London.
Ruekert, R.W. (1992), 'Developing a Market Orientation: An Organisation Strategy Perspective', *International Journal of Research in Marketing*, vol. 9, pp. 225–45.
Sachs, W.S. and Benson, G. (1978), 'Is It Time to Discard the Marketing Concept?', *Business Horizons*, vol. 21, August, pp. 68–74.
Saren, M. and Brownlie, D. (1995), 'Beyond the One-Dimensional Marketing Manager', in Bergadaa, M. (ed.), *Marketing Today and for the 21st Century*, Proceedings of the 24th Annual Conference of the European Marketing Academy, vol. II, pp. 1077–96.
Saren, M. and Brownlie, D. (ed.) (1995), The Commodification of Marketing Knowledge, *Journal of Marketing Management* Special Issue, vol. 11.
Schwartz, G. (1971), 'Marketing: The Societal Concept', *University of Washington Business Review*, vol. 31, pp. 33–8.
Sheth, J.N. (1992), 'Toward a Theory of Macromarketing', *Canadian Journal of Administrative Sciences*, vol. 9, no. 2, pp. 154–61.
Shuptrine, F.K. and Osmanski, F.A. (1975), 'Marketing's Changing Role: Expanding or Contracting?', *Journal of Marketing*, vol. 39, no. 1, pp. 58–66.
Silverman, D. (1985), *Qualitative Methods in Sociology*, Gower, London.
Smith, N.C. (1987), 'Consumers' Boycotts and Consumer Sovereignty', *European Journal of Marketing*, vol. 21, no. 5, pp. 7–19.
Sykes, W. (1991), 'Validity and Reliability in Qualitative Market Research: A Review of the Literature', *Journal of Market Research Society*, January, vol. 32, no. 3, pp. 32–42.
Takas, A. (1974), 'Societal Marketing: A Business Man's Perspective', *Journal of Marketing*, vol. 38, no. 4, pp. 2–7.
Tamilia, R.D. (1992), 'Issues and Problems in the Development of Contemporary Macromarketing Knowledge', *Canadian Journal of Administrative Sciences*, vol. 9, no. 2, pp. 80–97.
Tauber, E.M. (1974), 'How Market Research Discourages Major Innovations', *Business Horizons*, vol. 17, June, pp. 22–6.
Trustrum, L.B. (1989), 'Marketing: Concept and Function', *European Journal of Marketing*, vol. 23, no. 3, pp. 48–56.

Veblen, T. (1912 and 1953), *The Theory of the Leisure Class: An Economic Study of Institutions*, Mentor Books, New York.
Webster, F.E. (1981), 'Top Management's Concerns About Marketing Issues for the 1980s', *Journal of Marketing*, vol. 45, Summer, pp. 9–16.
Webster, F.E. (1988), 'The Rediscovery of the Marketing Concept', *Business Horizons*, vol. 31, no. 3, pp. 29–39.
Webster, F.E. (1994a), 'Defining the New Marketing Concept', *Marketing Management*, vol. 2, no. 4, pp. 22–31.
Webster, F.E. (1994b), 'Executing the New Marketing Concept', *Marketing Management*, vol. 3, no. 1, pp. 8–16.
Whittington, R. and Whipp, R. (1992), 'Marketing Ideology and Implementation', *European Journal of Marketing*, vol. 26, no. 1, pp. 52–63.
Williamson, J. (1978), *Decoding Advertisements, Ideology and Meaning in Advertising*, Marion Boyars, New York, London.
Wright, S. and Pickton, D.W. (1995), 'What Marketers Can Learn From Photography', in S. Brown, J. Bell and D. Carson (eds), *Proceedings of the Marketing Eschatology Retreat*, University of Ulster, Belfast, pp. 202–12.
Zeithaml, C.P. and Zeithaml, V.A. (1984), 'Environmental Management: Revising the Marketing Perspective', *Journal of Marketing*, vol. 48, Spring, pp. 46–53.

4

APOCALYPTUS INTERRUPTUS

A tale by parables, apostles and epistles

Douglas Brownlie and John Desmond

HOWLING AT THE MOON

Once upon a time, two itinerant scholars sought temporary respite from the demands of their intensive researches into marketing eschatology through taking the bracing air along the golden ribbon of dune and rock known as Malin Beg. As they meandered across the wildly beautiful strand, all of a sudden, there standing before them was a knotted whisper of a man who announced, without questioning or introduction, that his favourite way of revealing understanding about eschatology was to howl and hoot at a full moon, whilst reciting extracts from Faust. It then came to pass that, just as they were telling him about the Marketing Eschatology conference (Brown, Bell and Carson 1995) they had attended only a few days previously, his image began to slowly dissolve before their eyes. As it was doing so, the scholars heard the fading echo of a lilting melody ringing somewhere in the distance. The lyric was carried along by the scurrying breeze that darted between cliff and shore; and although it was barely audible, the scholars agreed that it seemed to be singing

> in the darkness of the milling throng
> where ignorance and prejudice hold kingly court
> there's yet a voice casts a lonely light upon
> the cant and capers of derivative thought . . .

And so it was that later that same day those earnest scholars of marketing eschatology found themselves howling and hooting at a gloriously full orb of a silver moon on a deserted beach somewhere in south Donegal, reciting the only quotation from Faust they could, at that time, muster from the murky depths of their collective memories:

> I have, alas, studied philosophy,
> Jurisprudence and medicine, too,
> And, worst of all, theology
> With keen endeavour, through and through –
> And here I am, for all my lore,

The wretched fool I was before.
Called Master of Arts, and Doctor to boot,
For ten years almost I confute
And up and down, wherever it goes,
I drag my students by the nose –
And see that for all our science and art
We can know nothing.

No dog would want to live longer this way!
Hence I have yielded to magic to see
Whether the spirit's mouth and might
Would bring some mysteries to light,
That I need not with work and woe
Go on to say what I don't know;
That I might see what secret force
Hides in the world and rules its course,
Envisage the creative blazes
Instead of rummaging for phrases.

Faust, Part 1, Goethe

The marketing scholars wailed and moaned at the skipping orb until they found themselves meditating on what eschatology might be coming to mean in the context of marketing scholarship. Their meditations evoked formative experiences of an ethnocentric religious institutionalisation, with its own peculiar forms of meaning and settled truths. They conjured up Dickensian nightmares of vengeful spectres, harrying and menacing the living in their lust for retribution, bringing foreboding of the perpetual agony and eternal damnation awaiting the sinful in hell-fire. The ocean wash, whistling breeze, racing clouds and fleeting moonshadows provided an ideal backdrop for images of the terror and chaos immediately preceding the announcement of the end of time by the Angel of The Lord from the rainbow on high.

It occurred to the diligent scholars that whilst those visions easily fed off and excited their feelings of guilt and angst, as well as their fear of death and the temptation of evil, similar visions have also inspired some of the greatest painters, philosophers, poets and composers of the classical era to dizzying heights denied to most mortals. This pleased the scholars, leaving them flushed with the warming glow of self-importance. And they hooted with mischievous glee at the thought that such visions have also inspired many prophets of doom to announce that the end of the world is nigh, most notably David Icke; and likewise many other Numerologists, Jehovahs Witnesses, and Charismatics as they avidly dig for signs of the end, or other intimations of divine intervention. However, their torrent of hooting hilarity soon dwindled to a trickle when it occurred to them that those visions may also summon hope against hope that perhaps *Genesis*, *Daniel* and *Revelations* should be read literally as pronouncements of fundamental truths; and that one day there will indeed be a Second Coming, when the New Jerusalem will descend to earth from heaven. It was then that the earnest scholars made a pact, one with another, that they would strive to long cherish the capacity to suspend disbelief and easy judgement. At this point they observed that their capacities for thought were temporarily disabled by the burdens of hunger and thirst, which they agreed no diligent scholar should ever endure for more than two hours. It was then clear to them what they had to do.

FERGUS MAGROARTY'S BAR

As the scholars waited patiently on their reviving food and drink, they mused awhile on the bullying bigot, spitting brimstone and damnation, who, they agreed, would be laughable, but for our tendency to take him seriously. They recalled with much mirth Spike Milligan's human, but more powerful eschatological vision in his novel *Puckoon* (1963), where the Sligo priest, Father Rudden, determined to convince his flock of impending doom and damnation, and in so doing greatly relieve his own penury, calls his own bluff in a way that Descartes (1968) never dreamt of in his ontological meditations:

> *(Priest chooses the right psychological moment to mount the pulpit and announce . . .)* 'I command fire to fall from heaven . . .'
>
> *(pregnant pause and an expectant hush from the flock that eagerly packed the church, now repeating his invocation louder and raising his beseaching eyes heavenwards)* 'I COMMAND FIRE TO FALL FROM HEAVEN . . .'
>
> *(voice of the verger from the loft on high, just above the priest's head)*
> 'Just a minute Fadder . . . I'm thorry, but de cat'th pithed on de matches . . .'
>
> Milligan 1963: 2

With the welcome arrival of the libation, the fog rose and it seemed obvious to the scholars that there is something exclusive and final about any doctrine of final endings. It was at this defining moment in their conversation that the barmaid announced that the entertainment for the evening was about to begin. Fergus Magroarty himself was about to lead the karaoke recital with his rendition of Frank Sinatra's famous version of Cole Porter's ballad, I've Got You Under My Skin. The diligent scholars listened intently as the publican heartily sang along to the deft pulse of the karaoke, offering the following reading of the original lyrics:

Believe me if you dare, but it don't mean I'm serious.
(sung to I've got you under my skin)

'Believing', what could it mean,
'believing', let's set the record straight,
between you and me,

who's to say that we've got it right, for
'believing', let's read control.

So let's not, deceive ourselves so,
that our search for the truth,
sets our efforts above it all.
Disciples we may be, we wish,
but we're well paid and don't we know,
that believing's really for show.

We'd reify anything, come what might,
for the sake of getting in print,
the small ideas that besott us so,
they set us apart,
and the truth's a commodity too.

How could it be, we'd interpenetrate so,
its not just the loot or fame, that
inscribes our ideas so tame.
But, the fear of connecting, local prose and its passion, yes
our buttons are tight to the top,
are we losing our bubble and pop?

We've analysed, till we've petrified,
what it is that we cannot contain,
within the bars of the iron cage,
we've built for ourselves,
yet believe me, the centre won't hold.

Oops, there we go again, closing things down,
keeping the world at bay,
the eschatological way,
with signifiers floating, absent structures decentring,
it's time to learn some new tricks,
our art's bigger, than the marketing mix . . . On believing, we're out to lunch.

The rapturous applause that greeted this rendition warmed the scholars to their conversation on a theme of eschatology in marketing studies. Despite their easy images of heaven and hell, they agreed that they had no ready universal language and grammar to call upon in dealing with questions of ontology, belief and faith in the context of marketing. Yet, the night was moving on and as the throb and thrum of the gathering rose, the everyday life of the local inhabitants began to reveal itself to the scholars; and it seemed clear that matters of belief transcend disciplinary settings and take us back to the possibilities of identity and language. It struck the scholars that there is no escape from language; that we are formed by the language we speak; that we see through it. In between singers and songs, Fergus, who was something of a para-anthropologist, was overheard saying that no interpretation can ever be final; that it is always provisional and contingent on social and cultural circumstances. It then struck the scholars that religious fundamentalism and the rationality of marketing, and science in general, may be part of the same problem, the same desire to subject the world to our mappings in exhaustive, efficient and exact ways. They wondered how are we to grow beyond this urge, to convey in our language the sense of being engaged by the everyday activity of living in this world as we experience it, whilst maintaining a sense of humility and provisionality? So it was that the earnest scholars of marketing eschatology were reminded of the elemental need to believe. As they made their way homewards, they wondered what to make of this call to apply to marketing the doctrine of the end of ends, of death, final judgement, heaven and hell and the cosmic. Were they to laugh at the (apparently) preposterous suggestion that there is a link between the cosmic and marketing, or that one can indeed be forged?

ON BELIEF AND BELIEF

And this parable leads us to questions of belief and their relation to the practices of marketing academics. In one sense, Belief is eschatological in that it reflects a response to a person's desire for meaning and relevance within some form of cosmic order. For some, this desire is served by religions, old and new. Others have either hedged their bets, or have fully embraced a humanistic belief in the transcendent power of science; and here Marxists and capitalists alike can find themselves to be (strange) bedfellows. Eco (1994) refers to such humanists as 'Modernolators', those inspired with an unbounded enthusiasm for the upward progression of the human spirit. Of course, this view has found its detractors: for example, Eco also refers to the 'Apocalyptics', or those who have dared to question the transcendent power of science. Each of these cosmic belief systems has become conditional; they are no longer unquestioned, but are subject to unending speculation and scrutiny.

From these positions marketers have defined their own stances. The consumer researcher Engel (Bartels 1988: 313) defines himself and his view of marketing in relation to his Christian beliefs. By contrast, Bartels (1988: 7) allies himself in the scientific rationalist tradition. Recently a tradition of critical marketing has brought notions of a marketing apocalypse to the fore. The cosmologies which underpin marketing belief have also become conditional, subject to scrutiny and endless debate. As a result, the desire to live without a cosmology has become more appealing, if unattainable. We wonder if there is not another side to belief. Something equally important, but usually dismissed as 'everyday', 'mundane', 'inconsequential' within the cosmic worldview? Here we are referring to belief in its day-to-day form, as given expression in everyday practice. To what extent can we believe what others tell us? Or to put the question another way, to what extent can we believe what we tell them? How much belief do we invest in our identities as academics, in manufacturing credibility as opposed to 'truth'; and does it matter anyway? If accounts are constructions of surfaces is it possible for us to get beneath these constructions to the 'truth'?

And yet the relation between realms of Belief (Cosmic/Eschatological) and belief (everyday, mundane) are tightly woven and recursive. By considering the mundane day-to-day aspects of belief we are thrown back into reflections on the cosmic, of the nature of the 'discipline' of marketing itself and whether we are to invest in its veracity as a science or should regard it as a mere ideology. Of course, for many belief is not a question of freedom, but of positions and interests. We argue that it is important therefore to reflect on the seemingly mundane aspects of our daily lives when contemplating final ends. We are of the world and yet part of it. We are also of the world of markets and of marketing, and part of it too. And if we are 'doing' marketing, must we not believe in it? Or, is there a crisis of faith, or worse, bad faith present in what we marketers do?

Should we then take the call to consider eschatology literally? In other words, should our investigation encompass the so-called parlous state of the Church of Marketing, of schisms, idolators and heretics; of new sects and cults arising with new orthodoxies to pursue; of the possibilities for retreat into fundamentalist doctrines; and of the raising of a Harvard Inquisition? Should we see what may usefully be 'borrowed' from other world religions in our bid to fashion a history, a theology, a teleology for ourselves in marketing? What if all this activity were to mask the fact that there is a dark void at the centre of what we do; that there is a brutality, a horror and a terror that we dare not speak of, a tacit capitulating cowardice that binds us, for fear of what our Gods might do? Our next parable begins here, by reflecting on some of the everyday practices we engage in as marketing academics.

A PARABLE BY EPISTLES BETWEEN APOSTLES

Epistle 1, from apostle A to apostle B

I was interviewing the marketing director of a large engineering company the other day and we wandered on to the topic of his involvement in company marketing strategy activities. He'd told me that he'd done an MBA in 1988 and was familiar with marketing strategy theory. He could even cite a few authors and wondered whether he might get a job as a visiting lecturer sometime. I wanted to know what use he made of the typical marketing techniques in his strategy and planning work, you know, the SWOT, BCG, Marketing Audit, Environmental Scanning, etc. Anyway, he knew my agenda. I didn't know his – at least not at the outset. He said that he'd found the ideas useful. He'd used them and told me this interesting story as a way of relating the hows and whos. After his MBA he'd been promoted out of sales and into his current job – the first board member with direct marketing responsibilities. He saw this as his finest moment. He'd been disagreeing with the sales director for some time over the direction of their European sales effort, which was costing the company serious money. The sales director had spearheaded their efforts with, initially, the support of the MD and the finance director, who ruled supreme. Their disagreements were kept internal to sales, and were never really aired at company level, at least while my informant was studying his MBA. The problem seemed to be that the company was happy to push for sales development overseas – whilst its product technology and quality seemed to suffer. He saw it as too much hassle to get involved in the wider discussions and felt that events would eventually take their toll anyway. He was, however, a bit concerned that he might become the scapegoat if events arrived more quickly than he expected. So he said he really never took his eyes off the ball.

Anyway, after his MBA, the sales director suggested to him that he'd better begin to look elsewhere for promotion, as it wasn't going to come to him just because he'd gone back to university for three years – and anyway a shake-up was coming in the company and his position would be under review. According to my informant, he seemed to be taking an active interest in making things difficult for him, by cutting him out of discussions. In the meantime his sales work and his attitude seemed to have suffered – at least that was my informant's representation of the sales director's view at the time. My informant said that he foresaw that some sort of realignment was in the offing and that the sales director must have been threatened by something to be so public in his defence, by dint of attack.

The story went that the bleeding sore of European sales had reached a crisis and the company had to decide whether to stay in Europe, or retrench and rationalise. But, meanwhile, events had rather overtaken them. The company finances were in poor shape. Advances had been made by a predator company and were being actively pursued. European customers were getting upset at the company's problems and were raising some serious concerns about future relationships. The company was involved in some long-term supply deals with those customers which the sales director had taken them into. It was having to fight the predators off and raise some serious money to do so, as well as to fund the retrenchment. And at this time the finance director left, and there was a rumour that he had taken up with the predator. A team of consultants were brought in by the MD as a condition of going to the city for more capital. The informant saw his opportunity and managed to get involved in their work through some careful politicking with the MD, who was really isolated since losing the finance guy and he didn't really trust the sales director. The informant said he could speak the consultants' language. He had learnt it through his MBA. Anyway, the MD could see the sense of having someone from the company involved with the consultants. And this he did. The consultants were critical of the European strategy. They quickly detected the lack of direction.

Their incisive cost/contribution analysis showed the problem with margins, product quality and delivery performance. They drew attention to the threats. And fingers were pointed.

During his MBA studies, the informant had made contact with an engineer in the same line of business, as a supplier of small high machined parts that went into their down-hole pumps. He had mentioned that some Japanese company had developed a new alloy that vastly improved bearing life in the highly corrosive conditions of down-hole operation. Post MBA he looked into the Japanese company. So when it came to the internal battling over European strategy, he built on what the consultants had done, speaking their language and using their concepts. In addition he put forward the idea of seeking a licence from a Japanese company to use its alloy and some of its designs in their pumps. This would up-date their product line as well as their management practices, particularly on quality. He had also received, off the record, some positive signals from one of their major European customers.

So, after the bloody coup, he was promoted to marketing director on the back of his contribution. He more or less designed his own job. The sales director left, as did two of his appointees, and the sales team was totally restructured. After some pretty tough negotiations a licensing deal was set-up with the Japanese company. He said that all that would never have happened if he had not been able to link up with the consultants and subtly shift the agenda from defence to attack. The language of the BCG and marketing strategy analysis had been a major resource for him. It allowed him to appropriate the discussions of marketing options and to cleverly de-personalise the issues.

I took what he said seriously. He was really convincing and seemed glad to be able to tell someone else about his success, as if he was getting some sort of kick out of it. At times I felt like a voyeur. Not in a predatory way, almost as if I was being manipulated by my intended victim. Do you think I should believe him though? Was he telling me the truth? I mean, I couldn't really go and publish this stuff if he wasn't telling the truth, could I? It seems to open up too many cracks that have been plastered over. No one has really considered the conceptual colonisation. During the interview, I was trying to be the objective outsider. But, I was a conspirator, a participant in the discussion we had. I provided cues which he responded to. He also provided me with cues which I responded to. And so he was interviewing me as much as I was interviewing him.

After the interview, when I was transcribing it, I wondered about the story he told me. During the interview I felt I had to believe him, or at least to feign it, just to keep engaged in the discussion. But now as I sit here trying to make sense of it all, I wonder was he having me on? After all, if he had been able to outflank some senior people in the company, could he not easily outflank me? He easily seemed to speak a language I could understand. In retrospect, he often spoke to me just as another academic would do. I felt he was organising me, just as he probably would do his colleagues. My ethnography was his impression management test. The idea that he might have been spinning me a clever yarn never entered my head until I sat down to analyse the transcript. And you know, I have conducted many research interviews. But, I've always ended up taking what was said at face value. I mean, in my papers I pontificate on the basis of the results of my empirical work as if they confer on me the privilege of giving the last word on things. *Do you think it's necessary to believe what someone says in order to take what they do say seriously?*

Epistle 2, from apostle B to apostle C

Well, I remember an interview I did for my PhD with a marketing manager of a leading computer manufacturer. I was looking for the secrets of success when launching new products. He told me everything I wanted to hear. He told me how his company was the fastest growing company in the world and what was special about it in achieving this. I transcribed his comments verbatim and used examples he gave as quotes in my thesis. I really felt I had got something from that interview. The interview was done six months before the press announced that the company had suffered a dramatic decline in profitability. The causes for this were described as being related to the company's rapid growth and an expanding cost base. It did not necessarily mean that their marketing strategy was at fault, but it changed the way I viewed my data. Looking back I am amused at how naïve I was. I was getting the standard sales motivation pitch. He was probably reeling off what he told his sales people every day. *Even so, does that mean I shouldn't have taken what he said seriously?*

Epistle 3, from apostle C to apostle A

Both epistles 1 and 2 are instructive reminders that there are two fields of activity, that of the so-called reflective academic and that of the practitioner. However, focusing on one side of the divide, we know research marketers are trained to wear academic white coats and value-free glasses. They make occasional forays into the practitioner's world, seeking data, often captured and retained in a portable data collection and retention unit, known as a tape recorder. When they get out there, horror of horrors, they are treated not as an academic, but as a human being, subject to the usual niceties and conventions as everyone else. Worst of all, they do not get data. They get some guy's story and he's basically boring and has been living with his story for years. He's been boring his wife and friends with the story for years. No one listens to him any more, except for obsequious subordinates with an eye on the main chance. Even his dog won't listen anymore and hides just before walkies. And then along comes these bozos who not only listen to the story, they transcribe it and pore over it, dip their fingers in its entrails and then come back to the guy with more questions. He must be important. Just as film stars have their perverted followers, so managers must have their tame researchers. No doubt stories relate to events. However, our accounts of them are always and everywhere subject to language and interpretation.

So, should we believe what people tell us? I don't know whether we are up to this. But, I think we must consider language first. The traditional view of language as a neutral, objective mirror of reality has been challenged by Wittgenstein, Rorty and Derrida. They emphasise the constitutive role of language, the fact that language does much more than describe the world. If we view language as a form of code, then language provides a sense of belonging, a sense of who 'we' are and 'not-we' are. Codes also have moral force, or some normative capacity in addition to providing resources of power. This point is made neatly in both epistles. The MBA deploys his linguistic resource in a way that gains him power. The moral is that we as researchers should not be blind to the way that language is deployed by those we talk to, nor should we be blind to our own usage. Strangely enough, this may account for why ultra-rational matrices are used as political weaponry – maybe that is their only real worth in an age that venerates rationality.

Epistle 4, from apostle A to apostle B

So, if in certain contexts, it is necessary to believe what someone says in order to take what they say seriously, should the manager providing the account be held responsible for its impact? *And when Levitt, Kotler, McCarthy and Drucker talk of the marketing concept as the guiding philosophy of business, is it necessary to believe what they say in order to take what they say seriously?*

Epistle 5, from apostle B to apostle C

I was recently involved in preliminary negotiations for a consulting job with a local government department. They said they wanted to bring a marketing orientation to their activities. I told them that they had to examine the objectives their leader had set for the department and ask themselves whether or not they were satisfying their own and their customers' needs. Four weeks later I heard they had gone to an advertising agency instead. Are Hewlett Packard and Harley Davidson responsible for Tom Peters? Is the fact that ICI drastically cut its range of operations because it wanted to 'stick to the knitting' to be pinned on Peters and Waterman?

Epistle 6, from apostle C to apostle A

Epistle 4 asks whether the manager responsible for the account should be made responsible for its impact. Epistle 5 responds that they should. This is an interesting point. I think that we should not take the consultant's role literally, but symbolically. Consultants play a role in creating the myth that cultures are collectivities of shared values. Schultz argues that the superficiality of the pragmatic concentration on shared values has tended to erode the originality of organisations as they seek to become copies, or simulacra of the blueprints of excellence of the managerialists. These prescriptions were always idealisations, there being no real-world original to copy, resulting in a proliferation of simulacra false to themselves and their model. So we can take consultants seriously at more than one level. The veracity, credibility, believability of what they do varies depending on the contextual code which we use to make sense of their activities. Also, many consultants pass on the received wisdom of marketing and in so doing are selling the unattained and therefore the unattainable, thus maintaining the illusion generated by this powerful ideology. As an ideology the marketing concept has recently been linked more and more in managers' minds with neo-classical economics, so obfuscating market-ing and the market. That said many sins have been committed in its name. Marketing, like any other academic dogma, becomes an alibi for whatever change the CEO, chief surgeon or head of department wants to introduce next. It is a convenient pretext. Substance is the last thing that matters.

Epistle 7, from apostle A to apostle B

If the attribution of veracity, credibility or believability of an account is a question of interests, then thought and deed can never be consistent. But talk and deed can. So, accounts cannot reveal the deeper structure of meaning that underlies the apparent disorder of the organisational surface. *So, is the understanding of marketing inseparable from the marketing of understanding?*

Epistle 8, from apostle B to apostle C

I've just been reorganising a working paper I wrote a while ago. What the data says seems pretty straightforward to me. Doubtless I will have imposed my own beliefs and prejudices on the way I analysed it, so that it says what I might expect it to say. But, then again, it was me who had a major part in the creation of that data, since I designed the research. My problem is in writing it all up. The same data can say different things to different audiences. I know, from previous hard experience, that if I write it up in the straightforward way I see it, the reviewers won't touch it. They'll say it lacks focus, or is not interesting enough. That's because it will not touch their prejudices and preferences. The only reviewer who would publish my paper is someone with the same background as me. So I write for my target audience. I generalise what the characteristics of my audience are, lumping their diversity of interests into seemingly suitable categories and then return to my data. From my generalisations I extract points of focus and write the paper around those, teasing the data in their direction. My paper will not say what I believe it to say because it has been corrupted by the preferences and prejudices of others, as I understand them. I understand my piece of marketing, but I must market that understanding to others, and in so doing make it less believable in my eyes.

Epistle 9, from apostle C to apostle A

We need to clarify how it is that belief is a question of interests, why thought and deed can't be consistent and how talk and deed can be? On the point that the understanding of marketing is inseparable from the marketing of understanding:

To be
Believed
We must, must we
Tell somebody something
They already know
To be true?

No – when celebrity is attained
it is sufficient to be recognised
then you can say what you like
take your drawers off in public
tell them it's a joke
they will detect deep profundity
in your fundament
a person can reach the stage where they
cannot not be credible

It's just that we haven't got there yet!

What about marketing? In 'On Seduction' Baudrillard (1988) uses the example of the Japanese Cyclorama, where women are displayed on a revolving pedestal, wide open to the gaze of men who can literally stick their noses in it! Modernity has a fixation with exposing reality to the gaze, with uncovering its fine-grained detail. This preoccupation with reality is (ob)scene as ultimately 'reality' is displaced from its context and floats free, as a form of hyper-reality is created in its place. Academia plays a fundamental role in the modern project. Put another way, it is a fundament of modernism. Academics are obsessed with uncovering the real. There are only two directions in which they can proceed. One, they can seek to 'uncover' the real by generating theory. In order to do this it is absolutely necessary not to believe what anyone tells you, or at the very least to treat accounts as indications of something else, some wonderful 'substructure' which 'explains' everything. This opens up the potential for all sorts of theoretical positions, certain in the knowledge that no one will ever be able to put what they say to the test. And so the great web of theory spins out and gradually begins to wind itself around the spider.

A second way is opened up for those, who, through belief in Comte and the great promise of positivism, have learned that to theorise is a sin. This recursion revolves around a web of method. This web is spun so fine and so many times that it can create a hyper-reality which is so divorced from its referent, that it begins to approach the virtuosity of some of the theories in recursion 1. Some of the best examples may be found in the *Journal of Marketing Research*, where signifiers have floated well away from any link with 'real' concepts into their own hyper-space, where only initiates can decode the many wonderful signs; the methodological amulets are hung around data to protect it, to guarantee its reality and veracity. But what reality does it correspond to? *Isn't that unbelievable?*

Epistle 10, from apostle A to apostle B

In the final para of epistle 8, our apostle argues that belief is a question of interests, and that what's in his interest can align with those of a reviewer. They don't have to overlap. Notions of authority and privilege (i.e. the attribution of believability) do not reside with the authors, or the readers of accounts. Authors do not write accounts. Accounts write them. And readers write accounts too through re-presenting the accounts of others and de-centring the subject. It's a matter of staging *truth effects* and readers and writers both do that. Belief is also a question of *attention*, of attending to something. You have to see something to believe it. Not necessarily in a perceptual, cognitive sense, but in a conceptual, pre-cognitive sense. We learn to see. Our vision is culturally determined. The West is a bright culture, concerned with illuminating truth, as epistle 9 implies in his use of the Baudrillard quote. The East is a dark culture, concerned with the *shadows between things*, as T.S. Eliot called them.

And so many things remain invisible to us. We don't notice them, or attend to them. Nor do we see *how* failing to notice what we don't notice shapes our thoughts and deeds. So, as Kant argues, *we see things not as they are, but as we are.* Belief is self-referential and also intersubjective. It's another form of identity crisis. At one level you could say that we are guided by interest, or belief, or rationality – you know the self-interest of the invisible hand. However, belief is not a mere projection of self-interest, for, as Lacan argues, individuals are limited in the extent to which they can know themselves and their thoughts . . . *I am where I think not. So I think where I am not.* As Weick observes, *how can I know what I think, until I hear what I say*? The structures of language provide the conditions of possibility of our thoughts. Language shapes our thoughts and various shapes are possible. And so you could argue that epistle 9's contextual codes (our structures/institutions) use us to make sense of their activities. And so it is that thought and deed can not be consistent. They are incommensurable. Does thought precede and define deed? How could it be? Does deed precede and define thought? How could it be? The world of praxis, of belief, resides at the nexus of thought and deed. How could it be? You can tell someone, yourself included, what you think you are going to do, why you think you are going to do it, and how you think you are going to do it. And if you can judge the expectations of your audience, you can tell them what you think they want to hear – i.e. that which is consistent with their expectations and beliefs as you think you know them. You anticipate, or prejudge, or re-present what it is they need to hear in order to elicit the reaction which is in your interests. It is not a matter of truth, but of truth effects. So talk can be consistent with deed. But, all these matters are ultimately undecidable. Through the spiralling process of the production and consumption of commodified marketing knowledge, sense and sensibility become transient and transformed. So belief can only be understood with respect to disbelief at the nexus of thought and deed.

The difference between taking what someone says seriously, and believing what someone says is not a simple matter of choosing how to react in a given situation, but of reading, and re-reading, writing and re-writing, or re-presenting meaning – i.e. staging truth effects. And this meaning resides at the nexus of thought and deed, intersubjectively, between participants. Therein lies intertextuality. Laws of correspondence and evidence are staged truth effects. There is no deep structure to be uncovered through apprehending and transforming reality into edited accounts. It is not a question of interpretation, but of re-presentation.

Epistle 11, from apostle B to apostle C

I'm currently writing distance learning study units on elementary marketing. You know, 'you are doomed if you do not apply the marketing concept to your organisation' sort of stuff. The process I have to use is to create a fine-grained hierarchy of objectives, starting with the objective of the entire programme, and dividing it down to the objectives of each sub-sub-section in a unit. For each of them I then trace out a linear line of argument, each point of which represents one idea, which in turn is one paragraph of text. For each paragraph I can either write the paragraph myself, or refer to a paragraph someone else has written, in a book or journal. Is this a case of re-presenting meaning for a different audience? Perhaps the most interesting part of this process is the need to create a hierarchy of objectives. This is essential. Without it the document will never get past the editor, who insists on a clear rational structure to the materials, where every paragraph is an illustration or extension of a logical argument.

As it happens, fitting Kotleresque texts into this structure is very easy. Marketing knowledge has already been packaged this way in such textbooks, and in effect all I am doing is propagating the great marketing paradigm through the linear hierarchy of educational objectives. In fact, in writing these materials, I have no alternative but to propagate the marketing paradigm, whether I believe in it or not, since unless I come up with an alternative hierarchy of objectives, my editor will not print my work. This hierarchy that defines marketing knowledge is tinkered with, refined and re-worked by an army of marketing academics. Anyone who chooses to disbelieve marketing know-how, must therefore take on this army by implication. *Thus, you may not choose to believe marketing knowledge, but you do have to take it seriously.*

Epistle 12, from apostle C to apostle A

Since I last wrote, my head has been buzzing from a seminar given by Gibson Burrell. I think he is grappling with some of the ideas we are, but in a more clearly focused way. In epistle 10, I can tune into the notions of the relationships between brightness and shadows and the ways these are tied into ideas of selective attention. The point made about the fragmentation of the self and the notion of belief is also very relevant. The notion of language speaking us, of the formation of the human subject by discourse, is something which I can buy into at one level, but which I am constantly seeking a way out of. There must in my view be some room for agency and so I will go to great lengths to find writers who can promise some form of rescue for this. People such as deCerteau seem to provide a limited promise of this.

Reading epistle 11, I was reminded of two books: Eco's *The Name of the Rose*; the other by Ivan Illich *et al.* on society as it might have existed before writing came into the world. Both books contain extensive sections on copying text, on the need to be faithful to the text and take as their model the scriptorium of the medieval monasteries and the ways in which monks passed their time making copies. Epistle 11 also adds another dimension to the notions of light and darkness raised in epistle 10, and that is the imprisoning, yet guiding linearity of the book. The notion of tinkering and reworking by an army of academics brings the medieval scene alive in my mind.

Gibson Burrell's seminar was based around his forthcoming book *Pandemonium.* In it he seeks to put his postmodernist ideas into action, so far as possible. For example, each double page will be split into two halves with a line drawn across the middle of the page. The text on both sides of this divide will be 'about' different things, although there will be serendipitous coincidences between them on occasion. The text on the top half is written in a linear script which moves from left to right; that on the bottom half, from right to left. The book will focus on 'retro' organisation theory: that is, he examines pre-modern modes of 'management' from the tenth to the twelfth centuries. The logic behind the book is simple: the disruption of modernist scientific rational approaches to life and the world. He has devised this set of 'rules' to guide him:

1 Search for the superficial secret

Modern science, in particular structuralism, has focused on trying to dig out the deep truth in the workings of the id, etc. This has spilled over into society at large, where truth needs to be uncovered everywhere. The notion of taking things seriously and believing is strongly implicated in the context of 'uncovering' the truth. We must turn away from this and search instead for the superficial secret.

2 Anything goes

The notion of one rational true discourse must be abandoned. Instead we must listen to Feyerabend and ask ourselves, is our knowledge, that which is generated in universities, any better than any other kind of knowledge? We must also be aware of the alternative discourses which have been subjected to the shining light of our western scientific rationality and snuffed out. Had they no value, nothing to say?

3 Distrust scepticism
Why not learn instead to trust?

4 Twist history till it groans
If history is not the history of all, but rather of the select few (of the white, male, anglo-saxon carrying phallus) we need to challenge this account. We need to challenge historical accounts and use them to construct a history of the present, of what is going on in the world now, as opposed to trying to make sense of the past in our own terms.

Burrell says he wants to unearth the suppressed, that which has been shoved down by our modern approach. He uses Greece/Crete as a metaphor. Greece became known for grace, beauty and linearity, the search for wholeness. The focus on straight lines and linearity led us to the Panopticon, of space cut through by shafts of light which help maintain surveillance and discipline. Greece, the birthplace of philosophy and science. Set against this Crete (suppressed), the labyrinth, dark tunnels, mystery, Bacchus (Dionysius) as opposed to Apollo. Of course, nowadays the very word Cretan is an abomination.

So far we've been dealing with all sorts of aspects related to this. But we've yet to ask: who are the contemporary cretans? What about this notion of progress? How can we evaluate and challenge it in marketing? Belief is seductive. Belief in progress brings us closer to the goal of modernism, which to a cold critical eye may be an imaginary progress towards an illusory end. *Can we work out what progress is and whether or not this is being attained in any way, and if so for whom?*

Epistle 13, apostle A to apostle B

Epistle 11 brings us back to earth. Where's that? You know, that strange place where submissive workers toil ceaselessly on the shop floor, or in the scriptorium, overseen by draconian supervisors, circumscribing and controlling their activity, rewarding good performance and productivity. You know – dark satanic Taylorian mills where we sacrifice ourselves to the god of production.

The output of this factory is knowledge, intellectual capital. Knowledge is manufactured. It is *produced* from raw ingredients which are hewn from the hillsides of experience and of existing knowledge and speculations; moulded, assembled, fashioned and packaged in a linear process, in terms of inputs and outputs, with the needs of a target market in sight. It is purposive and the purpose is progress, greater competitive advantage and market share. There are commercial pressures. There are competitors, customers, distributors and suppliers. There is gain. There is self-interest. And yes, there is a knowledge industry, an army of marketing labourers, and various markets and supermarkets for knowledge involving various competing/collaborating producers and consumers of knowledge: consultants, academics, practitioners, the media, students, the community. And using this analogy, apostle B provides another illuminating example of belief being a question of interests. Within this perspective knowledge exists independently of the observer, as if there is an external position of certainty *out there* waiting to be discovered. Knowledge is seen to be somehow external to, or detached (i.e. abstracted) from what Foucault calls the *clash of petty dominations*. It is produced. We miners go out there and chip away at the edifice of truth – we apprehend reality and return to our respective tribes with our trophies. It is then codified and captured in text. And *meaning* resides there too. It is congealed and fixed in text for all to see and grasp through consultation. There is an overwhelming sense of closure. But, what about the *will to knowledge* – the interests that often underlie the use people make of knowledge, of concepts such as gender, belief, truth, reality, justice, agency, environment, health, sexuality, ethics and, of course, marketing.

Apostle C desperately seeks the reconciliation of agency and discourse and perhaps that's his role as the catcher in the rye. Maybe we don't need to take a stand on whether it is necessary to believe what someone says in order to take them seriously. Two notions of belief have emerged. First, the legitimising and universal idea of belief as being something that is invested by someone in something else. This anticipates an ideal underlying structure, a grand narrative, that makes belief possible. For how else could we recognise belief if we couldn't know disbelief? We must have some prior structure, some insight that makes belief possible. Where does that structure come from? The divine? Genetics? Human nature? Second, that the concept of belief is itself man-made, not divine, and is put to work in society as an instrument of power. How is the concept of belief put to use in the market-ing social? This makes more sense to me, especially when we contextualise belief and we see that it is contingent, not fixed, and clearly so in our everyday life, as apostle B's examples illustrate.

We have already begun to consider the social functions that such concepts as belief, reason, truth, presentation and interpretation seem to play in the context of the social practice we marketing academics engage in. The idea of discourse is not that it is spoken, or written, or heard or seen. It has to do with the conditions of formation which make certain talk or text, or other representations possible – the set of taken-for-granted conceptual markers, or categories that underpin our practice. The conditions of possibility of our brief exchanges on marketing are set within the marketing discourse – which is not spoken or written and that's why, I suppose, apostle C facetiously refers to himself as being constructed through the discourse. It speaks of him. It produces him. Our imaginations are continually being captured. And yes we are socialised. Perhaps it is the role of a Derryman to seek reconciliation, or to be sought out by it. This is the process of self-formation that constructs our dear C.

It is through *the* agency of our experience and technique as marketing academics that we extract data and translate it into a meaningful account. But, I feel that in marketing circles the interpretive process whereby reality is apprehended, transposed and reconstituted is taken to be unproblematic. What do we *not* see about this process? What is it that makes this form of knowledge production possible? What has captured our imaginations? Are the institutions that construct us really neutral and independent? How is it that we take a literal reading of marketing texts as narrative accounts, as the idea of linearity suggests? Are we merely the retailers of FMCGs (i.e. fast moving current generalisations)? At the present there are many Greeks in marketing, and very few Cretans.

I like Gibson's idea of disruption, of the diabolical. It is a central idea of Foucault and Derrida to be suspicious of claims to universal truths. Foucault, like Neitzsche before him, refuses to separate off knowledge from power. He argues that we should cast aside utopian schemes, such as the search for first principles, and instead ask ourselves how knowledge works in our society. Is it our duty as marketing academics to criticise the workings of our institutions (i.e. journals/conferences/texts/courses, etc.) which often appear to be neutral and independent, when they are not. As apostle B very plangently demonstrates, those institutions do exercise power, indirectly perhaps. I think the marketing project would be healthier if this power, and the various staged truth effects of those institutions was unmasked and talked about openly.

One way of being disruptive and yet being constructive is to demonstrate the link between reflexivity and creativity through exploring the potential of various forms of re-presentation to raise interesting angles on our taken-for-granteds. Take apostle B's current project. There he is working away to an agenda he says is defined for him. The potential of what he can say, or what can be said, is circumscribed by the textual format (structure, style) he must adhere to. And this does say something about B's interests at the moment – it constructs him. At least I can choose to construe his interests on the basis of the account he provides and the various strategies he seems to be employing to stage truth effects. Yet, who knows what insights might be possible through adopting different textual formats – even in the context of distance learning modules. Pastiche is all the rage in ethnography at the moment – and perhaps Gibson is in the vanguard of attempts to bring those ideas to the world of organisation theory at the moment. Various re-presentational devices are used – text, poetry, film, song, dance, theatre, etc. (the medium is the message?). The goal seems to be to reassert the importance of ambiguity, of plurality of meaning; to encourage disruption, i.e. openings, rather than foreclosure.

And in our own small way, I think we have come to see the power of various rhetorical devices to raise questions, to open things up, rather than to assert closure through adherence to the typical format of paper development, with all its restrictive conventions on structure, style and content. At least we are still talking to each other and reflecting, not only on what we are attempting to say, but also about what we say says about us. Yes, we are taking what we say seriously, even if we don't believe it. It is not necessary for us to believe it, to begin to see what it is that makes what we say possible. *So, is it necessary to believe what someone says in order to see what it is that makes what they say possible?*

Epistle 14, from apostle B to apostle C

Everything I've researched leads me to disbelieve the validity of the marketing concept in emerging markets for high-technology products. Yet I cannot get around the fact that it can be used to explain all that I have researched.

Epistle 15, from apostle C to apostle A

How believable is marketing? How credible is it? How credible can anything be that seeks to deny its other? You can try to apply some of the questioning principles of Bourdieu's study of academic life in France to marketing. A brief foray yields many examples of the 'bad faith' to which he refers. How can marketing be credible, if on the one hand it claims to be an objective and scientific discipline, while on the other it treats its object of study as a predator studies a meal? Are authors really dispassionately interested in studying exchange relationships 'objectively'? Several authors have supported the contention that marketers have traditionally taken the view of the 'channel captain', studying consumers in much the same way that fishermen study fish, rather than as marine biologists study them.

How can marketing be credible, if marketing authors conveniently ignore some of the most damning critical theories in their 'appraisals' of various critiques? To believe in the validity of what someone says, but to ignore what they say is to render them invisible within your discourse. Marketers have tended to vanish people that they take seriously. One can say that marketers have experienced a profound myopia where theories which do not fit their worldview are concerned. For example, consumer behaviourists have tended to play down the effects of psychoanalytic theory and to highlight others, such as cognitivism, which accord more closely to their world view. Pollay's otherwise exhaustive review of critical literature specifically excluded a consideration of the European Marxist tradition. An article provocatively entitled *Desire: Induced, Innate, Insatiable*, which purports to constitute a history of the culture of consumption, ignores most of the European critical literature relating to desire. It is as if Jacques Lacan, Judith Williamson and Jean Baudrillard had never set pen to paper. But, why continue to kick a dead dog? The tautological nature of the marketing concept and its lack of specificity mean that it can be interpreted in any number of ways to justify whatever interests might be in play at a particular point in time. It has been invoked by the Tories' continuing privatisation programmes. It has been used to justify the implementation of 'total quality' programmes. It has been used to apply new concepts in 'strategic human resource management' in hospitals, schools and universities. It is so wonderful because it works at such a basic emotional level in everyday practice. It is simply beyond doubt. *Does that also mean that it is beyond belief?*

SITTING ON A CORNFLAKE

In this chapter we have tried to capture the *eschatological* as we believe it manifests itself in some of our everyday practices as marketing academics. Through this we have considered matters of belief and faith as they are embedded in those practices. However, we have no final answers; nor was it our intention to offer such a teleology and eschatology. But for those of you who feel the need for such guidance we offer the following advice, which was given to us by Fergus Magroarty that night at the karaoke party; sing along with this:

Detectives of Knowledge
(sung to The Lady is a Tramp)

lines of inquiry, they're such a thrill,
motives and evidence, the scent of the kill,
successful convictions, the proving of points,
detectives of knowledge, let's raid the joint.

The crafting of questions, gives us a buzz,
taping our interviews, we do it because,
words we can conquer, and meaning we'll force,
grounded detection, opens doors.

Some people get lost, in the qual-quant debate,
but disillusion's their fate,
break out, yes doubt,
That vested positions, are what it's really about,
the discourse is conviction,
it's not doubt.

Discrete observations, they give us a hit,
the richness of being there, the thickness of it,
but meaning's at question,
and we can't capture it,
with signifiers floating
we forfeit,

the right to say that, people mean what they say,
for the meaning's away,
floating high, bye bye.

So contrive a position,
do it if you will,
suspending suspicion, suspending suspicion,
suspending suspicion's, it's a bitter pill.

REFERENCES

Bartels, J. (1988) *The History of Marketing Thought*, Publishing Horizons, Columbus, Ohio.

Baudrillard, J. (1988) 'On Seduction', in Poster, M. (ed.) (1988) *Jean Baudrillard: Selected Writings*, Polity Press, Cambridge.

Brown, S., Bell, J. and Carson, D. (1995) *Proceedings of the Marketing Eschatology Retreat,* University of Ulster, Belfast.

Descartes, R. (1968) *Discourse on Method and the Meditations*, Penguin, Harmondsworth, translation by F. Sutcliffe.

Eco, U. (1994) *Apocalypse Postponed* (ed. R. Lumley), Bloomington, Indiana University Press.

Goethe, J.W. von (1979), *Faust*, trans. P. Wayne, Penguin Classics, Harmondsworth.

Milligan, S. (1963) *Puckoon*, Penguin, Harmondsworth.

5

ON AURA, ILLUSION, ESCAPE, AND HOPE IN APOCALYPTIC CONSUMPTION

The apotheosis of Las Vegas

Russell W. Belk

> And the kings of the earth, who have committed fornication and lived deliciously with her, shall bewail her, and lament for her, when they shall see the smoke of her burning. Standing afar off for the fear of her torment, saying, Alas that great city Babylon, that mighty city! for in one hour is thy judgment come. And the merchants of the earth shall weep and mourn over her; for no man buyeth their merchandise any more: The merchandise of gold, and silver, and precious stones, and of pearls, and the linen, and purple, and silk, and scarlet, and all thyine wood, and all manner vessels of ivory, and all manner vessels of most precious wood, and of brass, and iron, and marble. And cinnamon, and odours, and ointments, and frankincense, and wine, and oil, and fine flour, and wheat, and beasts, and sheep, and horses, and chariots, and slaves, and souls of men. And the fruits that thy soul lusted after are departed from thee, and all things which were dainty and goodly are departed from thee, and thou shalt find them no more at all.
>
> (*Revelations* 18: 9–14)

It requires less and less of a stretch of the imagination to see the city of Las Vegas as Babylon epitomised. This glittering oasis in the desert was created in a shadow of its contemporary character in 1946 when underworld figure Bugsy Siegel opened the Flamingo hotel and casino. Besides its links to organised crime and legalised gambling, Las Vegas is also the home of luxury shopping malls, all-you-can-eat cut-rate pseudo-gourmet buffets, and nearby legalised prostitution. With its neon-lit 24-hour casino-palaces, gargantuan spectacles, and blatant temptations to lust, gluttony, envy, and greed, Las Vegas makes the biblical luxuries and vices of Babylon pale by comparison. If Armageddon threatens the modern Babylon, what better metaphorical enactment of the End could there have been than the dawn parties of the 1950s when the denizens of Las Vegas stayed up to watch and toast the mushroom clouds of the nearby above-ground nuclear testing (Lang 1995). And in telling Las Vegas fashion, rather than fear and trembling, the bombs instead inspired such exaltations as the 'Atomic Hairdo', the 'Atomic Cocktail', and the 'Atomic View Motel' where guests could enjoy an unobstructed view of the bomb blasts (Ventura 1995).

But if to some Las Vegas is a modern Babylon of sinful luxury, licentiousness, and lust, to others it is a postmodern paradise of fantasy, freedom, and fun. Where the former vision forebodes the city's immanent apocalyptic destruction, the latter foreshadows its apotheosis as a sacred site for playful pilgrimage and worship of its goodly things. In this positive vision Las Vegas is the 'temple town of the American Dream' (Tosches 1995). I argue in this chapter that the second, positive, prophesy is clearly ascendant as the millennium approaches. Moreover, I contend that this apotheosis of Las Vegas is a prototype of changes taking place more broadly in world consumption. We increasingly venerate and celebrate a materialistic style of consumption long condemned as sinful and damning (see Belk 1983). In seeking to understand how and why this apparently radical recasting of luxury consumption is taking place, it is necessary to consider the parallel transformation of commercialism from profane and evil to sacred and good. For behind both transformational processes lies a dramatic shift in the locus of our hopes: from redemption to consumption. And rather than resulting from a monumental battle between good and evil like that prophesied for Armageddon, the ascendance of commercialism and consumerism has been gradual and quiet, evoking T.S. Eliot's revised revelation that the world ends with a whimper rather than a bang.

COMMERCIALISM AND LOSS OF AURA

As a starting point for examining the sacralisation of commercialism, consider Walter Benjamin's (1936/1968) concern for the fate of the (sacred) work of art in an age of (commercial) mechanical reproduction. He feared a loss of magical aura when art images are separated from their creators. He felt that churning out prints, film copies, and photographs would take something vital from us. He prophesied that it would doom us to a less authentic experience of the sacred when cheap reproductions substitute for the real thing. And he suggested that life itself would become less meaningful under these circumstances. Others have expressed the same fear that mass production and mass marketing negate authenticity, but use different labels: fakelore (Dorson 1976), staged authenticity (MacCannell 1989), invented tradition (Hobsbawm and Ranger 1983), pseudoevents (Boorstin 1961), spectacle (Debord 1970), carnivalisation (Twitchell 1992), trivialisation (Corwin 1986), Cocacolaización (Nuñez 1989), Disneyfication (Terrell 1991), McDonaldisation (Ritzer 1993), and the malling of the marketplace (Kowinski 1985). In each case there is concern that creating something for the commercial purposes of mass consumption, somehow robs us of true experiences and in their place we are left with a shallow simulacrum of surface without depth, spectacle without substance, sizzle without the steak.

In a nearly opposite take on postmodern consumer culture, Venturi, Brown, and Izenour (1972) argued that the vernacular architecture of Las Vegas and franchise-laden commercial strips are the epitome of that which is desirable, good, and authentic. The popularity of these locales is testimony to their worth. The analysis of Las Vegas by Venturi *et al.* offered a populist alternative to Benjamin's implicit elitism and anticipated their own postmodern architectural project. In the twenty-five years since this study, the vernacular architecture of Las Vegas has helped to transform the city into a postmodern fantasy playground. Moreover, in the sixty years since Benjamin's essay, marketing and art have moved from mechanical reproduction to virtual reality and hyperreality. The latter term is taken to mean both more real than reality and hyped reality (Baudrillard 1988; Eco 1986). The hyperreal is steeped in illusion. If Benjamin was concerned with copies, what should we make of a present and future in which fantasy has become blurred with reality? If increasingly we confuse the two or embrace fantasy over reality, perhaps we are not far from the hypothetical experience machine that Nozick (1974) feared might prove too alluring to ever separate ourselves from in order to return to our quotidian lives.

The fact that such alternative realities (or unrealities) are an integral product of contemporary marketing efforts, prompts us to ask whether marketing has become too adept at delivering illusory images and has thereby sown the seeds of its own demise. For if all is illusion and we have come unequivocally to embrace such illusions, perhaps we have reached a point where our fear is (or should be) the opposite of Benjamin's. We no longer fear that these reproduced illusions will have too little magical aura, but rather that they have too much. If so, then marketing may have outlived and outreached its usefulness. In this paper I explore these shifts in the locus of the sacred with particular attention to marketing as a maker of illusions, to Las Vegas as a postmodern capital of illusions, and to the implications of these concerns for the future of marketing.

AURA HYGIENE

While Walter Benjamin was concerned with high art, I am concerned with low art, particularly art involving the sort of consumer goods that became so important in Pop Art (e.g. Kunzle 1984; Maharaj 1992; Mamiya 1992; Schroeder 1992; Spiggle 1985; Varnedde and Gopnik 1990) and subsequent art genres (e.g. Cotter 1988; Janus 1992; Joselit 1988; Lurie 1986; Smith 1988). As Claes Oldenburg once said, 'I am for Kool-art, 7-UP art, Pepsi-art' (Varnedde and Gopnik 1990: 150–1). The irony is that while Benjamin feared that commercial reproduction would destroy the sacred aura that only the individual artist could impart to his or her work, more recent artists have sought the aura of potent consumer brands in order to empower their art. The Campbell's Soup cans, Coca Cola bottles, Volkswagens, Cadillacs, Hoover vacuum cleaners, Spalding basketballs, and other icons of Pop and post-Pop Art have immediate resonance to and a strong emotional impact on their American and Western audiences. We now visit museums of modern art not just to worship art, but to celebrate the commercial goods this art so often venerates (Belk 1995). But before this magical commercial aura could be appropriated by artists, it had to somehow first be imparted to these goods by manufacturers, marketers, and merchants. In order to understand how this is done, let us consider several historical moments when magic seems to have become firmly attached to consumer goods.

While we could start earlier with the madness of the marketplace in the carnivalesque fair (Bakhtin 1968; Buttimer and Kavanagh 1995), the first such moment I will address is found in the eighteenth-century peddler depicted by William Beckford in his 1786 novel, *Vathek* (Beckford 1970). This is an ostensibly Orientalist tale about the Caliph Vathek, although Beckford's rather detailed knowledge of Islam and Suffism as well as his use of the novel to attack occidentalism make him less subject to Said's (1978) criticisms that Westerners render the East as an exotic and inferior Other, as is typical of other authors of this genre (see Svilpis 1990). Beckford's tale of fantasy, magic, and treasure begins when a peddler arrives in an Eastern city offering 'extraordinary wares'. Assendorf (1993) describes these fantastic goods:

> The supposed peddler is revealed as the possessor of wondrous utensils – slippers that assist the feet in walking, knives that cut without requiring a movement of the hand, etc. The goods, all of them adorned with precious gems, are therefore utopian machines that relieve human beings of labor; and all without the obtrusive mechanism of anything like a steam engine. The Caliph Vathek is especially interested in a collection of sabres, 'whose blades emitted an abiding shine,' and on which are engraved apparently indecipherable foreign letters. Such are the wares that cast a spell on Vathek. And here begins a seduction by things whose quality is connoted doubly – the ware is a commodity and simultaneously a magical object; it materializes utopian possibilities, for which it is the reified substitute.
>
> (p. 11)

The ultimate power of this magician-peddler is shown in Vathek's willing sacrifice of fifty children to obtain these glittering goods. For their treachery and avarice, Vathek and his minion are ultimately condemned to an eternal damnation: 'Their hearts immediately took fire, and they, at once, lost the most precious gift of heaven: – HOPE' (Beckford 1970: 119).

The itinerant peddler's role as a magician offering incredible goods and casting a spell on those who behold them is a role that Lears (1989) suggests played an important part in the history of American consumption:

> For many Americans, particularly those outside the urban upper classes,

> the market was personified in the itinerant peddler. The primal scene of the emerging market culture in the mid-nineteenth century was the peddler entering the isolated village or rural community, laden with glittering goods that were ornamental as well as useful: scissors, knives, tools, tinware, clocks, patent medicines, jewelry, perfumes, and fabrics. The peddler embodied a multitude of cultural associations. Certainly he was a trickster figure, a confidence man who achieved his goal through guile rather than strength, particularly through a skillful theatricality. What was perhaps most striking about the peddler was his liminality. He was constantly on the move, scurrying along the fringes of established society. He occupied the threshold between the village and the cosmopolitan world beyond but also between the natural and the supernatural. He was an emissary of the marvelous, promising his audience magical transformations not through religious conversion, but through the purchase of a bit of silk, a pair of earrings, or a mysterious elixir. Like the traditional conjurer multiplying rabbits, doves, or scarves, the peddler opened his pack and presented a startling vision of abundance.
>
> (p. 78)

We see here the beginning of the shift of faith and inspiration from religion to commerce. It is significant, Lears notes, that Santa Claus 'looked like a peddler opening his pack' in Clement Moore's (1822) familiar poem, 'A Visit From St. Nicholas'. An abundance of magical delights are evoked in Moore's peddler simile from which children have learned to expect small miracles from Santa Claus each Christmas, even if their 'visions of sugarplums' are now far more grand (Belk 1987). What is salient in each case is the hopeful anticipation of wonder, surprise, and joyful ecstasy from the burgeoning cornucopia of the peddler's pack of commercial goods. Moreover, as Campbell (1987) suggests, with modern hedonism it is the anticipation more than its realisation that brings joy, suggesting that it is the bearers and not the goods themselves that create pleasure.

If Santa Claus offers a benign portrayal of the peddler's magic, a more sinister portrayal is found in Stephen King's (1991) *Needful Things*. Instead of peddling his wares, the central character, Mr Gaunt, opens a small shop called Needful Things in a New England village. At the end of the book, his departure from town in a horse-drawn medicine-show wagon demonstrates the evolution of marketplace magicians from itinerant peddlers to more permanently located merchants. In this Faustian tale Mr. Gaunt has the ability to search the souls of his prospective customers for their deepest material wishes and to fulfil them magically. Whether the desideratum is a Sandy Koufax baseball card, Elvis Presley's sunglasses, or a carnival glass lampshade, this is exactly what the proprietor offers. What he asks in exchange for these irresistible delights is a token amount of money, a mischievous 'favour' (that leads to murder and mayhem in the town), and, implicitly, the buyers' souls – the same souls where their consumer desires presumably reside. What is sinister in this tale is thus not the goods themselves, for as long as their new owners continue to believe in their magical power they really do bring delight. The evil is instead seen to be in the extent of their immersion in these illusions and what they are willing to give up to have these goods.

The next historical moment in the evolution of aura production in consumer goods is found in the development of the department store. While peddlers, fairs, country stores, and merchandise catalogues were the sources of magical goods in earlier eras and rural communities (Schlereth 1989), the department store became the magical merchandise mecca of the city in the latter half of the nineteenth century. Rosalind Williams (1982) calls the atmospheres created in these stores 'dream worlds' and 'fairylands'. Others have called early department stores 'palaces' and 'cathedrals' of consumption (e.g. Benson 1979; Hutter 1987; Miller 1981). These stores presented fantasyland displays in magically alluring grandiose settings. They provided the exotic, the erotic, and the wonderfully new in such enticing ways that seduction seems an apt description of the hold they gained on consumers (Reekie 1993). Such treatments and labels capture some of the magical attraction of department store goods, but novels like Dreiser's (1981) *Sister Carrie* and Zola's (1958) *Au Bonheur des Dames* offer richer portraits of the consumer desire they inspired. In Dreiser's novel, Carrie, fresh from the farms of Wisconsin, marvels at the still unaffordable luxuries of a turn of the century Chicago department store modelled on Marshall Fields:

> Carrie passed along the busy aisles, much affected by the remarkable display of trinkets, dress goods, shoes, stationery, jewelry. Each separate counter was a show place of dazzling interest and attraction. She could not help feeling the claim of each trinket and valuable upon her personally and yet she did not stop. There was nothing she could not have used – nothing which she did not long to own. The dainty slippers and stockings, the delicately frilled skirts and petticoats, the laces, ribbons, haircombs, purses, all touched her with individual desire, and she felt keenly the fact that not any of these things were in the range of her purchase.
>
> (p. 22)

In Zola's novel, set in late nineteenth-century Paris with the Bon Marché as its model department store, Denise is similarly overwhelmed by the attraction of consumer goods displayed in this new and wonderfully alluring setting.

> They had awakened in her flesh new desires and had become an immense temptation to which [she] fatally succumbed, yielding first to the purchases of a good and careful housewife, then won over by coquetry, finally devoured.
>
> (Zola 1958: 83)

In both of these novels too, the danger is not in the goods themselves, but in what these young women were willing to give up to obtain them: their chastity and virtue. These seductions by goods encapsulate the power of marketing in the new and majestic department store displays. The change in the locus of commercial magic from the peddler to the shop to the department store (and eventually the shopping mall) is one that Lears (1994) calls 'the modernisation of magic'. Significantly, Lears notes that similar magical thinking is commonly found in gambling.

Another locus of magic, and a contemporaneous moment to the department store in the historical evolution of attaching aura to consumer goods, is the rise of advertising. As Raymond Williams (1980) suggests, advertising is a magical system imparting power to goods. Not only are certain types of new products made magically desirable, but certain brands of these goods are more magical and more desirable than others, thanks to the transforming abilities of advertising, packaging, and other promotions. The most successful of these brands may become quintessential (Cornfeld and Edwards 1983; Sudjic 1985) or sacred (Belk, Wallendorf, and Sherry 1989). Like the mysterious markings on the sabres that enthral Vathek, these brand markings and embellishments offer a magical promise that the object is something far more than it would be without them.

Branded goods were still uncommon at the start of the nineteenth century, but were quite common by the century's end (Strasser 1989). Like the wares of the peddlers and medicine shows that preceded them, branded goods become magical elixirs once they are successfully mystified and mythologised by advertising (e.g. Barthel 1988). They represent the hope for transforming us and our lives from something drab and ordinary to something exciting and extraordinary. Moreover, they represent the power to transport us to a wonderful world of fantasy in which our lives are joyful, satisfying, hopeful and fun. Thus, the transcendent power once confined to religion and high art is now alive and well in the branded, advertised, displayed consumer good. The aura that Benjamin feared was lost has instead made a remarkable shift to mass produced, mass marketed, mass mediated consumer culture (see Belk 1991, 1995). Our primary source of hope has shifted from religion, to art and science, and finally to consumption.

VIVA LAS VEGAS

The magic that characterises the marketing moments just described and that creates and sustains the transcendent aura of consumer goods, has undergone further evolution in the present postmodern age. Much of this change is epitomised in the city of Las Vegas. While Los Angeles is sometimes called Babylon and capital of the postmodern world, due to such surreal features as Disneyland, Forest Lawn Cemetery, and Hollywood, it should probably be placed a distant second to Las Vegas. Consider some of the attractions found on the Strip (Las Vegas Boulevard South). With 5000 rooms and an eighty-eight-foot high golden lion that could swallow all the guests these rooms accommodate, the new MGM Grand Casino and Hotel is the world's largest hotel, centred around four separately themed towers and casinos (Morocco,

Hollywood, Monte Carlo, and the Emerald City of Oz). It also has an adjacent thirty-three-acre theme park, 'MGM Grand Adventures' with a Mississippi steamboat, Grand Canyon Rapids, a haunted mine, Casablanca, and a Hollywood Back Lot River Tour. As one reviewer observed, the complex represents 'a billion dollars' worth of building dedicated to Dorothy and Toto' (Drucker 1994).

Just down the Strip from the MGM is the second largest hotel in the world, the Excalibur hotel, with a mere 4000 rooms as well as a draw bridge, turrets, battlements, indoor jousting, fire-breathing dragon, Sherwood Forest Cafe, Camelot Restaurant, Robin Hood's Snack Bar, Little John's Snack Bar, Hansel and Gretel's Snack Bar, Lance-a-Lotta Pasta, Sir Ghalahad's Prime Rib house, Roundtable Buffet, King George's Bar, Jester's Lounge, Minstrel Theater Lounge, Medieval Village Restaurants and Shops, Fantasy Faire, Wizard's Arcade, Canterbury Wedding Chapel, and King Arthur's Arena dinner theatre and tournament site.

A short monorail ride from the Excalibur brings the visitor to the Luxor hotel, complete with thirty-storey pyramid, ten-storey sphinx, 100-foot obelisk, 2500 rooms, a lobby big enough for nine stacked Boeing 747s, an indoor Nile River on which guests pass in barges, talking animatronic dromedaries, chariot races, a replica of King Tut's tomb, entertainment including a linen-shrouded acrobatic team called 'the Flying Mummies', a water and light show with gigantic holographs, and a ground-shaking three-site show, 'The Secrets of the Luxor Pyramid Trilogy'. The 40 billion candlepower laser beam that is projected up from the peak of the pyramid can be seen 250 miles away in Los Angeles on a clear night and initially proved hazardous to aircraft in the area.

In the other direction up the Strip from the MGM, Caesar's Palace has only 1600 rooms, but it has three moving sidewalks, reproductions of classic statuary in genuine Carrera marble (see Venturi, Brown, and Izenour 1972: 50), the Cleopatra's Barge cocktail lounge, the Circus Maximus showroom, the Bacchanal restaurant, an Omnimax Theater, and an upscale shopping arcade, the Forum, complete with animated talking statues and an ever-changing blue and white ceiling of Mediterranean sky and clouds. Caesar's is currently expanding and recently spent $6 million each on two 10,000 square-foot penthouses for high rollers.

A bit further up the Strip, The Mirage resort hotel stops traffic with its spectacular volcano that erupts in shooting flames and thunderous noise every fifteen minutes. With over 3000 rooms and 100 acres, it is smaller than Excalibur, but offers a pricier set of fantasies. Guests and other gamblers are treated to an aquarium complete with sharks and stingrays, a 1.5 million gallon dolphin tank, a ninety-foot high atrium filled with exotic flora, and a menagerie that houses the rare white Bengal tigers of entertainers Siegfried and Roy. But currently the biggest free show in town is the six-times-a-day sea battle between the eighteenth-century British frigate 'Britannia' and the ninety-foot pirate ship 'Hispaniola' on the artificial sea in front of Treasure Island Casino (2900 rooms). The ships sail toward each other, exchange noisy cannon fire, and host a battle between thirty pirates and sailors who clash amid flames with bold sword play, culminating in a loudly cheered finale in which the frigate sinks into the lagoon.

These spectacular highlights almost render pedestrian such lesser attractions as the live circus, animated dinosaurs, and 90-foot waterfall at Circus Circus and its Grand Slam Canyon Adventuredome, the 750-car exotic automobile collection at the Imperial Palace (including Hitler's Mercedes-Benz and Elvis Presley's Cadillac), the nude review of the *Lido de Paris* at the Stardust hotel, the 2000 video poker and slot machines at the Gold Coast, the 1500-foot canopy being built over Fremont street with 1.4 million computer-synchronised lights and lasers, the constant parade of 'big name' entertainers, and the more than fifty mass production mini wedding chapels, like the Little Chapel of the West where my daughter was married after having to forgo her first choice of Disney World. Planned future attractions will compete for even more spectacular effects, including a 100-foot-tall glass Coke bottle at the Coca-Cola Oasis, the Hard Rock hotel and casino (with state-of-the-art concert stage), a simulation of New York (including the Statue of Liberty, Empire State Building, and Coney Island) at New York-New York hotel and casino, and an artificial fifty-acre lake with boating, waterskiing, and (on a seventeen-acre island) the 3000-room Beau Rivage resort (see Smith 1995; Wolkomir 1995). For Las Vegas is a city where fantasy is the norm. Your cocktail may be served by a Nubian slave, a cowgirl, a centurion, a swashbuckling pirate, a South Seas temptress, or a buxom medieval maiden. Hollywood entertainers, show girls, live elephants, trained tigers, and prostitutes offer further fantasy diversions in this year-round combination of Mardi Gras, Carnival, Halloween, Samhain, Saturnalia, and New Year's Eve.

As Venturi, Brown, and Izenour (1972: 14) note, 'Las Vegas is to the strip what Rome is to the Piazza'. The Strip concept is itself a derivative of the carnival midways that originated in the World Fairs – another building block of consumer culture and one also emphasising sex, exoticism, and Orientalism (Rydell 1993). Neon lights are another element borrowed from the World's Fair (of 1933 in Chicago – Hess 1993) that have found their full glory in Las Vegas. While Venturi *et al.* compared Las Vegas to Rome, Fontana and Preston (1990) call it a nouveau riche Versailles. They note as its distinguishing features a bigger-is-better design ethos, nostalgia, pastiche, liminality (aided by boundary-less interior spaces and lighting plus windowless and clockless separations from outside world as well as from constraints of day and night), parody, kitsch, wealth, glitter, glamour, gambling, and sex. The city is also an oasis (or mirage) in an otherwise improbably stark Mojave Desert location. Illusion is everything and the illusion continues to grow more grand and elaborate. There are even illusions of illusions, as with the Emerald City of the MGM Grand, drawing on MGM's film version of Frank Baum's master of illusion, the Wizard of Oz. Appropriately, Baum was also a pioneer in decorating department store windows and wrote tales of the life of Santa Claus (see Baum 1902; Culver 1988; Leach 1993). The effect of this atmosphere is a willing seduction into a fantasy of easy money, sex, sin, alcohol, and bigger than life fantasies; a Disneyland for adults; a hyperreal experience. As Fontana and Preston (1990: 10–12) characterise this milieu:

> The signs became icons of wealth and all that is the city; neon itself, with its flashing, on-off set of signifiers, signifies pulsating, fastpaced, controlled, on-the-edge living. The lights light up darkness, contain darkness in light, temporarily stretch out the day, minimize risks, while sharing risk-taking as the ordinary activity that defines action and where the action is for the humdrum life the players leave behind. The lights signify the bareness of the everyday. They awaken and quicken the pulse, while they draw the person as player into the dreamlike world of gambling, fun, entertainment, and time-out experiences. Like the city that stands on the edge of the desert, the end of the world, the lights invite the traveler into a city of light where the dark side of the player's life can be awakened, controlled, rewarded, and valued.

Even though the consumer's life is in these ways controlled by the dream world illusions of the casino-cum-themepark marketers, for the consumer this is a willing letting go, a welcome loss of control, a joyous succumbing to popular fantasies.

What is the nature of these fantasies? Hunter Thompson (1971) offered that Circus Circus is what we would all be doing on Saturday nights if the Nazis had won the war. The seductive activities to which we lose control may be crass, banal, decadent, sinful, or mind-numbing, but all this misses the point and reverts to the sophisticated elitism of Benjamin and others like Horkheimer and Adorno (1972). The traditional attraction of Las Vegas is 'a formula combining opulent accommodations, gourmet food and the titillation of gambling and sex' (Wright and Snow 1978: 42). There is also a giganticism (the resort casino hotels), a miniaturism (the mini wedding chapels), and an Orientalist exoticism (take your pick) that fascinate us the way 'freak shows' once did (see Bogdan 1988; Fiedler 1978; Stewart 1984). But there is more to the attraction than this. Baudrillard (1993: 246) calls Las Vegas (as well as Disneyland, Disney World, and Biosphere2) 'a matrix for tourist hallucinations and leisure activities'. Hallucinations are a particular type of fantasy comprised of superficial illusion and surface. Not only the Mirage hotel, but the entire Las Vegas tourist façade may be regarded as a shimmering and unlikely mirage in the desert. Unlike hallucinations however, to post-Puritan sensibilities there is little that is frightening or nightmarish about Las Vegas.

The postmodern Xanadus that support this hallucination in the desert offer a particularly attractive paradise of the popular. This is the American Dream distilled: get rich quick and have all your desires fulfilled. Dress and do as you wish at any hour of the day or night on any day of the year. Indulgently eat too much of everything bad for you at the obligatory all-you-can-eat buffets. Satisfy your sexual impulses vicariously at the shows or more actively via numerous Las Vegas 'escort' services and the legal brothels of adjacent counties. Get married or divorced with equal ease. Have your whims catered to, tan at the pool, see big name entertainers, retire to an inexpensive luxury suite, play, enjoy, gamble, take risks; let all your inhibitions go. The air conditioned, stimulating, shimmering, and seductive pleasure palaces of Las Vegas make such activity seem perfectly normal. And at any time of the year there are thousands of others (staying in the world record 87,000-plus Las Vegas hotel rooms) doing the same thing. Increasingly these are not just adults, but entire families, as the newer resorts provide something for everyone in order to compete with a rapidly increasing number of world theme parks and gambling venues. But rather than diminish Las Vegas revenues, the explosion of legalised gambling has simply increased primary demand and, as Mecca, Las Vegas has benefited greatly.

LAS VEGAS AS PROTOTYPE OF POSTMODERN CONSUMPTION

In all of these ways Las Vegas offers an escape from the ordinary that makes the mere extraordinary mundane (Pastier 1978). As gambling explodes in popularity throughout the world and as more of our time and money is spent on commercial entertainment, Las Vegas appears in the vanguard of the vernacular, offering what more and more people want more and more of – a hyperreal fantasy experience. This same desire is seen in the growth of malls and megamalls (e.g. Belk and Bryce 1993; Davis 1991; Hopkins 1990; Jacobs 1984; Kowinski 1985, 1986; Langman 1992; Shields 1989), theme parks (e.g. Fjellman 1992; King 1991), megachurches and religious theme parks (e.g. Heelas 1994; Niebuhr 1995; O'Guinn and Belk 1989), international tourism (e.g. Feifer 1986; Urry 1990) and in film and television (e.g. Doane 1987; Friedberg 1993). As might be expected of a postmodern generation brought up in the fragmented world of television, these forms also offer a fragmented and rapidly changing panorama of spectacular images (Langman 1992). In driving down the Strip of Las Vegas we move quickly from one fantasy world to another. This is increasingly like driving down the commercial strips of any city within an automobile culture (MacDonald 1985). Similarly moving from one shopping mall store to another is 'like flipping T.V. channels' (Davis 1991). Kowinski (1985) calls the mall three-dimensional television and Langman (1992: 49) explains how television helps prepare us for the shopping mall experience:

> The unusual impositions and juxtapositions of unending spectacles already presuppose the habits of televiewing in which rapid changes of spectacular disconnected images are the norm. The adjacent positioning of contradiction need not be resolved. Thus a weight-loss centre may be

> found between an ice-cream shop and a large-size apparel store, a diamond merchant is next to a salami shop while across the hall may be a bank and video arcade and tax or legal service. This is little different from the media coverage of a war or disaster sandwiched between Hemorrhoid relief and the new improved car (the latter causing the pain in the ass).

The increasingly popular international package tour, with its ten countries in twelve days, offers a similar constantly changing panorama of fantastic peoples, places, and things. In the process we theme countries. Peru becomes Incaland, Brazil is year-round samba and carnival, Norway is the land of trolls, and Mexico becomes a multi-themed tourist park we might call Gringolandia (Belk forthcoming; Shacochis 1989).

Whereas a theme park plans these discontinuities, they are more a matter of competition for bigger and more spectacular extravaganzas in Las Vegas and the shopping mall. The effect as well as the themes are similar however.

> The themes seen today on the Strip parallel, not coincidentally, those at Disneyland as well as in literature, movies, and advertising. These are the long-running myths of our culture: knightly chivalry, adventure among the heathen, the winning of a West, Victorian homesteads, utopian futures, fabulous riches; a mix of lands near and far, times past and future, imagined and remembered, civilized and uncivilized, familiar and strange, real and fabulous, peaceful and violent. At Disneyland they were plotted by one man; in Las Vegas they were evolved by the collective vernacular design process.
>
> (Hess 1993: 119)

The most striking thing about all of this is that the fantasy world of the Las Vegas Strip is becoming normal; it is what we have come to expect; and it may be a vision of our future. Hess (1993) also notes that while the Strip, where 'form follows fantasy', is an exaggerated version of the commercial strips in most American cities, it is no longer an anomaly and offers a way to study these 'populist, sprawling, postindustrial cities' (pp. 8, 120).

TRANSGRESSION, ESCAPE, HEAVEN, HOPE, AND CHILDHOOD

If Las Vegas today is a world of fantasy providing compelling hyperreal images of other times, places, and people (including other selves), and if such worlds are becoming less and less of an anomaly in our daily lives, what should we make of this triumph of fantasy? If Las Vegas is the unintended prototype for the future world city, how should we react to such a prospect? And if marketing, more generally than Hollywood, is now our dream factory, what does this portend for the future of marketing? Have we perhaps regressed to a childhood state of living in the dream worlds of Barbie, Ken, GI Joe, Mickey and

Minnie, Big Bird, Robin Hood, pirates, knights, magicians, circus clowns, Ronald McDonald, the Marlboro man, the Michelin man (Bibendum), and Santa Claus? As we become more adept at creating virtual realities and hyperrealities, will living in actual reality lose its appeal? If so, has marketing become too successful in creating alluring fantasies?

Since Las Vegas is known as 'Sin City', one thesis worth entertaining to explain the growing popularity of the city is that the Puritan roots of America have finally given way to the titillation of guilty pleasures. This perspective is that of transgression, developed by Georges Bataille (1991) and amplified by Pasi Falk (1994). In this view, the 'forbidden fruit' of sex for sale, nudity, gambling, alcohol. gluttony, luxury, and other 'sins' characteristic of Las Vegas, makes them all the more alluring. The transgression of the carnivalesque is exciting, tempting, and tinged with a hint of evil that we relish in our otherwise pedestrian lives. Where once we needed priests and artists to overcome such prohibitions (Goldberg 1995), we now embrace transgression and need only the crowd effect and carnival atmosphere of Las Vegas in order to pursue it. The thrill comes from not only the transgression itself, but also the risks, fears, and fantasies of winning and losing (Oates 1995). Appealing as this thesis is, it seems more relevant to an earlier era of Las Vegas (and perhaps to an older generation of its current visitors). In the view of one observer,

> Las Vegas remains a place unconstrained by the bounds that define most communities. As a result, Las Vegas has been free to reinvent itself as the market dictates. In its rapidly evolving history, Las Vegas has gone from 'mobster and starlet hideaway, to haven of sin and vice, to its present incarnation as low-roller heaven.' This hyperhistory is presented . . . from the modern-day pioneers who opened the Flamingo in the '40s, to today's fanny-packers who come by the tens of millions each year to visit 'Disney in the Desert'.
>
> (Tronnes 1995: xii)

Where there would once have been endless tables for craps, cards, and roulette, there are now endless rows of electronic slot machines. Half of all Americans have now been in a casino (4 per cent more than 1991 – Cooper 1995), AIDS fears curb sexual abandon, and increasing health consciousness makes all-you-can-eat meat buffets a bit anachronistic. In the new trend toward family-oriented megahotel-casinos, the lure of sin and vice is being supplanted by a Disneyesque appeal to fun and fantasy.

This suggests a second explanation of the appeal of the hyperreal experiences of Las Vegas: Escape. If our work lives are tedious and alienated, if our home lives are boring and lacking in surprises, why not escape into the illusions of Arthur's roundtable, Tut's tomb, Caesar's Rome, the circus, the yellow brick road, pirates, tigers, and myriad other fantasies served up so appealingly in Las Vegas? It is easy to escape to the illusion of another time and place in Las Vegas. If these illusions offer an escape from reality, it has been suggested that such escape is often good for us and conducive to a healthy state of mind (Taylor 1989). I find this escape explanation a useful one in understanding the appeal of contemporary Las Vegas, but I also think there is something more than escape involved. Films, books, and television all offer momentary escape, but come nowhere near the enveloping and thematic nature of contemporary Las Vegas. For a more complete understanding of the Las Vegas experience I think it is necessary to return to the concept of paradise.

Heaven may seem an improbable description of Las Vegas, but consider some of the elements of the Las Vegas Fantasy:

> And why come to Vegas for it? Maybe it has something to do with Heaven. For to do nothing special in Paradise, to have all your needs tended while you stare and twiddle your thumbs (or pull levers) . . . is pretty much the image most people have of heaven. Bugsy's idea of Paradise has mingled with the Mormon family idea of Paradise to attract Christians who've given up all hope of Paradise.
>
> (Ventura 1995: 192)

Shopping, entertainment, and the illusions of readily accessible riches, luxury, and exotic sex all have a part in this paradise as well. These elements accord well with the vision of heaven depicted by Julian Barnes in the concluding chapter of his novel, *A History of the World in 10½ Chapters* (1989). When the narrator dies and learns that he remains fully embodied in a heaven where he can have anything he wants, he immediately embarks on a programme of luxury shopping, incredible sex, heroic sports feats, and all manner of new and challenging interests and adventures:

> I went on several cruises; I learned canoeing, mountaineering, ballooning; I got into all sorts of danger and escaped; I explored the jungle; I watched a court case (didn't agree with the verdict); I tried being a painter (not as bad as I thought!) and a surgeon; I fell in love, of course, lots of times; I pretended I was the last person on earth (and the first). None of this meant I stopped doing what I'd always done since I got here. I had sex with an increasing number of women, sometimes simultaneously; I ate rarer and stranger foods; I met famous people all the way to the edges of my memory.
>
> (Barnes 1989: 299)

But as George Bernard Shaw once suggested, 'There are two tragedies in life: one is to lose your heart's desire, the other is to gain it.' And so it goes with Barnes' hero:

> I worked seriously on my golf. After a while I was going round in 18 shots every time and my caddy's astonishment became routine. I gave up golf and took up tennis. Pretty soon I'd beaten all the greats from the Hall of Fame on shale, clay, grass, wood, concrete, carpet – any surface

> they chose. I gave up tennis. I played for Leicester City in the Cup Final and came away with a winner's medal (my third goal, a power header from twelve yards out, clinched the match). I flattened Rocky Marciano in the fourth round at Madison Square Garden (and I carried him a bit the last round or two), got the marathon record down to 28 minutes, won the world darts; my innings of 750 runs in the one-day international against Australia at Lords won't be surpassed for some time. After a while, Olympic gold medals began to feel like small change. I gave up sport. I went shopping seriously. I ate more creatures than had ever sailed on Noah's Ark. I drank every beer in the world and then some, became a wine connoisseur and despatched the finest vintages ever harvested; they ran out too soon. I met loads of famous people. I had sex with an increasing variety of partners in an increasing variety of ways, but there were only so many partners and so many ways.
>
> (Barnes 1989: 307)

What eventually becomes clear to the bored hero is that what he lacks is dreams: something to hope for.

As we saw with the Caliph Vathek, eternal damnation was operationalised as a flaming heart and a loss of HOPE. On the other hand the good Gulchenrouz in Beckford's novel is admitted to a heaven of hope in which he enjoys perpetual childhood. Childhood is a time when we make fervent wishes as we blow out birthday candles; when we deliver hopeful wishes to Santa Claus and the Tooth Fairy; when all things seem possible. Such an empowerment of possibility exists among children because we have not yet disillusioned them and bound them to a more restrained code of 'adult' behaviour. As Tom Wolfe (1965) recognised, Las Vegas is a place of childhood liberation where dreams are reawakened and nobody can make us go to bed. Because of its irrationality, gambling is also a child-like indulgence, as Allen (1995) explains:

> In short, gambling invites me to take an hour's recess from adulthood, to play in a well-demarked sandbox of irrationality and to look at the world as a magical place, which of course it is when the light hits it at the right angle. Those people who stubbornly remain adults and who look upon gambling's happy meaninglessness from within will see a phalanx of games controlled by the indomitable law of averages, games that from an adult's wintry perspective you cannot hope to master. Those adults will see me, and the people sitting next to me, [as] giving our money away week after week to people who do not love us.
>
> (p. 315)

The new Las Vegas, far more than the old, is taking on a childlike Disneyesque character. And as one analyst concludes, this is not fully due to the discovery of the family target market:

> with so many Egyptian mummies, swashbuckling pirates, and dancing

> munchkins taking up residence on the Vegas Strip I might get the same wrong impression that other reporters have recently gotten, that this new adolescent-minded Vegas is up to something really dirty, like hooking a new generation of gamblers by getting them into the hotels while still in diapers – you know, the Joe Camel strategy . . . I mean, sure, Las Vegas *is* trying to hook the kiddies. But . . . that's not the real point. Nor is the signal truth here that American grown-ups have kids lurking inside them. Simply, it's that America's adults have become kids.
>
> (Cooper 1995: 334–5)

While Walter Benjamin would no doubt be alarmed, I suggest that regressing to childhood is not altogether a bad thing. Without becoming overly nostalgic about a golden age of youth (see McCracken 1988), childhood is a time when we find it rather easy to suspend disbelief and imagine things that are wonderful and terrible. Imagining these things helps us imagine other selves with infinite possibilities. From fairytales through virtual reality, imagination is itself a wonderful and terrible thing. Without imagination we live in an impoverished world with fewer possibilities for spiritual experiences, love, creativity, and other forms of transcendent joy. Even terrible imaginary possibilities may help us master our fears and better deal with our futures. McCracken (1988: 110) suggests that 'Goods serve as bridges when they are not yet owned but merely coveted. Well before purchase an object can serve to connect the would-be owner with displaced meaning.' The hyperreal fantasy worlds of Las Vegas and elsewhere in consumer society also act as a bridge to our hopes and dreams; it is a gossamer bridge that leads somewhere over the rainbow. In all of these respects, a reversion to a childlike state of fantasy is not such a bad thing.

This is not to suggest that a life of illusory brand promises, instant fantasy gratification, commercialised dreamworlds, fantasy resorts, voyeuristic travel, and gambling Xanadus that lure the compulsive is entirely healthy or good for us either. Nevertheless, we must face the fact that for many of us, perhaps all of us in one way or another, some of our strongest and most readily available hopes for transcendent and transformational experiences lie in consumer goods and services. It is through such hope and its accompanying suspension of cynicism and disbelief that we create that excited, if ultimately illusory state of anticipatory desire that sustains and nourishes us.

According to a traditional defence of marketing and advertising illusions, believing in these illusions may make them real. For instance, believing that a certain perfume will make us irresistible, certain shoes will help us run faster, or a certain car will gain us more respect, could be the key to a self-delusion that helps us believe and thereby actually become more beautiful, athletic, or self-confident. There is no doubt some truth in this Wizard-of-Ozian power of positive thinking (see Leach 1993), but it is not the real payoff of the fantasies engendered by the marketing of these products. What is created more assuredly than the actual payoff promised is the hope that it may occur. Alluring fantasies provide us with something to believe in and hope for. It is this hope that sustains us, even though it may well not be realised. It is for this reason that we devour catalogues, advertisements, and magazines about our areas of special leisure interest. For the act of imagining is an enlarging and empowering one. In an age of abundance, it is the sizzle rather than the steak that nourishes us.

This then is what I believe we may learn from Las Vegas: the work of art in an age of hyperreality is the branded, marketed, fantasy-laden consumer good and service. To say that there are better things than this to put our hope and faith in is a value judgement toward which we will all have our own prejudices. Some will argue for 'higher' forms of inspired hope from religion, visual art, music, literature, poetry, nature, or nation, and most likely certain forms of each. But these judgements are susceptible to charges of elitism and ethnocentricism. Others may argue that the source of hope should be the individual or our significant other or our children or our family. It is harder to argue with placing our hopes in people rather than things. However, while people may be a source of hope-inspiring fantasies, people need nourishment for their fantasies and many of us need reified artefacts that act as symbols of these hopes.

Hope is the essential element of Christian eschatology, Kasper (1994) suggests:

> For hope is not a commodity that people either have or do not have; hope is the very essence of human existence. When there is no hope for the future, life becomes meaningless.
>
> (pp. 8–9)

This is the force behind much art and religion, and yes, consumer goods and services as well. The peddler knew this as well as do the casinos of Las Vegas. Babylon, the peddler, merchant, advertiser, and casino have all been targets of condemnation because of the power this realisation provides. This is the power of the magical aura. It has been a part of marketing for a very long time and promises to be the key to its future as well. If we ever conclude that marketing has gained too much magical power through fantasy creation, it will be because we have found a better source of hope. For the consumer's part, we would do well to remember the moral tales of *Vathek*, *Needful Things*, *Sister Carrie*, and *Au Bonheur des Dames*, and not become too immersed in fantasy or give up too much in order to pursue it. But pursue it we should. For in the end, we can only hope.

REFERENCES

Allen, E. (1995), 'Penny Ante', in M. Tronnes (ed.), *Literary Las Vegas*, New York: Henry Holt and Company, pp. 313–24 (original in *Gentlemen's Quarterly*, May, 1992).

Assendorf, C. (1993), D. Reneau (trans.), *Batteries of Life: On the History of Things and Their Perception in Modernity*, Berkeley: University of California Press (original 1984).

Bakhtin, M. (1968), H. Iswolsky (trans.), *Rabelais and His World*, Cambridge, MA: MIT Press.

Barnes, J. (1989), *A History of the World in 10½ Chapters*, London: Jonathan Cape.
Barthel, D. (1988), *Putting On Appearances: Gender and Advertising*, Philadelphia: Temple University Press.
Bataille, G. (1991), R. Hurley (trans.), *The Accursed Share: An Essay on General Economy, Volumes II and III*, New York: Zone Books.
Baudrillard, J. (1988), M. Poster (ed.), *Jean Baudrillard: Selected Writings*, Stanford, CA: Stanford University Press, pp. 119–48, 166–84.
Baudrillard, J. (1993), 'Hyperreal America', *Economy and Society*, 22 (May), pp. 243–52.
Baum, F.L. (1902), *The Life and Adventures of Santa Claus*, New York: The New American Library.
Beckford, W. (1970), R. Lonsdale (ed.), S. Henley (trans.), *Vathek*, Oxford: Oxford University Press (original 1786).
Belk, R.W. (1983), 'Worldly Possessions: Issues and Criticisms', in R.P. Bagozzi and A.M. Tybout (eds), *Advances in Consumer Research*, 10, Ann Arbor, MI: Association for Consumer Research, pp. 514–19.
Belk, R.W. (1987), 'A Child's Christmas in America: Santa Claus as Deity, Consumption as Religion', *Journal of American Culture*, 10 (Spring), pp. 87–100.
Belk, R.W. (1991), 'The Ineluctable Mysteries of Possessions', in F. Rudmin (ed.), *To Have Possessions: A Handbook on Ownership and Property*, special issue of *Journal of Social Behavior and Personality*, 6 (6), pp. 14–55.
Belk, R.W. (1995), *Collecting in a Consumer Society*, London: Routledge.
Belk, R.W. (forthcoming), 'Hyperreality and Globalization: Culture in the Age of Ronald McDonald', *Journal of International Consumer Marketing*.
Belk, R.W. and Bryce, W. (1993), 'Christmas Shopping Scenes: From Modern Miracle to Postmodern Mall', *International Journal of Research in Marketing*, 10 (3), pp. 277–96.
Belk, R.W., Wallendorf, M. and Sherry, J.F., Jr. (1989), 'The Sacred and the Profane in Consumer Behavior: Theodicy on the Odyssey', *Journal of Consumer Research*, 16 (June), pp. 1–38.
Benjamin, W. (1936/1968), 'The Work of Art in the Age of Mechanical Reproduction', in H. Arendt (ed.), H. Zohn (trans.), *Illuminations*, New York: Harcourt, Brace & World, pp. 219–53.
Benson, S.P. (1979), 'Palace of Consumption and Machine for Selling: The American Department Store, 1880–1940', *Radical History Review*, 21 (Fall), pp. 199–221.
Bogdan, R. (1988), *Freak Show: Presenting Human Oddities for Amusement and Profit*, Chicago: University of Chicago Press.
Boorstin, D.J. (1961), *The Image or What Happened to the American Dream*, New York: Athenium.
Buttimer, C.G. and Kavanagh, D. (1995), 'Markets and Madness', in S. Brown (ed.), *Proceedings of the Marketing Eschatology Retreat*, Coleraine, Northern Ireland: University of Ulster, 1995, pp. 60–71.
Campbell, C. (1987), *The Romantic Ethic and the Spirit of Modern Consumerism*, London: Basil Blackwell.
Cooper, M. (1995), 'Searching for Sin City and Finding Disney in the Desert', in M. Tronnes (ed.), *Literary Las Vegas*, New York: Henry Holt and Company, pp. 225–50.
Cornfeld, B. and Edwards, O. (1983), *Quintessence: The Quality of Having It*, New York: Crown Publishers.
Corwin, N.L. (1986), *Trivializing America*, revised ed., Secaucus, NJ: Lyle Stuart.
Cotter, H. (1988), 'Haim Steinbach: Shelf Life', *Art in America*, 76 (May), pp. 156–63, 201.
Culver, S. (1988), 'What Manikins Want: *The Wonderful Wizard of Oz* and *The Art of Decorating Dry Goods Windows*', *Representations*, 21 (Winter), pp. 97–116.
Davis, T.C. (1991), 'Theatrical Antecedents of the Mall that Ate Downtown', *Journal of Popular Culture*, 24 (Spring), pp. 1–15.

Debord, G. (1970), *Society of the Spectacle*, Detroit: Red and Black.

Doane, M.A. (1987), *The Desire to Desire: The Woman's Film of the 1940s*, Bloomington, IN: Indiana University Press.

Dorson, R.M. (1976), *Folklore and Fakelore: Essays Toward a Discipline of Folk Studies*, Cambridge, MA: Harvard University Press.

Dreiser, T. (1981), *Sister Carrie*, Harmondsworth, Middlesex: Penguin Books (original 1900).

Drucker, S. (1994), 'Las Vegas, Theme City', *New York Times*, 13 February, section 5, p. 15.

Eco, U. (1986), W. Weaver (ed.), *Travels in Hyperreality: Essays*, San Diego, California: Harcourt Brace Jovanovich.

Falk, P. (1994), *The Consuming Body*, London: Sage.

Feifer, M.P. (1986), *Tourism in History: From Imperial Rome to the Present*, New York: Stein and Day.

Fiedler, L. (1978), *Freaks*, New York: Simon and Schuster.

Fjellman, S.M. (1992), *Vinyl Leaves: Walt Disney World and America*, Boulder, CO: Westview.

Fontana, A. and Preston, F. (1990), 'Postmodern Neon Architecture: From Signs to Icons', in N.K. Denzin (ed.), *Studies in Symbolic Interaction*, Vol. 11, Greenwich, CT: JAI Press, pp. 3–24.

Friedberg, A. (1993), *Window Shopping: Cinema and the Postmodern*, Berkeley: University of California Press.

Goldberg V. (1995), 'Testing the Limits in a Culture of Excess', *New York Times*, 29 October, pp. 43, 46.

Heelas, P. (1994), 'The Limits of Consumption and the Post-Modern "Religion" of the New Age', in R. Keat, N. Whiteley, and N. Abercrombie (eds), *The Authority of the Consumer*, London: Routledge, pp. 102–15.

Hess, A. (1993), *Viva Las Vegas: After-Hours Architecture*, San Francisco: Chronicle Books.

Hobsbawm, E. and Ranger, T. (1983), *The Invention of Tradition*, Cambridge: Cambridge University Press.

Hopkins, J.S. (1990), 'West Edmonton Mall: Landscape of Myths and Elsewhereness', *Canadian Geographer*, 34 (Spring), pp. 2–17.

Horkheimer, M. and Adorno, T.W. (1972), J. Cummings (trans.), *The Dialectic of Enlightenment*, New York: Herder and Herder.

Hutter, M. (1987), 'The Downtown Department Store as a Social Force', *Social Science Journal*, 24 (3), pp. 239–46.

Jacobs, J. (1984), *The Mall: An Attempted Escape from Everyday Life*, Chicago: Waveland Press.

Janus, E. (1992), 'Material Girl', *Art Forum*, 30 (May), pp. 79–81.

Joselit, D. (1988), 'Investigating the Ordinary', *Art in America*, 76 (May), pp. 149–56.

Kasper, W. (1994), 'Individual Salvation and Eschatological Consummation', in R.E. Brown, W. Kasper, and G. O'Collins, *Faith and the Future: Studies in Christian Eschatology*, J.P. Galvin (ed.), New York: Paulist Press, pp. 7–24.

King, M.J. (1981), 'Disneyland and Walt Disney World: Traditional Values in Futuristic Form', *Journal of Popular Culture*, 15 (Summer), pp. 116–40.

King, S. (1991), *Needful Things*, New York: Viking.

Kowinski, W.S. (1985), *The Malling of America: An Inside Look at the Great Consumer Paradise*, New York: William Morrow.

Kowinski, W.S. (1986), 'Endless Summer at the World's Biggest Shopping Wonderland', *Smithsonian*, 17 (December), pp. 35–43.

Kunzle, D. (1984), 'Pop Art as Consumerist Realism', *Studies in Visual Communications*, 10 (Spring), pp. 16–33.

Lang, D. (1995), 'Blackjack and Flashes', in M. Tronnes (ed.), *Literary Las Vegas*, New York: Henry Holt and Company, pp. 25–39 (original in *The New Yorker*, 20 September 1952).

Langman, L. (1992), 'Neon Cages: Shopping for Subjectivity', in R. Shields (ed.), *Lifestyle Shopping: The Subject of Consumption*, London: Routledge, pp. 40–82.
Leach, W. (1993), *Land of Desire: Merchants, Power, and the Rise of a New American Culture*, New York: Vintage.
Lears, J. (1989), 'Beyond Veblen: Rethinking Consumer Culture in America', in S.J. Bronner (ed.), *Consuming Visions: Accumulation and Display of Goods in America, 1880–1920*, New York: W.W. Norton, pp. 73–97.
Lears, J. (1994), *Fables of Abundance: A Cultural History of Advertising in America*, New York: Basic Books, especially chapter 2, 'The Modernization of Magic', pp. 41–74.
Lurie, D.R. (1986), 'Consumer and Connoisseur: On the New Museum's *Damaged Goods: Desire and the Economy of the* Object', *Arts Magazine*, 61 (November), pp. 16–18.
MacCannell, D. (1989), *The Tourist: A New Theory of the Leisure Class*, 2nd ed., London: Macmillan.
MacDonald, K. (1985), 'The Commercial Strip: From Main Street to Television Road', *Landscape*, 28 (2), pp. 12–19.
Maharaj, S. (1992), 'Pop Art's Pharmacies: Kitsch, Consumerist Objects and Signs, The "Unmentionable"', *Art History*, 15 (September), pp. 334–50.
Mamiya, C.J. (1992), *Pop Art and Consumer Culture: American Super Market*, Austin, TX: University of Texas Press.
McCracken, G. (1988), *Culture and Consumption: New Approaches to the Symbolic Character of Consumer Goods and Activities*, Bloomington, IN: Indiana University Press.
Miller, M.B. (1981), *The Bon Marché: Bourgeois Culture and the Department Store, 1869–1920*, Princeton, NJ: Princeton University Press.
Moore, C. (1822), 'A Visit From St. Nicholas', reprinted as *The Night Before Christmas*, New York: Simon and Schuster, 1949.
Niebuhr, G. (1995), 'Where Shopping-Mall Culture Gets a Big Dose of Religion', *New York Times*, 144 (50033), 16 April, pp. 1, 12.
Nozick, R. (1974), *Anarchy, State, and Utopia*, New York: Basic Books.
Nuñez, T. (1989), 'Touristic Studies in Anthropological Perspective', in V.L. Smith (ed.), *Hosts and Guests: The Anthropology of Tourism*, 2nd ed., Philadelphia: University of Pennsylvania Press, pp. 265–74.
Oates, W.E. (1995), *Luck: A Secular Faith*, Louisville, KY: Westminster John Know Press.
O'Guinn, T.C. and Belk, R.W. (1989), 'Heaven on Earth: Consumption at Heritage Village, U.S.A.', *Journal of Consumer Research*, 16 (September), pp. 227–38.
Pastier, J. (1978), 'The Architecture of Escapism', *American Institute of Architects Journal*, 6 (December), pp. 26–37.
Reekie, G. (1993), *Temptations: Sex, Selling and the Department Store*, St. Leonards, New South Wales: Allen and Unwin.
Ritzer, G. (1993), *The McDonaldization of Society*, Thousand Oaks, CA: Pine Forge Press.
Rydell, R.W. (1993), *The World of Fairs: The Century-of-Progress Expositions*, Chicago: University of Chicago Press.
Said, Edward W. (1978), *Orientalism*, New York: Pantheon.
Schlereth, T.J. (1989), 'Country Stores, County Fairs, and Mail Order Catalogues: Consumption in Rural America', in S. J. Bronner (ed.), *Consuming Visions: Accumulation and Display of Goods in America, 1880–1920*, New York: W.W. Norton, pp. 339–75.
Schroeder, J.E. (1992), 'Materialism and Modern Art', in *Meaning Measure, and Morality of Materialism*, in F. Rudmin and M. Richins (eds), Provo, UT: Association for Consumer Research, pp. 10–13.
Shacochis, B. (1989), 'In Deepest Gringolandia; Mexico: The Third World as Tourist Theme Park', *Harper's*, (July), pp. 42–50.
Shields, R. (1989), 'Social Spatialization and the Built Environment: the West Edmonton Mall', *Environment and Planning D, Society and Space*, 7, pp. 147–64.

Smith, J.L. (1995), *Destination Las Vegas: The Story Behind the Scenery*, M.L. Van Camp (ed.), Las Vegas: KC Publications.

Smith, R. (1988), 'Rituals of Consumption', *Art in America*, 76 (May), pp. 164–71.

Spiggle, S. (1985), '7-UP Art, Pepsi Art, and Sunkist Art: The Presentation of Brand Symbols in Art', in E.C. Hirschman and M.B. Holbrook (eds), *Advances in Consumer Research*, Vol. 12, Association for Consumer Research, Pravo, UT, pp. 11–16.

Stewart, S. (1984), *On Longing: Narratives of the Miniature, the Gigantic, the Souvenir, and the Collection*, Baltimore, MD: Johns Hopkins University Press.

Strasser, S. (1989), *Satisfaction Guaranteed: The Making of the American Mass Market*, New York: Pantheon.

Sudjic, D. (1985), *Cult Objects*, London: Paladin Books.

Svilpis, J.E. (1990), 'Orientalism, Fantasy, and *Vathek*', in K.W. Graham (ed.), *Vathek and the Escape from Time: Bicentenary Revaluations*, New York: AMS Press, pp. 49–72.

Taylor, S.E. (1989), *Positive Illusions: Creative Self-Deception and the Healthy Mind*, New York: Basic Books.

Terrell, J. (1991), 'Disneyland and the Future of Museum Anthropology', *American Anthropologist*, 93 (March), pp. 149–53.

Thompson, H.S. (1971), *Fear and Loathing in Las Vegas: A Savage Journey into the Heart of the American Dream*, New York: Random House.

Tosches, N. (1995), 'Introduction: The Holy City', in M. Tronnes (ed.), *Literary Las Vegas*, New York: Henry Holt and Company, pp. xv–xx.

Tronnes, M. (1995), 'Preface', in M. Tronnes (ed.), *Literary Las Vegas*, New York: Henry Holt and Company, pp. xi–xiii.

Twitchell, J.B. (1992), *Carnival Culture: The Trashing of Taste in America*, New York: Columbia University Press.

Urry, J. (1990), *The Tourist Gaze: Leisure and Travel in Contemporary Societies*, London: Sage.

Varnedde, K. and Gopnik, A. (1990), *High & Low: Popular Culture, Modern Art*, New York: Museum of Modern Art.

Ventura, Michael (1995), 'Las Vegas: The Odds on Anything', in M. Tronnes (ed.), *Literary Las Vegas*, New York: Henry Holt and Company, pp. 175–94 (original *Letters at 3 A.M.: Reports on Endarkenment*, Spring Publications, 1993).

Venturi, R., Brown, D.S. and Izenour, S. (1972), *Learning from Las Vegas*, Cambridge, MA: MIT Press.

Williams, Raymond. (1980), 'Advertising: The Magic System', in R. Williams, *Problems in Materialism and Culture: Selected Essays*, London: Verso, pp. 170–95.

Williams, Rosalind. (1982), *Dream Worlds: Mass Consumption in Later Nineteenth-Century France*, Berkeley: University of California Press.

Wolfe, T. (1965), *The Kandy-Kolored Tangerine-Flake Streamline Baby*, New York: Farrar, Straus and Giroux.

Wolkomir, R. (1995), 'Las Vegas Meets La-La Land', *Smithsonian*, 26 (October), pp. 51–9.

Wright, D.E. and Snow, R.W. (1978), 'Las Vegas: Metaphysics in the Technological Society', *Centennial Review*, 23 (Winter), pp. 40–61.

Zola, E. (1958), A. Fitzlyon (trans.), *Ladies' Delight*, London: Abelard-Schuman (original 1883 [*Au Bonheur des Dames*]).

Part II

JUDGEMENT

6

IN SEARCH OF THE HIDDEN GO(O)D

A philosophical deconstruction and narratological revisitation of the eschatological metaphor in marketing

Benoît Heilbrunn

INTRODUCTION

The 'hidden god' refers to a very influential book in the field of literary criticism, in which Goldman (1964) analyses tragic vision and its implicit religious structure in the *Pensées* of Pascal and the *Tragédies* of Racine. Tragic vision, he contends, is deeply influenced in the works of Pascal and Racine by a jansenist model of religious experience. The aim of this chapter is to illustrate the implicit influence of a religious paradigm on marketing thought, even though these two fields seem at first glance totally separate. Marketing, as will be shown, and especially one branch of it which is consumer behaviour is largely structured by primitive metaphors borrowed from the Judeo-Christian religion. As a field of investigation, marketing constantly imports concepts from other disciplines such as psychology, sociology, anthropology, semiology, etc. It is now accepted that most of our normal conceptual system is metaphorically structured, that is, most concepts are partially understood in terms of other concepts. This assumption, largely developed by Lakoff and Johnson (1980) raises an important issue concerning the roots of our conceptual system. Each stream of concepts carries a number of metaphors by which heteroclit ideas are interrelated. Marketing thought is thus largely influenced by metaphors which have been developed in other disciplines. Standard theories of meaning generally assume that all of our complex systems can be analysed into decomposable primitives. Such primitives can be taken to be the ultimate 'building blocks' of meaning (Lakoff and Johnson 1980: 69). The aim of this chapter is to show that marketing thought, as any other conceptual framework, derives from implicit original blocks of meaning that still have to be identified. One of these ultimate blocks, that is eschatology, will be specifically analysed as an essential metaphor which implicitly governs marketing thought. In other words, eschatology will be shown to be a hidden metaphor of classic marketing thinking and especially the way marketing views the relationship of consumers to goods. After having established the predominance of the eschatological scheme in marketing thought, philosophical approaches will be suggested to help deconstruct this paradigm which in many regards appears as fallacious, because it is unhelpful to account for most consumer decisions. Finally, a narrative approach will be used to propose an alternative approach to consumption and to reconstruct the idea of marketing on a non-eschatological basis.

THE CONCEPT OF ESCHATOLOGY IN THE JUDEO-CHRISTIAN RELIGION

The concept of 'eschatology', derived from the Greek '*eschatos*' ('last') and '*eschata*' ('the last things'), refers to the 'science or teachings concerning the last things, and/or with the consummation of all things'. It is thus related to a system of beliefs linked to the ultimate destiny of man (individual eschatology) and/or the universe (universal eschatology). Human eschatologies exist through such forms as metempsychosis, nirvana, soul migrations in oriental religions, individual judgement after death for the Aegyptians, etc. Universal eschatologies result either from an inescapable destiny, or from the intervention of a divinity. Two fundamental conceptions can be outlined: a cosmological type of eschatology based on a cyclical vision of time (eternal return) and an historical eschatology, based on a linear vision of time which ultimately ends with the Day of Judgement. Hence, any system of beliefs linked to eschatology is thus strongly related to a given conception of the universe, and therefore has a very strong influence on human behaviours (Kleiber 1980).

Eschatology is ultimately based on the experience shared by all human beings concerning the contradictory aspects of existence. Human existence is full of contradictions in the sense that contradictory principles – truth and error, good and bad, justice and injustice, joys and sorrows – continuously co-exist. Such a situation, which seems at first glance absurd, could only be understood by designing another 'principle'. Two orientations were thus historically designed to escape from absurdity (Kleiber 1980). First, using the category of space, an eternal world, where all contradictions have disappeared, was substituted to our temporal world. This is the gnostic or mystical tendency. Second, using the category of time, human situation was considered by comparison with either an original state (paradise) where contradictions did not yet exist, or with a final state where these contradictions would be solved. The first attitude which is ethically characterised by nostalgia of the golden age, that is, Lost Paradise, goes along with regrets, inaction, flee out of the world, etc. The second attitude which is continuously oriented towards a better future life is related to hope and action towards the avenement of this promised state. Strictly speaking, only this second attitude, which comprehends both a mythical and an ethical dimension, can be said to be eschatological (Kleiber 1980).

The most pregnant type of eschatology in occidental societies is largely influenced by Christianity in which moral transcendent values have long been used as a means to impose the social and economic power of Church on people. Christian eschatology has nevertheless borrowed its main conceptual framework from other cultural sources. First, Christian theology assumes the existence of two orders: human and divine. This distinction between the world of the natural desires and the realm of divine order goes directly back to Plato, whose philosophy is based on an essential dichotomy between the world of sense perception and the realm of Forms. This platonic dichotomy was Christianised by theologians like St Augustine, for whom man is conceived as undergoing a permanent conflict between *Cupiditas,* the desire for earthly things, and *Caritas,* the desire for heavenly (see MacIntyre 1966: 117). The second, as MacIntyre (1966: 116–17) reminds us, is the borrowing from feudal social life of concepts of hierarchy and role: 'when St Anselm explains man's relationship to God, he does so in terms of the relationship of disobedient tenants to a feudal lord . . . The theories of atonement and redemption, not only in Anselm but in other medieval theologians, depend on their conception of disobedience to the will of God.' A third source of interest, to quote only a few, is the Aristotelianism of Aquinas, who was essentially concerned 'not with escaping from the snares of the world and of desire, but with transforming desire for moral ends' (MacIntyre 1966: 117).

In this perspective, eschatology goes along with a duty of obedience to God. It thus stems from a morality principle, in the sense morality refers to the Judgement of God as the most important system of judgement. In this perspective, man is supposed to obey God, by respecting certain values such as love, ascetism, charity, etc. in exchange of the right to be redeemed and to gain access to eternity. Judeo-Christian eschatology is related to an ideology, being thus supported by a system of values which can be basically summarised as follows. First, it is based on an opposition between two modes of assessment of the values of life: temporal–human and eternal–divine. Prerequisite for this is the abrupt cleavage betweeen this world and the transcendent world of God. Temporal life can in this perspective only gain value and meaning by comparison with eternal life. Therefore, any human action is orientated towards a definite end, that is to gain access to eternal life. Third, any human action is assessed according to a hierarchical (and thus implictly orientated) system of values which transcend men and human life. These values are legitimised by and organised around the idea of fault, culpability, and/or redemption. Furthermore, the assessment of the value of life, as well as the value of any act, occurs only in the end with the Day of Judgement. This implies a temporal and causal approach to events, in the sense that any act is only viewed as a possible 'cause' or justification for redemption. Finally, this model is essentially a moral ideology in the sense that the value of any act is assessed through its adequation to transcendent values. Any human act does not have a value per se but by reference to an obedience to a strict system of values.

The next move is now to show that these principles in which eschatology is grounded also govern marketing thought, especially in the way it explains the relationship between consumers and products.

FROM THEOLOGY TO TELEOLOGY: AN ARISTOTELIAN INTERPRETATION OF CONSUMER BEHAVIOUR

There seems to be a consensus among academics about the role, goals and definition of consumer behaviour. Those have been clearly summarised by Holbrook (1987: 128) who gives a definition of consumer behaviour notably based on the following key points: '(1) consumer behaviour entails consumption (which) involves the acquisition, usage, and disposition of products; (2) products are goods, services . . . or any other entities that can be acquired, used, or disposed of in ways that potentially provide value; (3) value is a type of experience that occurs . . . when a goal is achieved, a need is fulfilled, or a want is satisfied; (4) such an achievement attains consummation . . .'. This approach is now widely accepted, even though slightly adapted, by most consumer behaviour textbooks. It can be condensed in the following manner: consumer behaviour is 'the mental, emotional, and physical activities that people engage in when selecting, purchasing, using, and disposing of products and services so as to satisfy needs and desires' (Wilkie 1994: 14; a similar definition is formed in Solomon 1994: 7). As any other definition, this approach is ideological in the sense that it implies a hidden paradigm, which we will now try to point out.

Consumer behaviour, as defined above, is viewed as a process made of the various contacts existing between consumers and goods. This process develops through different stages: acquisition, usage, etc. It can thus be read as a linear process in which each stage follows the other through a temporal and causal principle. The process is essentially seen in a chronological and mechanistic manner, that is one action is caused by another, the other by a third, and so on. Second, this process is based on the concept of 'value' considered as the ultimate reason for the process to start and end: the consumption process starts when a need is fulfilled and the product can be said to be valuable only if this original need is satisfied. Consumption is, in this perspective, essentially perceived as a goal-oriented activity, a goal being defined as the aim or end of an action, or more specifically as 'an end point representation associated with affect toward which action may be directed' (Pervin 1989: 474 quoted in Pieters *et al.* 1995: 228). This approach to consumer behaviour is hence deeply influenced by the theory of the final cause which grounds teleology: 'the "final cause" of an occurrence is an event in the future for the sake of which the occurrence takes place. When we ask "why?" concerning an event, we may mean either of two things. We may mean :"what purpose did this event serve?" or we may mean "what earlier circumstances caused this event?". The answer to the former question is a *teleological* explanation, or an answer by final causes; the answer to the latter is a mechanistic explanation' (Russel 1994: 84).

Teleology is a grounding principle of Aristotelian philosophy, in which a thing is constantly moved towards its end, that is the sake for which it exists. As Aristotle says, a creature in the natural course of its existence is subject to privation and to restoration processes. Therefore animals, plants and simple bodies have an internal process of motion, motion being the fulfilling of what exists potentially (see Russel 1994: 214–15; and Broadie 1991). Any human action is, in an Aristotelian perspective, essentially teleological, that is oriented towards an end. Teleology appears to be, in this perspective, a grounding principle of consumer behaviour, as outlined by Wilkie: 'consumer value research stresses the *important goals* most people are seeking' (Wilkie 1994: 159).

This teleological assumption leads to another very important dimension involved in Holbrook's definition of consumer behaviour, which is the determinant role of the value concept. If we accept the fact that consumer behaviour is in essence teleological, then it becomes essential to look for what is seen as the ultimate goal of consumer behaviour.

BASIC ESCHATOLOGICAL PRINCIPLES IN CONSUMER BEHAVIOUR

The next stage is to analyse more precisely how the concept of value is studied and approached in the consumer behaviour literature. The idea is now to consider a very popular conceptual model which is to be found in any consumer behaviour textbook. This model is the list of values designed by the socio-psychologist Milton Rokeach (1960, 1968), which is a good example of a conceptual model borrowed from various other disciplines. It is nevertheless important to realise that, by importing this model into consumer behaviour thought, marketers not only explicitly borrow a psychological framework but also implicitly borrow a Judeo-Christian metaphor. Rokeach distinguishes two main types of values: (1) *terminal (or means) values*, which are beliefs we have about the goals or end-states for which we strive; and (2) *instrumental values*, which refer to beliefs about desirable ways of behaving to help us attain the terminal values. The two lists of values appear in Table 6.1.

This model, when analysed precisely, supports an implicit system of values which can be summarised as follows: first, the value of goods is viewed at the end only: goods are valuable insofar as they are related to the terminal values which are important for the consumer. Second, the consumption of goods is a temporal process which is organised around a teleological and eschatological principle: the choice of the good is ultimately driven by long-term (terminal) values which are a-temporal and not specific to any product or situation. In cognitive terms, instrumental and terminal values can be considered as 'mental representations of the most basic or fundamental needs, and end states that consumers are trying to achcive in life' (Peter and Olson 1993: 97).

This list of values has been very much influenced by the pyramid of needs designed by Abraham Maslow (1943, 1954) in which is assumed a hierarchical

Table 6.1 Instrumental and terminal values in the Rokeach Value Survey

Instrumental values (preferred modes of behaviour)	*Terminal values (preferred end states of being)*
Ambitious	A comfortable life
Broadminded	An exciting life
Capable	A sense of accomplishment
Cheerful	A world at peace
Clean	A world of beauty
Courageous	Equality
Forgiving	Family security
Helpful	Freedom
Honest	Happiness
Imaginative	Inner harmony
Independent	Mature love
Intellectual	National security
Logical	Pleasure
Loving	Salvation
Obedient	Self-respect
Polite	Social recognition
Responsible	True friendship
Self-controlled	Wisdom

Source: Rokeach 1973

type of relationship between the various needs to which human beings are confronted. A second source of influence is the American philosopher Arthur Lovejoy who designed as early as 1907 a distinction between what he calls *terminal* and *adjectival* values. Lovejoy explains quite clearly the teleological paradigm inferred from his approach to human values: 'given a desire for some end, a reasoned knowledge of the relations of cause and effect may show us how to satisfy it by adopting the means without which the end can not be attained' (Lovejoy 1950: 595). Once again this approach refers to Aristotelian philosophy, for whom 'goods are ends (*tele*) of human action (and) we do seem to have many ends, but some of these are sought only for the sake of others, so they are not final (*teleios*) . . . One end is more final than another if it is pursued for its own sake, and the other only for the sake of something else, or if it is pursued for its own sake whereas the other is pursued for itself and also for something else' (Broadie 1991: 30). This reference to Aristotle shows very clearly that the conception of behaviour implied by the Rokeach Value Survey is essentially teleological.

Furthermore, this list of values can be said to be eschatological because it assumes that there is a common definition accepted by all people on such values as love, happiness, wisdom, etc. This can only be understood if we accept that these values are transcendent values and not personal values. The transcendence of values implies a pernicious moral system which is ideologically biased. The assumption is clearly made that if values are generally shared and understood by everybody, then they are implicitly considered to be 'good' values. Let us quote for instance from Wilkie: 'since values are transmitted through culture . . . most people in a society will agree that they are good' (Wilkie 1994: 159). This extremly vicious and ideological sentence clearly means that such a list of transcendent values is strongly related to a moral system which imposes on any individual a sense of morality, a sense of duty, that is, it gives a strict vision of what is 'good' and what is 'bad'. It is for instance interesting to remark that 'salvation' is mentioned by Rokeach as part of the terminal values. This in some way confirms the hidden eschatological nature of the Rokeach Value Survey.

This is why the Rokeach model implies both a hidden *god* and a hidden *good*. First it refers to a transcendent system of values from which man has disapeared and human values have been dethroned by divine values. In so doing, it imposes a vision of the good by providing us with a system of values which is ideologically orientated. It is implicitly obvious that all the terminal values can be said to be 'good'. This model does not leave room for a criterion of what is 'good'. The good is 'hidden' in the sense that this moral system is supposed to be widely and implicitly accepted by everybody. Moreover the 'good' is hidden, in the sense that the pragmatic and qualitative value of goods is assessed thanks to a moral system which proposes more a value judgement than a value assessment. The static concept of 'value' has replaced the dynamic process of valuation. This model thus ultimately implies a hidden 'god' linked to a hierarchical system of values which relate neither to the consumer (the evaluator) nor to the goods which are evaluated.

The second principle which grounds this eschatological theory of human behaviour is a principle of continuity which is established between consumption values and product attributes. One good example of the way this continuity principle is established is laddering which attempts to trace the linkage between a consumer's values and a particular product's attributes. These linkages, which are often called the means–ends chain, usually contain three basic steps (Attributes, Consequences, Values). This theory proposes a way to analyse 'product meaning structures' which consist of 'a chain of hierarchically related elements' (Claeys *et al.* 1995: 193); this chain starts with the product attributes and establishes a sequence of links with terminal values. Means–end chain theory is extremely representative of both a teleology and teleological way of considering man's relation to things, because it is based on the assumption that 'the consumption of a product is ultimately a means to achieving important values' (Pieters *et al.* 1995: 228). This goal-oriented approach to consumption assumes that a consumer values end-states, and he/she chooses among alternative means (i.e. goods) to attain these goals. The underlying assumption is that product concrete attributes are linked, through a continuity principle, at levels of increasing abstraction to terminal values (see Figure 6.1).

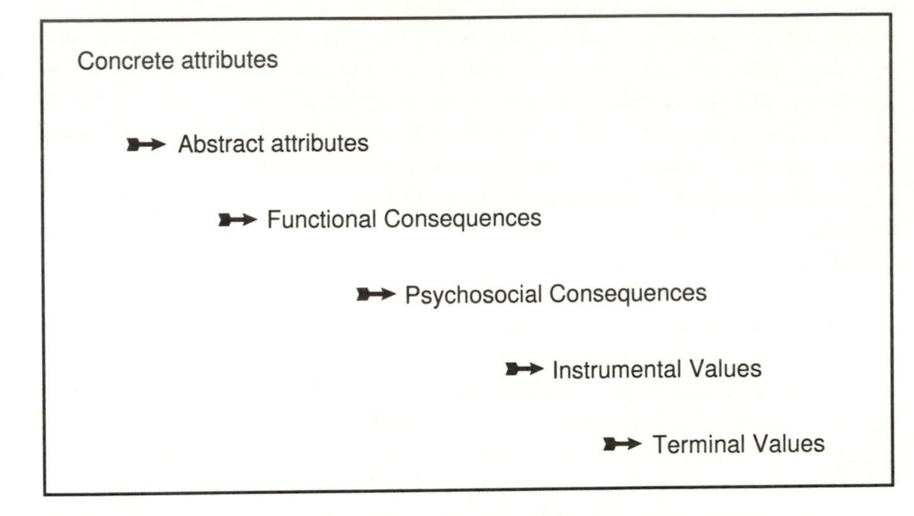

Figure 6.1 The expanded A–C–V model
Source: Olson and Reynolds 1983

A NIETZSCHEAN CRITIQUE OF THE ESCHATOLOGICAL PARADIGM IN MARKETING

After having established the predominance of the eschatological scheme in marketing thought, it seems important to help deconstruct this paradigm which in many regards appears fallacious, because it is unhelpful to account for most consumer decisions. Specific decisions such as impulse purchase or browsing obviously contradict most of the eschatological premises. The eschatological paradigm, as stated above, is very strongly related to a cultural way of thinking which has been very deeply criticised by Nietzsche: 'what is at stake . . . is not only the status of morality insofar as it depends upon divine sanction, but also a whole range of valuations pertaining to everything . . .' (Schacht 1992: 353). As Nietzsche reminds us, 'consider the damage all human institutions sustain if a divine and transcendent higher sphere is postulated that must first sanction these institutions' (*The Will to Power*: 245).

The first criticism to be directed at the paradigm stated above is that it evaluates every action thanks to values which transcend goods and situations, as if the evaluation of a given object was the result of a divine type of sanction imposed on the individual. This theory thus hides the biological and vital concept of instincts behind sublimated motives of behaviour which are called values. In some way instincts, desires and needs which are considered as granted in main consumer behaviour theories, are in fact largely inhibited from discharging themselves, through a process of internalisation and sublimation.

What is first described as an instinctive process (Wilkie 1994; Solomon 1994) is culturally transformed into a more sublimated model in which what counts is ultimately the attainment of certain states conceived in abstract and metaphysical notions such as a sense of accomplishment, a world of beauty, a world at peace, etc. The denaturalisation of values is, according to Nietzsche, an illustration of the same mistake repeated over and over again, that is, the transformation of 'a means to life into a standard of life' (Schacht 1992: 350).

Furthermore, the consumption process is often described as a mechanistic and causal process in which various stages are precisely identified as systematically following from one another. This causality link between two events is an unrefined simplification of the real psychological phenomenon; it attempts to explain a complex process, which occurs at various levels (Assoun 1980), by a unidimensional and abstract chain of events along which each stage is arbitrarily isolated from the others. Such a duality between cause and effect thus never truly exists, and we are in fact confronted by a *continuum* out of which we isolate a couple of pieces. This mechanistic interpretation of the world, as Nietzsche would say, is a falsification of the real processes at stake, even though it makes the interpretation of actions and attitudes more readily susceptible to quantitative treatment and thus enhances their calculability. Any phenomenon is, in a Nietzschean terminology, essentially determined by a plurality of 'forces' endowed with different meanings; one can thus not elucidate the meaning of a phenomenon if one does not know what forces are at stake in this particular phenomenon (Deleuze 1983: 4). The meaning of any action or decision is therefore extremely complex and difficult to assess, because there is in fact always a co-existence of various meanings in a given phenomenon, depending on the various forces in operation. It is therefore extremely fallacious to ascribe a specific meaning or value to a given consumption decision, because such a phenomenon is in fact largely conditioned by a set of forces and values, some of which are sometimes contradictory. The interpretation of any action or decision should therefore not go beyond the delimitation or visualisation of a certain type of 'value orientation' which may influence the process.

It is Nietzsche's position that there is no such thing as cause; and he argues that 'the belief in cause and effect which man applies whenever anything happens is an atavism of the most ancient origin' (*The Gay Science*: 127). Nietzsche takes this position both with respect to the understanding of causation in terms that 'something that causes' and 'something upon which an effect is produced' and with respect to its construal in terms of states of affairs of which one is taken to be the cause of the other. The concept of causation leads to another 'metaphysical mistake', in the sense it presupposes an author and someone upon whom 'change' 'is effected' (*The Will to Power*: 546). The cause–effect chain is thus intimately related to the concept of agent because the implicit belief is: all changes are effects, and all effects suppose an agent who would perform the action. The concepts of 'ego' or 'self' as autonomous units relate in fact to some kind of fiction which mostly results from a grammatical habit (Williams 1995: 69; Schacht 1992: 140), that is, the need to ascribe a grammatical agent to a will. But 'willing' is in fact a complex of sensations, thinking and affects; 'the experiences involved in "willing" do not reveal and may conceal, the shifting complex of psychological and physiological forces that lies behind any action, the constant, unknown, craving movements that make us, as he puts it, a kind of polyp' (Williams 1995: 70). The world is seen, in this perspective, as a collection of 'matter in motion', that is, a world 'consisting of material units, which have certain properties, are possessed of varying and changing amounts and kinds of forces' (Schacht 1992: 169). Nietzsche proposes to view any process, not as a 'manifold one-after-another', but rather as a 'flow of becoming'. Therefore, he proposes to abandon the concepts of agent, action and causation which can only be regarded as serviceable categories of interpretation. Nietzsche's interpretation of any type of process is to get rid of the 'cause and effect' construal in terms of things acting upon and being changed by agents, in favour of construing this pair of concepts in terms of *sequence of events* (see Schacht 1992: 183). Thus, decoding any process requires us to grasp the regular ordering of various sequences of events, and to point out the underlying values which infuse each sequence.

ELEMENTS FOR A NARRATOLOGICAL DECONSTRUCTION OF THE CONSUMMATION PARADIGM

Towards a new approach to the concept of 'value'

A redefinition of the concept of value seems essential to escape from the eschatological paradigm. The concept of value is nevertheless hard to conceptualise because it implies many dimensions. Philosophical enquiries into the complex concept of value have pointed out two main properties of values (see Heilbrunn 1996). First, values are not elements of things but properties, qualities, *sui generis,* which certain objects that we may call valuable objects possess. In other words, values do not possess substantiveness (Frondizi 1963). A product does not have an intrinsic value; its value depends on the evaluator, that is to say in our context: the consumer. Therefore the value only exists through an interaction process. Second, the value of a thing depends partly on the circumstances under which it is evaluated: 'value is not a fixed, inherent property . . . A thing may have different values for different purposes, at different times, to different people, under different conditions (the physical environment in which the evaluator finds himself), and in different circumstances (the personal, physical, emotional, psychological and social situation of the evaluator at the time he makes the valuation)' (Sinden and Worrell 1979: 4–5). Value can thus be defined as 'all factors, both qualitative and quantitative, subjective and objective, that make up the complete shopping experience' (Zeithaml 1988). Therefore a strictly objective approach focusing on an object, its price, or the functional utility may be too narrow to account for all value provided by consumption experiences (Hirschman and Holbrook 1982). On the other hand, a concept of value which largely goes beyond the real and 'total shopping experience' and transcends the consumer as well as the consumption situation may be too large to account for the valuation process during the consumption experience. It appears thus necessary to consider that an object's value occurs through (1) a temporal perspective, and (2) an interaction with a subject. The underlying hypothesis is that goods do not have intrinsic value for the consumer, but are rather submitted to an evaluation process from the consumer at different stages. In other words, an object may be simultaneously or successively endowed by a consumer with different values.

A narrative approach to the consumption process

Let us now consider that goods are essentially objects which provide value to the consumer along the consumption process. From the consumer's perspective, goods are value providers, which means they are endowed with a programme within which they have to perform, that is, essentially to satisfy the consumer's expectations. Goods in this perspective play the role of magic objects in fairy tales, in the sense that they provide the hero (the consumer) with powers (invisibility, ubiquity, omniscience, etc.) and help or even replace him/her in his/her quest for values. In other words, these objects do not have value *per se*, but they can only be understood as mediators between a mythical destinator and the person to whom they are provided (Greimas 1983: 20). Therefore, these objects can be mythically analysed as degraded and figurative forms of the main spheres of divine sovereignty, that is, at an imaginative level, essential attributes of human competency which institute and justify human actions (see Greimas 1983: 20; Dumézil 1968: 541–2).

The interactions existing between consumers and goods can in fact be 'read' as a story (Heilbrunn 1996). Rethans and Taylor (1982) have for instance proposed the idea that the consumer decision making process could be decoded into various stages, so as to form a script, a script being defined as 'a coherent sequence of events expected by the individual involving him either as a participant or as an observer' (Abelson 1976: 33). Floch has also brilliantly illustrated the fact that consumers' accounts of their expeditions to the hypermarket could be metaphorically compared to 'micro-tales with structures and sequences lending themselves to semiotics analysis, so long as they are analysed as complex programmes of action performed in the function of value systems' (Floch 1988: 235). Hence the consumption process can be described as a narrative programme which develops itself through several possible stages (Heilbrunn 1996). The 'goods' have to go through various stages in order to be evaluated by the consumer; they are thus endowed with a narrative programme, in the sense narrativity essentially refers to a sequence of events of which the final event is semantically connected with the unitial event (Nöth 1990). The consumption can therefore be studied as a text (Hirschmann and Holbrook 1992) using a narratological approach.

The Russian folklorist Vladimir Propp published in 1928 *Morfologija skazki* (*Morphology of the Folktale*) which exercised a decisive influence upon the semiotics of narrative structures. He attempted to solve the historical problem of the origin and evolution of the fairy tale by working out a morphological description. Propp rapidly came up with the idea that the variable part of the motif deals with the names and qualitative attributes of the *dramatis personae,* whereas the invariant part deals with their actions. In other words the question of knowing who performs which role and how does not concern the invariant part of a given tale. On the contrary, the invariant element of the motif consists of its function in the plot. Applying this principle to the study of hundreds of Russian fairy tales, Propp pointed out a definite number (thirty-one) of functions in the plot. He searched for minimal units of the tale, called functions which serve as stable 'constant elements in a tale independent of how and by whom they are fulfilled' (Propp 1928: 21). The plot consists in fact of a sequence of functions (absence, interdiction, violated interdiction, . . .) which usually follow in a definite order for their aesthetic effects. He thus pointed out the fact that the structure of folklore tales revealed a number of recurrences and repetitions of moves, that is, a number of minimal invariant stages in the tale, considered as narrative minimal units which when linked would become the syntagmatic process which is the tale. In any tale, three main kinds of moves can be stressed:

- a *qualifying move*: goods have to acquire competency through trials, competitions, and initiation rituals;
- a *decisive move*: goods accomplish themselves by going through a certain number of actions; and
- a *glorifying move*: goods are recognised for what they have accomplished and thus for what they are.

The narrative scheme applied to the consumption process integrates the following functions (after Floch 1988):

1 The *Acquisition of Competency*: acquiring the ability required to carry out the programme;
2 The *Contract*: proposal and acceptance of a programme to carry out, within the framework of a value system;
3 *Performance*: carrying out the programme by conquering the object of value of one's desire; and
4 The *Sanction* is the comparison of the realised programme with the programme that had to be accomplished.

This narrative scheme is the logical sequence of the major episodes which comprise the basic structure of all tales (Floch 1988: 236). This scheme can for instance be applied to the narrative trajectory of a consumer product (see Heilbrunn 1996). First the product has to acquire *competency*, that is, to prove its ability to perform through communication contact (advertising, word of mouth communication, product contact in the store, etc.). The product has to appear as desirable and valuable to target customers and thus, at this stage, its value is a competence value which derives essentially from all the so-called beliefs the consumer holds about the goods. The second stage might be a *contract*, that is, an exchange of value. The value of the product (as perceived by customers) derives in this stage from a comparison between the 'give' components (time, effort, money) and the 'get' components. The *contract* usually occurs if the product was able to prove its competence, which means its exchange-value was perceived by the consumer to be acceptable. The *performance* stage then deals with the various dimensions of the consumption experience, that is, the series of contacts and interactions which may involve such actions as storage, transportation, preparation, disposal of the product. Then comes the *sanction* through which the customer compares what he got from the goods with what he expected. The product's performance is evaluated according to the consumer's expectations and to the consumer's experiences with other comparable goods. It is then seen as an a-posteriori evaluation of the experience with the product which can result in several outcomes: if the consumer is satisfied, the resulting outcome can be a further purchase and loyal behaviour in the case of a branded product; on the other hand, if the consumer is dissatisfied, the sanction can be the creation and development of negative attitudes towards the product, as well as resulting behaviours.

Narrativity and the redefinition of consumption

This narratological perspective offers new insights on the consumption process. First, it suggests that consumer behaviour should not be read as a linear and causal process, but rather as a sequence of functions which are interrelated. It is important to mention three aspects of the narrative scheme:

1 The functions do not necessarily follow the same order: *impulse purchasing* implies a process in which the contract comes first and no acquisition of competency is necessary.
2 Each function in the narrative chain implies a specific approach adopted by the consumer to evaluate goods. The consumption process can be read as a series of evaluative rituals by which the consumer projects simultaneously and/or alternately various categories of meaning on to the object. This approach is consistent with a ritualistic approach of consumer behaviour which holds that consumer goods exist through their ability to communicate and create cultural meaning (Douglas and Isherwood 1978; McCracken 1981) and that rituals such as *exchange* rituals, *possession* rituals or *divestment* rituals, are used to transfer meaning from goods to individuals (McCracken 1981). The

process by which consumers endow products with meaning equates to an evaluation process, and each function in the narrative or consumption chain involves a specific type of value ascribed to the product.

3 All functions need not be present within the process. For instance *browsing*, or more generally *flânerie*, can be analysed as consumption processes which are complete without any *contract* or any *sanction*. They illustrate the fact that consumers might derive disinterested pleasures from consumption objects without using or consuming them, which is consistent with the Kantian approach to aesthetic pleasure. For Kant, an object might be associated with three types of delights: delight in the 'agreeable' which is based on inclination, delight in the 'good' based on 'respect', and delight in the 'beautiful' based on 'favour'. The first two delights are 'interested', that is, the relationship of the desire involves a desire either because the object renders immediate 'gratification' (the agreeable sensual pleasures), or because the object is defined as 'good' due to an external (for example moral) purpose. In contrast to these two, the third delight is 'disinterested' in the sense it represents a contemplative delight which is indifferent to the possession or use of the object (Falk 1994; Guyer 1979: 170–87; Kant 1987: 51). This anti-utilitarian or pro-aesthetic approach to consumption might easily be related to numerous works which have contributed to show the essential hedonic aspect of consumption (Hirschman and Holbrook 1982). This field of research considers that the consumption of products no longer refers to an act of destruction effected by the consumer, but rather to an 'experience' in which the priority is given to affective and emotional factors.

The value and quality of a consumption experience can therefore not be assessed only with objective values and/or utilitarian criteria which solely refer to the destruction of the product. Consumption is more a construction of meaning than a destruction of products. Douglas and Isherwood have for instance illustrated that consumption is a ritual process whose primary function is to make sense of the inchoate flux of events (Douglas and Isherwood 1978: 65). Goods are therefore essentially conceived as markers which are used to create and communicate meaning and therefore create value. This leads to a totally new conception of the consumption process. The universalistic approach equates consumption with the satisfaction of needs and therefore 'naturalize(s) the dynamics of consumption into an abstract principle which is not very far from the definition of matter/energy transformation offered by physics. In this universalistic sense, consumption is viewed as synthesis of enthropic and negenthropic processes; matter dissolving into energy . . . through an endless chain of transformations – of destruction and construction –' (Falk 1994: 93). This approach is consistent with the etymology of 'consumption' which derives from the Latin '*consumere*', that is, to use up entirely, which involves destruction of matter, and '*consumare*', to sum up, to carry to completion (see Falk 1994: 93; Barnhart 1988).

The approach proposed here is to consider consumption, not as an act of destruction, but rather as a sequence of events by which an object's value is created and transformed. Consumers may project on goods, at each stage of their consumption, a subjective meaning which (1) differs from one stage to another and (2) exceeds by far the functional attributes goods may actually possess. This approach is consistent with a very comprehensive definition of value given by Holbrook and Corfman: value is seen as an 'interactive relativistic preference experience . . . characterizing a subject's experience of interacting with some object' (in Babin *et al.* 1994: 645).

After considering consumption as an evaluation process, it becomes crucial to determine and categorise the main value orientations which can guide and inspire the process. Sheth *et al.* (1991a, 1991b) have in this regard designed an interesting theory of consumption values as impacting market choice behaviours by defining five types of value orientations: functional value, conditional value, social value, emotional value and epistemic value. This theory is based on three main assumptions: (1) consumption choices are functions of multiple values; (2) these values make differential contributions in any given consumption situation; and (3) these values are independent. Another interesting stream of research is to be found in the structural semiotics literature and especially in Floch who was able to categorise the main values potentially ascribed to a hypermarket (Floch 1988), or to cars (Floch 1990). The four values potentially ascribed to any consumption object (product, store, service, etc.) are the following: utilitarian or practical values (money, time, physical effort, etc.); existential or 'life' values (experience, adventure, etc.); ludic values (fun, fantasy, etc.); and critical values (value for money, perceived quality, etc.). This axiology of consumption was carried out through the analysis at a deeper level of consumers' discourses and their classification into semio-narrative structures by reference to a semiotic square. The main implication of this approach, apart from providing an exhaustive classification of values ascribed to consumption objects, is to illustrate the fact that consumption is articulated through a number of signifying 'practices' by which consumers endow objects with meaning. In other words, any 'consumption practice' (Holt 1995) is related to a search for, and construction of, meaning or, to speak in semiotic terms, to the conquest of the object of value of one's desire.

ACTANTS, VALUE AND DESIRE: TOWARDS A NARRATOLOGICAL RECONSTRUCTION OF THE UNIVERSALISTIC CONSUMPTION PARADIGM

Instead of considering consumption as a process oriented towards the reduction of a need from the consumer's perspective, let us consider, from a more general point of view, that consumption is a narrative process through which an object's value is both created (through the projection of meaning on goods) and transformed. This approach sets a riddle which concerns the *prime mover* –

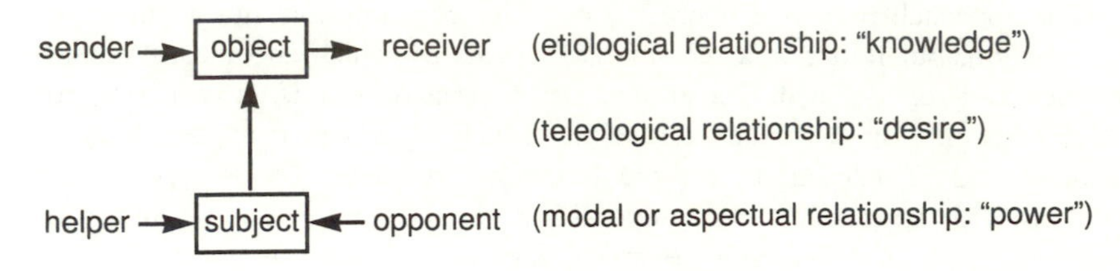

Figure 6.2 The actancial model
Sources: Greimas 1966; Schleifer 1987

to speak in Aristotelian terms – of this process. As illustrated by Falk, the 'riddle of consumption confronts us with questions concerning (a) the constitution of desire exceeding the "necessary", and (b) the limitlessness of the desire . . .' (Falk 1994: 94). As desire appears to be a key word by which to read consumption 'practices', the issue is now to reintegrate the 'desire problematic' within the narrative paradigm. Part of the answer is given by Greimas, for whom 'the relation of man to the object of his desire and its inscription within the structures of interhuman communication seems sufficiently general to furnish the basis of an initial articulation of the imagination' (Greimas 1983: 51; Schleifer 1987: 88).

In order to provide a more general framework to read narratives than Propp's (which was exclusively based on the study of tales), Greimas developed an actancial model (Figure 6.2) which is a redefinition of Propp's narrative functions as relationships between actants. This model is based on the following scheme: subjects want (or desire) an object; they encounter an opponent; they find a helper; they obtain the object from a sender; and they give it to the receiver (Greimas 1966; Nöth 1990: 372).

This model is based on the assumption that the object and the subject do not exist independently but are related by *disjunction* and/or *conjunction.* In other words, any narrative is the process by which the subject and the object who are originally 'disj*u*ncted', gradually come to be 'conjuncted'. This move from the *disjunction* to the *conjunction* of the subject and the object occurs through the various interactions between actants, which are 'characters' considered from the point of view of their narrative role and of their mutual relations. Any narrative can thus be interpreted as the coexistence of three axes: (1) a *desire axis*: the story of a subject questing for an object; (2) a *knowledge axes*: the object is also transmitted from a sender to a receiver; and (3) a *power axis*: the helper helps the subject to obtain the object while the opponent is an obstacle to this quest.

This model functions if one keeps in mind the following rules (Everaert-Desmedt 1988: 29):

- an object might be a material possession as well as a non-material value (e.g. quest for knowledge);
- an actant is not an actor but rather a fictive narrative unity which exists at a

more abstract level than the actor – an actancial role might be played by a human character but also by a material object;

- an actant might be represented by several actors;
- an actor might play several actancial roles; and,
- within a given narrative, the actancial model might appear at different levels, because several actants might be searching for objects simultaneously.

This scheme, which can be used as a general macrostructure for any narrative, might very well be applied to the understanding of most consumption practices, as illustrated in the following two examples.

> *'I've started to take a new "miracle drug" for my arthritis, and I'm feeling a lot better now. I thank Dr. Reed for prescribing it for me.*
> *The cost? It's expensive, I bet, but my medical plans cover most of it.'*
>
> Wilkie 1994: 12

Let us now briefly decode this consumer's words in narrative terms by reference to the actancial model. Semiotically, this story is the narrative programme of a *subject* (the consumer) who is searching for – state of *disjunction* – an *object* (a pain-relieving medicine); this *object* of desire is potentially transmitted (prescribed) by a *sender* (the doctor) to a *receiver* (the consumer). The *subject* finds a potential *opponent* (the high price of the medicine) in his/her search for the *object*, but the *opponent*'s action is thwarted by a *helper* (the social security system). The story ends with the release of the pain, that is the consumer found the *object* of value he/she was looking for – state of *conjunction* between the *subject* and the *object*.

The second example illustrates further issues raised by the metaphorical use of the actancial model to interpret consumption practices:

> *'Dad, no offence, but you really don't get it about shoes . . . we have to wear the new Nikes 'cause they really are the best. Besides, the kids at school do notice what someone wears, you know!'*
>
> Wilkie 1994: 12

What is first demonstrated in this story is that actors may play several actancial roles. The kid's father might for instance be alternatively and/or successively an *opponent* (he refuses to buy the Nikes) and a *sender* (he finally accepts to get the Nikes for his son).

It also illustrates the fact that the desire for a given consumption object is socially constructed by the various actants. The Nikes are considered as valuable by the child insofar as they are perceived as desirable by his/her schoolmates. In other words, the value of an object, that is, its propensity to suscitate desire to a subject, is created and negotiated by the various actants within the narrative process. A narrative can be understood as the story by which an object's value is created, transformed and appropriated by the various actants. Thus, the important consequence is that the value of an object, conceived in a narrative perspective as its desirability, is co-constructed and negotiated by the various actants. This approach refers to the theory of *mimetic rivalry* proposed by Girard (1972, 1977) to explain the way things are socially desired insofar as they are desired by a rival; there is no immediate desire for a given object; by desiring an object, the rival signifies to the subject what is desirable. 'In other words, a desire expressed towards an object is not constituted due to its representational role – as "standing for", being "symbol of", or representing something valued and desired. An object is desired only derivatively on the basis of an intimate relation to (an) other subject . . . or by adopting the other's desire and resulting in a rivalry concerning the other's object of desire' (Falk 1994: 119). Girard describes the process of mimetic rivalry in the following manner: 'Rivalry does not arise because of the fortuitous convergence of two desires on a single object; rather, the subject desires the object because the rival desires it. In desiring an object the rival alerts the subject to the desirability of the object' (Girard 1977: 145).

This actancial model hence seems extremely valuable to reconstruct marketing thought on a non-eschatological basis. First, this approach helps to get rid of the traditional unitary view of the consumer as a conscious and single unit by introducing the concept of actant. A consumer might play several actancial roles and therefore has no fixed role. More generally, consumption can only be decoded as a system constituted by various actants who are in an interdependent situation: actants do not exist as isolated entities, but only through their interaction with other actants, these interactions being governed by three kinds of forces which are *desire*, *power* and *knowledge*.

Second, the value of an object does not exist *per se*, but results from an interaction process. This postulate is consistent with the main assumption which grounds structuralism, that is, meaning resides in the differences apprehended between the various elements of a system and the values of the elements are only relative and determined by the relations existing between the elements of the system. Therefore, an object's value can only be apprehended in a differential perspective, which means it is constructed and transformed by the interactions of several actants. Therefore, the value of an object is not a fixed property, but exists through operations of transformation and transfer among actants.

CONCLUSION

This narrative reinterpretation of consumption proposes to escape from any morality principle in marketing and to replace it by ethics. For Spinoza, ethics elaborated as a 'topography of immanent modes of existence, replaces Morality, which always refers existence to transcendent values . . . Ethics overthrows the system of judgement. The opposition of values (good–evil) is supplanted by the qualitative difference of modes of existence (good–bad)' (Deleuze 1988: 23). In other words, universalistic marketing thought promotes a hidden eschatological way of valuing goods thanks to transcendent values which relate more to abstract truths than to the interrelated spheres of consumer experience (White 1966: 101). An eschatological view of consumer behaviour thus implicitly replaces *consumption* by *consummation* in the sense that eschatology can be related to the consummation of all things. It was therefore proposed to replace this static conception of value by the dynamic approach of evaluation. Such thinking refers to the original meaning of consumption as construction, production and/or reproduction rather than as a destructive process, but it also returns us to a dynamic and pragmatic conception of value. Narrativity was presented as a key concept to account for the way objects become invested with value so as to become desirable objects. Consumption is not the way by which consumers try to conform themselves to absolute and transcendent values but, on the contrary, the process by which value is created and transformed by various actants and the desirability of consumption objects narratively co-constructed and negotiated. A narrative perspective thus provides a way to escape the eschatological view of consumption. It could be said that this escape is philosophical. As Nietzsche questioned the essence of philosophy as a search for truth and wisdom and substituted new forms of activities which aim at interpreting, evaluating and experimenting (Deleuze 1983), a narrative approach permits us to de-eschatologise consumption by reading it as a constructive and evaluative process by which an object's value is created, transformed and negotiated.

REFERENCES

Abelson, R.P. (1976), 'Psychological Status of the Script Concept', *American Psychologist*, 36, 7, pp. 715–29.

Assoun P.-L. (1980), *Freud et Nietzsche*, Paris: Presses Universitaires de France.

Babin, B., Darden, W.R. and Griffin, M. (1994), 'Work and/or Fun: Measuring Hedonic and Utilitarian Shopping Value', *Journal of Consumer Research*, 20, March, pp. 644–56.

Barnhart, R.K. (ed.) (1988), *The Barnhart Dictionary of Etymology*, New York: Wilson.

Barthes, R. (1966), 'Introduction à l'analyse structurale des récits', in *Communications*, 8, Paris, Seuil, pp. 1–27. Translated in 'Introduction to the Structural Analysis of Narratives', in Barthes, R. (1994), *The Semiotic Challenge*, Berkeley: University of California Press, pp. 95–135.

Broadie, S. (1991), *Ethics with Aristotle*, Oxford: Oxford University Press.

Claeys, C., Swinnen, A. and Van den Abeele, P. (1995), 'Consumers' Means-Ends Chains for "Think" and "Feel" Products', *International Journal of Research in Marketing*, 12, 3, pp. 193–208.

Deleuze, G. (1983), *Nietzsche and Philosophy*, The Athlone Press. Translated from *Nietzsche et la philosophie*, Paris: PUF (1962).

Deleuze, G. (1988), *Spinoza: Practical Philosophy*, San Francisco: City Lights.

Douglas, M. and Isherwood B. (1978), *The World of Goods*, New York: Basic Books.

Dumézil, G. (1968), *Mythe et Epopée*, Paris: Gallimard.

Everaert-Desmedt, N. (1988), *Sémiotique du récit*, Editions Universitaires, De Boeck Université.

Falk, P. (1994), 'Consuming Desire', in P. Falk, *The Consuming Body*, London: Sage, pp. 93–150.

Floch J.-M. (1988), 'The Contribution of Structural Semiotics to the Design of a Hypermarket', *International Journal of Research in Marketing*, 4, pp. 233–52.

Floch, J.-M. (1990), 'J'aime, J'aime, J'aime . . .', in J.-M. Floch, *Sémiotique, marketing et communication. Sous les signes, les stratégies*, Paris: Presses Universitaires de France, pp. 119–52.

Frondizi, R. (1963), *What are Values: An Introduction to Axiology*, La Salle, LL: Open Court.

Girard, R. (1972), *La violence et le sacré*, Paris Grasset; English translation: *Violence and the Sacred* (1977), Baltimore: The Johns Hopkins University Press.

Girard, R. (1977), *Des choses cachées depuis la fondation du monde*, Paris, Grasset; English translation: *Things Hidden Since the Foundation of the World* (1987), London: Athlone.

Goldman, L. (1964), *The Hidden God: A Study of Tragic Vision in the* Pensées *of Pascal and the Tragedies of Racine*, London: Routledge and Keegan Paul.

Greimas, A.J. (1966), *Sémantique structurale. Recherche de méthode*, Paris: Larousse. English translation: *Structural Semantics: An Attempt at a Method* (1983), Lincoln: University of Nebraska Press.

Greimas, A.J. (1983), *Du Sens II*, Paris: Seuil.

Greimas, A.J. and Courtés, J. (1979), *Dictionnaire raisonné de la théorie du langage*, Paris: Hachette. English translation: *Semiotics and Language: An Analytical Dictionary* (1982), Bloomington: Indiana University Press.

Gutman, J. (1982), 'A Means–End Chain Model Based on Consumer Categorization Processes', *Journal of Marketing*, 46 (summer), pp. 60–72.

Guyer, P. (1979), *Kant and the Claims of Taste*, Cambridge, MA: Harvard University Press.

Hartman, R. (1967), *The Structures of Values: Foundations of Scientific Axiology*, Southern Illinois Press.

Heilbrunn, B. (1996), 'My Brand the Hero: A Semiotic Analysis of the Consumer–Brand Relationship', in M. Lambkin, G. Foxall, W.F. Van Raaij and B. Heilbrunn, *European Perspectives in Consumer Behavior*, Hemel Hempstead: Prentice Hall (forthcoming).

Hirschman, E. and Holbrook, M. (1982), 'Hedonic Consumption: Emerging Concepts, Methods and Propositions', *Journal of Marketing*, 46 (Summer), pp. 92–101.

Hirschman, E. and Holbrook, M. (1992), *Postmodern Consumer Research: The Study of Consumption as a Text*, London: Sage.

Holbrook, M. (1987), 'What Is Consumer Research?', *Journal of Consumer Research*, 14 (June), pp. 128–31.

Holbrook, M. and Hirschman, E. (1982), 'The Experiential Aspects of Consumption: Consumer Fantasies, Feelings and Fun', *Journal of Consumer Research*, 9 (September), pp. 132–40.

Holt, D. (1995), 'How Consumers Consume: A Typology of Consumption Practices', *Journal of Consumer Research*, 22 (June), pp. 1–16.

Kant, I. (1987), *Critique of Judgement*, Indianapolis: Hackett Publ. Co. (originally published in 1790).

Kearney, R. (1994), *Modern Movements in European Philosophy*, 2nd ed., Manchester: Manchester University Press.

Kleiber, M. (1980), 'Eschatologie', in *Encyclopaedia Universalis*, vol. 6, Paris.

Lakoff, G. and Johnson, M. (1980), *Metaphors We Live By*, Chicago: The University of Chicago Press.

Lovejoy, A. (1907), 'The Desires of the Self-Conscious', *The Journal of Philosophy*, 4, pp. 29–39.

Lovejoy, A. (1950), 'Terminal and Adjectival Values', *The Journal of Philosophy*, 47 (21), October 12, pp. 593–608.

MacIntyre, A. (1966), *A Short History of Ethics*, New York: Macmillan.

Maslow, A. (1943), 'A Theory of Human Motivation', *Psychological Review*, 50, pp. 370–96.
Maslow, A. (1954), *Motivation and Personality*, New York: Harper.
McCracken, G. (1981), 'Culture and Consumption: A Theoretical Account of the Structure and Movement of the Cultural Meaning of Consumer Goods', *Journal of Consumer Research*, 13 (June), pp. 71–84.
Nietzsche, F. (1968), *The Will to Power*, trans. W. Kaufmann and Hollingdale, New York: Vintage (originally published in 1883–8).
Nietzsche, F. (1974), *The Gay Science*, trans. W. Kaufmann, New York: Vintage (originally published in 1882).
Nöth, W. (1990), *Handbook of Semiotics*, Bloomington: Indiana University Press.
Olson, J.C. and Reynolds, T.J. (1983), 'Understanding Consumers' Cognitive Structures: Implications for Advertising Strategy', in L. Percy and A. Woodside (eds), *Advertising and Consumer Psychology*, Vol.1, Lexington, MA: Lexington Books, pp. 77–90.
Pervin, L.A. (1989), 'Goal Concepts: Themes, Issues and Questions', in L.A. Pervin (ed.), *Goal Concepts in Personality and Social Psychology*, Hillsdale, NJ: Erlbaum, pp. 473–9.
Peter, J.P. and Olson, J.C. (1993), *Consumer Behavior and Marketing Strategy*, 3rd ed., Homewood: Irwin.
Pieters, R., Baumgartner, H. and Allen, D. (1995), 'A Means-End Chain Approach to Consumer Goal Structures', *International Journal of Research in Marketing*, 12 (3), pp. 227–44.
Propp, V. (1928), *Morfologija skazkii*, coll. Voprosy poetiki, n°12, Gosudarstvennyj institut istorii iskusstava, Leningrad. English translation: *Morphology of the Folktale* (1968), Austin: University of Texas Press.
Rethans, A.J. and Taylor, J.L. (1982), 'A Script Theoretic Analysis of Consumer Decision Making', in Walker, B.J. (ed.), *Proceedings of the American Marketing Association Educator's Conference*, Vol. 48, American Marketing Association, Chicago, pp. 71–4.
Reynolds, T. and Gutman, J. (1988), 'Laddering Theory, Method, Analysis, and Interpretation', *Journal of Advertising Research*, 28, February/March, pp. 11–34.
Rokeach, M. (1960), *The Open and Closed Mind: Investigations into the Nature of Beliefs Systems and Personality Systems*, New York: Basic Books.
Rokeach, M. (1968), *Beliefs, Attitudes and Values*, Josey Bass.
Rokeach, M. (1968–9), 'The Role of Values in Public Opinion Research', *Public Opinion Quarterly*, 32, (4), Winter.
Rokeach, M. (1973), *The Nature of Human Values and Value Systems*, Free Press.
Ross, Sir D. (1995), *Aristotle*, London: Routledge (originally published in 1923).
Russel, B. (1994), *History of Western Philosophy*, London: Routledge (first published in 1946).
Schacht, R. (1992), *Nietzsche,* London: Routledge.
Schleifer, R. (1987), *A.J. Greimas and the Nature of Meaning. Linguistics, Semiotics and Discourse Theory*, Lincoln: University of Nebraska Press.
Sheth, J., Newman, B. and Gross, B. (1991a), *Consumption Values and Market Choices. Theory and Applications*, Cincinnati, OH: South-Western Publishing Co.
Sheth, J., Newman, B. and Gross, B. (1991b), 'Why We Buy What We Buy: A Theory of Consumption Values', *Journal of Business Research*, 22, pp. 159–70.
Sinden, J. and Worrel, A. (1979), *Unpriced Values. Decisions Without Market Prices*, Chichester: Wiley.
Solomon, M. (1994), *Consumer Behavior. Buying, Having and Being*, 2nd ed., New York: Allyn and Bacon.
Vinson, D., Scott, J. and Lamont, L. (1977), 'The Role of Personal Values in Marketing and Consumer Behavior', *Journal of Marketing*, April, pp. 44–50.
Weblowsky, R. (1987), 'Eschatology: An Overview', in Eliade, M. (ed.), *The Encyclopedia of Religion*, New York: Macmillan & Free Press, vol. 5, pp. 148–51.

White, I. S. (1966), 'The Perception of Value in Products', in Newman, J. W., *On Knowing the Consumer*, New York: Wiley, pp. 90–106.
Wilkie, W. (1994), *Consumer Behavior*, 3rd ed., New York: Wiley.
Williams, B. (1995), 'Nietzsche's minimalist moral psychology', in *Making Sense of Humanity and Other Philosophical Papers*, Cambridge: Cambridge University Press, pp. 65–76.
Zeithaml, V. (1988), 'Consumer Perceptions of Price, Quality and Value: A Means–End Model and Synthesis of Evidence', *Journal of Marketing*, 52 (July), pp. 2–22.

7

THE PROTESTANT ETHIC AND THE SPIRIT OF MARKETING

Visions of the End

Ray Kent

INTRODUCTION

Marketing was nurtured within the cradle of modern capitalist enterprise, an economic system based on the deliberate and systematic adjustment of economic resources for the attainment of monetary profit. It required an attitude of mind that ran counter to the traditional view that regarded the unrestrained and unlimited desire for monetary gain as anti-social and immoral. Explaining why such a change in values should have come about has provided sufficient scope for equally unrestrained and unlimited debate and controversy. One answer that provoked early disputation was that put forward by Weber, generally regarded as one of the founding fathers of sociology, between 1904 and 1906 in Germany and translated by Talcott Parsons in 1930 as *The Protestant Ethic and the Spirit of Capitalism.* He proposed that the spirit of capitalism – the pursuit of profit in a rational and systematic fashion from the utilisation of peaceful opportunities for exchange that are underpinned by a sense of duty, hard work and asceticism – was unique to the West and the rational outcome of a particular form of Protestantism that began with Calvin and his Presbyterian followers in the late-seventeenth century.

While Weber's characterisation of the spirit of capitalism and his account of the nature of Protestant beliefs have been questioned, and although the methods he employed to establish the connection between the two have been much criticised (see Green 1959 for a summary), it is clear that, if we sought to unearth the 'essence' or spirit not of capitalism but of marketing, the Weberian thesis is likely to offer the basis for some fundamental insights. This chapter sets out in pursuit of such a spirit by utilising a phenomenological approach; it goes on to argue that it is this spirit, rather than particular perspectives or theories that are its manifestations, that has endured and survived onslaughts from a number of directions, and that visions of the end of marketing are, like the end of history in the apocalyptic literature, based on false premises.

THE WEBER THESIS

Weber saw his thesis as but a preliminary to a much wider investigation into the relationship between religious ideas and the economic order. He saw it also as an illustration of a method of social research that entailed combining interpretive understandings with causal explanations. He attempted to justify his thesis from two angles: he tried to demonstrate why, a priori, we might expect or at least understand as reasonable and meaningful, why beliefs relating to the Protestant ethic were conducive to the development of the spirit of capitalism, and he then went on to show, using the comparative method of causal analysis based on historical data, that such a relationship did in fact exist and that all other explanations were, for one reason or another, inadequate.

The outstanding and essentially unique feature of Protestantism, particularly of the Calvinist sect, was its conception of the 'calling'. This was a life-task, and, according to Weber, a concept unique to Protestant peoples. It emphasised the fulfilment of duty in worldly affairs as the highest form that the moral behaviour of the individual could assume. While in its earlier manifestations the concept of the calling meant a state of life to which the individual had been assigned by God or Heaven, to the Calvinist it was more a strenuous and exacting enterprise to be chosen personally and pursued with a sense of religious commitment. Everyday worldly activity was thus endowed with a religious, or at least moral, significance. This belief emphasised virtue in the industrious pursuit of one's business or occupation, and thereby became a moral justification for the pursuit of profit. Other features of Protestantism, for example its worldly asceticism and the idea of predestination, which eliminated all intermediaries between God and man in a tremendous emphasis on individualism, underpinned a similar goal.

The result of such beliefs was a metamorphosis in moral standards that converted a natural frailty – economic self-interest – into an ornament of the spirit, canonising habits that in earlier times had been denounced as vices. Acquisitiveness – even covetousness – if a danger to the soul, was at least a less formidable menace than sloth. The antidote to sin became hard work. Poverty, far from being meritorious, was to be avoided by dint of profitable occupation. Piety and money-making became natural allies – the virtues of the one (diligence, thrift, sobriety and prudence) becoming the passport to the other. The pursuit of worldly goods, once feared as the enemy of religion, assumed the mantle of a moral imperative; success became a sign of virtue. Prosperity and salvation were now to go hand-in-hand.

THE SPIRIT OF EMPATHY

In his methodological writings, Weber saw sociology as a science that aimed at 'the interpretive understanding of social behaviour in order to gain an explanation of its causes, its course, and its effects' (Weber 1962: 29). The subjectively intended meaning in an action is a causal component of it – but not necessarily the only one. Furthermore, to the extent that behaviour is meaningful, it is understandable since it can be linked with reference to underlying motives.

There are two ways of gaining interpretive understanding: through logical deduction, where direct and unambiguous intelligibility is possible, and empathic, where proof and understanding is supplied by complete sympathetic emotional participation. Such empathy is facilitated where the behaviour concerned is rational and it is possible to comprehend the link between the means and ends of action, in short, we can understand why an individual has behaved in a particular way. Empathy and understanding may also be facilitated through the construction of 'ideal-types'. These are unified analytical constructs (like the 'perfect market' in economics) that are fully rational, but may not be found anywhere empirically. Irrational and emotional behaviour may be seen as deviations from such constructs.

Understanding is a tool of social research which aims at providing more insight than can be had, even with the most precise statistical proof, from the correlation between events. It is not, however, a complete method in itself. Although adequate at the level of meaning, it still requires verification, or else it remains only a 'particularly plausible hypothesis'. Verification is through causal analysis – a demonstration of a calculable probability that some event is either followed or accompanied by another event (Weber 1962: 40). A scientifically balanced explanation requires *both* understanding *and* causal verification; the first establishes why a connection between motives and behaviour is meaningful, and the second tries to demonstrate that this is, in fact, the case.

THE GHOST OF PHENOMENOLOGY

Phenomenology is the investigation of the ultimate 'essence' of phenomena using direct intuition and deliberate and self-conscious reflection to produce absolute knowledge. Its founder is generally regarded as Husserl (1859–1938), although the quest for immutable and fundamental principles by way of 'insightful' mental processes may be traced back to Descartes. The focus of phenomenologists is the point of contact between lived experience and consciousness of mind in the individual knower. The essence of what we perceive is a reflection of our experience, and all phenomena – whether empirical or cultural – need to be 'reduced' to the world of immediate experience.

The early phenomenologists were philosophers who were concerned, for our purposes somewhat unfortunately, to apply their method to discover answers to such fundamental questions as the essence of life, of consciousness, of being or of existence. The application of phenomenological analysis to sociology was largely the result of the work of Schutz (1899–1959). In his *The Phenomenology of the Social World* (1967) Schutz, like Weber, argued that the essential function of social science is to understand the subjective meaning of social action. However, it is necessary to distinguish between the subjective meaning of the social actor and the observer's interpretation of the actor. The problem for social science is how to map the latter from the former. Any 'action' is a lived experience that is guided by some goal or motive and is distinguished from all other lived experiences by an act of attention. This is what gives 'meaning' to behaviour. The social scientist can understand that meaning only indirectly through the construction of an ideal-type – a typification of behaviour that is endowed with meaning.

Berger and Luckman (1967), building on the work of Schutz, forge a new link between phenomenology and sociology by looking at the ways in which realities – both everyday and scientific – are socially constructed. For the individual the world consists of multiple realities. Everyday reality is experienced as ordered, objective and as having an existence independently of the individual's apprehension of it. Above all it is intersubjective – 'commonsense' knowledge is shared with others in the normal, self-evident routines of everyday life. It is taken for granted. Intersubjectivity becomes much closer during face-to-face interaction – but even this is 'managed' by using typificatory schemes that enter into ongoing and reciprocal negotiation.

'Society', according to Berger and Luckman, exists as both objective and subjective reality. The former is created from the latter as a result of three processes: externalisation (society is a human product), objectivation (society is an objective reality), and internalisation (man is a social product). Each, however, is an ongoing accomplishment. Externalisation is achieved chiefly through language; objectivation through institutionalisation, role-playing, legitimation and reification; internalisation through socialisation. Berger and Luckman, unfortunately, do not consider the implications of their analysis for research methodology, but it is possible to move towards a phenomenological analysis of the spirit of marketing by applying their method of analysis to the marketing world.

THE SPIRIT OF MARKETING

Like its holy counterpart, the spirit of marketing is embodied in a trinity: in the producer as marketer, in the consumer, and in the marketing academic (the father, the son and the Holy Ghost?). What is required is an analysis of the spirit of all three and their interrelationships. Each needs to be recognised as both a subjective and an objective reality, and that the study of the processes involved in creating one from the other will include a phenomenological analysis along the lines suggested by Berger and Luckman.

Weber's original link between the Protestant ethic and the spirit of capitalism was, in reality, about production rather than consumption. Subjective reality at the point of contact between lived experience and consciousness of mind for the capitalist is viewed as an ethic of hard work as a moral duty, but for the marketing practitioner this manifests itself as an aggressive, purposeful and rational search for ever-renewed innovation and growth. Externalisation of this subjective reality is accomplished through the rhetoric of marketing and the dramaturgical, even theatrical, specification and communication of marketing goals that often have more to do with the presentation of self in everyday life than with the vigorous pursuit and cultivation of markets. Objectivation is achieved through the institutionalised ceremonies and rituals of marketing planning, the planning of an advertising campaign, or the conduct of marketing research. The role of marketing manager thus becomes both legitimated and reified. The 'ideal-type' marketing role becomes experienced by the neophyte marketer as an objective reality that is handed down by way of instruction, initiation, the provision of role models, the celebration of accomplishments and the discipline of appraisal. This spirit of modern producer marketing was not, however, necessarily the *outcome* of the Protestant ethic, but it nevertheless provided the cradle in which it could be nourished.

Any explanation of the emergence of the spirit of producer marketing is, however, likely to be inadequate to explain also the development of the spirit of modern consumerism without which capitalism could not have flourished. The most characteristic feature of modern consumerism, according to Campbell (1987), is its insatiability – an apparently endless pursuit of wants and an inexhaustibility of wants themselves. There is, he says, no adequate theory of consumption that can explain this phenomenon. It is not just a result of the growth in population or the rise in disposable incomes. Existing theories tend to treat wants as unproblematic – as a by-product of exposure to the media, the stimulation of emulative desires, or as a basic instinct. Instead they concentrate on the rationality of product selection, taking wants as given. The origins of this new propensity to consume clearly stemmed from changes in attitudes and values, being in some way related to such innovations as the rise of modern fashion, romantic love and the novel, but extant explanations for these changes were, argues Campbell, either reductionist or circular.

The modern consumer treats consumption as a luxury which is for the pursuit of pleasure; but the concepts of 'luxury' and 'pleasure' do not figure in theories of consumption and consumer behaviour and cannot be accommodated within the framework of utility maximisation. There needs to be, Campbell argues, a corresponding theory of modern hedonism.

Hedonism is the pursuit of or devotion to pleasure, particularly pleasures of the senses. It can also be seen as an ethical doctine which asserts that only that which is pleasant is intrinsically good. Modern hedonism manifests itself as conduct being pulled along by desire for the *anticipated* quality of pleasure that an experience promises to yield. The anticipation is imaginatively created through fantasy and day-dreaming. In consequence, people do not so much seek satisfaction from products as pleasure from the self-illusory experiences that they construct from their associated meanings. The essential activity of consumption is thus not the actual selection, purchase or use of products, but the imaginative pleasure-seeking to which the product image lends itself. Viewed in this way, the modern emphasis on innovation and novelty combined with the ethic of insatiability becomes more susceptible to interpretive understanding in the Weberian sense.

It is difficult, however, to see how this spirit could have flourished in the mind of the ideal type Protestant described by Weber, particularly given its asceticism. However, Campbell (1987) argues that there were, in fact, two powerful cultural traditions of thought and associated 'ethics' that developed out of English Puritanism in the eighteenth century. The first, which corresponds to that identified by Weber, stressed rationality, instrumentality, industry and achievement, and is more suspicious of pleasure than of comfort. This is Weber's asceticism. An alternative tradition, however, and one that Weber did not consider – his sources only took him up to about 1700 – is traceable to the Arminian revolt against the idea of predestination and the Cambridge Platonists. This incorporated an optimistic, emotionalist version of the Calvinist doctrine of signs and developed first into the cults of benevolence and melancholy, and then into a fully fledged sentimentalism, leading finally to Romanticism. This provided the highest motives with which to justify day-dreaming, longing and the rejection of painful reality.

The nature of the connection between Romanticism and modern consumerism, like that between Protestantism and the spirit of marketing, was essentially ironic. The spirit of modern consumerism was an unintended consequence; an incongruity between what might have been expected and what actually occurred. For the Romantic, pleasure is not an end in itself, but rather a path to moral renewal – a way of becoming emotionally sensitive to the plight of others. The spirit of romanticism is the consumer's subjective reality. It is the point of contact between lived experience and consciousness of mind. It is not materialistic, but rather manifests itself as a desire to experience in reality the pleasurable dramas that people have already enjoyed in imagination.

'Objective' consumer realities are, as the phenomenologist would argue, created through the processes of externalisation, objectivation and internalisation. The language of advertisers feeds our desire for drama, fantasy and day-dreaming. It provides our images of products, and facilitates our imaginative pleasure-seeking. Objectivation creates our 'image as reality' and provides for the presentation of self in everyday life (see Goffman 1959), while internalisation creates the 'you-are-what-you-buy' syndrome, underpinned by socialisation and peer group pressure.

The spirit of the marketing academic is also a constructed reality, both subjective and objective, that has been through the processes of externalisaton, objectivation and internalisation. The concepts they employ establish 'realities' that are experienced by others as objective, but are in fact subjective inventions that are created and recreated as ongoing accomplishments that continuously need to be negotiated and renegotiated (e.g. 'above-the-line' and 'below-the-line' advertising expenditure). Objectivation is accomplished through the institutionalisation of many of marketing's concepts and theories, many of which are sustained by the making of a marketing faith, the establishment of churches of marketing thought and by the role played by the marketing guru. Legitimation, reification, even sanctification, are key processes in objectivation. As far as internalisation is concerned, the socialisation of the marketing practitioner and of the marketing academic creates marketers as social products, playing by whatever are the rules of the organisation in which they are employed, whether this is the sanctity of sales volume, or the volume of publications in refereed journals.

The spirit of academic marketing is embedded in faith – faith in the efficacy of its preachings; faith in the catechisms of its teachings; faith in the textbooks of marketing dogma. Through the process of guru creation and the making of a marketing mythology, concepts and principles suggested by a single author have, if they have been in tune with the times, had a remarkable tendency readily to become accepted as articles of faith, unchallenged and unresearched, rather than treated as hypotheses to be tested. This tendency in respect of the four Ps has already been noted elsewhere (Kent 1986). The result is a church of marketing based on dogma and holy scripture, institutionalised, ritualised, and customised for appropriate congregations.

VISIONS OF THE END

The spirit of marketing is a durable concept. It has survived onslaughts from several directions – from those who have seen it as the sanctimonious ally of sharp practice, from those who have doubted the very possibility of any objective science of marketing, from the postmodernists who espoused pluralism and even nihilism, and from those who have prophesied the marketing apocalypse.

Marketing has sometimes been portrayed as the unacceptable face of unbridled profit-seeking – with shoddy and unsafe goods on the shelves and in the showrooms, salesmen's malpractices of pyramid selling and unethical promotional activity. Its 'clean linen' has been washed in public – specific firms and industries have been accused of being guilty of negligence (Beem 1973; Kotler 1972), deceptive advertising (Jacoby and Small 1975; Gardner 1976), non-disclosure of product information (Resnik and Stern 1977), the mistreatment or neglect of minority or disadvantaged groups (Kassarjian 1969; Andreasen 1965) and customer dissatisfaction and consumer complaints (Oliver 1988; Churchill and Suprenant 1982).

Peter and Olson (1983) have cautioned that the 'aura of objectivity has been steadily eroding for years' across all sciences, and that marketers should be converted to the Reformist church of relativism and constructionism. Mick (1986) advocated semiotics for marketing research because 'objectivity is impossible'. Fullerton (1986) endorsed historicism, claiming that researcher objectivity and intersubjective certifiability are 'chimeras – they cannot be achieved'. The critical relativists, according to Hunt (1990), saw 'truth' itself as a subjective construction (Peter and Olson 1983) and could play no role in any science. Its pursuit in marketing was a 'Quixotic idea' (Anderson 1988).

Postmodernism, which made a somewhat dramatic entry into the marketing scene in 1993 (Brown 1994) is, by contrast, sceptical, subversive, anarchistic, and quite often negativistic, even nihilist (Brown 1993). It is a reaction to everything that is 'modern'. Postmodernism in marketing, however, is clearer about what it is against than what it is for. It is against the search for objectivity, causality and universal truths; it is hostile towards generalisations or what it describes as 'metanarratives'; it is against rationality, 'progress', reason, authority and control. Postmodernists accept that knowledge is bounded, and that attempts to produce universal truths are, at best, leading us into temptation. The world is ephemeral, contingent, diverse, disordered and ambiguous. Postmodernists are prone to debunk modern marketing theory, which they see as counterproductive, with believers in the product life cycle eliminating perfectly sound products; followers of the 'Boston Box' failing to appreciate its restrictive assumptions; whole congregations in the Church of modern marketing taking the sacrament of the four Ps without confession or recantation.

Postmodernists are less clear, or less in agreement, about what they are for and what they advocate. On the whole they are in favour of accepting a plurality of epistemologies. They force us to take seriously issues concerning the foundation of knowledge in the discipline and could just provide a path towards paradigm dialogue. Postmodernism does provide a philosophical basis for more creative, spontaneous and adaptable approaches to marketing that fit more happily with the trend towards treating customers as individuals to be nurtured over long periods (as in 'relationship' marketing) or treated as a market segment of one (as in database, direct or 'micro' marketing, and, more recently, 'mass customisation').

Despite postmodernism's emphasis on creativity, intuition, spontaneity, emotion, uniqueness and its focus on local narratives, and despite its 'fit' with trends in marketing towards individualism, fragmentation, hyper-reality, and dedifferentiation (Brown 1994), nevertheless, maintaining a position of extreme relativism is, in the long run, self-defeating. No research is possible or worthwhile since no findings can be evaluated against others. Indeed, it becomes impossible to distinguish between science and religion. The very basis of the relativist rhetoric is self-contradictory: to announce that there are no universal truths is to state a universal truth. Relativism and postmodernism, in fact, have no more foundation than any other perspective.

Ironically, the postmodern condition, according to Brown (1993), has affected more the practice than the theory of marketing. If postmodern scepticism were to be applied to all extant theory, there could be few survivors. Is this, asks Brown (1993), the end of marketing – either as in finish or as in destination?

Visions of the end of marketing are not recent phenomena. In 1983 Austen, for example, argued that in a period of turmoil and accelerating change, what was required was a business application that was more responsive than marketing; that certainly the older formulations of the marketing concept were obsolete. By 1987, Gummeson was confessing that the marketing concept was unrealistic and needed to be replaced. By the early 1990s visions of the apocalypse were becoming commonplace. According to Rapp and Collins (1990) traditional methods of marketing were no longer working. Brownlie and Saren (1992) argued that it is questionable whether the marketing concept as it has been propagated 'can provide the basis for meaningful business at the end of the twentieth century'. Marketing was seen to be teetering on the brink of a serious intellectual crisis (Marion 1993).

Despite decades of theorising, years of dedicated research and the steady accumulation of research 'findings', the reliability, validity and applicability of many marketing principles were regarded by many as being far from established. By 1995 a Marketing Retreat in Belfast was grappling with Marketing Eschatology and such concepts as 'onanist scatology', 'honest catology', 'catalytic catechism' and the parable of 'apocalyptus interruptus'.

The word 'apocalypse' in fact means 'revelation' – the unveiling of a divine secret. It has not, consequently, always been used to describe visions of the end, or even visions of ultimate destruction, but a final state of grace, glory or peace. It is a particular version of eschatology that has to do with the end of history – and what lies beyond it. It is a different kind of eschatology from that of the prophets, which is a consciousness of living in the last age of history. The apocalyptic version amounts to a conviction that the last age is itself about to come to an end. It tends to be pessimistic and determinist rather than, as the prophets would have it, optimistic and with a view of history that sees it as capable of being subverted. Apocalyptic eschatology is typically presented in a rich, distinctive style, with heavy use of symbols, allegorical figures and rhetorical devices. It is a drama of the conflict between good and evil with a scenario that contains the elements of crisis, judgement and salvation. The last of these elements clearly links with the Protestant vision of predestination, the calling and the hope of joining the ranks of the selected few.

Apocalyptic materials can be traced back to the period c. 200 B.C. and early Christian apocalypticism continued up to A.D. 400 (McGinn 1979). It has since been a distinctive element and an unfolding phenomenon in both Judaism and Christianity for many centuries. An apocalyptic eschatology for marketing would envisage, then, not just a crisis, not just a day of judgement, nor even a Second Coming, but a vision of salvation – a life after death. The source of such knowledge – the gnosis – was in ancient literature and in the Old Testament always a Revelation from God. Unfortunately, then, as now, each apocalyptist had his own vision, each with no more sanctity than the last, each based on the false premise that the divine was right. Today, in marketing, we have 'Coca Kotler: over-wrought, over-rated and over here' (Brown 1995). We have a Church of Marketing and the catechism of the four Ps. Faiths, dogmas, beliefs, theories and perspectives come and go, but like the Holy Ghost, the spirit lives on.

THE CUSTODIANS OF THE SPIRIT

If the spirit of marketing is such a durable concept, who are its custodians? In the religious world priests are the primary custodians of faith, keeping the congregation in touch with 'reality' through the mediation of the community's tradition in symbol and ritual. In marketing there is a parallel priestly mode that has a presumptive faith in order – an order that can be predicted, is governed by regularities, and can be approached through the use of the correct ceremonies that embody the church of marketing. The priesthood is abstemiously dedicated to the prediction of regularities and patterns over time, thereby, ultimately, to reach the Holy Grail – total knowledge. The priest mediates between the reliably ordered marketing system, which is composed of interrelated parts that have structures that can be observed, and the somewhat messy flux that characterises the everyday world of the marketer at the sharp end. Initiation to the priesthood requires preparatory rituals and a language of communion so specialised that it needs to be interpreted and rendered in sermon and worldly advice for the layman. The analogy of a 'priestly' mode in science, incidentally, is not totally idiosyncratic. Fitch (1958) and Lapp (1965), for example, have both used it to refer to the world of natural scientists.

The main threat to the priestly mode in marketing is the prophetic mode. Prophets seek to change the world by using their projections of past behaviour into the future to alter that future; to use such extrapolations as a weapon to divert its actual fulfilment. Commitment and intervention are imperative to the prophetic mode; partisanship is strongly endorsed. The prophet always aims to be part of the solution, not part of the problem. The cloak of neutrality and the mask of objectivity are removed. The prophetic mode in marketing is all about achieving goals and attaining objectives through competitive strategy. The marketing world is viewed not as a system of interrelated parts; rather it is an arena in which marketing warfare takes place (e.g. Kotler and Achrol 1981). Marketing is pursued on behalf of organisations, whether in-house or on behalf of a client. The established churches of the priestly mode are anathema to the prophet, who would question or attack the priestly edifice that is the church of marketing. Visionaries and utopians rub shoulders with moneymakers and wealth-seekers in a church that is more Presbyterian than Episcopalian. In sociology the prophetic mode, whose origins go back to Karl Marx and beyond, was an instrument of social reform; in marketing it is a gospel of corporate success.

The prophetic mode is subjectivist rather than relativist. There is still a reality 'out there' to be observed, but not one that can be brought to light by utilising the specialised rituals and rhetoric of the priestly mode, but through a focus on the subjective world of the participants in marketing exchanges. If we return to Weber and his methodology in *The Protestant Ethic*, however, then it is clear that he would argue that you need both the pursuit of causal connections and subjective understanding. It is, furthermore, not just a question of each having its own contribution to make or that each has a role, but that both are necessary conditions and must be *combined* for an adequate explanation to emerge. It is clear, too, that from the phenomenologists we learn that reality is a constructed reality that is both subjective and objective. To understand how we move from the subjective to the objective, it is necessary to understand the processes of externalisaton, objectivation and internalisation. The trinity of the spirit of marketing can be arrived at only through the phenomenological grid. It is this spirit that has survived the onslaughts of the consumerists, the radical relativists, the postmodernists, and the apocalyptic eschatologists. Visions of the End, whether apocalyptic or prophetic, contribute to a proliferating Babel, a growing confusion of 'revelation' and divine message.

REFERENCES

Anderson, Paul F. (1988), 'Relativism Revidivus: In Defense of Critical Relativism', *Journal of Consumer Research*, vol. 15, December, pp. 403–6.

Andreasen, Alan R. (1965), 'Attitudes and Consumer Behaviour: A Decision Model', in Lee, E. Preston (ed.), *Research Program in Marketing: New Research in Marketing*, Berkeley: Institute of Business and Economic Research, University of California, pp. 1–16.

Austen, Alfred (1983), 'The Marketing Concept – is it Obsolete?', *The Quarterly Review of Marketing*, vol. 9, Autumn, pp. 6–8.

Beem, Eugene R. (1973), 'The Beginnings of the Consumer Movement', in William T. Kelly, *New Consumerism: Selected Readings*, Columbus, OH: Grid, pp. 13–25.

Berger, Peter L. and Luckman, Thomas (1967), *The Social Construction of Reality*, London: Allen Lane, The Penguin Press.

Brown, Stephen (1993), 'Postmodern Marketing?', *European Journal of Marketing*, vol. 27, no. 4, pp. 19–34.

Brown, Stephen (1994), 'Marketing as Multiplex: Screening Postmodernism', *European Journal of Marketing*, vol. 28, no. 8/9, pp. 27–51.

Brown, Stephen (1995), 'Coca Kotler: Over-wrought, Over-rated and Over Here', *Irish Marketing Review*, vol. 8, pp. 134–9.

Brownlie, Douglas and Saren, Mike (1992), 'The Four Ps of the Marketing Concept: Prescriptive, Polemical, Permanent and Problematical', *European Journal of Marketing*, vol. 26, no. 4, pp. 34–47.

Campbell, Colin (1987), *The Protestant Ethic and the Spirit of Modern Consumerism*, Oxford: Basil Blackwell.

Churchill, Gilbert A. and Suprenant, Carol (1982), 'An Investigation Into the Determinants of Consumer Satisfaction', *Journal of Marketing Research*, vol. 19, November, pp. 491–504.

Fitch, Robert E. (1958), 'The Scientist as Priest and Saviour', *Christian Century*, vol. 75, 26 March.

Fullerton, R.A. (1986), 'Historicism: What It Is and What It Means for Consumer Research', in M. Wallendorf and P. F. Anderson (eds), *Advances in Consumer Research*, Association for Consumer Research, Provo, UT, pp. 431–4.

Gardner, David M. (1976), 'Deception in Advertising: A Receiver Oriented Approach to Understanding', *Journal of Advertising*, vol. 5, Fall, pp. 5–11.

Goffman, Erving (1959), *The Presentation of Self in Everyday Life*, New York: Doubleday.

Green, Robert W. (1959), *Protestantism and Capitalism. The Weber Thesis and its Critics*, Boston: D.C. Heath and Company.

Gummeson, Evert (1987), 'The New Marketing – Developing Long-term Interactive Relationships', *Long Range Planning*, vol. 20, no. 4, pp. 10–20.
Hunt, Shelby D. (1990), 'Truth in Marketing Theory and Research', *Journal of Marketing*, vol. 49, Summer, pp. 11–23.
Hunt, Shelby D. (1993), 'Objectivity in Marketing Theory and Research', *Journal of Marketing*, vol. 57, April, pp. 76–91.
Jacoby, Jacob A. and Small, Constance (1975), 'The FDA Approach to Defining Misleading Advertising', *Journal of Marketing*, vol. 39, October, pp. 65–8.
Kassarjian, Harold H. (1969), 'The Negro and American Advertising, 1946–1965', *Journal of Marketing Research*, vol. 2, October, pp. 28–31.
Kent, Raymond A. (1986), 'Faith in Four Ps an Alternative', *Journal of Marketing Management*, vol. 2, no. 2, Winter, pp. 145–54.
Kotler, Philip (1972), 'What Consumerism Means for Marketers', *Harvard Business Review*, vol. 50, May–June, pp. 48–57.
Kotler, Philip and Achrol, Ravi S. (1981), 'Marketing Warfare in the 1980s', *Journal of Business Strategy*, vol. 1, Winter, pp. 30–41.
Lapp, Ralph E. (1965), *The New Priesthood*, New York: Harper and Row.
Marion, G. (1993), 'The Marketing Management Discourse: What's New since the 1960s?', in Michael J. Baker (ed.), *Perspectives on Marketing Management, Volume Three*, Chichester: John Wiley and Sons, pp. 143–68.
McGinn, Bernard (1979), *Visions of the End. Apocalyptic Traditions in the Middle Ages*, New York: Columbia University Press.
Mick, D.G. (1986), 'Consumer Research and Semiotics: Exploring the Morphology of Signs, Symbols, and Significance', *Journal of Consumer Research*, vol. 13, September, pp. 196–213.
Oliver, Christine (1988), 'The Collective Strategy Framework: An Application to Competing Predictions of Osomorphism', *Administrative Science Quarterly*, vol. 33, no. 4, December, pp. 543–61.
Peter, J.P. and Olson, J.C. (1983), 'Is Science Marketing?', *Journal of Marketing*, 47 (Fall), 111–25.
Rapp, S. and Collins, T. (1990), *The Great Marketing Turnaround*, New York: Prentice Hall.
Resnick, Alan J. and Stern, Bruce L. (1977), 'An Analysis of Information Content in Television Advertising', *Journal of Marketing*, vol. 41, January, pp. 50–3.
Schutz, Alfred (1967), *The Phenomenology of the Social World*, trans. G. Walsh and F. Lehnert, Evanston: Northwestern University Press.
Weber, Max (1930), *The Protestant Ethic and the Spirit of Capitalism*, trans. Talcott Parsons, London: George Allen and Unwin.
Weber, Max (1962) *Basic Concepts in Sociology*, trans. H.P. Secher, London: Owen Press.
Weber, Max (1969) *The Methodology of the Social Sciences*, trans E.A. Shils and H.A. Finch, New York: Free Press.

8

MARKETS, EXCHANGE AND THE EXTREME

Cornelius G. Buttimer and Donncha Kavanagh

BEYOND THE END OF MARKETING

Marketing is contemplating its End, in at least two senses of the word (Brown 1993; Brownlie and Saren 1992, 1995). Ruminations on its demise are unsurprising, since crisis and images of death are primal parts of our attempt at making sense of the world (Kermode 1967). Such apocalyptic visions occur with particular sharpness at *fin de siècle* times, not to mention towards the close of a millennium, which might explain the recent flurry of announcements of the End: of the world (Meadows *et al.* 1972); industrial society (Touraine 1974); capitalism (Lash and Urry 1987); the social (Baudrillard 1988); history (Fukuyama 1989); and work (Rifkin 1995). Latter-day predictions of marketing's imminent downfall can be seen as prototypical of this phenomenon. Moreover, these declarations are singularly characteristic of modernity, with its passion for re-invention, for new Ends and new Beginnings. But histrionic proclamations of the End often fail to deliver on their promise of finality: for beneath the cloak of eschatological language is modernity's ongoing teleological project of rampantly re-visioning the future. We prefer, therefore, to demur from the current discussion on the End *of* Marketing. Rather, we shall focus, in this chapter, on the End *in* Marketing. Here, we interpret End as meaning limit, extreme or margin, and, in particular, the extremes of the human condition. We posit that these extremes are pervasive in the market-place, which we view as a site where human limitations can be quite overtly articulated. This chapter, then, contributes to our understanding of market phenomena through a study of the complex inter-relationship between markets, exchange and the extreme.

This interest in Ends is, in effect, an interest in boundaries, and this awakens us to some of the philosophical and methodological borders within marketing itself. Marketing's recent concern with matters apocalyptic also highlights issues and edges that have been largely ignored within the field, such as the metaphysical, eternity and time (Kavanagh 1994). With regard to the latter, we agree with Fullerton's (1987) assertion that marketing is paradigmatically averse to history, existing in a temporal dimension best described as permanently present. In what follows we seek to transcend this temporal boundary. We also see value in breaching disciplinary constraints and merging a range of empirical data and theoretical viewpoints. Hence, we have deliberately embraced a *pastiche* approach in our research. We believe that this eclecticism is appropriate and even necessary if we are to deepen our appreciation of markets and marketing activity which, in our opinion, is the marketing scholar's ultimate goal or end.

EXEGESIS

Our work is based on a hermeneutic study of texts and visual records that pertain particularly, although not exclusively, to pre-modern markets. We attempt to make both categories of evidence as comprehensive as space constraints permit. We take the reader from comparatively recent testimony to the medieval period, the classical world and forwards again towards modernity; voyage across north-west European culture, the Mediterranean region, North America and the East; and sample the riches of art-work, poetry, saga and other forms of prose narrative, derived from literate societies or recorded latterly during ethnographic field-work. The communities delved into vary from aristocratic to multi-class to peasant cultures, and there is corresponding variation in the tenor of the events described.

Picturing the market

Barrell (1980) has noted that commercial exchange and work, which occupy such a major place in individual and collective life, are very under-represented in art. However, if there are relatively few paintings of pre-modern markets, what there is is challenging, especially the output of artists such as Peter Bruegel in the sixteenth century. Bruegel's *The Fight Between Carnival and Lent* (Figure 8.1a), painted in 1559, portrays the festivities in the market square of a late-medieval town. Significantly, the piece depicts a commercial transaction – a woman buying fish (Figure 8.1b) – at the very centre of the image, the locus around which the picture's other features are arranged. Circumscribing this interchange is a catalogue of extremes, including inversions (women taking the role of cart-horses), grotesque realism (protuberant, incomplete, over- and under-sized depictions of the body), dissimulation (cheating, masks and make-believe), music, gambling, and dance. Around the margins of the painting a procession of sombre, dark characters intrudes, highlighting the conflict between the profanity of the carnival and the sanctity of Lent. Such Bruegelian perspectives on the market also occur in later periods, as in the nineteenth-century illustration of Donnybrook Fair (Figure 8.2), a well-known popular gathering held near Dublin until its decline towards the end of the last century (Ó Maitiú 1995), where we can again witness the intermixing of the commercial and the carnivalesque.

Figure 8.1a Peter Bruegel, *The Fight Between Carnival and Lent* (1559)
Source: Kunsthistorisches Museum, Vienna

Figure 8.1b Peter Bruegel, *The Fight Between Carnival and Lent* (detail)

Figure 8.2 George du Noyer, *Donnybrook Fair in the Year 1830*
Source: Reproduced with the assistance of the Irish Academic Press

Writing the market

Traversing media, we see a similar expression of tumult and turbulence in the world of poetry. These features are well expressed in *Tuairisc Amhailt Uí Iartáin*, a late eighteenth-century Gaelic verse composition from a south-east Ireland manuscript, offering a panorama of a localised, village or small-town fair in its sixty-four lines (Buttimer 1992). Prices seem excessive in relation to the live-stock on offer; commodities such as food and drink are readily available for consumption on the spot; these combine with music, dancing and sporting to produce an atmosphere of noisy abandon: youths chase and seduce girls, one sees pick-pocketing, faction-fighting and drunken disputation, in which conditions animals go astray. The following excerpts convey, in English translation, the atmosphere of the original rhythmical Gaelic:

> . . . a mangy ewe six and six,
> a hedgehog-sized pig thrice sixpence . . .
> There was play below by the old road valley,
> violin and pipe at the wood-sorrel fence,
> with rough dancing killing beatles,

the lower orders' old shoes squeaking,
running contests at the shamrock field
and chancers and gamblers crying foul . . .
Honor was chasing George Cusack
because he uncovered her knee and her hem
as she lay on her rear in a nettle-bush recess . . .
Pick-pockets there were chased and run after,
there was fighting, striking and commotion . . .
At the custom's gap jackets were opened,
shouts of lies, falsehood and exclamation,
oaths sworn without warning or reservation.

Oath-taking is heard at the tolls as dealers conceal the value of their purchases from the customs authorities. The last laugh is on the individual reporting the various incidents. In his distraction he has failed to sell his wares and is left impoverished, unable to obtain a consoling draught to 'wet his old throat'. Throughout this relatively nonchalant piece, the persona reveals an attitude of bemusement on his part at his own foibles as well as those of his fellow human beings.

If nonchalance is the dominant feature of this eighteenth-century fair, then crisis and catastrophe feature more prominently in an earlier description of an *oenach*, which is the Old Irish term for an assembly or fair. The source here is the ninth-century saga *Noínden Ulad*, 'The Debility of the Ulstermen' (Hull 1968), which forms part of a major cycle of stories about the pre-Christian heroic province of Ulster in north-eastern Ireland (Thurneysen 1921). *Noínden Ulad* describes significant *failure* of a kind also evident in other Ulster legends like the famous Deirdre story later re-worked by W. B. Yeats and J. M. Synge (Buttimer 1994–5). The 'Debility of the Ulstermen' tells how a woman, Macha, inflicted a crippling weakness on the fighting men of Ulster leading them to lose their energy in times of crisis, such as an invasion of their territory. Macha's husband, Crunnchu, a wealthy commoner, boasted of her superior speed at an *oenach*, presided over by the king, of whom it was stated that no horses were swifter than his. Although pregnant, the woman was obliged to race against the ruler's steeds to prove the assertion or else see Crunnchu killed. Having outpaced the animals she gave birth to twins in the following dramatic encounter:

> ba sisi boí urtharsna ara cinn i cinn na láithre. La sodain at-racht a screit n-esi ar tíachra in galair. Ro-glé Día dí fo cét-óir, ocus berid mac 7 ingin i n-óen-tairbirt. Amail ro-cólatar in slúag uile a screit inna banscáile, fos-ceird fóo combo inann nert dóib uli 7 in banscál boí isin galur . . .

> at the end of the course she was across in front of [the horses]. Thereupon a scream arose from her on account of the pain of the travail. Forthwith God cleared it away for her, and she bore a boy and a girl at

> one birth. As soon as all the people heard the scream of the woman, it laid them low so that the strength of all of them was the same as [that of] the woman who was in travail . . .

Macha's capacity to impose so powerful a sanction on Ulster's warriors probably reflects divine attributes associated with her elsewhere in the literature. Nonetheless the story employs the vocabulary of everyday experience rather than that of mythology to explore its major theme. The story shows that Macha adhered strictly to the requirements of domestic propriety when establishing herself in Crunnchu's homestead. She also reminded the messengers, who came to compel her to attend the *oenach*, of the legal rights to delay pregnant women were allowed in complying with a request (Kelly 1988). She was nonetheless constrained to attend the event. The violation of her dignity suggests the saga is concerned with an inability to maintain the appropriate distinction between life's private and public spheres (Buttimer 1995), a dilemma recalling a critical preoccupation of Sophocles' Antigone (Steiner 1984). Tellingly, the *oenach* is the locus of this confusion of categories and the resultant cataclysmic impact on the Ulster community.

Moving across cultures, we see that the market-place and an apocalyptic moment coincide in another major early civilisation, that of Israel at the commencement of the Christian period. We refer to the famous episode of Christ driving the traders from the temple. This is probably the only occasion one witnesses Jesus engage in an act of physical aggression in the Gospels. Indeed the outburst's physicality is emphasised in later medieval and early modern iconographic portraits of the scene by such artists as Ghiberti, El Greco and Rembrandt (Suchaux and Pastoureau 1994: 243). Their art-work is effectively an interpretation of passages like the following in the Gospel of St John (2:13–17), cited here from the King James' version:

> (13) And the Jews' passover was at hand, and Jesus went up to Jerusalem, (14) And found in the temple those that sold oxen and sheep and doves, and the changers of money sitting: (15) And when he had made a scourge of small cords, he drove them all out of the temple, and the sheep, and the oxen; and poured out the changers' money, and overthrew the tables; (16) And said unto them that sold doves, Take these things hence; make not my Father's house an house of merchandise. (17) And his disciples remembered that it was written, The zeal of thine house hath eaten me up.

Significantly, the market episode is at the heart of an apocalyptic event. It reflects the long-standing tension between Jesus and the Pharisees on matters of mendacity (Mt 11, 12, 15, 19, 20; Mk 2, 7; Lk 5, 7, 11), and brings relations between Christ and the religious establishment to a new level of tension, a debate that continues in the temple after his frenzy (Mt 22, 23; Mk 11, 12; Lk 20). More importantly, this is the incident that ultimately triggers the Pharisees' will to suppress him, which, in turn, is the fulfilment of Christ's predictions of his own death and the symbolic destruction of the temple which will later be re-embodied in himself (Mt 12:6, 26:61, 27:40). It is ironic that the same clergy are not slow to exploit the market for their own ends: scribes and pharisees, who are said to crave places of honour at feasts and the best seats in the synagogues, seemingly go there to receive public adulation (Mt 23:7; Mk 12:38; Lk 20:46). At the same time, the market is seen as a likely source of contamination; it is stated of clerics that when they come from the market-place they do not eat unless they purify themselves (Mk 7.4). The importance of the market episode is further highlighted by its narrative location: in three of the gospels it is at the start of the death and resurrection sequence, while in John's gospel the equivalent incident is prominently placed, out of the dominant narrative order, at the start of his public life (Powell 1990: 36–8).

The intensity of Christ's temple outrage contrasts with the relative calm with which matters of commerce are dealt with elsewhere in the Gospels. It is clear that references to various types of exchange need not necessarily be so emotionally charged. Trade is clearly a facet of daily life: the statement about paying Caesar his dues (Mt 22:21; Mk 12:14) appears to be an acknowledgement of public finances, with advice to tax-collectors to take no more than is appointed to them (Lk 3:13). Even if the highest values transcend quantification (the lilies of the field are better clad than Solomon because of God's will (Mt 6:28–9)), Jesus frequently uses parables (Bailey and Vander Broek 1992) with a mercantile dimension to illustrate in practice what constitutes acceptable or unacceptable behaviour towards the divine, such as in the model of proper stewardship of an estate (Lk 16). It is interesting to observe that the story of Christ's troubled entry into the temple is preceded by a parable on a nobleman's just chastisement of his subjects for failure to manage correctly his and their financial affairs (Lk 19:11–17).

Subsequent events in place and time, which can only be mentioned here in passing, conjoin certain of the characteristics noted in our initial examples. Thus the municipal authorities sponsored a race for prostitutes on the feast day of St Mary Magdalene (22 July) at the fair in the Languedoc town of Beaucaire during the 1400s (Otis 1985: 10 and 71). In the present century, Balinese cockfights, with their elaborate, symbolic wagering systems, coincide and interact with local markets (Geertz 1971: 32–3, note 18). Bauman has similarly described how dog owners come to engage in an interchange of wits and words, in 'creative exaggeration' and downright lying, at a popular dog trading fair (dating from the seventeenth century and still active) in the town of Canton, south of Dallas, Texas (Bauman 1986: 11–32, 117–27).

THE END IN THE MARKET: SOME PERSPECTIVES

These various examples reveal a connection between exchange and extreme behaviour of all sorts: the inversions and carnivalesque in Bruegel's painting, the falsehoods of the hound fair, the rage of Jesus as he drove the traders from the temple, the race between Macha and the steeds in the ninth-century saga, excessive consumption of food and drink, displays of the diseased and deformed, noise and music, varieties of dissimulation, inversions, profanity, prostitution, cheating, stealing, fighting, gaming and the suspension of other social mores. What is striking is the range *and* collocation of this conduct. For us, it is ultimately of no import that the behaviour can be construed as foolish, irrational, deviant, immoral or criminal; rather it is significant because it is *extreme*. More arresting is the possibility that the market is a primary forum where extremes of human experience are manifest. This, then, is why we say that the End is *in* the market, since the market is a site where conduct that is reaching the limits of comprehension is concentrated. We have also used the term madness (Buttimer and Kavanagh 1995) to describe such behaviour, for madness may be construed as that which is beyond theory, beyond knowledge, beyond reason: the mad are deranged, past the limits of classification and comprehension. In Foucault's words:

> Madness has become man's possibility of abolishing both man and the world – and even those images that challenge the world and deform man. It is far beyond dreams, beyond the nightmare of bestiality, the last recourse: the end and the beginning of everything.
>
> (1967: 281)

Foucault did not shirk the paradoxical task of attempting to describe what he regarded as the undefinable. Neither have others. In the following section we search through literatures and domains that might offer a satisfactory account of the madness of markets. We review etymology, economics, psychiatry and psychoanalysis, Marxist social theory, the sociology of deviance, anthropology, ethnology and the works of writers such as Nietzsche and Canetti. Each field brings a greater or lesser potential for understanding the connection between market exchange and the extreme. We have sought to present, in condensed form, these primary insights, and have also, where necessary, delineated the perceptible lacunae. We follow this investigation by drawing on these and other literatures to present our own conceptualisation of the market.

Etymology

Etymology provides us with a first linkage between market and madness, suggesting that extremes were widely recognised as cognate elements of exchange, even in ancient times. For example, medieval glossators associate the Old Irish term *oenach* with the Greek word *agón,* which also denotes an assembly held for trials and contests (see Huizinga 1955: 30–1). The extreme dimension is arguably clearer in its derivative, the verb *agónió* which means 'to be in agony'. Similarly, an early link between the market and dissimulation is evidenced by the fact that Mercury, the god of trade (and source of the word merchant), is also the king of thieves. However, the resonances of these terms have not been systematically exploited, even by students of the early Greek economy, who tend to focus more on issues like trade (Finley 1982) rather than the topic in question here.

Psychiatry and psychoanalysis

Other fields have recognised the register of early words, such as *psyche* in the twin fields of psychiatry and psychoanalysis. These two disciplines have focused on extreme or mad behaviour since their inception, but they provide, from our perspective, a somewhat limited view of madness: psychiatry sees it as a form of deficiency, while the psychoanalytic outlook is that madness is a manifestation of a primitive, infantile state of mind caused by a defect of the ego. Sass (1992: 16–21) has recently provided a powerful critique of both positions, arguing that they have each constructed the mad as 'inferior' and oversimplified the phenomena they purport to explain. More important for present purposes, however, is the apparent absence of any sustained theory in either field linking exchange and the extreme. Hence, despite the scale of both literatures, they would seem to contribute little to our study.

Economics

Classical micro-economic theory provides one explanation: namely, 'irrational' behaviour can be rationalised if analysed using an alternative logic. For example, giving away money might be regarded as mad or irrational, but economics can account for such altruism by arguing that one cannot pre-ordain utility, and, therefore, if giving money away is considered useful by an individual, such an activity must be deemed to be rational. But by appealing to self-serving concepts such as rationality and utility, economic theory ultimately loses its explanatory power on a tautological merry-go-round. If every action may conceivably have some rational explanation, the term rationality ends up meaning nothing. This is one reason why it has been argued that conventional economic wisdom has presented so few insights into 'primitive economies' and phenomena like the ritual gift-giving or potlatch of some Indian tribes (Dalton 1968). Furthermore, economic theory makes no meaningful distinction between extreme and irrational behaviour. Extreme behaviour, as we understand it, is not necessarily irrational; rather it is extreme in the particular context where it is manifest. Indeed economics has little real visualisation of the extreme, preferring instead to see the market as essentially stable and at, or close to, 'equilibrium'. In contrast, the markets we have described are sites in which factors that are far from equilibrium – extremes – oppose and interweave with one another. Similarly, the Frankfurt School critique – that consumer irrationality is caused by the manipulative character of marketing and advertising – seems inadequate, because it is a thesis of irrationality rather than of extreme behaviour.

Marx

Marx ((1867) 1954) was probably the first writer to envisage an overlap between commercial exchange and extreme conduct when he developed his theory of alienation. In this he posited that such behaviour arises as a response to a sense of alienation which in turn is caused by the characteristics of modern capitalist markets and society. While Marx identified a series of causes for this development – such as the structural nature of modern society, industrialisation, the loss of community, the division of labour, technological change, increasing rationalisation, and the ownership of property – we shall focus solely on the role played by market exchange in his argument.

Central to Marx's thesis was his view that human identity is created through productive and creative activity. In his words, man, by 'acting on the external world and changing it . . . at the same time changes his own nature' (Marx (1867) 1954: 177). He further posited that capitalist markets are characterised by a process through which the products of human labour are reduced to abstract 'exchange values'. Capitalist markets, therefore, are a great circulating web of transubstantiating commodities and money in which workers 'appropriate the produce of the labour of others by alienating that of their own labour' (Marx (1867) 1954: 108–9). Accordingly, for the market to operate, man – retaining Marx's wording for consistency and convenience – must become detached from the product of his labour, and, since humanity is founded on productive activity, this detachment necessarily results in the type of disorientation he terms alienation. Marx also identified uncertainty and crisis as bedfellows of market exchange, a theme later more fully developed by Heidegger (1978). Uncertainty arises because parties to an exchange are never sure that what they receive will adequately compensate for their loss. In particular, the capitalist system, with its emphasis on efficiency improvements and change, provides no guarantee as to the utility of any commodity brought to the market, or that the worker will get his anticipated return for his labour. This uncertainty, in turn, may contribute to tension and foreboding in the marketplace.

Sociology of deviance

Marx developed his theory to posit that alienation and uncertainty would be resolved through proletarian revolt. This, in hindsight, proved not to be the case. Yet Marx's insights endured and strongly influenced Durkheim, whose work spawned an extensive field of enquiry called the *sociology of deviance*. If Marx was optimistic about the prospects for de-alienation through revolution, Durkheim ((1897) 1970) was considerably less sanguine. In his theory of *anomie* he posited that *deviant* behaviour, rather than social upheaval, would be the outcome of the dysfunctions within capitalism.[1] This perspective was thus concerned with 'deviant' phenomena such as suicide and crime. At the same time, Durkheim dwelt less on the exchange process itself and instead stressed that anomie is caused by structural contradictions in modern society. Despite these and subsequent observations, the sociology of deviance is today riddled with self-doubt, to the extent that Sumner has recently written its 'obituary', classifying it as a 'corpse', rather than a corpus, of knowledge (Sumner 1994). While an obituary may be premature, it is worth noting that, in essence, sociologists came to agree that the term 'normal' had lost true significance and that consequently any study of abnormality was logically incoherent. Also, as with psychiatry and psychoanalysis, the sociology of deviance was dominated by a view of deviance as 'socially inadequate' and therefore concentrated on classification, control, and censure of the abnormal. In time, many sociologists became uncomfortable with this paternalistic, if not oppressive, approach. Here, they were partly influenced by the Surrealists, who provided an alternative understanding of madness to the mainstream view of 1930s psychiatry and psychoanalysis by celebrating the deviant as part of the normal rather than as a form of inadequacy.

Nietzsche

In *The Birth of Tragedy*, Friedrich Nietzsche ((1872) 1993) introduced the stimulating idea of the opposed forces of the active (the mad, Dionysiac tendency) and the reactive (the rational, Apolline tendency). In particular, he emphasised that the active, or potentially mad element, is foundational. Poignantly, this celebration of the extreme came from a man who himself later became insane, though the formulation had a beneficial and enduring effect on many of the literary, intellectual and artistic *avant-garde* of the twentieth century. In the context of the market, his work throws doubt upon the presumption of causality underlying much of the social theory inspired by Marx and Durkheim, namely that the market is primordial and that madness or extreme behaviour result from market activity. Instead, it indicates that the reverse causality is equally possible, providing a novel interpretation of the *market as an outcome of madness*. Furthermore, his ideas imply that extreme behaviour is a feature of *all* markets and not just modern capitalist markets, with which Marx, Durkheim, and later critical theorists such as Fromm (1956) and Habermas (1987), were almost exclusively concerned. As we noted above, Marx, and especially Durkheim, saw alienation and anomie primarily as the product of logical defects and structural instabilities associated with industrialisation and modernisation. At heart, 'aberrant conduct' is viewed as a 'symptom of dissociation between culturally defined aspirations and socially structured means' (Merton 1938: 674). However, Nietzsche's ideas suggest that madness is an innate characteristic and not just a by-product of structural contradictions. Moreover, our historical examples tend to support this view.

Anthropology and ethnology

In anthropology and ethnology we also find connections between market exchange and extremes or madness. The common etymological root of the words sanity and sanitation suggests that the separation of the normal from the mad is related to the division between the sacred from the profane, a topic that has been of keen interest to anthropologists (Douglas 1966) and, less frequently, to scholars of contemporary consumer behaviour, most notably in the Odyssey project of the 1980s (Belk *et al.* 1989). Indeed anthropology's *raison d'être* – the study of the Other – is essentially an investigation of the limits or ends of the human condition, which is why the comparative study of boundary rituals, taboos, religious beliefs, the sacred and profane have always been central to the field. But sacred–profane and normal–mad are not equivalent dimensions, and conflating them may be particularly inappropriate for our purposes. For example, gift-giving could be interpreted as a ritual in which objects are taken from the profane world of commerce and converted, through the ritual of decorative wrapping, into sacred gifts (Waits 1978). However, applying the normal–mad dimension to gift-giving yields no similar insights. Furthermore, gift-giving is not market exchange, a distinction that is well known in anthropology and especially in the rich domain of economic anthropology.

Within this field, the work of Karl Polanyi and his student, George Dalton, is important, providing valuable views regarding the collocation of extreme behaviour and the market (Bohannan and Dalton 1962; Dalton 1968; Polanyi 1944; Polanyi *et al.* 1957). Polanyi emphasised that market exchange is only one particular form of transactional mode by which goods, services, land and labour are re-allocated. He identified and comprehensively analysed two other broad transactional modes or 'patterns of integration': *reciprocity* (obligatory gift-giving between kin and friends) and *redistribution* (obligatory payments to a central authority which uses this wealth to support the community). Drawing on his deep knowledge of 'primitive economies', which were based on these systems, he was thus quick to dismiss Adam Smith's suggestion that markets, and man's propensity to barter, truck and exchange, were in some way axiomatic. Instead, he emphasised the *unimportance* of economic organisation in primitive society and the embeddedness of economic transactions in social and institutional structures (see also Granovetter 1985). Moreover, he stressed that privileging the market is singularly inappropriate when interpreting the nature of primitive societies, which suggests that we may be investing too much weight in the commercial transactions depicted in our examples. Nonetheless, he took the socialist position that uncontrolled market exchange, based as it was on a view of man as a free, utilitarian 'atom' rather than a societal animal, led to social disunity, destroying the underlying cohesion of communities founded on either reciprocity or redistribution. He thus agreed with Robert Owen's view that the laissez-faire system will necessarily lead to extremes and 'will produce the most lamentable and permanent evils, unless its tendency be counteracted by legislative interference and direction' (Owen (1815) 1927: 121). Consequently, he supported government 'interference' in the economy and the 'welfare state', both of which he interpreted as an attempt to contain, control and normalise the market's inherent extremes.

The market as crowd

Elias Canetti's (1962) seminal study of crowds, and the extreme behaviour that characterises mobs, suggests that we might usefully see the market as a form of *crowd*. This shifts our attention away from society and the individual located within it to an intermediate construct – the crowd – in which there is an a priori equality between all participants. Canetti lists a number of defining attributes of crowds, one of which reveals a possible explanation for the madness of the market. This is that crowds constantly fear disintegration, which means that they will accept *any* goal, no matter how irrational or extreme, to ensure their continued existence. He also described how the crowd, which like the market appears composed of multi-faceted elements, imposes a regularity which temporarily subjugates individuality to the mindlessness of the moment. However, Canetti's primary concern was with mobs, audiences and congregations, and consequently he over-emphasised *homogeneity*, which is hardly a feature of the markets that we have described (for further criticism see Rudé (1964) 1995: 3). In contrast, we have seen that markets are heterogeneous and diverse. Furthermore, one of his four defining attributes of crowds is that they 'love density' (ibid.: 29), which is hardly a *defining* attribute of markets.

EXPLICATION

All these literatures, in their various ways, provide different levels of insight into the peculiar co-occurrence of extreme or mad behaviour and commercial exchange. However, none of them comprehensively explains the form and range of extreme behaviour in the markets that we have described. This, we believe, is because each theory provides only a partial image of the market. Our aim, therefore, is to offer a more inclusive conceptualisation of the latter which adequately incorporates its extreme dimension and articulates the relationship with commercial exchange. We propose that the following six key features are essential aspects of the market: hybridity, illusion, agon, recursive transformation, elusive harmony, and tragedy.

Hybridity

As we saw from Canetti's work, the most significant distinction between a crowd and a market is that crowds are homogeneous while markets are heterogeneous. However, markets are not only heterogeneous, they are also *hybrid* places, a distinction that may warrant further explanation. Heterogeneity implies a *mixture* of two pure forms; hybridity, in contrast, is best understood as a heterodox *fusion*, rather than a mixture, of elements usually perceived as incompatible. Sand and salt mixed together produce a heterogeneous mixture, while oxygen and hydrogen *fuse* to form a hybrid – water. Latour (1993), in his study and characterisation of hybrid phenomena, has further proposed that, rather than beginning with poles of purity and imposing these on one's data, these poles are better understood as explanatory *outcomes* that are wrested out of the hybrid. This hybrid vision of the market might be described as pre-modern, for the pre-moderns, in contrast to the moderns, saw the world as saturated with combinations of divine, human and natural elements. 'The native is a logical hoarder', writes Claude Lévi-Strauss; 'he is forever tying the threads, unceasingly turning over all the aspects of reality, whether physical, social or mental' (Lévi-Strauss (1962) 1966: 267, quoted in Latour 1993: 42).[2] This concept of hybridity also echoes the ideas of Stallybrass and White (1986), who studied carnivals and other sites of contradiction and transgression in the eighteenth and nineteenth centuries. In particular, it resonates through their valuable characterisation of the market, which also clearly links commercial exchange and extreme behaviour:

> At the market centre of polis we discover a commingling of categories usually kept separate and opposed: centre and periphery, inside and outside, stranger and local, commerce and festivity, high and low. In the marketplace pure and simple categories of thought find themselves perplexed and one-sided. Only hybrid notions are appropriate to such a hybrid place.
>
> (Stallybrass and White 1986: 27)

This interpenetration of opposing categories is vividly depicted in the markets we have examined, from the sacred and profane in Bruegel's painting, to the exchange and the extreme in Jesus's outburst in the temple. Moreover, the concept may also be extended to encompass hybridisation of the body – 'grotesque realism' – and hybridisation of language – the curses, profanities, and improprieties of the fair – that Bakhtin ((1968) 1984) documented in his interpretation of the world of carnival depicted by Rabelais.

Illusion

Nietzsche's writings suggest that market exchange may be understood as a manifestation of the surface order that the Apolline element seeks to impose on the Dionysiac foundation. This occurs because the operation of the market demands and emphasises quantification, rationalisation, abbreviation and control (Cooper 1992). While the common-sense view might see stable, bounded, finite information as a prerequisite for exchange, we can now contemplate an inverse relationship. In this, exchange can be seen as a mechanism that *creates an illusion* of stability, form, certainty and finiteness, which in turn forms part of the conscious protective shield around the primordial, chaotic, uncertain, infinite, mad, unconscious Dionysiac component. In other words, it is not so much that surprise must be suppressed for the market to operate, but rather that the market must operate to suppress surprise.

This illusion of stability is well illustrated in Edgar Degas' painting, from 1873, of the New Orleans Cotton Exchange (Figure 8.3), one of a series he produced as a pictorial assessment of the business world. His *A Cotton Office* constitutes one of the most important visual representations of nineteenth-century capitalism (Brown 1993a: 264), and, interestingly, it depicts a market that is apparently stable, sombre, refined and leisurely. This, however, is *illusory*. In a careful analysis of the work and its context, Brown (1993a) highlights the extremes that the representation of the market only barely masks. The picture shows a cotton office belonging to Degas' American uncle, which, despite the aura of restfulness and tranquillity, was actually going *bankrupt* when he was painting the piece. More broadly, world markets for cotton were shaken by an international stock market crash during the same year. Furthermore, the sobriety of the cotton office hides the extremes and inhumanity of the American South's cotton industry, built as it was on slavery and the slave trade with Africa.

Degas saw his painting as both a representation of the market and as a

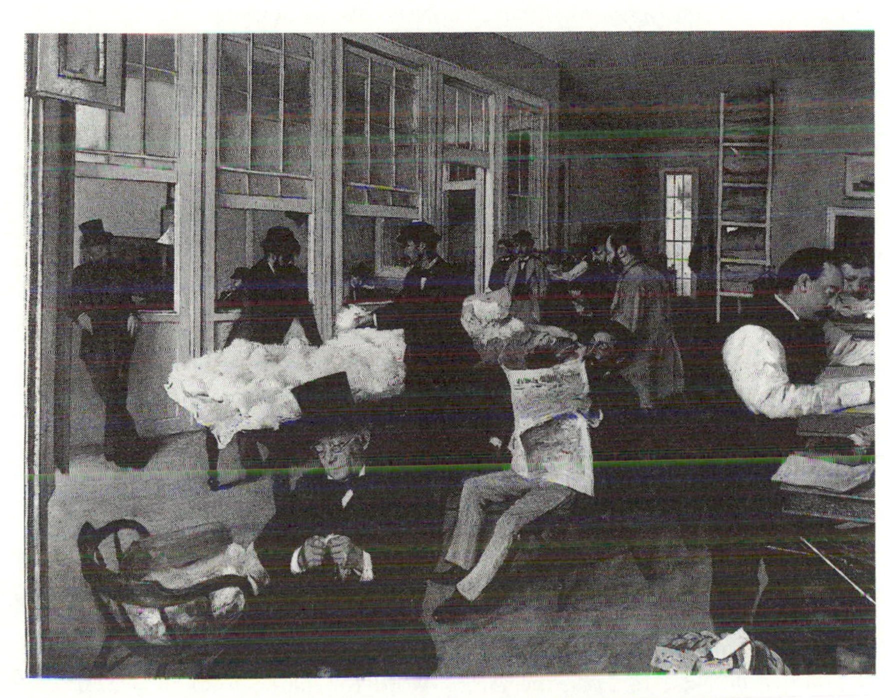

Figure 8.3 Edgar Degas, *A Cotton Office, New Orleans* (1873)

commodity *in* a market (the art market). Thus, the *tableau* was a reflection of the artist's own entrepreneurial venture and, significantly, this enterprise, like the cotton office it portrayed, *also failed.* Despite, or maybe because of, his involvement with the market, Degas was well-known for his blistering diatribes against the art market, commerce in general and the market-minded bourgeoisie in particular. This perspective is more obvious in another painting from the series, *Sulking* (occasionally called *The Banker*) which, according to Brown, is 'an expression of modern psychological tensions owing something to the experiences of the Degas family business' (ibid.: 278). Degas' own quip about the art market: 'there are successes that take the form of a panic', also shows his cognisance of the latter's extreme and irrational dimension, a feature that was particularly acute in the context in which he himself operated. Indeed elements in *A Cotton Office* suggest that Degas was subtly expressing some of these more aberrant market attributes in the painting. There is, for example, 'perspectival disjunction' which led one critic to see in the picture 'an uneasy image of his own prosaic world thrown out of joint' (ibid.: 270). Allied to this is the work's exclusion of women, its 'asymmetry', and the displacement of important signs, such as the safe and the framed art, to the picture's rightmost margin, all of which contribute to the painting's 'unsettling' effect (ibid.: 279).

Degas' *A Cotton Office* is thus an *illusion of order.* In addition, the exclusion of madness and inhumanity from the painting is itself a form of misrepresentation or *dissimulation.* Dissimulation was also a dominant feature of the other markets that we described earlier: Bruegel's use of masks and other devices, the 'creative exaggeration' of the twentieth-century dog-fair, the overcharging for pigs ('as small as hedgehogs') and the 'shouts of lies, falsehood and exclamation' recounted in the Gaelic poem. More broadly, the concept of illusion is intrinsic to acting and the theatre, which have both provided helpful interpretive perspectives on organisational life (Höpfl 1995).

Agon

The aforementioned Nietzschian view also emphasises the essentially *agonistic* character of the world in general and the market in particular. Nietzsche stressed that it is the abnormal, mad Dionysiac element that is legitimate, primary, and active. This thinker, especially in his later compositions, clearly saw the Dionysiac as primordial, implying that commercial exchange (the manifestation of the rational, Apolline tendency) must be seen as reactive and inferior. However, we prefer to see the market as a forum in which there is ongoing conflict between opposing categories, none of which should be regarded as essential or privileged. The market, for us, is a site of hybrid phenomena where categories meet, mingle and *oppose* one another. We use the term *agon* to represent this conflict. *Agon* means a struggle between two protagonists, and is etymologically close to *agora*, the Greek word for market, and to *agonistic* and *antagonism* which both indicate contest and opposition. It is also the source of the word *agony* which suggests human extremes of suffering and humiliation that are potentially the outcome of such aggression.

This strife is evident in our earlier textual and visual evidence: we may recall the disputes in Donnybrook Fair (Figure 8.2), the 'fighting, striking and commotion' in the Gaelic poem, the challenge and race in *Noínden Ulad*, the Balinese cock-fights, the violence of Jesus in the temple, and the battle between carnival and Lent in Bruegel's painting (Figure 8.1). Bruegel's piece also depicts a number of *inversions* – such as a woman taking the role of a horse – which can also be interpreted as a manifestation of conflict. Bakhtin ((1968) 1984: 109) suggests that these inversions – such as a commoner acting as a king – are best seen as attempts by the lower orders to subvert and challenge the dominant social hierarchy. Other writers have also claimed that it is precisely because carnivals and fairs were sites of (potential) revolt that they were suppressed, especially in the nineteenth century (see Ó Maitiú (1995) for a description of the State and Church suppression of Donnybrook Fair, for example). An alternative, less utopian, view is that the carnival was a location where social protest was *licensed* and thus controlled (Sales 1983). The carnival also provided the emerging bourgeoisie in the nineteenth century with a depiction of a profane Other, and encoded 'all that which the proper bourgeois must strive *not to be* in order to preserve a stable and "correct" sense of self' (Stallybrass and White 1986: 178). Hence, it was both contained and sanctioned to ensure that this 'sense of self' was maintained. Moreover, the lower social orders, while using the carnival as a forum for *their* particular form of social protest, were as likely, if not more likely, to use it ritually to re-assert their status above the most marginalised – such as women and minorities (ibid.: 19).

Nietzsche's thesis is that the reactive Apolline or ordering tendency continually attempts to deny the existence of the active Dionysiac. In the context of the market, this means that commercial exchange seeks to confirm its dominance over the essentially mad character of the market (Deleuze 1983: 40–2). Control, classification, and identification can each, then, be interpreted as reactions against the informal, self-referential, active that is innately beyond such exercises. This presents an alternative interpretation of many of the enterprises that we previously classed as deviant, such as gambling. Gambling might now be better viewed as a project or a technology in which uncertainty is rationalised and computed, a rational attempt to formalise the informal. We may thus explain why the Athenian *agora* was circumscribed by various centres of public administration erected over the course of time: the senate building (*bouletreion*), the kingly *stoa* or location of royal magistracy, and the prison in which Socrates died (Camp 1986). Similarly, our very attempt at classifying the mad could be interpreted as just another project to suppress the truly mad which is beyond understanding, beyond good and evil, beyond classification.

Recursive transformation

The textual and visual evidence we have repeatedly returned to thus far illustrates a variety in both the form of commercial exchange and in the range of extreme behaviour exhibited. Bruegel and Degas both depicted quite different markets (one in the sixteenth and one in the nineteenth century) and significantly the form of dissimulation also differed in each case. What we now require is a thesis on the dynamic process by which both the form of exchange and extreme behaviour can be understood to change over time.

A way forward is presented by the concept of *recursion.* This relates to how a change in one category folds back to change other categories in the market. There are two forms of recursion operating: *immanent* and *extrinsic. Immanent recursion* occurs solely through the cyclical and repetitive character of the market. The constant repetition of extreme or abnormal behaviour eventually blurs the distinction between the normal and the abnormal; what was previously extreme becomes merely unusual and finally normal, a phenomenon encapsulated in the Latin aphorism *communis error facit ius* (common error makes the law). Thus repetition of the extreme necessitates a redefinition of the abnormal as normal, providing the potential for new forms of madness or extreme behaviour to emerge.

Extrinsic recursion, in contrast to immanent recursion, is a dynamic change in the nature of one category caused by a change in another category, over and above simple transformation due to repetition. For example, we saw, in the early part of this century, profound alterations in the nature, location and scale of commercial exchange as capitalist markets replaced the medieval fair as the dominant locus of commerce. In this case, old, legitimised forms of madness are ostensibly marginalised as the spread of capitalist markets destroyed not only the fair but also the carnival and the particular and peculiar form of extreme behaviour of the carnivalesque. What is important, however, is that the extreme behaviour or madness was not eliminated. Instead it fragmented, transformed and migrated, re-emerging in new forms in different places. In the case of the nineteenth-century carnivalesque, its madness re-surfaced in the Surrealist art of the period and in the hysteria first documented by the psychoanalysts of the early twentieth century (Stallybrass and White 1986: 181).

This recursive dynamic may also involve a *spatial* displacement. For example, Detroit was an important engine driving the expansion of the market in the early twentieth century, but its madness was transplanted to Chicago, where deviance of all sorts, ranging from gangsterism to prostitution, was rampant, and which was, according to Rudyard Kipling, 'inhabited by savages'. This transmutation and relocation of the extreme has not, however, disguised the essentially mad character of contemporary markets, and the connection is invariably rediscovered. For example, the Pop Art movement of the 1960s was an explicit attempt to depict or represent a large-scale capitalist market, similar to Degas' project during the late nineteenth century. Critically, and in contrast to Degas, Pop Art sought to reflect the banality and inhumanity – the madness – of the growing American consumer market. In keeping with this view of the market, this art-form produced banal, repetitive and apparently meaningless images.[3]

At the same time, other social mechanisms – the civilising process referred to by Elias (1982) – also develop to counteract and control the extreme behaviour brought about by either immanent or extrinsic processes. Thus, side by side with the changes in the market and mania earlier in the present century, accounting systems developed in an attempt to restructure and circumscribe the individual (Miller and O'Leary 1987). Similarly, postmodern society is characterised not only by madness, but also by a craving for control.

Elusive harmony

In the previous section, the dynamic inter-relationship between exchange and extreme behaviour was articulated. Nevertheless, we do not seek to reduce the market to these two simple constructs, nor to imply some sort of Hegelian dialectic between them. The market, instead, consists of a heterogeneous mixture of hybrid categories, tending towards extremes, eluding any attempt to reduce it to a simple binary opposition or to a single unity.

This elusive attribute of the market does not, however, necessarily imply that it is chaotic or anarchic. Markets pulsate with a dynamic *harmony*. Here, we distinguish between the harmony of the market-place and the *homogeneity* of the crowd, as described by Canetti (1962). The market-place consists of heterogeneous elements that can vibrate and mingle, in harmony, and it is this dynamic interaction that provides the natural order of the market. Pre-modern fairs and carnivals provide good illustrations of this feature, since they were occasions when the unity of the primordial chaos was symbolically repeated and re-created. These assemblies sought to conjoin the Alpha and the Omega into a sacred unity allowing the temporary suspension of the profanity of human existence (Nowotny 1994: 103). This search for wholeness is further illustrated in the Irish word for fair, *aonach*, whose Old Irish root *oenach* is itself derived from the numeral *oen* 'one'.

The process by which unity or harmony is achieved deserves investigation because it is complex and counter-intuitive. Fundamental to the perception of unity is the process and act of separating; it is only through dividing that we can perceive the undivided whole. So the *oenach* can be seen as an attempt – through separating the finite and infinite, the ordered and chaotic, the market and madness – at re-creating a unity. The market, therefore, necessarily requires both the commingling and separation of categories to present the illusion of completeness. The unity is an illusion because it is both *lost* and *unattainable*. It is lost because it is an attempt to re-create the primordial oneness of the Alpha and the innocence of the Garden of Eden. It is unattainable because unity necessarily implies its duplication – one implies, indeed requires, two.[4]

Tragedy

Our re-examination of the market has emphasised its antagonistic, dynamic, extreme and illusory nature. The confluence of each of these traits in the market also means that the latter may become a locus of *tragedy*. Most especially, *tragedy* may be born out of the conjuncture of fundamental opposing impulses, such as the Dionysiac and the Apolline. For example, our ninth-century saga indicates that the pre-Christian *oenach* was a site where the public and private domains, which were normally kept separate, were confused. This resulted in both the death of Macha and social turmoil in the society in question. In the biblical text, Jesus is the central tragic figure and again we find that the market is at the epicentre of his apocalyptic moment. Here, the tragedy is sparked by the confusion of the sacred and the profane in the temple. What is of interest is that this commingling creates tension, extreme behaviour, leading potentially to tragic schism.

Tragedies in the theatre provide an illuminating contrast to the tragedy inherent in the market-place. Tragedy, more than any other form of drama or representation, focuses on the very limits of the human condition, of extremes in suffering, elation, failure, agony and death. It is the site where the physical and the metaphysical meet – the early Greek tragedies were performed in honour of the god Dionysus – and where weird and *hybrid* characters and phenomena occur – such as horses turning cannibal in *Macbeth*. In this sense tragedies are *eschatological* since they, like the markets we have described, are the site in which limits, extremes and margins are potently articulated. This cosmic and eschatological dimension was developed to the full by Shakespeare in a set of masterful plays. These, like the market, are founded centrally on *illusion*. His tragedies centre on a powerful hero such as Lear or Macbeth, but this power is illusory because it masks a fatal flaw that eventually leads to failure and disaster. Similarly, human frailty is suggested in Bruegel's depiction of human characters at a small scale relative to the overwhelming expanse of the market-place they inhabit.

Tragedy is as likely to occur today in matters concerning the market as demonstrably happened during times past. The current transformation of East-European societies from command to exchange-driven economies may be taken as a case in point. The market is either offered to, or perceived by, former communist states as a secular panacea for societal well-being. The model at issue is that of an orderly exchange whose rationality promises liberation from centralising tyranny. However, extremes likely to be found in the contemporary western market may not be revealed by its exponents or sufficiently appreciated by its recipients. A classic gap between perception and reality common to all tragic experience is thus in danger of emerging. This also provides the necessary ingredients for new forms of deranged behaviour to emerge, bewildering, as a result, whole nations. The latter is not a normative judgement on either western or eastern economic systems. Rather, it shows how thinking about the market opens up another window on the polarities of human existence. Tragedy, by expressing our limitations and the perceived extremes of humanity, is ultimately revealing and potentially redeeming. As Kermode has noted in his insightful distinction between myths and fictions, tragedy is 'a fiction that inescapably involves an encounter with oneself, and the image of one's end' (1967: 39).

THE END IN THE PRESENT

The market's tragic dimension may possibly explain the deliberate *separation* of the festive (the mad) from the commercial in modern capitalist markets. This endeavour was especially worked on by the bourgeoisie of the nineteenth century who 'laboured *conceptually* to re-form the fair as *either* a rational, commercial, trading event or as a popular pleasure-ground' (Stallybrass and White 1986: 30, emphasis in original). Our study proposes, however, that such efforts at containing and suppressing the mad are futile, illusory and themselves doomed to fail. This belief is reinforced when we consider that madness is possibly *the* defining attribute of modernity in so far as the notion of progress necessarily celebrates deviance from past norms. Many factors suggest that madness is a dominant feature of contemporary markets, whether it be the craziness of Las Vegas or the dissimulation at the root of the Barings Bank collapse. Indeed, writers on management and marketing have regularly emphasised the importance of deviant, ludicrous behaviour, for instance March and Olsen (1979) on the technology of foolishness, Peters (1989, 1994) on chaos and crazy organisations, Pascale (1991) on conflict and 'managing on the edge', or the current infatuation with disorganisation, chaos, catastrophe, and 'virtual' reality. Further back in time we find similar themes in old aphorisms such as Shaw's 'all progress depends on the unreasonable man', Kierkegaard's 'the instant of decision is madness', or Nietzsche's 'to renounce false judgement would be to renounce life'. Even more intriguing is the fact that the *market* has become a central feature of modernity. Indeed, modern intellectual history pivots around fundamental re-conceptualisations of the market: from Adam Smith's theory of the invisible hand, to Marx's profound insights into capitalist markets, to Baudrillard's writings on postmodern society, engulfed and consumed by the market.

*Post*modernity is at once besotted by late capitalist markets and the extreme (Brown 1995; Featherstone 1988; Jameson 1991; Lyotard 1986; Poster 1988). Nietzsche's impact on the post-structuralists is particularly noteworthy, all of whom have embraced meaninglessness, the unreasonable, the ludic, the libidinal, and the mad. Thus, Derrida's concept of *différance* carries with it the notion of deferred, different and absent meanings, implying a celebration of deviance, meaninglessness and madness. Nietzsche's notion of the Dionysiac resonates through Cooper and Burrell's comment that *différance* 'is more than a theoretical concept', it is 'a kind of prime energizer' (Cooper and Burrell 1988: 99). The post-structuralists' style of writing is further evidence of their infection. It is usually and deliberately at or beyond the limits of comprehension: deranged. More positively, the postmoderns, in centralising madness, can be seen as attempting to *re-suture* the artificial conceptual divisions that we have inherited from modernity (Latour 1993), and especially the illusory exclusion of madness from the market. Therefore, we can welcome much of the playful and nonsensical discourse of postmodernism, seeing it as part of a project of *re*-construction rather than of *de*-construction.

CONCLUSION

In this chapter, we have sought to examine and understand the peculiar interrelationship between commercial exchange and human extremes. Our study and methodology are founded on the opinion that the marketing academic can and should study markets, in their widest sense, unencumbered by normative or managerial agenda. We recognise that our effort at conceptualising the market may be doubly flawed: like the theories it draws on, it is partial and provisional, and the interpretation of 'primitive economies' is unavoidably prejudiced and ethnocentric. There is also the further danger that our montage of ninth- and eighteenth-century Gaelic assemblies, medieval markets and the economy of the United States will be viewed as legitimating superficial comparison. Nonetheless, we believe that there are major opportunities for future research along these lines. We look forward, for instance, to a much more rounded study of representations and depictions of markets in the historical record. Others might decide to focus on particular aspects of the range of extreme behaviour that pervade the exchange, such as the by now familiar catalogue of prostitution, wagering, dissimulation, inversions, noise, music, or drinking. Each of these is a substantial field of study in its own right, but marketing has largely ignored them as a collective: there is an absence of synthetic investigation describing the interweaving of these extremes in the market. It is appropriate and opportune that we examine such conditions, since societies tend to locate powerful symbolic repertoires at borders, margins and edges, as well as at accepted cores of the social body. In truth, therefore, our study of the End in the market is only a beginning.

ACKNOWLEDGEMENTS

Thanks to Luis Araujo, Joan Buckley, Bob Cooper, William Gallagher, Eileen Kavanagh, Diarmuid Kavanagh, Majella O'Leary, Don O'Sullivan, Brian Patterson, Terry O'Reilly, Colin Rynne, John Sheehan and particularly Sebastian Green for his constructive and supportive comments.

NOTES

1 In contrast to both these positions, Baudrillard (Poster 1988) has suggested that in a postmodern world of hyper-exchange there is nothing left to be alienated from, and so the concept of alienation disappears through redundancy. Paradoxically, hyper-exchange destroys alienation.

2 Interestingly, the 'postmodern' questioning of modernity and the simultaneous study of modernity's artefacts has created a new interest in hybrids, cyborgs and the in-human (Callon and Law 1995; Haraway 1991; Kavanagh and Araujo 1995; Latour 1993).

3 The Pop Art movement, and Andy Warhol's work in particular, also highlights some of the other features of the market that we have already addressed. For example, Warhol's paintings of soup cans conflated the divisions of high and low art, and, by mass-producing his own work, he also subverted the a priori categories of art and commerce. Thus, his work was a form of *hybrid*. Furthermore, like Degas, he was acutely aware of his own output as both a representation *of* a market and a commodity *in* a market. This double perspective provided more opportunities for inversions: for example, he delighted in subverting the law of supply and demand by re-issuing 'limited' editions of his work. According to the law of the market this increase in supply should decrease the price of his work. However, this act of dissimulation only added to his notoriety, *increasing* both the demand for and the price of his products.

4 The vision of the market we have presented here echoes some of the ideas of Deleuze and Guattari and their notion of the 'desiring machine' which is also 'irreducible to any form of unity' (Deleuze and Guattari 1983: 42). Recently, Jordan (1995) has used their concept of 'desiring machines' to present an interpretation of rave dances, which many see as a form of madness, as a 'collective body'.

REFERENCES

Bailey, J. and Van der Broek, L.D. (1992), *Literary Forms in the New Testament*, SPCK, London.

Bakhtin, M. ((1968) 1984), *Rabelais and his World*, Indiana University Press, Bloomington.

Barrell, J. (1980), *The Dark Side of the Landscape: The Rural Poor in English Painting*, Cambridge University Press, Cambridge.

Baudrillard, J. (1988), *In the Shadow of the Silent Majorities*, Semiotexte, New York.

Bauman, R. (1986), *Story, Performance and Event*, Cambridge University Press, Cambridge.

Belk, R.W., Wallendorf, M. *et al.* (1989), 'The Sacred and the Profane in Consumer Behaviour: Theodicy on the Odyssey', *Journal of Consumer Behaviour*, vol. 16 (June), pp. 1–37.

Bohannan, P. and Dalton, G. (eds) (1962), *Markets in Africa*, Northwestern University Press, Evanston.

Brown, M.R. (1993a), 'An Entrepreneur in Spite of Himself: Edgar Degas and the Market', in T.L. Haskell and R.F. Teichgreber (eds), *The Culture of the Market*, Cambridge University Press, Cambridge, pp. 261–92.

Brown, S. (1993b), 'Postmodernism . . . The End of Marketing?', in D. Brownlie *et al.* (eds), *Rethinking Marketing*, Warwick Business School Research Bureau, Coventry, pp. 1–12.

Brown, S. (1995), *Postmodern Marketing*, Routledge, London.

Brownlie, D. and Saren, M. (1992), 'The Four Ps of the Marketing Concept: Prescriptive, Polemical, Permanent and Problematical', *European Journal of Marketing*, vol. 26(4), pp. 34–47.

Brownlie, D. and Saren, M. (1995), 'On the Commodification of Marketing Knowledge: Opening Themes', *Journal of Marketing Management*, vol. 11, no. 7, pp. 619–27.

Buttimer, C.G. (1992), 'Tuairisc Amhailt Uí Iartáin: an Eighteenth-Century Poem on a Fair', *Eighteenth-Century Ireland*, vol. 7, pp. 75–94.

Buttimer, C.G. (1994–5), 'Longes mac nUislenn reconsidered', *Éigse: A Journal of Irish Studies*, vol. 28, pp. 1–41.

Buttimer, C.G. (1995), 'Noínden Ulad: Private and Public', unpublished paper presented at *Tionól* Conference, School of Celtic Studies, Dublin Institute for Advance Studies, 25 November.

Buttimer, C.G. and Kavanagh, D. (1995), 'Markets and Madness', in S. Brown *et al.* (eds), *Proceedings of the Marketing Eschatology Retreat*, University of Ulster, Belfast, pp. 60–71.

Callon, M. and Law, J. (1995), 'Agency and the Hybrid Collectif', *South Atlantic Quarterly*, vol. 94(2), pp. 481–507.

Camp, J.M. (1986), *The Athenian Agora: Excavations in the Heart of Classical Greece*, Thames and Hudson, London.

Canetti, E. (1962), *Crowds and Power*, Gollancz, London.

Cooper, R. (1992), 'Formal Organization as Representation: Remote Control, Displacement and Abbreviation', in M. Reed and M. Hughes (eds), *Rethinking Organization*, Sage, London, pp. 254–72.

Cooper, R. and Burrell, G. (1988), 'Modernism, Postmodernism and Organisational Analysis: An Introduction', *Organisation Studies*, vol. 9(1), pp. 91–112.

Dalton, G. (1968), 'Introduction', in G. Dalton (ed.), *Primitive, Archaic, and Modern Economies: Essays of Karl Polanyi*, Beacon Press, Boston, pp. ix–liv.

Deleuze, G. (1983), *Nietzsche and Philosophy*, University of Minnesota Press, Minneapolis.

Deleuze, G. and Guattari, F. (1983), *Anti-Oedipus: Capitalism and Schizophrenia*, University of Minnesota Press, Minneapolis.

Douglas, M. (1966), *Purity and Danger: An Analysis of the Concepts of Pollution and Taboo*, Routledge, New York.

Durkheim, É. ((1897) 1970), *Suicide*, Routledge & Kegan Paul, London.

Elias, N. (1982), *The Civilizing Process: State Formation and Civilization*, Basil Blackwell, Oxford.

Featherstone, M. (ed.) (1988), *Postmodernism*, Sage, London.

Finley, M.I. (1982), *Economy and Society in Ancient Greece*, Viking Press, New York.

Foucault, M. (1967), *Madness and Civilization*, Routledge, Cambridge.

Fromm, E. (1956), *The Sane Society*, Routledge & Kegan Paul, London.

Fukuyama, F. (1989), 'The End of History?', *The National Interest*, vol. 16 (Summer), pp. 3–19.

Fullerton, R.A. (1987), 'The Poverty of Ahistorical Analysis: Present Weakness and Future Cure in U.S. Marketing Thought', in A.F. Firat *et al.* (eds), *Philosophical and Radical Thought in Marketing*, Lexington Books, Massachusetts, pp. 97–116.

Geertz, C. (1971), 'Deep Play: Notes on the Balinese Cockfight', in C. Geertz (ed.), *Myth, Symbol and Culture*, W.W. Norton & Company, New York, pp. 1–37.

Granovetter, M. (1985), 'Economic Action and Social Structure: The Problems of Embeddedness', *American Journal of Sociology*, vol. 91(3), pp. 481–510.

Habermas, J. (1987), *The Philosophical Discourse of Modernity*, Polity Press, Cambridge.

Haraway, D.J. (1991), *Simians, Cyborgs and Women: The Reinvention of Nature*, Free Association Books, London.

Heidegger, M. (1978), *Basic Writings from Being and Time (1927) to the Task of Thinking*, Routledge and Kegan Paul, London.

Höpfl, H. (1995), 'Performance and Customer Service: The Cultivation of Contempt', *Studies in Culture, Organizations and Societies*, vol. 1(1), pp. 47–62.

Huizinga, J. (1955), *Homo Ludens: a Study of the Play Element in Culture*, The Beacon Press, Boston.

Hull, V. (1968), 'Noínden Ulad: the Debility of the Ulidians', *Celtica*, vol. 8, pp. 1–42.

Jameson, F. (1991), *Postmodernism, or, the Cultural Logic of Late Capitalism*, Verso, London.

Jordan, T. (1995), 'Collective Bodies: Raving and the Politics of Gilles Deleuze and Felix Guattari', *Body and Society*, vol. 1(1), pp. 125–44.

Kavanagh, D. (1994), 'Hunt v Anderson: Round 16', *European Journal of Marketing*, vol. 28(3), pp. 26–41.

Kavanagh, D. and Araujo, L. (1995), 'Chronigami: Folding and Unfolding Time', *Accounting, Management and Information Technologies*, vol. 5(2), pp. 103–21.

Kelly, F. (1988), *A Guide to Early Irish Law*, Dublin Institute for Advanced Studies, Dublin.

Kermode, F. (1967), *The Sense of an Ending: Studies in the Theory of Fiction*, Oxford U.P., Oxford.

Lash, S. and Urry, J. (1987), *The End of Organized Capitalism*, Polity, Cambridge.

Latour, B. (1993), *We Have Never Been Modern*, Harvester Wheatsheaf, New York.

Lévi-Strauss, C. ((1962) 1966), *The Savage Mind*, University of Chicago Press, Chicago.

Lyotard, J.-F. (1986), *The Postmodern Condition: a Report on Knowledge*, University of Manchester, Manchester.

March, J.G. and Olsen, J.P. (eds) (1979), *Ambiguity and Choice in Organizations*, Universitetsforlaget, Bergen.

Marx, K. ((1867) 1954), *Capital: A Critical Analysis of Capitalist Production: Volume 1*, Foreign Languages Publishing House, Moscow.

Meadows, D.H., Meadows, D.L. *et al.* (1972), *The Limits to Growth*, Universe Books, New York.

Merton, R.K. (1938), 'Social Structure and Anomie', *American Sociological Review*, vol. 3, pp. 672–82.

Miller, P. and O'Leary, T. (1987), 'Accounting and the Construction of the Governable Person', *Accounting, Organizations and Society*, vol. 12(3), pp. 235–66.

Nietzsche, F. ((1872) 1993), *The Birth of Tragedy*, Penguin Books, London.

Nowotny, H. (1994), *Time: The Modern and Postmodern Experience*, Polity Press, Oxford.

Ó Maitiú, S. (1995), *The Humours of Donnybrook: Dublin's Famous Fair and its Suppression*, Irish Academic Press, Dublin.

Otis, L.L. (1985), *Prostitution in Medieval Society: the History of an Urban Institution in Languedoc*, The University of Chicago Press, Chicago.

Owen, R. ((1815) 1927), *A New View of Society and Other Writings*, Everyman, New York.

Pascale, R.T. (1991), *Managing on the Edge: How Successful Companies use Conflict to Stay Ahead*, Penguin, London.

Peters, T. (1989), *Thriving on Chaos*, Pan Books Ltd., London.

Peters, T. (1994), *The Tom Peters Seminar: Crazy Times Call for Crazy Organizations*, Macmillan, London.

Polanyi, K. (1944), *The Great Transformation*, Rinehart, New York.

Polanyi, K., Arensberg, C.M. *et al.* (eds) (1957), *Trade and Market in the Early Empires: Economies in History and Theory*, Free Press, Glencoe.

Poster, M. (ed.) (1988), *Jean Baudrillard: Selected Writings*, Polity Press, Cambridge.

Powell, M.A. (1990), *What is Narrative Criticism? A New Approach to the Bible*, SPCK, London.

Rifkin, J. (1995), *The End of Work: the Decline of the Global Labor Force and the Dawn of the Post-Market Era*, Jeremy P. Tarcher, New York.

Rudé, G. ((1964) 1995), *The Crowd in History*, Serif, London.

Sales, R. (1983), *English Literature in History 1780–1830: Pastoral and Politics*, Hutchinson, London.

Sass, L.A. (1992), *Madness and Modernism*, Harvard University Press, Cambridge, MA.

Stallybrass, P. and White, A. (1986), *The Politics and Poetics of Transgression*, Methuen, London.
Steiner, G. (1984), *Antigones: The Antigone Myth in Western Literature, Art and Thought*, Clarendon Press, Oxford.
Suchaux, G. and Pastoureau, M. (1994), *The Bible and the Saints*, Flammarion, New York.
Sumner, C. (1994), *The Sociology of Deviance*, Open University Press, Buckingham.
Thurneysen, R. (1921), *Die irische Helden – und Königsage bis zum siebzehnten Jahrhundert*, Max Niemeyer, Halle.
Touraine, A. (1974), *The Post-Industrial Society*, Wildwood Press, New York.
Waits, W.B. (1978), *The Many-Faced Custom: Christmas Gift-Giving in America, 1900–1940*, unpublished dissertation, History Department, Rutgers University, New Brunswick, NJ.

9

THE FALL AND RISE OF MARKETING FUNDAMENTALISM

The case of the 'Nature & Découvertes' distribution concept

Patrick Hetzel

INTRODUCTION

In a previous study (Hetzel 1993), we demonstrated just how useful the concept of postmodernity could be in analysing recent developments in distribution concepts within a sector such as, for example, the distribution of women's lingerie products in France. Indeed, it is clear that, in our 'display society', value systems are undergoing radical change. Hence, stores have gradually progressed from emphasising the product offering to displaying the offering as a whole. In the space of only a few years we have gone from the store as a setting for staging the object to the point of sale as the object of the setting. As a result the work of the distributor has become continually more complex since nowadays he must not only stage the products but also beforehand reflect on how best to stage the setting itself through its architecture, spatial layout, etc.

In a more recent study (Hetzel 1995), we also showed that it was becoming necessary, more and more, to review research methods in order to understand the behaviour of consumers at the point of sale, for two reasons. The first is that to an increasing degree consumers are in search of emotions, of new experiences as has been demonstrated for just over ten years now by authors such as Hirschman and Holbrook. The second is that distributors, who for a long time worked on the visual dimension of the offering, are taking the other organoleptic dimensions more and more into account: the senses of hearing, smell, touch and taste.

It is worth noting, in fact, that in so doing they are merely renewing the ties with a more traditional mode of marketing products: namely the souk markets, where all the senses are stimulated. There is however one major difference: indeed, the souk is not the result of a previously thought-out and defined marketing approach; instead, it draws its roots from an entire history and culture, while our contemporary distribution concepts drawn up by marketing people are created from scratch, virtually from nothing. Today, certain distributors in the West are drawing up highly sophisticated distribution concepts and even go as far as to work systematically on the five senses. This is the case of the brand Ralph Lauren in France but also that of a retail name such as 'Nature & Découvertes', which in fact looks very much like the American firm name of 'Nature Company'. This firm markets a wide array of products more or less closely connected with nature: rucksacks for hikers, geographical maps, decorative objects, etc.

What we shall be trying to do here is unravel the concept of 'Nature & Découvertes', show how it works and explain why it is highly characteristic of the postmodernist era since it has within it a philosophical dimension, to which in fact it probably owes its success. To sell today, then, may well be more than to exchange goods; it can be to display particular values, not to say resolve philosophical issues. All this will enable us to demonstrate that marketing is an increasingly present factor in companies and on the market, contrary, for example, to what Tedlow and Jones (1993) had to say when they spoke of the rise and fall of mass marketing (it will be noted that the title of the present chapter is the very opposite of theirs). Thus in our opinion, marketing is not about to meet its Apocalypse; rather marketing techniques are tending to become more and more sophisticated. And if today marketing practices are less readily seen in certain consumer sectors, it is precisely because they are increasingly sophisticated. To the eschatological utterances of some people, we would hasten to reply that marketing, far from disappearing, is currently undergoing a transformation. It is always in the process of adapting very subtly to the post-modern environment (Hetzel 1994). Even if certain ideas become outmoded and gradually replaced by newer concepts, that does not mean the end of marketing; like the phoenix (a creature very dear to the hearts of the alchemists), marketing always rises rejuvenated from its ashes. Others reject it since it reflects the very nature of our society. Because marketing is not simply a discipline whereby needs are satisfied, but, more important, a systematic procedure of reflection on the creation and production of what is on offer. Hence we shall be successively examining the three aspects displayed in Figure 9.1.

METHODOLOGICAL AND EPISTEMOLOGICAL FOREWORD

This research is based on data acquisition at several levels:

- interviews with the directors of 'Nature & Découvertes'
- literature and other information put out by the company: catalogues, videocassettes, etc.
- visits to and analyses of a number of points of sale, notably in Lyon and Paris
- interviews with regular 'Nature & Découvertes' clients

The status of this research is very specific. In the following pages, we shall only

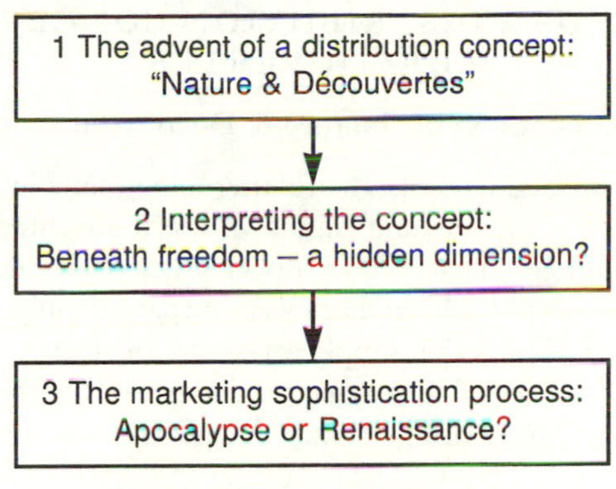

Figure 9.1 Nature & Découvertes
Source: Musée Municipale de Pau

be taking the case of 'Nature & Découvertes' to point to a number of recent developments in respect of distribution marketing, and more especially to put into perspective the marketing sophistication process in our postmodern society. Thus we do not claim to have made an exhaustive analysis of a distribution concept, nor to maintain that what can be observed in the specific case of 'Nature & Découvertes' can necessarily be applied to the distribution sector as a whole. The only purpose of taking this particular company is to illustrate and sustain our point of view. We are aware that an approach of this nature poses problems in respect of the researcher *vis-à-vis* his subject and his field of investigation; some would contest the idea of basing theoretical and scientific postulates on a single case. Needless to say, that is not an opinion we share; rather we feel that a case of this sort can stimulate the researcher to further reflection.

We are persuaded that the time has gone when market researchers could build awkward quantitative and statistical methodologies creating the illusion of total knowledge. As Laufer and Paradeise (1982) have very rightly shown in the early pages of their book: 'From now on, we'll say not that things are as they are, but that they are very similar to what they seem to be.' Today's market researcher no longer comes up with the right solution, no longer has an ontological insight, but is rather someone who acts as an aid to understanding, even composition of the senses, organising thoughts in order to help people see managerial and consumer society problems from a fresh point of view. That is what we hope to achieve here.

THE ADVENT OF A DISTRIBUTION CONCEPT: 'NATURE & DÉCOUVERTES'

The consumer context of 'Nature & Découvertes': 'green fever'

'Ecology, having emerged from its ghetto after a long time in the wilderness, is taking hold of people's hearts and minds all the more intensely since it had previously been ignored.' That is how Roger Cans (1992) describes this new 'green fever', whose rapid advent has been surpassed only by its expansion since the early 1990s. But is this simply a fashion, or does it reflect something deeper? French sociologists fail to agree on this point, but they are unanimous in saying that they have observed real changes in consumer attitudes and behaviour.

French ecological awareness has never been so high. The consumer study carried out in 1993 by Crédoc (a Parisian survey organisation) showed that from being an acute, but marginal, preoccupation, ecological awareness has become a preoccupation in France for the majority of consumers: 82 per cent of the population say that environmental problems are a concern, and 62 per cent that they are a major preoccupation. Thus from the early 1990s, virtually everyone in France has been alive to ecological questions.

For Félix Guattari (1989), the role of ecology is to reinvent new ways of living and new social habits. Ecology will, he says, be initially intellectual and social and then lead to changes in new family and social relationships, together with deep respect for life itself. This will ultimately affect the whole planet, with this new awareness producing a new ethic, a philosophy of mutual respect and solidarity between individuals, consisting of multiple relationships between them and their natural environment. Joël de Rosnay (1991) seems similarly convinced: 'Ecology is an integrating concept, a global way of thinking.' He says that 'ego-man', the completely inward-looking individual, selfish and wrapped up in his own concerns, must become 'eco-man', a true citizen of the world.

All this tells us to what a great extent this set of ecological themes made itself felt in the early 1990s in France; and it is precisely the same set of environmental and ecological themes that the founders of 'Nature & Découvertes' will be turning to advantage when they introduce their new store concept.

Target clientèle

As has been observed in the USA since the 1980s, a sociological movement that advocates a more balanced life-style, based mainly on respect for nature, has been making itself felt in France since the early 1990s. What people are reluctant to see as a return to traditional values is orienting consumer behaviour towards a 'new conservatism', which can be summed up in four points:

- From impulse buying to thoughtful buying: after the excesses of the 1980s as well as the recession, which people have not forgotten, the French are seeking a more balanced life-style and less indebtedness. So they are abandoning expensive and conspicuously displayed products (basically luxury products).
- Authenticity and quality: even in town, priority is being given to a return to nature, natural values, quality and the protection of the environment. Nature is again becoming the affirmation and the symbol of a more personal way of life. The product needs to be long-lasting, uncomplicated and user-friendly.
- A need for service and comfort: people who are mainly concerned with their income and their basically fairly useless activities are being replaced by thinking people who are more interested in making the best use of their time and looking after their health. We can see a genuine concern with the quality of life.
- Higher moral standards: there is an evident return to traditional and more edifying values. More attention is being paid to the family environment. Attitudes are changing from individualism to a rediscovery of both the human and the physical environment.

From the 1990s, then, social changes go beyond a purely ecological movement. Nature is doubtless at the root of these societal trends, but they take on a larger dimension with the restoration of fundamental values such as the meaning and the quality of life, tradition and authenticity. Thus the question that distributors need to ask themselves is how to introduce an offering that comes up to the expectations of these 'eco-citizens'. And that is exactly what 'Nature & Découvertes' is seeking to achieve by proposing a new distribution concept.

The 'Nature & Découvertes' project

'Nature & Découvertes' seeks to be regarded as the expression of 'real values rediscovered'. Its purpose is to help people better understand nature and so have respect for nature. Thus the store concept is not simply based on an environmental trend, but also the wish to make discovery of nature a 'daily habit'. This is set out very clearly in the 'Nature & Découvertes' corporate charter (Nature & Découvertes 1995):

> Nature & Découvertes exists in order to offer a wider public of all ages quality products designed to encourage the public to see, understand, share and enjoy the natural world in a positive educational spirit.
>
> We wish our stores to be places of wonder, harmony and a welcoming atmosphere, and in which our guides will enable you to share their enthusiasm for nature and the natural sciences.
>
> When you share our own wonder at the beauty and variety that our planet has to offer, we think that together, and day by day, we can better protect this oasis we call the Earth.

It is especially interesting to note that in the charter all three paragraphs refer to three complementary dimensions:

Paragraph 1: Corporate objective
Paragraph 2: The commitment to the consumer
Paragraph 3: How this commitment is to be fulfilled

It may be a short text, but there is a logical chain of ideas which clearly shows that the aim of the company is to reawaken the sense of wonder, of aesthetics and social interaction that is latent in everyone. 'Nature & Découvertes' owes its existence to an ideal. It is aimed at all age-groups, both children (tomorrow's consumers) and adults, so that all can enjoy the harmony nature offers. And to share this ideal, the stores (to quote one of the directors), 'should be as close to and as magic as nature itself'. This is why the layout and the fountains are the very embodiment of nature. The lighting, too, which is as close as possible to natural light, creates the illusion of a forest clearing. Not difficult to understand that the 'Nature & Découvertes' concept corresponds very exactly to the environmental thematic described above. Let us now look at this concept in more detail.

The 'Nature & Découvertes' distribution concept

'Nature & Découvertes', created to meet the 'back to our sources' societal urge, is a chain of medium-sized stores which specialise in science and nature and offer a wide range of products derived from nature (earth, sea, space) and associated phenomena. The aim of 'Nature & Découvertes' is to create some sort of escape from the modern world and the stress it causes by helping the consumer to discover, better understand and come close to nature and the universe. The range offered falls within the following subjects: astronomy, mineralogy, geography, oceanography, nature-watching, botany, and related subjects, together with the appropriate gifts and decorative objects. The target clientèle is mainly urban. Nature is reflected in objects and products that it alone has inspired. So it is not just a 'good idea'; it is a state of mind, a way of life, a new way of looking at things and of understanding the image of nature that 'Nature & Découvertes' seeks to present to the consumer. In the stores, the client can see, hear, feel and enjoy nature close at hand, a nature that city-dwellers have on their doorstep but which they never get to see. The purpose of 'Nature & Découvertes' is to open doors to emotions, a sense of wonder and a feeling of pleasure.

Reformulating the 'Nature & Découvertes' concept at the point of sale

The offer only exists through the stores and the display designed to highlight the offer. The contextual design provides information on how the company sees the interaction between the client and its system of offering. Thus the spatial layout and the point of sale in general help to place 'Nature & Découvertes' within the thoughts and the cognitive structures of the consumer. They are the expression of the information that is going to be interpreted by the consumer, and are an integral part of the offering system. The contextual design may therefore be regarded as the visible dimension, the concrete part of the value system and ideology of 'Nature & Découvertes'. If we look for the major thematics in play in the 'Nature & Découvertes' contextual design, there are five: abundance, magic, the awakening, authenticity and simplicity. For each of these, let us point to a number of elements that are found at the point of sale.

Abundance

- a very wide product range (2500 products)
- a large number of products within the store itself
- widely differing furniture
- several 'special areas' in the store that clients discover as they gradually progress towards the back of the store; this creates a strong feeling of infinite space.

Magic

- Indirect diffused lighting which creates the visual atmosphere of a forest clearing
- Lighting centred on products, giving the impression of the sun's rays penetrating a forest
- Natural fragrance given off by the wood and the plants, and artificial perfumes which are diffused to recreate all the scents of the undergrowth
- Above, mobiles and other objects designed to take the client back to childhood: these objects are out of reach, just as they were for the client when he/she was a child
- A peaceful and friendly nature that 'Nature & Découvertes' recreates in its stores, with a fountain, a celestial dome, a glass roof and fresh flowers: a place where people can let themselves dream.

The awakening

- An appeal to all five senses; the client is awakened by an environment in which scents, sounds, taste, sight and touch (all the products can be handled) all play a part
- Assistants dressed as mountain guides are on hand to inform the clients, to advise them, to give details of one or another product
- Products carrying information (both technical and cultural), to 'educate' clients and arouse their interest.

Authenticity

- A décor consisting of natural materials: wood, leather, plants, fresh flowers
- A place where the clients enjoy complete freedom: they can touch whatever they want, take their time, sit down for a while, relax
- Clients are offered an 'infusion', just as though they were guests at 'Nature & Découvertes'
- Information is made available on associations for the protection of nature, environmental protection, rambles and so on.

Simplicity

- A number of products are displayed 'jumbled'
- Sober natural materials are used for the furniture, the décor and very often the products themselves
- The lighting is discreet and unobtrusive.

Evidently, whilst all these themes could be considered individually, it must be borne in mind that collectively they make up a significant system: meaning lies in difference. Thus all these themes are the reflection of a wider ideology, the opposition of nature to culture. Thus the 'Nature & Découvertes' concept is not tied to the ecological sphere of influence but reflects something very much deeper. This is what we shall be examining in the second part of this chapter.

INTERPRETATION OF THE CONCEPT: A HIDDEN DIMENSION BENEATH THE FREEDOM?

'Nature & Découvertes', or a systematic appeal to the five senses

An appeal to all five senses is made to the client coming into 'Nature & Découvertes'. As in all stores, the eyes are immediately and highly stimulated. But what makes 'Nature & Découvertes' different is that there is more to it than that: all the other organoleptic canals are equally stimulated. The background music lets the client discover bird songs, the sounds of the forest, of nature itself. He or she can also listen to the sound made by some articles on sale by playing with them: bells, bird-calls and so on. Being able to handle all the products encourages the clients to familiarise themselves with new shapes, new materials, thus to have physical contact with the products. An appeal is also made to the clients' sense of taste as they are offered a herbal tea. And finally, the natural scents given off by the wood and the plants and the artificial scents diffused recreate all the delicious atmosphere of the undergrowth, to appeal to the client's sense of smell.

No mistake should be made beneath the appearance of unlimited freedom and a feeling of 'nature rediscovered': the environment is purely and simply contrived, and reflects a somewhat deliberately created design: one only has to imagine a company that has created nature in an urban context, that amounts to seeing itself as the 'grand architect of a small world'. To bring that back to reality, to make real what in fact appears unreal, it is essential to act upon all five senses so as to create the right impression on the client. It will be readily understood that the client will not just have seen, but also heard, touched, tasted and felt a number of things. And in a very real sense. There we have the first important factor, as developed by a philosopher like Virilio (1984): the real and the unreal can coexist in our postmodern civilisation. For nothing is more real than the experience the client can have in a 'Nature & Découvertes' shop. That said, the total environment is man-made, ultimately artificial, in short a sort of 'hyper-reality'. Compared with many other points of sale, there is at 'Nature & Découvertes' an 'overdetermined' motivation to create sensory effects, to the utmost extent possible, on all the senses simultaneously. Additionally, we might add that in this sort of situation the appeal is not so much to the clients' minds as to their perceptions: to their emotions; the appeal is not to their objective but rather to their subjective reactions.

'Nature & Découvertes': from order to chaos?

The concept is developed to the point where the staff are even shown how to achieve a methodical, ordered way of displaying a 'jumble' of products in order to give clients the impression that they have been laid out without much organisation. To us, that is the height of postmodernity: 'turn order into chaos', whilst the pre-modern concept was the opposite, whereby the idea was to create order from chaos, at least where the distributors were concerned. In short, the Latin dictum 'Order from Chaos' has turned into 'Chaos from Order'. There again, it can be seen that it is interesting when a company adopts marketing techniques completely in tune with the social demand: if consumers want to have the impression of freedom at the point of sale, there is no problem, a layout is methodically arranged so as to give the impression of 'non-organisation'. Thus 'Nature & Découvertes' can create 'organised chaos' (a concept the Club Méditerranée, for example, has been well aware of for several decades!).

'Nature & Découvertes': back to Rousseau or 'new-age' concept?

The foregoing interplay between order and disorder may appear of minor interest, but the whole purpose is to offer the consumer a new system of values beneath the surface of the distribution concept: the means of reconciling two supposedly opposite concepts, nature and culture. Like Rousseau's *Emile*, in which the author advocates an upbringing in direct contact with nature and growing up on the simple basis of one's own experiences, 'Nature & Découvertes' offers an experience whereby the individual becomes at one with nature – recreated by the company for the purpose in hand. In short, nothing is too good for the consumer since we can recreate on his doorstep a natural 'micro-universe' in which he can rediscover his roots.

All this means that at 'Nature & Découvertes' nature forms the subject of culture; and culture is a way of rediscovering nature. This is quite astute, as the image is obviously aimed at the urban population, eternally torn between nature and culture. The name, like most modern names, is a part of the times we live in, but at the same time it seeks to appeal to people's roots, their values, human nature and even basic philosophy. What the company has to say is of interest, because beneath the appearance of freedom, 'Nature & Découvertes' is offering a holistic vision which today is 'in the air', so that people (town-dwellers) who have never really lost touch with nature can in fact find nature again. Further, the idea is emphasised in much of the company's literature and catalogues, which quote the words of an Indian chief:

> We have not inherited the earth from our ancestors, we're simply borrowing it from our children. [The company's message in this respect is very evocative, with messages such as] 'Let's get back to simple enjoyments'; 'People need to re-experience childhood wonder'; The consumer needs to be encouraged to live in harmony with his world . . .

Some people in France feel that 'Nature & Découvertes' is a 'new-age' company. We feel that the situation is not as simple as that, as the company was happy to ride on the crest of a 'new-age' wave. The fact is that the founders' purpose was to create a profitable company, needless to say, and they realised very quickly that the 'green fever' was a major societal trend and could represent a market. They have, via the distribution concept, restored to a number of people who had become somewhat sceptical a taste for natural objects. 'Nature & Découvertes' realised long before many others the phenomenon described for example by Luc Ferry (1992): that there is not necessarily any juxtaposition between society's ecological concepts and political movements insisting on an ecological label; and that therefore the market for 'ecological' or so-called natural products was very probably more important quantitatively than the number of 'green' electors. The evidence would suggest that this sort of approach might be seen as 'societal' marketing (Gobbi *et al.* 1990).

'Nature & Découvertes': an animistic concept?

At 'Nature & Découvertes', each article has a life and its own story behind it, hence our use of the word 'animism'. Once inside the store, the clients can explore at leisure, just as though they were in a natural history museum. Every product gives the client an opportunity to widen his field of knowledge. In addition, the information cards show when and where the product was invented, a résumé of the manufacturer's background or else the natural phenomenon the product represents. So the products are not simply 'objects', they have a life of their own. Whenever possible, they are displayed on a base of natural wood to set them off to their best advantage; they are in a context, in their natural environment. They 'speak' to the client.

The entire sales area design is based upon nineteenth-century references. Pictures, nature descriptions look like scientific drawings of the last century. Therefore, the concept also has an implicit meaning which is to say that scientific progress goes too fast, too quick. The concept tries to bring the consumer back to the past. This is done very subtly and ingeniously because to understand this, the customer has to analyse the whole environment whereas everything is done to let him feel emotions rather than analyse things with 'reason'. The environment solicits more the affective dimension than the cognitive dimension. This allows us to say that there is a paradox in this distribution concept: 'découvertes' means discoveries. 'Nature & Découvertes' has a double meaning: it means discovering nature but also 'nature and discoveries' which can be understood as: 'how science contributes to discovering nature'. To assert that second meaning, we must add that the shop sells a lot of products of the scientific environment: microscopes, maps, etc., but all those products are well-known scientific products. There is a gap between the products of the scientific world that can be found at 'Nature & Découvertes' and the equipment used by scientists nowadays. Also, science usually means 'reasoning' rather than 'feeling'. Perhaps 'Nature & Découvertes' is the expression of an Apocalyptical feeling in the consumption system. In which case, the concept would only be the 'retranscription' in the offer system of a deep longing: 'Because the future is uncertain, let us look back . . .'

'Nature & Découvertes': nature versus culture or life versus death?

'Our only hope of salvation lies in respect for nature, otherwise it's the beginning of the end for humanity' – that is an ecological statement of belief. The interesting point here is that we are looking at pure eschatology. The same may be said of our consumer society. Beneath the nature versus culture dialectic, there is another: life or death, the whole future of our consumer society. It could well be possible, cynically, to see in 'Nature & Découvertes' a totally artificial creation. If indeed the company is simply riding on the back of an ecological movement, as it does with the 'new-age' wave, it comes back to saying that it is trying to reconcile nature and culture without resolving the basic problem – 'how do we keep the environment safe?'

That does not for a moment mean that 'Nature & Découvertes' is doing nothing to protect the environment. A glance at our catalogues will show that the company gives 10 per cent of its pre-tax profit to a foundation devoted to the protection of nature. So we are not in any way unmindful of the environment. 'Nature & Découvertes' is very simply a responsible company whose basic aim is commercial and economic and to which end it does all it can to exploit the target market.

Here we would also like to point out that the vision that 'Nature &

Découvertes' gives of nature is a very idyllic one – implicitly the shop considers nature as a 'benefactor'. It disguises an important part of the history of human beings, because it overlooks the idea that since the beginning there was a fight going on between nature and human beings. Nature was dangerous for humans. Human beings were always trying to protect themselves against nature. Therefore, we think that 'Nature & Découvertes' is an apocalyptical distribution concept, because it develops a unique way of looking at nature, a very urban way of looking at nature, where human beings forget that their ancestors were considering nature not only as a beneficial factor but also a malevolent one. To a certain extent, such a vision is a 'revision' of the history of mankind which definitely is an apocalyptical perspective of society (but not necessarily of marketing . . .).

Given the questions above, the big question is: in the final analysis do all the marketing techniques involved mean the Apocalypse or an ordered Renaissance? Which in turn means adopting a position between an eschatological and a prophetic-cum-evangelical stance. We shall be examining this point in the third and final section.

THE SOPHISTICATION OF MARKETING: APOCALYPSE OR RENAISSANCE?

In our view, marketing always rises like the phoenix from its ashes. It changes, it becomes more sophisticated. To put it in eschatological terms, it is the alpha and the omega, the beginning and the end of the present socio-economic system. Its legitimacy lies in exchange. Each time a client buys a product which results from a commercial operation, he or she gives legitimacy to the marketing process. Therefore, marketing eschatology is unacceptable. What we shall attempt to do here is to analyse in more detail certain aspects of the marketing sophistication process which in fact has been going on for some time and develop the reasons why marketing eschatology is unacceptable.

The postmodern consumer is increasingly aware

What never fails to strike us when we study consumer behaviour is the fact that the consumer is increasingly aware of marketing techniques: by no means the prerogative of the professionals. Over the years, consumers have become very skilled at seeing into marketing strategies. They can see causal relationships: 'If "Nature & Découvertes" does this or that, it's because . . .' The main reason for this heightened awareness on the part of the consumer is very probably that marketing techniques go back a long way; and also through TV programmes devoted to analysing the marketing strategies of one or another company. The end result is that companies need to redouble their thinking in order to develop original and increasingly sophisticated marketing strategies.

'Perception' and 'interpretation' by the consumer

For a long time, marketing experts have realised that there may well be a difference between the image the company would like to enjoy and the corporate image as perceived by the consumer. The result is the development of new tools that whenever possible can be used to measure the difference between these two factors and then do the maximum to reduce it. Additionally, the concept of 'perception' involves all five senses of the consumer, and there again, in the present economic context, more and more distribution concepts are being developed involving all five perceptual senses (as we have shown in the case of 'Nature & Découvertes').

Where consumer interpretation of the offer is concerned, the advent of semiotic theories in the domain of marketing has increased awareness of the interpretation process. There are in fact two separate areas which do not always coincide: the offer made by the company and the consumer's reception of that offer. Getting nearer consumers, understanding them better, involves an effort to interpret the offering system, defining the exact scope of possible meanings. It also means accepting the fact that at any given moment the product, the distribution concept or the offering system go beyond the aims of the company and into the consumers' world, the receptiveness of consumers, which has its own perceptual rules.

Marketing's extended field of action: the tendency towards totalitarianism and the creation of illusions

The case of 'Nature & Découvertes' is interesting for a number of reasons. First, it shows that more and more parts of the distribution mechanism seek to appeal to all five senses and not just to sight alone. This in turn shows that marketing's field of action is tending to expand and work in hitherto unexplored areas. So much so that a number of distributors are endeavouring to create a multidimensional impression (a simultaneous appeal to all five senses in order to make the maximum impression on the consumer).

Second, 'Nature & Découvertes' also makes us aware of the fact that marketing seeks to systematise the whole system of offering, as can be seen in the methodical and systematic display of products apparently just 'jumbled' together. This shows that there is no place for 'random' displays within the system. From a certain point of view, we have here the very height of marketing techniques: the client likes to 'browse', so products are displayed in a very carefully worked out jumbled way. So there is a big difference between intention, 'very much organised', and the image, 'random display'.

The danger here is a tendency towards a 'totalitarian' attitude. The urge to control and dominate raises the question of how much freedom the client actually has. It might be asked whether a given company wants to give the impression of freedom when in fact it is strongly tempted to keep a very tight rein on the client. Because in this sort of situation, whilst the illusion of freedom is created, it is an effect created by the company simply to win over the client.

Marketing: a closer relationship with philosophy

As we have seen above, 'Nature & Découvertes' is a meeting between nature and culture. In effect, the company seeks to resolve a real philosophical problem for town-dwellers hoping to rediscover nature. Trying to formulate and implement this concept means enormous skills as well as a thorough understanding of the societal questions involved. Not forgetting the sophistication and adaptation of marketing to the new conditions produced by our post-modern society.

It should also be noted that bringing marketing and philosophy together is not new; see Laufer and Paradeise (1982): 'Vous faîtes du marketcirc;ing'. They do seem to agree on at least one point: that is one of the most deadly and definitive insults that philosophers can hurl at each other today in France. It is very likely time that marketing experts get involved, even at the risk of 'playing philosophy . . .'

Marketing as a 'societal' factor

During the 'Glorious Thirties', there were basically two concepts of marketing. Some said that marketing manipulated people unscrupulously, others that marketing experts were able to anticipate the housewife's needs before she was aware of them. With that sort of approach, what predominated was detection of needs and the usefulness of products, because these needs pre-existed, and it was felt that consumers knew what they wanted and were able to express themselves. Given that situation, marketing studies could reveal these needs, and the market leader's job was to come up with an offering appropriate to the potential demand. It is quite obvious today that a marketing concept of that sort is outworn and obsolete, that marketing is changing and that what we are witnessing is the development of what has been called 'societal' marketing (Cova and Svanfeld 1993).

Indeed, social 'testing the water temperature' (cf. 'Nature & Découvertes' when the concept was introduced), consists of the following:

- See what the prevailing social tendencies are; they may well mean innovations in offering terms, and can themselves create trends (cf. slipping tendency with sports products)
- Study consumption and forward studies on decisions (looking not at consumers but at consumption)
- The company is permanently interacting with a number of recipients and always keeping aware of what is happening in society.

It is keeping aware of social trends and identifying 'societal' factors that are the key factors to success.

Marketing: ethical or not?

Marketing is not moral or immoral, it is quite simply amoral. That does not mean that marketing experts never need to ask themselves moral questions. On the contrary, ethics are becoming crucial in our economic system. If any proof is needed, one need only look at the USA, where companies whose operations are seen as 'politically incorrect' are boycotted by the consumer and can find themselves out of business and closed down virtually overnight, to the point where some American colleagues have been heard to say 'Ethics pay'. We do not see the problem as being as simple as that; there is no single answer. But certainly what has to be realised is that this idea is making itself more and more felt in the social requirements of the market. Marketing, as a discipline in its own right, cannot afford to overlook this fact. Which is doubtless why 'Nature & Découvertes' contributes 10 per cent of its pre-tax profit to a non-profit making organisation.

CONCLUSIONS

All that has been said leads us to feel that marketing is not at the beginning of the end. It is capable of adapting to a changing context, by very reason of the sophistication of its methods and tools. If we accept the idea put forward by Laufer and Paradeise (1982) that marketing is a modern bureaucratic form of sophistry, then certain conclusions must be drawn: that marketing can still look forward to a bright future. Marketing is not nearing its end; it is simply adjusting to new social demands, and a number of companies, among them 'Nature & Découvertes', have not been slow to adapt.

If we use the term 'eschatology', it is because this theme of 'the end' is very much a part of our consumer society (cf. the link between ecology and life or death). If here we talk of the eschatology of marketing, it is because eschatology is an integral part of society today (the twentieth century or the second millennium is not over yet). But it would be a mistake to think that only marketing is involved; society itself is at stake. And marketing will continue to be a fact for as long as our consumer society exists. Marketing is in fact a naïve technique with a far from naïve power. Marketing's greatest naïveté is to see itself otherwise. What does give cause for concern is the possibility of change in the political and economic powers that be, and thus in consumer patterns and marketing. But have we reached that point? For all the reasons given above, we do not think so.

REFERENCES

Cans, R. (1992), *Tous verts: la surenchère écologique*, Calman Lévy, Paris.

Cohn, N. (1993), *Cosmos, Chaos and the World to Come*, Yale University Press, New Haven.

Cova, B. and Svanfeld, C. (1993), 'Societal Innovations and the Postmodern Aestheticization of Everyday Life', *International Journal of Marketing Research*, 10 (3), pp. 297–310.

Crédoc (1993), 'L'engagement idéologique des fabricants séduit les consommateurs', *Consommation et Modes de Vie – Crédoc Journal*, 75, March 1993. pp. 1–4.

Ferry, L. (1992), *Le nouvel ordre écologique*, Grasset, Paris.

Genoud, V., Mazuel, F. and Valette, A. (1994), *Nature & Découvertes*, unpublished Student Report, University Jean Moulin Lyon 3.

Gobbi, L., Morace, F., Brognara, R. and Valente, F. (1990), *I boom: Prodotti e societé degli anni '80*, Lupetti and Co, Milan.

Guattari, F. (1989), *Les trois écologies*, Galilée, Paris.

Hetzel, P. (1993), 'The Development of Trade Environment Design in the Lingerie Sector in France or the Emergence of Postmodernist Concepts among French Distributors', *Architecture & Behaviour*, 9 (4), pp. 443–62.

Hetzel, P. (1994), 'The Role of Fashion and Design in a Postmodern Society: What Challenges for Firms?', in M. Baker (ed.), *Perspectives on Marketing Management*, 4, John Wiley, Chichester, pp. 97–118.

Hetzel, P. (1995), 'Systemising the Awareness of the Consumer's Five Senses at the Point of Sale: An Essential Challenge for Marketing Theory and Practice', in Bergadaa, M. (ed.) *Proceedings of the 24th European Marketing Academy (EMAC) Conference*, Essec, France, 1, pp. 471–482.

Laufer, R. and Paradeise, C. (1982), *Le Prince bureaucrate: Machiavel au pays du marketing*, Flammarion, Paris.

Nature & Découvertes (1995), Trade-catalogue, Toussus-le-Noble, Nature & Découvertes.

Rosnay (de), J. (1991), *Les rendez-vous du futur*, Fayard, Paris.

Tedlow, G. and Jones, G. (1993), *The Rise and Fall of Mass Marketing*, Routledge, London.

Virilio, P. (1984), *L'espace critique*, Christian Bourgeois, Paris.

Part III

RENOVATION

10

MARKETING ADIDIMUS

Michael J. Thomas

INTRODUCTION

Are marketers, scholars and practitioners the victims of Darwinian evolution, soon to decline into irrelevance? This chapter comments on three issues. Does marketing and market-driven behaviour add value? How will the functions of marketing be organised in the virtual corporation? What are the political perceptions of marketing?

Until marketing scholars can demonstrate empirically that marketing does add value and that market-driven companies are measurably more successful than other companies (The Holy Grail), marketing will remain suspect, seen as manipulative and exploitive in the short term, and condemned to Darwinian extinction in the long term.

Czeslaw Milosz is an exiled Polish poet who has always fascinated and challenged me. Writing in *Granta* in 1990, he made the following observations about the New Europe:

> What will happen next? Does the victory of the multi-party system in the countries of Central and Eastern Europe mean the end of their estrangement from the West? Will they, by introducing the classical division of powers – a legislature, executive and judiciary – recognize the supremacy of all Western values? Will the years of suffering under totalitarian rule be obliterated, erased and the people start from scratch? Should the thinkers, poets and artists join their Western colleagues in the somewhat marginal role assigned to them in societies busy with selling and buying?
>
> The failure of Marx's vision has created the need for another vision, not for a rejection of all visions. I do not speak of 'socialism with a human face', for that belongs to the past. I speak instead about a concern with society, civilization and humanity in a period when the nineteenth-century idea of progress has died out and a related idea, communist revolution, has disintegrated. What remains today is the idea of responsibility, which works against the loneliness and indifference of an individual living in the belly of a whale. Together with historical memory, the belief in personal responsibility has contributed to the Solidarity movement in Poland, the

> national fronts in the Baltic States, the Civic Forum in Czechoslovakia. I hope that the turmoil in these countries has not been a temporary phase, a passage to an ordinary society of earners and consumers, but rather the birth of a new form of human interaction, of a non-utopian style and vision.
>
> (Milosz 1990: 165)

As I contemplate the future state of things, the eschatology of marketing, Milosz's concerns stalk me and my thinking.

His concerns are echoed in another influential text (Bull 1995). Krishan Kumar in an essay entitled, 'Apocalypse, Millennium, and Utopia Today', observes

> Now the socialist utopia has lost its appeal. But, with the exception of certain sections of East European opinion, the capitalist utopia is likewise tarnished. Capitalism unleashed is seen to threaten the life-support systems of the planet. Left unchecked it bids fair to turn the world into a moral and material wasteland. Alternatives to capitalism, in the sense of whole new systems, are not currently on offer. But that still leaves capitalism as no more than the least worst rather than the best of even the good society. This is hardly the stuff of utopia.
>
> (Bull 1995: 209)

The text for my sermon comes from Stephen Brown's (1994) brilliant article 'Marketing as Multiplex: Screening Postmodernism':

> Many commentators on the current state of marketing have concluded that something is amiss, that the concept is deeply, perhaps irredeemably, flawed, that its seemingly solid foundations are by no means secure and that the discipline is teetering on the brink of a serious intellectual crisis.
>
> Piercy, for example, maintains that the traditional marketing concept 'assumes and relies on the existence of a world which is alien and unrecognizable to many of the executives who actually have to manage marketing for real'. Gummesson states the 'the present marketing concept . . . is unrealistic and needs to be replaced'. Nilson contends that 'a revision of the marketing concept is necessary'. Rapp and Collins suggest that 'the traditional methods . . . simply aren't working as well anymore'. Brownlie and Saren argue that 'it is questionable whether the marketing concept as it has been propagated can provide the basis for successful business at the end of the twentieth century'. McKenna concludes that 'there is less and less reason to believe that the traditional approach can keep up with real customer wishes and demands or with the rigors of competition'. And, Professor Michael Thomas, one of Britain's most respected marketing academics, has recently made the frank, and frankly astonishing, confession that, after 30 years of propagating the marketing concept, he is having serious doubts about its continuing efficacy.

Similarly, when it comes to long-established marketing principles like the product life cycle, Fishbein's behavioural intentions model, the wheel of retailing, the stages of internationalization concept, the information-processing paradigm of consumer behaviour and so on, broadly similar expressions of concern are discernible. The fact of the matter is that, despite decades of research and replication, the validity, reliability, universality and predictive power of these and many other prominent marketing principles are far from established. Worse, the concepts themselves may have a counterproductive or deleterious effect on marketplace behaviour. It is not unknown, for example, for perfectly sound products to be killed off because of management's belief in the existence of a product life cycle. The codification of the retailing hierarchy concept has contributed to decades of conflict between town planners and retail organizations and impeded the introduction of innovative retailing formats. And, as the 'co-operative' rhetoric of relationship marketing has come to prominence, academics are having to face the uncomfortable fact that *they* introduced generations of managers into the hostile – and now reputedly redundant – vocabulary of competitive advantage and marketing warfare.

This sense of exhaustion surrounding the marketing concept and the growing uncertainty about the practical worth of established marketing principles is exacerbated by the profusion of marketing panaceas that are being propounded at present. Apart from the plethora of self-styled 'postmodern' research procedures, which are in the process of supplanting the established positivist standpoint, in the sub-field of consumer research at least, a host of less philosophically robust catholicons is also on offer. These solutions to marketing's manifest ills come in numerous forms, though a suitably snappy, dynamic, macho, evangelical or alliterative title is common to all – maxi-marketing, turbo-marketing, neo-marketing, micro-marketing, after-marketing, value-added marketing, database marketing, transformational marketing, relationship marketing and so on *ad infinitum*. True, the marketing of marketing nostrums has always gone on to some degree – after all, it is only through the identification of latent shortcomings and the provision of an appropriate remedy that management gurus and marketing consultants can reap the rich financial rewards that are their due – but this process is arguably more prevalent than before and involves prominent, mainstream marketing scholars (Kotler, Sheth, Christopher, Piercy, etc.) as opposed to the lunatic fringe (the lunatic fringe, of course, is writing articles on postmodernism!).

(Brown 1994: 440–1)

I am not volunteering to join the lunatic fringe as they contemplate their millennial navels. I concur with Gellner's position:

Postmodernism is a contemporary movement. It is strong and fashion-

> able. Over and above this, it is not altogether clear what the devil it is. In fact, clarity is not conspicuous amongst its marked attributes. It not only generally fails to practise it, but also on occasion actually repudiates it. But anyway, there appear to be no 39 postmodernist Articles of faith, no postmodernist Manifesto, which one could consult so as to assure oneself that one has identified its ideas properly.
>
> (Gellner 1992: 22–3)

I agree with Kumar, who states in the essay already cited:

> The postmodernist retreat is one response. Postmodernity flattens time; it solves the problem of the future by simply denying the relevance of the concepts of 'past', 'present' and 'future'. It denounces modernity's belief in progress and attacks its faith in science and technology. To that extent it echoes the cultural conservatism of the earlier part of the century. But, unlike that, it refuses to replace modernity with anything; this denial of an alternative is indeed its principal characteristic.
>
> (Kumar 1995: 210)

I want to return to the mainstream, to challenge my fellow scholars to continue to seek answers to a number of questions. I do so because we intellectuals have a challenge to face, a promise to deliver.

> We should note that, even in Western societies, the pessimism of the intelligentsia has not been whole-heartedly endorsed by the mass of the population. A species of 'popular utopianism' thrives in the spaces of popular culture. Pop songs, Hollywood movies, and television soap operas are replete with utopian imagery. True, this is often nostalgic or escapist. The world of Australian soaps such as *Neighbours* and *Home and Away*, and even of more realistic English varieties such as *Coronation Street* and *East Enders*, is a fantasy world of community and neighbourly intimacy; while the glamorous and glossy settings of *Dallas* and *Dynasty* evoke images of wealth and power such as can satisfy the wildest desires. This is the 'poor man's utopia', the utopianism that is fed by the fantasies of the Land of Cockaygne. But it is none the less powerful for that; and it shows that, whatever jaded intellectuals might feel, images of the good life continue to appeal to a wide section of the population of Western industrial societies.
>
> (Kumar 1995: 216)

Has marketing not claimed that it serves capitalism by delivering the good life more effectively than any other economic system?

Eschatology – the doctrines of the future state (of things). I want to address three topics. Topic one. Does marketing and market-driven behaviour add value? Topic two. The future state of marketing organisation, in other words, how the functions of marketing will be organised. Topic three. I want to be dangerously political and raise some questions about political perceptions of what marketing and markets are all about.

DOES MARKETING AND MARKET-DRIVEN BEHAVIOUR ADD VALUE?

The Observer of 7 May 1995 carried an article on the success of New Saatchi in securing the £60 million British Airways account. I quote from the article because it raises, in a rather neat way, some of the issues that interest me.

> Life's a pitch and then you're reborn. Exiled from the Saatchi & Saatchi Agency they created, Maurice Saatchi and his 'barmy Armani army' of loyal executives marked their triumphant return to the advertising industry last week by winning the £60 million British Airways account for the New Saatchi Agency.
>
> But will a resurrected Maurice Saatchi again set the tone for the British advertising community he so long dominated?
>
> The BA success was all the sweeter because the account was taken from the old Saatchi & Saatchi, the agency Maurice and his brother, Charles, founded 25 years ago. They left abruptly at the beginning of the year, along with a host of defectors, after a boardroom rout removed Maurice from the chairmanship of his own company.
>
> The deal had much to do with the strong personal ties between BA's life president, Lord King, its chairman, Sir Colin Marshall, and Maurice Saatchi, but the pitch (against 'old Saatchi', J. Walter Thompson and Bartle Bogle Hegarty) showed the adman has not lost his legendary flair and retains a sense of humour.
>
> Saatchi's partner in the pitch, the French group Publicis, put together the boring details – the charts, the research and the worldwide network of agencies through which to run the business. Meanwhile, Maurice brought three cardboard cut-outs of the key executives – Bill Muirhead, David Kershaw and Jeremy Sinclair – who will be working with him as soon as they are released from their contracts with 'old Saatchi'. The three men's appointments are the subject of a bitter legal wrangle.
>
> While other agencies handed out their presentations in boring old briefcases, New Saatchi put theirs on CD-Rom. Adland rumour had it they handed out laptops, though one New Saatchi source insists that 'there was only one laptop and we lent it – we can't afford to give them away'.
>
> Champagne corks littered the pavements in Soho after last Wednesday morning's victory, but the New Saatchi Agency promises to be as much a model for the more puritan Nineties as Saatchi & Saatchi became a shrine to the excess and materialism of the Eighties.
>
> Gone are the million-pound salary cheques, the opulent suites of offices, the fleet of luxury company cars, the £40,000 taxi bills and £5,000 a year

> at the florists which characterised 'old Saatchi'. Gone even is the complete control of the brothers, replaced by a five-way equal split of equity, a reward for the three executives who risked most by following Maurice.
>
> New Saatchi executives are happy to be seen driving Fiat Puntos – or at the most a Toyota Corolla – and will be sharing an open-plan office in the smart but quiet buildings in Kingly Street, Soho, that Mr Saatchi is negotiating to rent.
>
> 'Maurice is absolutely insisting on open plan – he wants to be sitting in the middle of a buzzing office,' says one of the New Saatchi partners. Only a couple of years ago, Maurice occupied an enormous private suite of offices, complete with private bathroom, in Berkeley Square, 15 minutes' walk from the hurly burly of the Saatchi & Saatchi Charlotte Street Agency.
>
> However, New Saatchi has not fully embraced a Blairite future. Rumours are rife that Maurice's next coup will be to lure the Conservative Party away from Saatchi & Saatchi – the account which initially made the Saatchi name famous with its 'Labour Isn't Working' campaign for the 1979 general election.
>
> (Bell 1995: 12)

Merely note for future reference these points:

- The account was won by an agency that did not exist last year. It did so because a network was far stronger than an organisation.
- Saatchi won the account because unlike the almost successful agency Bartle Bogle Hegarty, it has as part of its network, access to Publicis, which gave BA assurance that it could gain worldwide media access, i.e. a global network won out over a primarily domestic network.
- The pitch was masterminded by Maurice Saatchi, three cardboard cutouts, and a CD-Rom.
- The old Saatchi (& Saatchi) was a perfect metaphor for the 1980s, Maggie Thatcher's favourite advertising agency, totally controlled by the Brothers, and brought to its knees by over-extension and just a little hubris. Fiat Puntos and Toyota Corollas now – we shall see. Open office plan replaces opulent office in flat (flatulent) organisation.
- Now Maurice wants the Conservative Party account back – does this suggest that this is the final refutation of the learning curve hypothesis?

I bring this glimpse of the postmodern world into my chapter to make a point, well made in another brilliant paper by Brown (will he never stop?). 'Marketing Scholarship . . . became increasingly divorced from reality and this has been followed by the fragmentation of the discipline into a multiplicity of hostile factions, retrenchment and a search for a new guiding paradigm' (Brown 1995: 15).

My search for a new paradigm has been motivated by my determination to demand that marketing scholarship remains wedded to reality, and my position as Chairman of the Chartered Institute of Marketing reflects my determination to remain credible to practising marketing managers and directors, 26,000 of whom elected me to this office. That is why the accusations levelled at the profession ('marketing is too important to be left to marketers') must concern me and I hope you. I am concerned with positioning, the positioning of the profession, within the changing organisational environment. I must therefore be concerned with issues of organisation. I am, at the same time very anxious that marketing scholars seek proof of the contention that the most successful organisations become so because they are market-driven, are close to their customers, and are adding superior value compared to their competitors. Unless we have 'scientific proof' that this is the case, our profession is vulnerable, accused by detractors and doubters alike of using the tools of hype and persuasion which others regard as our very own tools for manipulation and obfuscation of the truth. During my tenure of office in the CIM I have been instrumental in persuading CIM to sponsor research in this area, and the presentation of research findings has become the centrepiece of our last two Annual Conferences. If we cannot demonstrate adequate proof of the critical role played by the marketing function we will be sidelined.

I do not doubt that finding proof is complicated, for the environment in which marketing operates – dynamically changing markets, operating globally – is so multi-faceted, multi-functional, that the most sophisticated multiple regressions have difficulty in capturing secure relationships. Nevertheless, we must pursue this particular Holy Grail.

Does marketing add value, and are the most successful organisations successful because they are market driven, close to their customers and better at creating superior value? What evidence do we have?

I quote from Narver and Slater (1990: 34):

> Our study is an important first step in validating the market orientation/performance relationship. For scholars, the implications of the study are clear. The research must be replicated in diverse environments and over time to increase confidence in the nature and power of the theory. For managers, the implications of the study are less clear. Because of the exploratory nature of the research, the generalisability of the findings is limited. The findings do suggest that after controlling for important market-level and business-level influences, market orientation and performance are strongly related. These findings are entirely consistent with the intuition and expectations of both scholars and practitioners over the past three decades about the nature and effects of a market orientation. The findings give marketing scholars and practitioners a basis beyond mere intuition for recommending the superiority of a market orientation. If the findings in replications of our research support our findings, the

> message to managers is clear. A substantial market orientation must be the foundation for a business's competitive advantage strategy.

Jaworski and Kohli (1993: 64) address the same issue and conclude:

> The purpose of the study was to empirically test several hypotheses advanced in the literature regarding antecedents and consequences of a marketing orientation. The findings of the study suggest that the market orientation of a business is an important determinant of its performance, regardless of the market turbulence, competitive intensity, or the technological turbulence of the environment in which it operates. As such, it appears that managers should strive to improve the market orientation of their businesses in their efforts to attain higher business performance.
>
> Finally, this study employs a cross-sectional analysis of a large number of businesses. While providing important insights into the determinants of a market orientation, it does not shed much light on the change processes involved in improving a market orientation. For example, a relatively low level of market orientation may in fact lead managers to alter certain antecedents such as reward systems which, in turn, lead to a higher level of market orientation. In this regard, it would be useful to conduct in-depth studies of a few organizations engaged in the change process so as to better understand the factors that influence the initiation and the implementation of change efforts directed at improving the market orientation of a business.

Thus both papers call for more in-depth research. The publications record suggests that there has been a limited response. We must ask why this is the case. The subject is absolutely crucial to the future of our professional standing. Deliver empirical proof to support our claims that marketing is good for you and we need worry less about the hereafter. It has been done profitably for Guinness, why not for marketing?

Doyle and Hooley produced some very promising material in 1992, based upon research into British company performance (they claimed 379 responses from a sample universe of 1000). They explored eleven propositions:

> **Proposition 1**: A distinction can be drawn between long-term market share driven companies and short-term profit-driven companies.
>
> **Proposition 2**: A significant percentage of British companies will be in a 'transitionary' phase shifting from a short-term profit to a long-term share orientation.
>
> **Proposition 3**: Market share-orientated companies are more likely than profit orientated companies to be customer-led. Share driven companies are less likely to be product- or sales-led.
>
> **Proposition 4**: Long-term share and transitionary companies will be more likely than their counterparts to adopt a marketing orientation as a corporate philosophy.

Proposition 5: In the transitionary companies marketing can be expected to increase in importance in the near future more rapidly than in the short run profits companies and even the long-term share companies.
Proposition 6: In the long-term share companies marketing will generally enjoy a higher status compared with other functional areas than in the short-term profit companies. Transitionary companies might be expected to fall between these extremes.
Proposition 7: Long-term share-orientated companies will exhibit closer working relationship between marketing and the other functional areas.
Proposition 8: The major objectives of the short-term profit companies will be more associated with productivity improvement and survival compared with the more expansive objectives of the other companies.
Proposition 9: The long-term share and transitionary companies will adopt a more proactive approach to the future while the short-term profit companies are likely to be more reactive.
Proposition 10: Long-run share and transitionary companies are likely to adopt a greater degree of marketing planning than their counterparts.
Proposition 11: Short-term companies will more often measure performance in terms of profit while the market-share-driven companies will more often measure performance in terms of market share.

Their conclusions should be noted:

> Three different strategic orientations were observed amongst a large sample of British companies. The orientations were associated with different attitudes towards marketing, marketing relationships and strategic outlooks.

Attitudes

The short-run profit orientated companies are more likely to adopt a product orientation ('make what we can and sell to whoever will buy') and see marketing as primarily a sales support function confined to the marketing department. Their CEOs are more likely to see marketing as 'really selling' and the role of marketing has been least changed in the last five years and is expected to change little in the next five.

By contrast the long-run share-orientated companies are characterised by a marketing orientation ('marketing is identifying and meeting customer needs') adopted as a guiding philosophy for the whole organisation. This is echoed by their CEOs who see marketing as ' an approach to business that should guide all of the company's operations'.

The transitionary companies share many of the characteristics of the share-led companies, though to a lesser extent. The major discriminators of this group centre around the increased importance attached to marketing (both over the past five years and expected in the next five) and in their willingness to 'adjust products and services to meet market needs if necessary'.

Marketing relationships

Two issues were explored: the status of marketing compared with the other functional areas; and the extent to which marketing and the other functional areas work together.

In the profit-led companies marketing was more often seen as of lower status that finance, personnel, production and even sales. In both share-driven and transitionary companies marketing enjoyed a higher status and working relationships were reported to be much closer (i.e. marketing is not just confined to what the marketing department does). In the market share-orientated companies in particular, a more balanced status for marketing was noted.

Performance

Contrary to expectation the market share-driven companies were not found to pursue market-based goals at the expense of short run financial performance, but rather to reconcile the two. This reconciliation has resulted in companies that not only perform well today but promise to continue to perform well in the future. The transitionary companies share many of the characteristics of the longer-run share-orientated companies and perhaps promise a brighter future for British industry.

Doyle and Hooley 1992: 72–3

The authors call for further study. The ESRC had engaged in support of such research in the 1980s (The Marketing Initiative), but it must be said that the impact appears to me to have been minimal, partly because of poor marketing of its outcomes. The format of the final report, a 400-page book, appears without conclusions.

The Bradford research (1995) (Manufacturing – the Marketing Solution) sponsored by the Chartered Institute of Marketing attacks the subject anew. It uses an elaborate evaluation framework (probably too elaborate). The components of this framework are shown in Appendix 1.

If the dimensions of Bradford's marketing heaven can be effectively measured, it may be possible to demonstrate that marketing strategy, quality strategy, innovation, customer development, branding and supply chain management are the keys to superior performance, as long as manufacturing strategy is also determined by explicit reference to market needs.

What I want to know is why we, as researchers, are not devoting ourselves to the quest for this truth. The evidence for the existence of the Holy Grail is to hand, but proof is neither accepted and certainly not widely acknowledged. Is it because we know in our hearts that there is no hereafter, that we live in a truly Darwinian environment where real evidence points to our decline as a species?

HOW WILL MARKETING BE ORGANISED?

The organisational issue is itself a minefield, designed to blow management to the other place. Organisational solutions have to deal with a number of problems. It would be sensible to delineate them:

1 Strategy should determine structure. Too many examples can be produced to demonstrate marketing failure because structure has limited strategy. Strategy too often influences how an organisation perceives its environment, and frequently protects the status quo. I believe one factor that harmed Bartle Bogle Hegarty in its bid for the BA account was a failure by the client to believe that an agency without a worldwide network in place could handle its international business – it preferred an agency with a limited track record which claimed through its link with Publicis to have a global network. Structure prevailed over strategy. Too frequently British companies believe that they cannot compete internationally because they have no international structure. Relationship marketing claims to address the problem, and Maurice Saatchi may have proved the point.
2 Marketing channels are becoming more powerful – dealing with them is forcing organisational change.
3 Co-makership, preferred supplier relationships, JIT manufacture and the like are changing the relationships between producers and customers.
4 Information technology is the fundamental threat to hierarchical organisations; it is the reason why layers of managerial bureaucracy are being removed from large corporations. If information is power, then marketing should be enormously powerful, since the marketing function traditionally claims sovereignty over market research and the design of marketing information systems. Whether it has such power, I doubt.
5 When Procter and Gamble, and Unilever, Pillsbury and AT & T drop brand management and close marketing departments replacing them with project teams, category managers and some species called Integrators, we should at least take notice. Organisational change is burgeoning in the real world, hierarchies are becoming busted, self-managing teams consisting of multi-functional players are appearing, re-engineering places emphasis on process management not, emphatically not, on functional silos. Global marketing is the key to survival in the global village, hence new skills and structures are required (Thomas and Saxena 1995). Account management and learning organisations have become the fashionable concepts, networking and relationship marketing the components of the Final Solution, reality is the Virtual Corporation.

The agenda provided by Piercy and Cravens (1995) enables us to discuss the

Table 10.1 New organisational forms for marketing: a classification framework

Strategic level	*Units of analysis*	*Examples of major issues*	*Examples of new organisational forms*
Functional	Marketing subsystems	Organising and coordination, sub-functions of marketing such as advertising, marketing research and sales operations	Channel management Logistics services specialists Information/technology specialists
Business	Marketing department	The departmentation of marketing and internal structure of the marketing department The integration of marketing sub-functions Relationships with other functions	Sector/segment management Trade marketing Investment specialists Venture/new product departments
Corporate	Divisional marketing responsibilities and group-wide marketing issues	Centralisation Decentralisation of marketing decision making and relationships between central and peripheral marketing units	Marketing exchange and coalition companies Network organisations
Enterprise	Strategic alliances and networks	External relationships and boundary-spanning with strategic marketing partners Marketing 'make or buy' choices	Partnerships Alliances

Source: author, after Piercy and Cravens (1995)

implications of new organisational forms for the performance of the marketing function. The classification framework is shown in Table 10.1.

What we must do is to be sure we do not confuse strategic levels, and that solutions must encompass the enterprise, corporate and business level as well as the narrow marketing function level.

I like to set myself an agenda for thinking about the organisational problem in strategic terms. Contemplate the agenda in Table 10.2 and see what illumination it provides.

Thus far I have highlighted two issues that we need to address. Do we have proof that marketing driven companies are more profitable than those who are not? Do we have a real contribution to make to the organisational debate – are

Table 10.2 Advanced marketing capability – the bridge to the future

	Today's business	→	*Pre-empting the future*
1 Intelligence gathering	Collect data about existing markets and competitors	→	Create insights about emerging markets and competitors – develop 'early warning signals' capability
2 Strategy formulation	Employ technology for today's competitive advantage	→	Exploit technology for reformulating the strategic vision of the business–paradigm shift
3 Idea creation	Screen new ideas for fit to existing business	→	Nurture ideas for creating new business opportunities
4 New product development	Reduce time to market	→	Create new products and new markets
5 Technology development	Boost performance of today's technology	→	Exploit the potential for leapfrogging into new technologies
6 Technology sourcing	Tap and enrich the existing network	→	Set up new networks

Source: author, after Piercy and Cravens (1995)

there any principles to guide this debate, or do we merely stand by as observers reporting excitedly about the latest reported change in organisational philosophy at IBM, or Unilever or AT & T?

POLITICAL PERCEPTIONS OF MARKETING

My last point relates to political perceptions of marketing. In thinking about the future, in thinking eschatologically about where we are going, we should remember that the marketing profession must be seen to be addressing some of the great issues facing society, our society and other societies. Let me list just four questions:

1 Have we begun to understand the implications for markets of the information based, post-industrial society?
2 Market saturation is a common characteristic of Western developed economies, too many goods and services chasing too few discretionary spending customers – can marketers find solutions to this problem?
3 Too few discretionary spending customers – is this the beginnings of bi-polar society, with high income knowledge workers as a small minority, surrounded by a low income proletariat?

4 Do we have an answer to Milosz's charge? In a society busy with buying and selling, in a society of earners and consumers, who can guarantee civilisation and humanity? What is the meaning of personal responsibility in the late twentieth century? Are we contributing to a community of quality and taste, or encouraging frivolity and irresponsibility?

These are surely political questions.

I started by citing a tale about Maurice Saatchi's winning the BA account. I will close the circle with another cautionary airlines tale. The nature of competition in the airline business is itself fascinating. Some cynics would argue that at the end of the day, international airline competition is all about politics, particularly about control over landing slots and protecting quasi-monopolies. That is the substance, all else is trappings! I don't want to delve deeply into the questions, I merely want to place a footnote on the debate.

Again, let me quote from Piercy and Cravens (1995: 22):

> It is frequently suggested that networks represent ideals of equality and partnership, not power and conflict. It is for management in specific situations to take a hard-headed view of the real, practical conditions – we may see ourselves as the 'core' or 'leader' of a network of trusted and trusting partners, but this may not be the perception of those partners. As noted earlier, a characteristic of many channels of distribution is that dominant control has passed from manufacturer to retailer. The converse of partnerships and sharing is dependency and strategy vulnerability.
>
> Consider the recent experiences of Virgin Atlantic and Southwest Airlines. Virgin leased access to a computerized booking system, which had been developed for its own use and then marketed to other airlines by British Airways. This made it particularly simple for British Airways representatives to enter Virgin's computer system to poach passengers. In a related situation Southwest Airlines is dependent on other airlines' computerized booking systems utilised by travel agencies. Currently, Southwest is being shut out of these systems. The suggestion is that the overwhelming financial attractiveness of strategies of sharing, co-operation and collaboration may be somewhat less, if balanced against the strategic vulnerabilities created which may threaten our very survival in the market.

Is marketing about serving the customer, about adding value (Heaven delivered to the customer) or is it about manipulating the market, elegantly, technologically but still at the knell, about exploitation!, about a constructed reality consisting of Vegas, Disneyworld, shopping malls and soaps? It's enough to drive a man, woman or person to religion.

REFERENCES

Bell, E. (1995), 'Old flair's a winner for slimline New Saatchi', *The Observer*, 7 May, p. 12.

Bradford Management Centre in association with the Chartered Institute of Marketing Annual Conference (1995), 'Manufacturing – the Marketing Solution' (May).

Brown, S. (1994), 'Marketing as Multiplex: Screening Postmodernism', *European Journal of Marketing*, 28 (8/9): 27–51.

Brown, S. (1995), 'Life Begins at Forty? Further Thoughts on Marketing's Mid-Life Crisis', *Marketing Intelligence & Planning*, 13(1): 4–17.

Cranfield School of Management in association with the Chartered Institute of Management Annual Conference (1994), 'Marketing – the Challenge of Change' (May).

Doyle, P. and Hooley, G.J. (1992), 'Strategic orientation and corporate performance', *International Journal of Research in Marketing*, 9(1), pp. 59–73.

Gellner, E. (1992), *Postmodernism, Reason and Religion*, Routledge, London.

Jaworski, B.J. and Kohli, A.K. (1993), 'Market Orientation: Antecedents and Consequences', *Journal of Marketing*, 57(3) July, pp. 53–70.

Kumar, K. (1995), 'Apocalypse, Millennium, and Utopia Today', in Bull, M. (ed.), *Apocalypse Theory and the Ends of the World*, Blackwell, Oxford, pp. 200–24.

Milosz, C. (1990), 'The State of Europe', *Granta 30,* pp. 164–5.

Narver, J.C. and Slater, S.F. (1990), 'The Effect of a Market Orientation on Business Profitability', *Journal of Marketing*, vol. 54, October, pp. 20–35.

Piercy, N.F. and Cravens, D.W. (1995), 'The network paradigm and the marketing organisation', *European Journal of Marketing*, 29(3): 7–34.

Saunders, J. (ed.)(1994), *The Marketing Initiative*, Hemel Hempstead: Prentice Hall.

Thomas, M.J. (1994), 'Marketing – in Chaos or Transition?', *European Journal of Marketing*, 28(3): 55–62.

Thomas, M.J. and Saxena, N. (1995), 'The Unified Field of the Global Corporation', submitted to the *European Journal of Marketing*.

APPENDIX 1

COMPONENTS OF THE MARKETING EXCELLENCE FRAMEWORK

Marketing strategy	There is an extensive awareness of the need for external analysis and review of the company's competitive and market position
	There is a systematic process for the collection and use of marketing information
	Staff at all levels are actively involved in the collection of market information
	There is a well-defined strategic marketing planning process
	There are explicit strategies for developing and managing strategic alliances
	Resources are explicitly developed by reference to competitive information
	Organisational structures reflect the marketing strategy
	The company culture is marketing oriented
Quality strategy	Top management is committed to quality
	The company has a long-term commitment to improving quality
	The company has a culture which underpins quality
	The company uses systems, tools and techniques to monitor and control quality
Innovation	New product development is seen as a critical business process
	Systematic approaches are used in new product development
	External stakeholders are consciously and deliberately involved in new product development
	Product and process development are simultaneous considerations

	Cross-functional teams are consciously and deliberately involved in new product development
	New product development is time driven
	Quantified goals are established to manage and control new product development performance
Customer development	There is a conscious and explicit approach to segmentation, targeting and positioning
	The company explicitly manages through relationship marketing
	The marketing programme is regularly adjusted to reflect and anticipate customers' needs
	The company has an explicit programme to develop strategic partnerships with distributors, agents and other intermediaries
Branding	There is a clear understanding of the role of brands throughout the business
	Branding is seen as a source of strategic competitive advantage
Supply chain management	Supply chain management has a strategic role
	There are explicit systems in place for managing suppliers
	The company and its suppliers share the same strategic vision
Manufacturing strategy	Manufacturing's strategic role is explicitly recognised
	Manufacturing investment is determined by explicit reference to market needs and competitive strategy

11

ADVERTISING RESEARCH

Sins of omission and inaugurated eschatology

Stephanie O'Donohoe

INTRODUCTION

Eschatology refers to doctrine about the ultimate destiny of humanity and the world; it is a discourse about endings and the events surrounding them (Hayes 1994; McGrath 1993). As Patterson (1995) observes, it became a theological buzzword around the turn of the century when it was realised that Jesus's preaching as presented in the Gospels of Matthew, Mark and Luke is very much concerned with 'last things'. Theologians Johannes Weiss and Albert Schweitzer were particularly influential in this respect, arguing that Jesus preached an imminent apocalyptic reign of God, about to bring the world to a violent and cataclysmic end.

Current theological literature appears to have largely discarded the apocalyptic thesis in favour of an eschatology which has already been inaugurated but is not yet fully realised. This paper argues that there are strong parallels with the field of advertising research, where an experiential perspective increasingly intrudes on existing theory but has yet to develop its potential. The lack of an experiential underpinning for advertising theory until recently seems to be a grave sin of omission in the literature. A review of theory and empirical research bearing on advertising experiences finds other perspectives and methods poorly represented, and characterises these as further sins of omission. It is argued that these sins, together with the schism between academic and practitioner researchers, inhibit understanding of advertising consumption experiences. In order to make restitution, the paper proposes a programme of audience ethnography.

ESCHATOLOGY AND ADVERTISING RESEARCH

While the apocalyptic view of Jesus dominated for much of this century, Patterson (1995) argues that there is a new consensus, based on research into the early sources of Jesus's apocalyptic sayings and the context in which they were reported. The new consensus is that Jesus did not see the reign of God as a future apocalyptic event, but rather as a present reality breaking into the current world of human experience (see also Glasson 1980). In this sense, eschatology completes what is already taking place in human experience; it is the fulfilment of the process implicit in human hope and the flourishing of the innately human capacity to become (Lane 1995). According to this perspective, the Empire of God is neither a future, apocalyptic reality to be waited for constantly, nor is it fully present or realised. Its essence may be described only as potential (Patterson 1995). In this sense, McGrath (1993) talks about an inaugurated eschatology: the Kingdom of God has already been initiated, but it is not yet fully manifest.

Such twists and turns in interpretation not only offer different perspectives on the end of things; they also indicate that doctrinal formulations are conditioned by their social, historical and cultural contexts. For example, Patterson shows how European political instability in the early years of this century fostered a sense of pessimism conducive to the apocalyptic thesis, and how this spread to America from the 1950s onwards, thanks to the sense of dread inspired by two world wars, the Holocaust, the Cold War, and the spread of nuclear weapons.

The current fashion for theological pluralism reinforces a view of doctrine as socially and culturally situated. Existentialist philosophy, anthropology and sociology, for example, have led to an acknowledgement of non-theological factors at work in the definition of orthodoxy (McHugh 1994; Lindbeck 1995; Tanner 1995). Thus, even in the case of Scripture, we can see postmodern theories of language reflected: these texts are also produced, used and situated within other cultural practices, so that meaning is generated 'ephemerally and precariously' from the interaction of texts, contexts and the social activities of individuals (Graddol 1993).

Even this cursory review of eschatological thinking suggests useful parallels with current developments in advertising research. First, advertising and consumer research doctrines have certainly not evolved independently of their social and cultural environment, as Sherry (1991) illustrates in his account of the diffusion of 'alternative' methods into the American consumer research community. Second, in recent times there have been various prophesies of, and calls for, the end of academic research into advertising as we have known it. Indeed, if we look at some recent writings in this area, it seems that an eschaton has already been inaugurated; it is intruding into our current conceptualisations and practices, but is yet to be fully realised. Such realisation will involve atoning and making restitution for various sins of omission in the doctrines of advertising. These sins represent perspectives and methods which while not always absent, have been poorly represented in prior theory and research.

FIRST SIN OF OMISSION: CONSUMERS' EVERYDAY EXPERIENCES OF ADVERTISING

Many religious scholars emphasise the present day world of human experience as an important source of theology; indeed, Schillebeeckx (1977, in McHugh 1994: 670) argues that 'the interpretive experience is an essential part of the concept of revelation'. Until recently, however, a sense of human experience has rarely informed advertising doctrine, and this appears to be a grave sin of omission. As Meadows (1983) has pointed out, people consume advertising as well as products and brands. If this is so, then our theories should be able to account for advertising consumption experiences. Holbrook and Hirschman (1982: 132) have argued that consumer research has focused on information-processing and problem solving, to the neglect of experiential aspects of behaviour:

> Ignored phenomena include various playful leisure activities, sensory pleasures, daydreams, esthetic [sic] enjoyment, and emotional responses . . . This experiential perspective . . . regards consumption as a primarily subjective state of consciousness with a variety of symbolic meanings, hedonic responses, and esthetic criteria.

While they were particularly concerned with hedonic consumption, these authors suggested that a focus on consumer experiences may have implications for involvement, and for image-based and emotional responses to marketing phenomena. Subsequent treatments of consumption experience, while emphasising emotional or hedonic issues, have much in common with the cognitive–affective–conative approach of many attitude models. For example, Hirschman and Holbrook (1986) refer to thoughts, emotions, activities and values, and they point out that thoughts include dreaming, imagining and fantasising. Similarly, Lofman (1991) discusses experience in terms of settings, sensations, thoughts, feelings, activity and evaluation.

Thompson *et al.* (1989: 143) argue that the concept of 'experience' is still approached within the consumer research literature '. . . with some of the same metaphysical suspicions behaviouralists held for "mind"'. In an advertising context, however, several authors have recently shown how it is no longer possible to conceptualise advertising responses without recognising their experiential dimension. Perhaps the most well-known example is the work of Mick and Buhl (1992). These authors offered a meaning-based model of advertising experiences, and demonstrated how three Danish brothers' interpretations and experiences of particular ads were intertwined with their personal life themes and life projects, so that what appeared to be idiosyncratic meanings were

> demonstrably significant and relatively patterned when observed ads were analysed against the backdrop of the individual's life history and current life-world.
>
> (p. 333)

Other studies, conducted in Britain by researchers working outside the marketing discipline (Buckingham 1993; Nava and Nava 1990) as well as within it (e.g. Elliott and Ritson 1995; Ritson and Elliott 1995; O'Donohoe 1994a,b) have begun to explore the roles and meanings of advertising in everyday life; Buttle (1991) also reviews a range of studies touching on similar issues. These empirical studies indicate the active, sophisticated and socially situated nature of advertising reception. Many of their findings had been anticipated by several close readings of advertising texts such as those offered by Grafton-Small and Linstead (1989), Stern (1993) and Scott (1991; 1992; 1994a,b). For example, Grafton-Small and Linstead demonstrated how ads presume and require creative interpretations on the part of consumers, informed by their everyday social experiences and understandings. Scott's (1994a) analysis of images in print ads presents a devastating critique of the experimental tradition, and of 'central' and 'peripheral' processing theory, in advertising research. Indeed, she argues (1994b: 475) that

> The implied [advertising] reader in consumer research . . . is passive and lazy – but is remarkably interested in learning brand information for its own sake. This is not a reader any of us care to be, nor one that any of us probably know.

Such insightful analyses of advertising texts may be considered eschatological language events, in the sense that Patterson (1995) uses for the extended metaphors of Biblical parables. Reviewing the work of scholars such as Funk, Wilder and Crossan, Patterson explores the argument that parables draw listeners into a new world whose reality unfolds in their imagination. Through parables, listeners do not just hear of a new world, a new way of being: it actually becomes a reality to be experienced, with the power to shock and transform:

> [A parable] encounters the listener insofar as he or she allows the parabolic event to deconstruct the world as he or she has constructed it. As the conventional world of meaning(-lessness) is shattered by the parable, the reign of God comes breaking in.
>
> (Patterson 1995: 41)

Similarly, exegeses of advertising texts and their 'implied reader' (Scott 1994b) not only make a compelling case for rethinking the world of advertising consumption experiences; they also offer us tantalising glimpses of what this reconstructed world might look like.

The remainder of this paper is based on a literature review of marketing and consumer research conducted in pursuit of a more rounded account of consumers' advertising experiences, moving beyond the mechanistic 'processing' of message elements (O'Donohoe 1994a). As so little material addressed this topic directly, the review focused on three areas which seemed relevant. First, given the similarities between theories of experience and the cognitive–affective–conative attitude framework, it seemed useful to examine research on attitudes to ads and advertising. Second, the issue of involvement and advertising seemed to be worth examining. Much of this literature actually addresses the advertising implications of product or situation involvement. However, Krugman's (1965) initial notion of advertising involvement seemed to offer some useful directions, with its emphasis on consumers making connections between the content of ads and their own lives. Finally, several British advertising research practitioners had written about what was loosely termed 'advertising literacy' (Meadows 1983; Lannon 1985, 1992), and has only recently begun to be theorised and examined by academics (Ritson and Elliott 1995; O'Donohoe 1994a, 1995a). This also seemed to offer a useful perspective on advertising consumption experiences; for example, advertising literacy was seen to incorporate consumers' understanding of advertising styles, codes and conventions.

In focusing on these areas, the assumption was not that these would yield a definitive framework for conceptualising consumers' experience of advertising. Instead, it was hoped that addressing these issues simultaneously would indicate relationships between them, contributing to a less fragmented theoretical platform for examining consumers' advertising experiences. That review identified four further sins of omission in that literature, which may also be relevant to other areas of enquiry. It is argued that these impede the realisation of the advertising eschaton inaugurated by work 'putting consumer experience back into consumer research' (Thompson *et al.* 1989).

SECOND SIN OF OMISSION: EUROPEAN PERSPECTIVES

British-based researchers have examined consumers' advertising literacy and attitudes to advertising. However, most studies on the structure of beliefs about advertising, attitudes to particular ads, and involvement are American. Indeed, Buttle's (1990) bibliometric analysis of American and European journals in the field of consumer and marketing research concludes that the literature 'has an American accent': most articles written or cited in these journals were by authors with American affiliations. Buttle (1990: 137) asks:

> If 'European' knowledge about consumer behaviour is no more than reconstituted American knowledge based upon American observation of American subjects, how reliable, valid and utilitarian is it in other contexts?

Such concerns seem particularly relevant to the study of advertising experiences. First, there are some indications that American and British ads are different (Weinberger and Spotts 1989; Katz and Lee 1992). Second, it seems that consumers' attitudes to advertising are more positive in Britain than in America (O'Donohoe 1995b). Even more fundamentally, Carey (1992) argues that European and American communication models are based on different metaphors: American theory is dominated by a 'transmission' perspective, concerned with issues of effectiveness and control. In contrast, European theory is based on a 'ritual' perspective, bound up with a sense of shared culture. Thus, it seems that rather than being overawed by American evangelicalism, we should question our faith in the relevance of US models to different cultures.

THIRD SIN OF OMISSION: NON-MANAGERIAL PERSPECTIVES

Just as a church could usefully be researched from the perspective of its congregation as well as its ministers, our understanding of advertising may benefit from venturing beyond a managerial vantage point. Issues of involvement and attitudes to particular ads, however, have been almost exclusively addressed from the perspective of marketing 'effectiveness'. Much research on attitudes to advertising in general, and until recently, many studies of advertising literacy, have also been conducted within a managerial framework.

Several researchers have lamented this restricted perspective in the field of marketing and consumer behaviour. Sheth (1980) and Holbrook (1985), for example, have argued that if consumer behaviour is to be understood, theory must serve the purposes of the discipline as well as those of managers. Similarly, Anderson (1983) refers to marketing theory as a 'technology of influence', used largely for the benefit of marketers rather than consumers or society at large. More recently, Hirschman (1993) conducted an 'ideological analysis' of the 1980 and 1990 volumes of the *Journal of Consumer Research*. She reports that approximately one-third of articles were explicitly positioned as managerial aids, and argues that this places consumers 'in an even more vulnerable position'. It is not necessary, however, to consider marketers as Machiavellian manipulators, and consumers as their passive and defenceless prey, to agree with Anderson (1983: 28) that marketing – or advertising:

> is a generic human activity, which may be studied simply because it is an intrinsically interesting social phenomenon . . . The interest must lie in understanding and explaining the phenomenon itself, rather than understanding it from the perspective of only one of the participants.

Indeed, greater understanding of people's advertising experiences should be useful to those exploring advertising's social, cultural and public policy implications; it would be a sad reflection on our discipline if only those outside it concerned themselves with such issues.

FOURTH SIN OF OMISSION: QUALITATIVE METHODS

While the few empirical studies of advertising literacy have been almost exclusively qualitative, the reverse is true of the vast body of research on attitudes and involvement: much of this has been in the form of laboratory experiments using students, simulated ads and hypothetical products. The ecological validity of such approaches is questionable (see for example Allen and Madden 1989;

Sears 1986; Thorson 1990). Indeed, Wells's (1993) critique of 'myths' surrounding consumer research encompasses assumptions that students represent consumers, laboratories represent the environment, and statistical significance confers real significance. Wells is not the first to criticise the quantitative, statistical focus of much consumer research. For example, Jacoby (1978: 94) asked:

> what are we doing working three and four digits to the right of the decimal point? What kind of phenomena, measures, and data do we really have that we are being so precise in our statistical analysis?

One reason for the quantitative orthodoxy which has prevailed until recently may lie in the culture of graduate education in marketing and consumer research. In this context, Lull's (1990: 9–10) comments about his experience as a graduate communications student in the 1970s may provide a useful parallel:

> Learning to use statistics was the core ritual in the rites of passage for graduate students in communication studies. If you were clever with path analysis, and multi-discriminant analysis, you were a good student . . . The study of human communication was actually defined by our training in quantitative methods . . .

Consideration of such issues is not intended to undermine thoughtfully constructed quantitative research projects. It does, however, suggest the limitations which may be imposed on understanding when the study of human, social phenomena is dominated by a quantitative perspective. As Burns (1989) has pointed out, qualitative methods are particularly appropriate when the researcher seeks to 'experience the experience of others', as the focus is on exploring and understanding phenomena from the participant's perspective. With the emerging body of research incorporating interpretive analyses of advertising texts and qualitative studies of consumers' everyday advertising encounters, it appears that the potential of such methods is in the process of being realised.

FIFTH SIN OF OMISSION: NONPOSITIVISTIC PARADIGMS

As paradigms refer to the accepted procedures and ways of thinking within a particular discipline (Boronski 1987), they embrace not only beliefs about the nature of reality and what can be known, but also ideas about how what is knowable should be investigated. Thus, paradigms are deeply embedded in researchers' socialisation, telling them what is important and legitimate in their fields of study.

The positivistic paradigm may be compared to what Lindbeck (1995; see also McGrath 1993) describes as a cognitive-propositionalist theory of doctrine; this sees it as a set of 'informative propositions or truth claims about objective realities'. Although Hunt (1989, 1991) challenges the general view of positivism and the extent of its influence, there is a broad agreement that the dominant research paradigm for consumer research has been positivistic, focusing on objectivity and rigorous measurement in order to explain, predict and control phenomena (see for example Ozanne and Hudson 1989; Lutz 1989; Sherry 1991). Academic studies of attitudes and involvement with respect to advertising have been firmly located within a positivistic framework. Their emphasis on measurement and controlled experiments implies a belief in 'objective' research and an interest in predicting advertising effects. Attitude and involvement studies have frequently presented isolated subjects with simulated ads in laboratory settings, implying that reality is fragmentable and generalisations are possible beyond the research context. Buttle (1991: 97) for one finds this unacceptable, as:

> Those researchers who investigate individual effects appear to conceive of individuals as islands of cognitive and affective responses, unconnected to a social world, detached from culture, removed from history and biography. This is an impoverished model of humanity which can produce only barren theory.

Indeed, there are many grounds for contesting the nature of the individual as he or she is generally presented in experimental consumer research. As Lane (1995) points out, a view of the human subject as some kind of fixed, self-contained entity is not only challenged by disciplines as disparate as feminism, ecology and cosmology, but also seems to preclude the kind of transformation offered by eschatology. The emerging view is that the human self is, in Lane's terms, 'radically relational, [and] always in the process of becoming'.

Increasingly, consumer researchers are turning towards a naturalistic paradigm (Lincoln and Guba 1985), alternatively described as 'interpretive' or 'humanistic'. This paradigm challenges the axioms of positivism, and is more concerned with understanding than prediction or control. It is also consistent with what Lindbeck describes as a cultural-linguistic theory of doctrine, emphasising how human thoughts and actions are shaped by historical and cultural contexts. The fruits of such an approach are beginning to be seen in advertising research. Interpretive analyses of advertising texts, for example, offer some insights into the complex interactions between ads, individuals and the social and cultural environment; the few qualitative studies of consumers' advertising literacy and interpretations also address such issues. However, as Mick and Buhl (1992) observe, there is a lack of 'actual consumer data' informing studies of advertising meanings and encounters, and a need to look at advertising 'more thoroughly through the consumer's eyes'.

SCHISMATIC TENDENCIES: ACADEMICS VERSUS PRACTITIONERS

So far, it has been argued that our understanding of advertising consumption experiences is impeded by various sins of omission in the literature. It also seems to be hindered by schismatic tendencies in the community of advertising researchers, which fragment knowledge and understanding. While there may be some crossover between advertising academics and practitioners in terms of personnel, very little research overlap was evident in the literature reviewed. Involvement research appears to have been conducted almost exclusively by academic researchers, although attitudes to ads and advertising have been investigated by industry practitioners as well as by academics. Advertising literacy was initially a topic of interest to practitioners, although as we have seen, it has recently begun to interest academics.

Even within areas which have attracted the attention of academics and practitioners, however, there seems to have been little interaction between them. For example, in the case of attitudes to particular ads, practitioners have focused on Reaction Profiles, while academics have devoted attention to the construct of 'attitude towards the ad'. Where overlaps exist in this area, they have tended to take the form of academics testing the validity of practitioners' 'atheoretical' research instruments. In the case of literacy research, academics and practitioners appear to have worked largely independently of each other.

The lack of integration between the two approaches may be attributed to a sense of mutual suspicion. For example, Holbrook (1985: 146) suggests that business executives possess 'a resolute bias against scholarship and science', to the extent that they find words such as 'conceptual' or 'theory' distasteful. From the other side of the divide, Lannon (1985) observes that while she once regretted the lack of links between the worlds of business and academia in Britain, she had come to see it as a distinct advantage. Such mutual suspicion may in turn be explained in terms of different priorities. Brindberg and Hirschman (1986) suggest that academic research tends to be concept-driven, with strengths in the rigour brought to bear on measures and manipulations. However, this approach tends to sacrifice detailed analysis and comprehensive understanding of a phenomenon's features. Practitioner research, on the other hand, tends to be system-driven. It generally focuses on particular 'real world' phenomena or systems, and its strength often lies in its pragmatic relevance and detailed descriptions. However, it tends to sacrifice precision and control of measures and manipulations. This suggests that there is a need for both academic and practitioner orientations, so that the strengths of one may compensate for the weaknesses of the other. As an indication of this potential complementarity, practitioners' reflections on the phenomenon of advertising literacy have alerted academics to the possibilities for a fascinating stream of research grounded in the ways that consumers use and experience real ads in real life. Thus, it seems that rapprochement between those who practice and those who preach advertising could lead to a less fragmented understanding of advertising experiences.

DISCUSSION: INAUGURATING AUDIENCE ETHNOGRAPHY FOR A NEW ERA OF ADVERTISING RESEARCH

This chapter has argued that it is no longer possible to rely on advertising theories or research which deny the centrality of advertising consumption experiences. While exegeses of advertising texts have ushered in new ways of seeing these, Scott (1994b) also calls for a 'new research stream' beginning with observations of phenomena as we find them, and addressing actual everyday advertising discourse. This echoes Buttle's (1991) discussion of ethnographic research as the ideal means of understanding how the raw material of advertising is accommodated in the routine social actions of everyday life. Ethnographic research, rooted in anthropology, traditionally refers to:

> a written account of a lengthy social interaction between a scholar and a distant culture . . . an effort to observe and to comprehend the entire tapestry of social life.
>
> (Radway 1988: 367)

Similarly, Smith (1986) refers to ethnography as inductive and holistic, relying heavily on participant observation. Indeed, given the desired research emphasis on advertising consumption as a socially and culturally situated experience, participant observation seems a particularly appropriate way forward. As a research method, however, this is most suited to situations where there is a constant supply of the activities to be examined, including interactions between people playing particular roles. Sites such as shops, schools and hospitals are dedicated to particular activities and offer a range of formal and informal interactions to be observed. We may expect participant observation of consumers' everyday advertising experiences to pose problems, however. Such experiences are not necessarily public, and they are widely dispersed. They may occur while watching commercial television programmes in the home, but advertising is also encountered in many other media and locations, and may be experienced beyond the point of actual 'exposure' to particular ads.

Similar problems have been encountered in the fields of cultural and media studies. Much research in these areas addresses how mass media messages are consumed, interpreted, and integrated into people's everyday lives. At the same time, audience researchers taking the 'ethnographic turn' (Moores 1993) have faced the elusiveness of media audiences. Thus, Ang (1991) distinguishes between the concept of the television audience, and the dispersed, dynamic and contradictory social world of actual audiences. Similarly, Moores has observed that there is often no stable entity which can be isolated and observed as 'the media audience'.

Morley's (1980) research on the *Nationwide* audience was the first to take an ethnographic approach to audiences in the field of cultural studies. He showed a video of that current affairs programme to different groups of students, and asked for their responses. While this study is generally accepted as a landmark in audience research, there has been much discussion of its shortcomings as a piece of ethnography, not least by its author (Morley 1986); for example, the study put individuals into groups which would not normally have formed, and treated them as an audience for a programme which they may not otherwise have chosen to watch. Subsequent audience studies have broadened the scope of enquiry beyond interpretations of particular television episodes to patterns of media usage and preference. Hobson (1982) visited female viewers of the soap opera *Crossroads* in their homes, and watched an episode with them as a springboard for discussion. This indicated the context in which the programme was viewed, with many women juggling their viewing with preparations of the evening meal or feeding children. Lull's (1990) account of family television viewing is based on participant observation in many homes and in-depth interviews with each family member. Morley (1986) also visited families in their own homes, but his research on television viewing patterns was restricted to one-and-a-half-hour interviews. Other studies on media audiences have been restricted to discussions with children in schools and youth clubs, or even the analysis of solicited letters concerning people's likes and dislikes (Buckingham 1993; Ang 1985).

As Turner (1990) observes, the use of the term 'ethnography' in relation to some of this work is contentious. Indeed, Nightingale (1989) wonders whether one-and-a-half-hour interviews are sufficient for a detailed or 'thick description'. She also rejects accounts which are simply descriptive, unrelated to societal structures of power and inequality. Furthermore, she argues that even when audience research techniques are ethnographic, research strategies often are not. Many studies do not set out to gain a broad understanding of a culture, for example, but to address narrow issues such as the decoding of a text or the pleasures which it provides. The 'narrowly circumscribed' goals of much audience research have also been criticised by Radway (1988), as it often isolates a single medium rather than exploring how the media in general fit into 'the endlessly shifting, ever-evolving kaleidoscope of daily life'. In defence of audience ethnography, however, Moores (1993: 4) emphasises the private context of much media consumption and argues that many 'audience ethnography' studies:

> share some of the same general intentions as anthropological research. There may be a similar concern, for instance, with questions of meaning and social contexts – and with charting the 'situational embeddedness' of cultural practices . . .

Furthermore, as Morley and Silverstone (1991) observe, not all ethnographic research uses participant observation: the precise methods used depend on the demands of the research setting. In this context, McRobbie's (1984, in Turner 1990: 118) comments on cultural studies research are instructive. She argues that preoccupation with participant observation in cultural studies of young people restricts research to public acts. This in turn neglects many of their experiences as audience members, and:

> To ignore these is to miss an absolutely central strand in their social and personal experience . . . we are left with little knowledge of any one of their reading or viewing experiences, and therefore with how they find themselves represented in these texts, and with how in turn they appropriate from some of these and discard others.

This suggests that there is a place for the conventional qualitative methods of individual interviews and group discussions within an ethnographic research programme addressing advertising experiences. Indeed, given advertising research practitioners' expertise in these techniques, this offers one avenue for rapprochement between academics and practitioners.

It is important, however, that such techniques are applied in the spirit of ethnography, both in terms of a study's scope and its approach to participants. Thus, ethnographic studies of advertising experiences should not have narrowly defined goals, nor should they seek to isolate advertising consumption from the 'entire tapestry of social life', as Radway (1988) puts it. Furthermore, ethnographic studies should treat participants as informants rather than respondents. The importance of this apparently minor semantic distinction has been discussed by Spradley (1979), who shows its influence over how a study is framed. Treating participants as informants rather than respondents grounds a study in their language and culture, rather than those of the researcher, and it emphasises that their contribution extends beyond simply answering questions.

The Mick and Buhl study has shown how much individual interviews can yield in terms of interconnections between particular ads and the life-worlds of their audiences. That research, however, focused on how three brothers experienced particular ads selected by the researchers, albeit from magazines which the brothers actually read. Rather than imposing a set of ads on participants, O'Donohoe (1994a,b) based a combination of individual interviews and small group discussions on young adults' accounts of ads drawn from their own real-life encounters with advertising. This approach allowed the participants to offer many rich and extremely detailed descriptions and interpretations of ads drawn from their own everyday experiences. Advertising appeared to serve a wide range of purposes for the young adults, and many of these seemed to have little to do with traditional marketing transactions. For example, advertising appeared to be used as a means of scanning the environment, a source of entertainment and an outlet for creative play, and a means of reinforcing attitudes and values. Advertising also seemed to be used as a resource to be drawn upon in social interactions with friends, family and acquaintances, or as tokens in social exchange, as Willis (1990) puts it. This appeared to happen at different levels. At the most basic level, it provided common ground for talk; as one young adult put it, talking about ads was like talking about the weather, but a bit more cheerful! At the next level, advertising was seen as a legitimate and interesting topic of conversation in its own right, and at the highest level, talking about advertising was considered a distinct social skill, surrounded by a set of conventions and expectations. Many of the young adults' uses for advertising had a great deal in common with 'uses and gratifications' commonly identified with the mass media in general (O'Donohoe 1994b). Indeed, the boundaries between advertising and other communication forms were very fluid for the young adults, so that their experience of ads shaped and were shaped by their experience of films, music, and television programmes for example. Furthermore, as Mick and Buhl would expect, much of the young adults' talk about advertising was intertwined with comments about other aspects of their lives.

Such findings indicate the potential for using a wider range of ethnographic methods in advertising research. For example, if advertising is indeed used as a social resource, there is great potential for research among families, groups of friends or colleagues rather than just individuals or groups of people unknown to each other. Buttle (1991: 107) is pessimistic about the prospects for such research, suggesting that observing everyday conversations would be extremely time-consuming and require the researcher to be present:

> when the advertising-related talk occurs, whether that is at the breakfast table or in front of the television watching the Saturday morning cartoons.

This may well be true, although the extent of advertising-related talk in daily life may be greater than Buttle suggests. There are however other options. For example, there are many possibilities for opportunistic studies, if only researchers are alert to the possibilities as they go about their own daily lives. For example, Grafton-Small has written a great deal of 'deep ethnography', reflecting on the implications of his own encounters with marketing phenomena (see for example Grafton-Small 1993, 1995). Elliott and Ritson (1995) address 'the lived meaning of sexuality in advertising' in their analysis of the meanings and social actions constructed by a group of flatmates from print ads for Häagen-Dazs ice-cream. That study is based on interviews with a key informant, located through social talk about advertising. Another alternative to researchers conducting participant observation is to recruit advertising consumers as participant observers over time, for example by keeping diaries of advertising-related talk and social actions initiated by others in their daily lives.

Thus, with a little imagination it does indeed seem possible to usher in a new world of advertising research, one which, in Scott's (1994b: 478) terms is able to:

> situate advertisements in the world of our own experience, connecting the way we think about advertising in our work to the way we know it in our lives.

ACKNOWLEDGEMENTS

Caroline Tynan and Bob Grafton-Small provided helpful comments on an earlier incarnation of this material, although they are not implicated in any of this paper's eschatological heresy.

REFERENCES

Allen, C.T. and Madden, T.J. (1989) 'Gauging and explaining advertising effects: emergent concerns regarding construct and ecological validity', in P. Cafferata and A.M. Tybout (eds), *Cognitive and affective responses to advertising*, Lexington, MA: Lexington Books, pp. 327–51.

Anderson, P.F. (1983) 'Marketing, scientific progress, and scientific method', *Journal of Marketing*, 47, Fall, pp. 18–31.

Ang, I. (1985) *Watching 'Dallas': soap opera and the melodramatic imagination*, London: Methuen.

Ang, I. (1991) *Desperately seeking the audience*, London: Routledge.

Boronski, T. (1987) *Knowledge*, New York: Longman.

Brindberg, D. and Hirschman, E.C. (1986) 'Multiple orientations for the conduct of marketing research: an analysis of the academic/practitioner distinction', *Journal of Marketing*, 50, October, pp. 161–73.

Buckingham, D. (1993) *Children talking television: the making of television literacy*, London: British Film Institute.

Burns, C. (1989) 'Individual interviews', in S. Robson and A. Foster (eds), *Qualitative research in action*, London: Edward Arnold, pp. 47–57.

Buttle, F. (1990) 'Communication amongst marketing and consumer researchers: a bibliometric analysis of transatlantic traffic', in A. Pendlebury and T. Watkins (eds), *Proceedings, Marketing Education Group Conference*, Oxford Polytechnic: Marketing Education Group, pp. 124–42.

Buttle, F. (1991) 'What do people do with advertising?', *International Journal of Advertising*, 10, part 2, pp. 95–110.

Carey, J.W. (1992) *Communication as culture*, London: Routledge.

Elliott, R. and Ritson, M. (1995) 'Practising existential consumption: the lived meaning of sexuality in advertising', *Advances in Consumer Research*, vol. 22 [forthcoming].

Glasson, T.F. (1980) *Jesus and the end of the world*, Edinburgh: St Andrew's Press.

Gordon, W. (1982) 'Consumer trends in advertising – 1982', unpublished paper, London: The Research Business.

Graddol, D. (1993) 'Three models of language description', in D. Graddol and O. Boyd-Barrat (eds), *Media texts: authors and readers*, Clevedon: Multilingual Matters Ltd., pp. 1–21.

Grafton-Small, R. (1993) 'Consumption and significance: everyday life in a brand new second-hand bow tie', *European Journal of Marketing*, 27:8, pp. 38–45.

Grafton-Small, R. (1995) 'From goods to beast: consumer interpretations of order and excess', paper presented at the *Second Conference of the European Association for Consumer Research*, Copenhagen, June.

Grafton-Small, R. and Linstead, S. (1989) 'Advertisements as artefacts: everyday understanding and the creative consumer', *International Journal of Advertising*, 8:3, pp. 205–18.

Hayes, Z. (1994) 'Eschatology', in M. Glazier and M.K. Hellwig (eds), *The modern Catholic encyclopedia*, Goldenbridge, Ireland: Gill & Macmillan, pp. 285–7.

Hirschman, E.C. (1993) 'Ideology in consumer research, 1980 and 1990: a Marxist and feminist critique', *Journal of Consumer Research*, 19, March, pp. 537–55.

Hirschman, E.C. and Holbrook, M.B. (1986) 'Expanding the ontology and methodology of research on the consumption experience', in D. Brindberg and R.J. Lutz (eds), *Perspectives on methodology in consumer research*, New York: Springer-Verlag, pp. 213–51.

Hobson, D. (1982) *'Crossroads': the drama of a soap opera*, London: Methuen.

Holbrook, M.B. (1985) 'Why business is bad for consumer research', in E.C. Hirschman and M.B. Holbrook (eds), *Advances in Consumer Research*, 12, Ann Arbor, MI: Association for Consumer Research, pp. 145–56.

Holbrook, M.B. and Hirschman, E.C. (1982) 'The experiential aspects of consumption: consumer fantasies, feelings, and fun', *Journal of Consumer Research*, 9, September, pp. 132–40.

Hunt, S.D. (1989) 'Naturalistic, humanistic, and interpretive inquiry: challenges and ultimate potential', in E.C. Hirschman (ed.), *Interpretive consumer research*, Provo, UT: Association for Consumer Research, pp. 185–97.

Hunt, S.D. (1991) 'Positivism and paradigm dominance in consumer research: towards critical pluralism and rapprochement', *Journal of Consumer Research*, 18, June, pp. 32–44.

Jacoby, J. (1978) 'Consumer research: a state of the art review', *Journal of Marketing*, 42, April, pp. 87–96.

Katz, H. and Lee, W. (1992) 'Oceans apart: an initial exploration of social communication differences in US and UK prime-time television advertising', *International Journal of Advertising*, 11, part 1, pp. 69–82.

Krugman, H. (1965) 'The impact of television advertising: learning without involvement', *Public Opinion Quarterly*, 29, Fall, pp. 349–56.

Lane, D.A. (1995) 'Anthropology and eschatology', *Irish Theological Quarterly*, 61:1, pp. 14–31.

Lannon, J. (1985) 'Advertising research: new ways of seeing', *Admap*, vol. 20, October, pp. 520–4.

Lannon, J. (1992) 'Asking the right questions: what do people do with advertising?', *Admap*, vol. 27, March, pp. 11–16.

Lincoln, Y. and Guba, E. (1985) *Naturalistic inquiry*, Beverly Hills: Sage.

Lindbeck, G.A. (1995), 'The nature of doctrine: toward a postliberal theology', in R. Gill (ed.), *Readings in modern theology*, London: SPCK, pp. 188–202.

Lofman, B. (1991) ' Elements of experiential consumption: an exploratory study', in R.H. Holman and M.R. Solomon (eds), *Advances in Consumer Research*, 18, Provo, UT: Association for Consumer Research, pp. 729–35.

Lull, J. (1990) *Inside family viewing: ethnographic research on television's audiences*, London: Routledge.

Lutz, R.J. (1989) 'Positivism, naturalism, and pluralism in consumer research: paradigms in paradise', in T.K. Srull (ed.), *Advances in Consumer Research*, 16, Provo, UT: Association for Consumer Research, pp. 1–8.

McGrath, A.E. (1993) 'Doctrine and dogma', in A.E. McGrath (ed.), *The Blackwell encyclopaedia of modern Christian thought*, Oxford: Blackwell, pp. 112–19.

McHugh (1994) 'Theology', in W. Outhwaite and T. Bottomore (eds), *The Blackwell dictionary of twentieth-century social thought*, Oxford: Blackwell, pp. 669–71.

Meadows, R. (1983) 'They consume advertising too', *Admap*, vol. 18, July–August, pp. 408–13.

Mick, D.G. and Buhl, C. (1992) 'A meaning-based model of advertising experiences', *Journal of Consumer Research*, 19, December, pp. 317–38.

Moores, S. (1993), *Interpreting audiences: The ethnography of media consumption*, London: Sage.

Morley, D. (1980) *The Nationwide audience: structure and decoding*, London: British Film Institute.

Morley, D. (1986) *Family television: cultural power and domestic leisure*, London: Comedia.
Morley, D. and Silverstone, R. (1991) 'Communication and context: ethnographic perspectives on the media audience', in K.B. Jensen and N.W. Jankowski (eds), *A handbook of qualitative methodologies for mass communication research*, London: Routledge, pp. 149–62.
Nava , M. and Nava, O. (1990) 'Discriminating or duped? Young people as consumers of advertising/art', *Magazine of Cultural Studies*, 1, March, pp. 15–21.
Nightingale, V. (1989), 'What's ethnographic about ethnographic research?', *Australian Journal of Communication*, 16 (December), pp. 50–63.
O'Donohoe, S. (1994a) *Postmodern poachers: young adult experiences of advertising*, unpublished PhD thesis, Edinburgh: The University of Edinburgh.
O'Donohoe, S. (1994b) 'Advertising uses and gratifications', *European Journal of Marketing*, 28:8/9, pp. 52–75.
O'Donohoe, S. (1995a) 'Playtime TV: advertising literate audiences and the commercial game', in T. Meenaghan and P. O'Sullivan (eds), *Marketing communications in Ireland*, Dublin: Oaktree Press, pp. 585–603.
O'Donohoe, S. (1995b) 'Attitudes to advertising: a review of British and American research', *International Journal of Advertising*, 14:3, pp. 245–61.
Ozanne, J.L. and Hudson, L.A. (1989) 'Exploring diversity in consumer research', in E.C. Hirschman (ed.), *Interpretive consumer research*, Provo, UT: Association for Consumer Research, pp. 1–9.
Patterson, S.J. (1995) 'The end of apocalypse: rethinking the eschatological Jesus', *Theology Today*, 52:1, April, pp. 29–48.
Radway, J. (1988) 'Reception study: ethnography and the problems of dispersed audiences and nomadic subjects', *Cultural Studies*, 2 (3), pp. 356–76.
Ritson, M. and Elliott, R. (1995) 'A model of advertising literacy: the praxiology and co-creation of advertising meaning', in M. Bergadaa (ed.), *Proceedings, European Marketing Academy Conference*, ESSEC, Paris: European Marketing Academy, pp. 1035–54.
Scott, L.M. (1991) 'The troupe: celebrities as dramatis personae in advertisements', in R.H. Holman and M.R. Solomon (eds), *Advances in Consumer Research,* 18, Provo, UT: Association for Consumer Research, pp. 355–63.
Scott, L.M. (1992) 'Playing with pictures: postmodernism, poststructuralism, and advertising visuals', in J.F. Sherry and B. Sternthal (eds), *Advances in Consumer Research*, 19, Provo, UT: Association for Consumer Research, pp. 596–612.
Scott, L.M. (1994a) 'Images in advertising: the need for a theory of visual rhetoric', *Journal of Consumer Research*, 21, September, pp. 252–73.
Scott, L.M. (1994b) 'The bridge from text to mind: adapting reader-response theory to consumer research', *Journal of Consumer Research*, 21, December, pp. 461–80.
Sears, D.O. (1986) 'College sophomores in the laboratory: influences of a narrow data base on social psychology's view of human nature', *Journal of Personality and Social Psychology*, 51:3, pp. 515–30.
Sherry, J.F. (1991) 'Postmodern alternatives: the interpretive turn in consumer research', in T. S. Robertson and H.H. Kassarjian (eds), *Handbook of consumer behaviour*, Englewood Cliffs, NJ: Prentice Hall, pp. 548–91.
Sheth, J.N. (1980) 'The surpluses and shortages in consumer behaviour theory and research', *Journal of the Academy of Marketing Science*, 7:4, pp. 414–27.
Smith, D. (1986) 'The anthropology of literacy acquisition', in B.B. Schieffelin and P. Gilmore (eds), *The acquisition of literacy: ethnographic perspectives*, New Jersey: Ablex Publishing Corporation, pp. 261–76.
Spradley, J.P. (1979) *The ethnographic interview*, New York: Holt, Rinehart and Winston.
Stern, B.B. (1993) 'Feminist literary criticism and the deconstruction of ads: a postmodern view of advertising and consumer response', *Journal of Consumer Research*, 19, March, pp. 556–66.

Tanner, K. (1995) 'The difference theological anthropology makes', in R. Gill (ed.), *Readings in modern theology*, London: SPCK, pp. 43–57.
Thompson, C., Locander, W. and Pollio, H. (1989) 'Putting consumer experience back into consumer research: the philosophy and method of existentialist-phenomenology', *Journal of Consumer Research*, 16, September, pp. 133–45.
Thorson, E. (1990) 'Consumer processing of advertising', in J.H. Leigh and C.R. Martin (eds), *Current issues and research in marketing*, 12, Michigan: Michigan Business School, pp. 197–230.
Turner, G. (1990) *British cultural studies: an introduction*, Boston: Unwin Hyman.
Weinberger, M.G. and Spotts, H.E. (1989) 'A situational view of information content in TV advertising in the US and UK', *Journal of Marketing*, 53, January, pp. 89–94.
Wells, W.D. (1993) 'Discovery-oriented consumer research', *Journal of Consumer Research*, 19:3, pp. 489–504.
Willis, P. (1990) *Common culture*, Milton Keynes: Open University Press.

12

THE PATHETIC PHALLUSIES OF ST THOMAS AQUINAS AND WHY MARKETING SHOULD GIVE EVE A BREAK

Miriam Catterall, Pauline Maclaran and Lorna Stevens

INTRODUCTION

Marketing academics, like early theologians such as St Thomas Aquinas and St Augustine, are using false premises on which to build their theories. Just as these early Christian scholars did not question core beliefs such as the existence of God, Adam's (man's) superiority to Eve (woman), and Eve's blame for man's fall from grace so, too, marketing scholars and practitioners do not question that which they hold as sacred, nor challenge the patriarchal world-view upon which marketing knowledge is based. Phallocentrism with its misplaced 'sacred' ideals has led to an imperfect discipline; a discipline which through its 'profanities' is increasingly alienating marketing's followers. To illustrate, we will examine one of marketing's core tools – market(ing) research – and find it prejudiced at best and seriously flawed at worst. We will go on to propose that a feminist perspective is necessary to redress the balance and that market(ing) researchers need to shed their androcentrism, complacency and comfortable assumptions about research practice and rethink their relationship with the subjects of their research. Only then can marketing progress as a discipline.

SACRED PHALLUSIES

Marketing knowledge is founded on an empiricist positivist philosophical position which emphasises rationality and objectivity. As Holland (1990: 8) argues, this ontology is from an exclusively and exclusive masculine perspective. In effect '*men* create *the world from their own point of view, which then* becomes *the reality to be described*' (Mackinnon in Holland 1990: 8). According to Stanley and Wise (1993: 194) this ontology 'sees all of reality as characterised by two opposing principles, those of masculinity and femininity'. Maleness is associated with the mind, objectivity, science, culture and rationality and femaleness with the body, subjectivity, art, nature and emotion. In this world of Cartesian dualisms the values associated with maleness have been worshipped and held as sacred ideals to pursue above all else. The values associated with femaleness have been debased, held as profanities which can have no contribution to make to the pursuit of 'truth'.

This worldview is reflected in the early theological writings of St Augustine (fifth century AD) and St Thomas (twelfth century AD), amongst others, who interpreted the story of creation as providing divine sanction for male dominance and female subordination ad infinitum. Eve, Adam's 'help meet' (mate), by partaking of the fruit of the tree of knowledge and tempting Adam to do likewise, is responsible for man's fall from grace. As St Ambrose reminds us, 'Adam was led to sin by Eve and not Eve by Adam'. By her act Eve is forever condemned to a life of servitude and suffering. To these early Christian theologians women were objects of fear and loathing, to be shunned. Tertullian described women as 'the devil's doorway', and St John Chrysostom, in his discomfiture with the female sex, went so far as to declare that 'among all savage beasts none is found so harmful as woman'. Women were by their very nature perceived as profane, and man sacred. However religious writings also reflect an ambivalence man feels towards woman, symbolised by the two opposing images of woman perpetuated by them: the sacred (The Goddess) and the profane (The Whore). From earliest times these conflicting (male) images of woman continually oscillate and transmogrify, typifying the kratophanous power associated with sacred objects (Belk *et al.* 1989: 518); inspiring longing on the one hand and loathing on the other; at once revered and feared, both sacred and profane, tantalising yet taboo.

We argue that just as man simultaneously worships and profanes women so too marketers simultaneously worship and profane the customer. In man's relationship with woman and in marketers' relationship with consumers the claim is made to understand the needs and wants of the object of their desires, but in reality man's and marketers' own needs and wants predominate. To illustrate our argument we employ an overarching metaphor of sex as a commodity to show how the consumer is profaned through the marketing research process.

MARKETING PROFANITIES

There can be little doubt that marketing as a discipline has a worldview which is masculine in orientation (Bristor and Fischer 1993; Hirschman 1993; Joy and Venkatesh 1994), and we would argue that this dominant, patriarchal ideology is currently being exposed for all its shortcomings and inadequacies. Marketing is failing its disciples and leading to increasing numbers of doubters and unbelievers. The current spate of angst-ridden literature on marketing and the marketing concept (Brady and Davis 1993; Brown 1995; Brownlie and Saren 1992) questions the sacred tenets on which marketing is founded, and testifies to an identity crisis in the marketing brotherhood together with a sense of impending doom for the discipline.

One of the central tenets of the marketing concept is that the customer is worshipped, and much of the mid-life crisis literature emanating from the marketing brotherhood recognises a loss of customer focus and addresses a need to reassert a focus on the customer (Brady and Davis 1993; Webster 1988). Indeed Buttle (1994) goes so far as to suggest that consumer behaviour is a theoretical black hole, and to say that after fifty years of research we are no nearer to an understanding of consumer behaviour.

Traditionally, market(ing) research has provided the link between marketers and consumers. However, like the marketing discipline in general, market researchers are also experiencing an identity crisis, and many are calling for a reassessment of the role of marketing research and the relationship between researcher, client and respondent (Cowan 1994; Freeling 1994; Hodock 1991). We argue that a more fundamental reassessment is required; that market researchers need to re-dedicate their relationships with both clients and respondents.

Disenchantment with traditional quantitative market research has led in recent years to greater attention being given to qualitative research methods. One of the main advantages of qualitative research is that it is perceived to bridge the gulf between marketers and consumers; that it gets closer to the consumer and sees things from the consumer's point of view. However, we will suggest that this is not the case, and that qualitative market researchers' primary focus is on clients' needs and wants. To explore the extent to which qualitative market research is out of touch with respondents we will look at focus group research, that most popular and enduring form of qualitative research. In so doing we will develop our analogies of man and woman, marketer and consumer, the sacred and the profane, with imagery which we trust illustrates how the consumer is profaned through the market(ing) research process. We will then go on to argue that a feminist perspective may offer a solution to the present quandary in which marketing researchers find themselves. With its emphasis on research as a co-operative process, a partnership of equals, and researcher and researched collaborating to gain genuinely insightful knowledge (Fonow and Cook 1991), feminist research may go some considerable way to offering a solution to the current crisis.

ON THE ROAD TO HELL

Qualitative market researchers exploit and profane respondents in a manner not dissimilar to the rape model used by Reinharz (1979) to refer to academic researchers: 'researchers take, hit, and run. They intrude into their subjects' privacy, disrupt their perceptions, utilize false pretences, manipulate the relationship, and give little or nothing in return.' Market researchers do not operate in a state of blissful ignorance; indeed they confess to this shameful state of affairs with a mixture of guilt and self-justification (Templeton 1989). A more appropriate analogy than Reinharz' rape model might therefore be that qualitative market researchers are the pimps of marketing. For £15 and a couple of drinks, flesh-and-blood consumers are procured for the titillation of marketing and advertising executives. In this seedy underworld mutual manipulation and instant gratification are the norm. We may conclude from this scenario that qualitative market researchers have strayed a long way from the path of righteousness; indeed it is more likely that they are on the road to Hell.

A JUDGEMENT SAMPLE?

By way of a final judgement on the industry the research process is examined with specific reference to the relationship between researcher and researched. We question the 'sacred' assumptions on which this relationship is based, by addressing issues of power, exploitation and the lure of objectivity (and objectification) in qualitative market research.

The shifting boundaries, as Belk *et al.* (1989) have noted, between that which is perceived as sacred and that which is perceived as profane in consumption, are also evident in current marketing research practice. As sacred ideals prove to be inadequate, researchers look elsewhere for enlightenment and truth. So in their quest to understand buyer behaviour, that which is perceived to be most 'sacred', the consumer, is in turn sacrilised and profaned, in the name of marketing research.

In the discussion that follows we illustrate how the pursuit of a sacred 'truth' profanes both the research(er) and the researched. Specifically we demonstrate that:

- market research is technique rather than problem driven;
- is hierarchical and divisive with an unequal balance of power throughout the research process;
- is characterised by practices that demean respondents; and,
- is focused entirely on client demands and expectations.

Wham, bham, thank you, mam!

Time and money set the pace

Qualitative market research has become technique driven, a triumph of method over experience. It has become synonymous with the focus group regardless of the nature of the research issue or problem to be addressed. Although other types of groups exist, informed by a number of different theoretical traditions (Fleury 1984; Satow 1989; Sampson 1985), the focus group is undoubtedly one of qualitative research's 'sacred cows', and it prevails in both Britain and the USA (Cooper 1991; Schlackman 1989). Whilst focus groups are promoted as a flexible method, there is a limit to the types of 'qualitative' problems or issues that groups can address (Fern 1982; McQuarrie and McIntyre 1986; Schlackman 1984; Twyman 1973).

The attraction of the focus group for almost any 'qualitative' problem seems to be due largely to its saliency, speed, and convenience (Sargent 1989). Promoted as quick and cheap (Andreasen 1983), at least by comparison with other qualitative methods, focus groups guarantee instant satisfaction. After all, it is less time consuming, more convenient and thus less costly to interview four groups of eight than to go out to thirty-two different locations to interview thirty-two individuals, or to engage in a sustained period of human observation. These savings in time and cost benefit the researchers and clients, but do not consider the needs of respondents (Bloom 1989).

The house of sin

Feeling superior, the audio-recorder crackled with laughter

Qualitative research is often portrayed in the research literature as an holistic process, and one which is supposedly very different from a quantitative research process which proceeds in stages and involves a research hierarchy and strict division of labour (Morton-Williams 1993). However, focus group research, with its rules, roles and restrictions, is just as hierarchical and divisive as quantitative research, and this is particularly evident from personal interviews with recruiters for focus groups.

The role of recruiters is to enlist; the role of moderators is to control. In terms of recruiters' roles in particular, phrases such as 'hard to get', 'aim for', and 'get them', all emphasise their active role and the passive part played by respondents. In the perceptions of recruiters, uncertainty and insecurity prevail in focus groups. Their main fear is that the recruits will not turn up for the group session and the moderator's wrath will be incurred; the recruited fear the unknown, whether they will have anything to say and what the discussion will be about. The moderator worries that information will not be forthcoming and the group will have been a waste of the client's resources. Thus suspicion and anxiety dominate the whole proceedings.

As far as respondents are concerned the power is unquestionably with the moderator, perceived as a dominant and distant figure. This perception is actively encouraged by many moderators, who, like high priests, administer their sacred rituals to their flocks while maintaining a distance from them, liable to become angry if they encounter group members prior to the discussion or if too few recruits turn up for the group. The practice of moderators being in situ, awaiting respondents being led in by their 'hostess' leaves respondents in no doubt as to who is in control.

In contrast to moderators the respondents are somewhat wary, asking the recruiters' advice before a discussion, 'what am I supposed to say?' and 'will I have to talk on my own?' Respondents are kept in a state of ignorance and feel at a disadvantage; they are uneasy and nervous beforehand because they do not know what to expect and are deliberately given little information in order to avoid any advance preparation on the discussion topic. This ignorance is justified by one recruiter in the following terms: 'you get more out of them [respondents] when they're green'.

Admittedly recruiters make considerable efforts to relax respondents, if only in order to get a better response from them for their clients. The recruiters are friendly and encouraging, offering drinks to relax respondents, 'otherwise they [moderators and clients] will not get what they're after'. The madame of the brothel offers up her precious virgin recruits in order to satisfy the needs of her powerful clients. In so doing, that which is most sacred (the consumer) is thereby profaned, sacrificed on the altar of a research process which pays lip-service only to a qualitative paradigm.

The peep show

The mirror gave a dirty laugh

Client demands also lead to the exploitation and objectification of respondents. Nowhere is the quest for gratifying the needs of clients at the expense of the respondent more strongly emphasised than in client observation of focus group sessions. The questionable practice of one-way viewing mirrors has not yet become as widespread in the UK as in the USA (Greenbaum 1987; Robson and Wardle 1988) where focus groups take place largely in the living rooms of recruiters' homes, often under the watchful eye of silent observers. It is also the norm to take a video or audio recording of groups. The whole process reflects a secularisation of the sacred as ideals of objectivity lead to exploitation of the consumer. At the same time the profaned side, those attributes of subjectivity, emotionality and intuition, become sacrilised as 'flesh and blood' consumers become a useful learning experience for clients (Axelrod 1975). In principle observation may seem a good idea and may lead to greater understanding for both parties if the observer actually participates in the discussions (see Geddes 1987, reported in Robson and Wardle 1988; Wells 1974). In practice such dialogue rarely, if ever, occurs.

This voyeuristic aspect of focus group research is recognised by focus group moderators; Templeton (1989: 143) writes that 'much of the popularity of focus groups stems from their supreme qualities as a spectator sport', and there is 'something delightful and faintly illicit about observing a group of people who are seen and cannot see' (op. cit.: 144). The seediness of this voyeurism is suggested by Caruso (1976) who reports on a recruiting specification for 'attractive respondents', and of the voyeurs behind the mirror creating so much noise that it was disrupting the group but 'the client is paying for this and it is part of what he [sic] wants'. Gordon and Langmaid (1988: 129) state that 'eating and drinking (often too much) are the norm as are respondent baiting and criticizing the moderator' and this helps 'offset the boredom of the scene' for 'decision-oriented people who are unaccustomed to silently listening to others in the semi-darkness'.

In fact these decision-oriented people can be spared the effort of attending by having access to the video-tape or the audio recording. A video permits even more people to learn from the group experience: 'I had a client at a debrief recently asking where the video was as his children enjoyed watching them' (Robson 1991: 24). The video can be put to other uses. Templeton (1989: 144) claims that the video is 'used as a matter of course' by agencies in new business presentations and in meetings attended by sales staff, distributors and so on; 'the intoxicating power of eavesdropping carries over very well into video tape presentations'. The 'theatrical use' of the focus group is 'rarely mentioned in marketing textbooks' (op. cit.: 158) nor does it appear to be mentioned to the unsuspecting respondents. In these ways the consumer is yet again debased through the research process.

Normally the first the respondents hear about recording and observers is when they enter the discussion room and either see for themselves or are informed by the moderator. This is all part of keeping the respondent at arms length, retaining the balance of power firmly with the moderator and justifying this in the name of 'objectivity'. There is a general 'fudging' of information given to respondents, for example, ' the best way to handle . . . these issues is in a low-key manner so they do not get positioned in people's minds as significant issues' (Greenbaum 1987: 87).

Apart from raising ethical questions, the observation of groups also impacts on the outcome of the research. Robson and Wardle's research (1988) has confirmed that observers, whether behind the mirror or in the living room, have a significant impact on the discussion that takes place in the group. Specifically, respondents assume observers are there in an evaluation role and are more likely to self-censor their comments in their presence and present a public rather than a private face. Additionally, 'there are times when respondents suspect the moderator of lying: a client observer introduced as a colleague can still be seen as the client'; thus it may be 'less destructive to tell the truth than to lie' (Robson and Wardle 1988: 356).

Let me entertain you!

The earpiece hisses 'she's no virgin . . .'

One can be in little doubt as to where the power lies in focus group research. There is an overemphasis on client needs and expectations, specifically, that focus groups provide a good opportunity to observe real consumers, that groups should contain 'virgin' respondents who have not participated in a focus group before and, preferably, that groups should be composed of respondents who are not acquainted with each other.

There is general agreement that client observers have negative consequences on the moderator's 'performance'. Manipulating the respondents to put on a good show for the observers is commonplace (Greenbaum 1987; Templeton 1989), as is adhering more strictly to the discussion guide when the client is present (Caruso 1976; Templeton 1989; Robson and Wardle 1988). Focus group facilities have developed special communication devices such as 'ear-phones that the moderator wears so clients can provide ongoing direction' during the course of the discussion (Greenbaum 1987: 56). One might be forgiven for concluding that the only feature that is qualitative about this type of research is that the output is comprised of words!

Client demands for 'virgin' respondents, who have not participated in a group discussion before, are difficult, if not impossible to meet (Templeton 1989), and in any case the obsession with and sacrilisation of 'virgin' recruits may be a misguided one. Research on group attendance suggests that the quality of discussion can actually improve with more relaxed (experienced) respondents (Tuckel, Leppo and Kaplan 1993; Hayward and Rose 1990).

The stipulation that groups should not contain any respondents who are known to each other makes the recruiter's task very difficult; some refuse to be recruited unless they can bring a friend for support (not surprising since they are given so little advance information about what will be expected from them in a group), and as recruitment takes place within a limited geographic area of the facility or recruiter's home, it is difficult to find respondents who are not acquainted.

Focusing on clients' demands, controlling and exploiting respondents reinforces our analogy of researchers as pimps engaged in a corrupt exercise that benefits no one; certainly not the respondents, and certainly not the clients, who are offered research that falsely claims to achieve understanding of the consumer. Researchers' short term monetary gains from their procurement of flesh and blood 'virgin' respondents more than compensate for the transitory guilt many feel about their abuse.

THE END IS NIGH?

Few qualitative market researchers would accept or recognise our analysis of their practices, arguing that it is one-sided and partial. Indeed this is the very point we wish to make on research in marketing. We believe that it is simply not possible for researchers to take a neutral stance or to claim that research is value-free.

Marketing researchers within the academy should not take any comfort from the fact that our analysis concerns commercial market researchers and thus does not apply to those engaged in scholarly activity. Researchers in the academy take sides, and implicitly or explicitly they are on the side of marketing management (Anderson 1983; Parasuraman 1982).

Market researchers would also point out that our analysis fails to take account of the reasons why they engage in the practices we so readily criticise. They would argue that:

- respondents are given little information in advance of the focus group to discourage prepared, as opposed to natural, responses;
- identifying the client or being overly familiar with respondents would increase opportunities for biased responses;
- the specification of 'virgin' respondents deters professional respondents ('groupies');
- non-acquaintances deter censored responses that may occur in the company of friends; and
- observation and recording of groups helps avoid selective or partial interpretations on the part of the moderator.

Market(ing) researchers in qualitative research in their quest for the 'sacred cows' of 'objectivity' and 'truth' objectify the respondent. This leads them to profane that which is upheld as sacred, namely insight into the consumer. It is therefore hardly surprising that so much consumer research has been less than insightful or that there is increasing scepticism as to the value of market research (Freeling 1994). What is termed qualitative research adheres to a quantitative paradigm and belongs to a patriarchal and dualistic ontology.

For all these reasons we believe that the end of marketing research as we know it is nigh, and that the second coming is imminent. What form will this second coming take? Can Eve, once spurned and condemned to silence and powerlessness, be given a voice to redress the balance? Can she now break free from her enslavement in the dual roles of worshipped Madonna and profaned Whore?

ENTER THE DEVIL'S DOORWAY

Let us enter the 'devil's doorway' and explore the deep, dark mysteries of the feminist perspective. Let us confront man's fears and explore that so-called female side which has been rejected and profaned, to see how feminism can transform marketing research in particular and the marketing academy in general.

Feminist scholars recognise the value-laden nature of research, reject Cartesian systems of thought, and argue for a more co-operative relationship between the researcher and the researched.

Given that research is value-laden, the largely male dominated academy produces knowledge that reflects male interests and values. Female interests tend to be misrepresented or ignored or absent from theory. The Cartesian systems of dichotomous thought on which much of our knowledge is based are challenged. These encourage researchers to erase subjectivity and emotion from the research endeavour in favour of the supposedly superior objectivity and reason. Dichotomous thinking, which has been a feature of philosophy from its origins in ancient Greece, tends to essentialise dichotomous categories and to valorise one side of the dichotomy at the expense of the other. In Liberalism for example, the social contract is based on prior assumptions about human essence or human nature. Thus it is not uncommon to find that women are categorised as emotional and men as rational as if these were essential or natural categories as opposed to categories that reflect social and political values (Gatens 1991).

Dichotomous thought results in one side of the dichotomy being valorised; thus reason is considered superior to emotion which in turn is defined only in relation to reason, that is, by what it is not (Jay 1981). Similarly, male and female have been defined dichotomously with male the valorised term and female defined only in relation to male; by what female is not, is deficient in, or lacks.

In research, objectivity is considered superior to subjectivity to the extent that subjectivity has been demonised, associated with distortion and bias and ought to be erased from the research process. We do not argue that objectivity should be discouraged but that subjectivity should not be defined only in terms of what objectivity is not. Subjectivity can be seen as a unique, useful and personal quality of the researcher (Jansen and Peshkin 1992). When feminists reject the Cartesian dualisms, they are not arguing that one set of categories should be replaced by another, namely subjectivity for objectivity; rather that these categories can operate co-operatively without the researcher having to make a false either/or choice. The choice is false because subjectivity, emotion, and involvement cannot be erased from the research process though they tend to be erased from our accounts of how research should be done and from our accounts or reports of research. For example, researchers are discouraged from reporting in the first person to avoid any suggestion that there is a person or 'self' preparing the account. As Eisner (1988: 18) argues, 'we distance ourselves from phenomena we wish to understand so that we can see them from the knee of God – or at least somewhere close by'.

Paradoxically, including the 'self' in research is more likely to increase the objectivity of research making research accounts more complete and less distorting (Harding 1991). This is achieved through constant reflection by the researcher on how the self is impacting on the research and vice versa. Various terms conceptualise this process including reflexivity (Stanley and Wise 1993), conscious subjectivity (Duelli Klein 1983), and feminist objectivity (Haraway 1991).

Once the involvement of self is seen as producing positive rather than negative consequences, the traditional researcher/researched dichotomous relationship can be re-examined. Traditionally, it has been considered proper for the researcher to distance herself from the researched in order to preserve objectivity and reduce distortion and bias. However, as we demonstrated earlier in our discussion on focus groups, this distancing is more likely to lead to distorted research accounts, to mistrust, withholding of information, and the objectification of subjects. A more collaborative and co-operative relationship is more likely, and perhaps the only way, to achieve the research subject's perspective (Fonow and Cook 1991; Harding 1991; Oakley 1981).

Feminists question whether the power relationships in research are inevitable, and argue that respondents in research should be treated as subjects rather than as objects from whom data are captured. The hierarchical power relationships in research which distance the researcher from the researched are demolished, and Oakley (1981), Finch (1984), Kelly *et al.* (1992), and Stacey (1988) have demonstrated that unstructured interviewing, surveys and ethnographic research can reduce the distance between researcher and respondents.

Finally, feminist scholars argue that theory should be grounded in the everyday lived experiences of research subjects; that is, that personal experience can be theorised. This is not to imply that researchers simply mirror the experiences or views of research subjects uncritically or take these at face value. The data are made meaningful through theory, and theorising involves the engagement of the researcher's own personal presuppositions with the data (Henwood and Pigeon 1995).

Similarly marketing researchers can reassess their relationship with the consumer. Are not all those involved in research both researchers and consumers? Can marketing researchers not acknowledge and utilise this subjectivity?

EVE AND THE NEW JERUSALEM

We propose that salvation for market researchers lies in the dialectic resolution of the patriarchal dualisms embodied in Cartesian systems of thought with neither the so-called masculine nor feminine sides given superiority. Researchers, in trying to achieve the ideals of objectivity, science and rationality, have rejected subjectivity, nature and emotion as aberrations to be controlled and disguised by strict adherence to method and analysis. One of the unfortunate outcomes of this stance is that it creates an artificial distance between researcher and researched, and objectifies the latter. We suggest that subjectivity and emotion should be given equal credence with objectivity and reason. This would reflect research as it is actually done rather than encourage researchers to try to attain some ideal conception of how research should be done. The feminist perspective represents a more wholesome and trusting approach to research, with all parties benefiting from the research process.

Additionally, we need to embed our research in consumers' lived experience rather than looking at consumers only through marketers' and clients' perspectives. In so doing, we can alter our conception of research problems, and the way we implement and write accounts of our research.

The pathetic fallacy is a literary term referring to the attribution of life to inanimate objects. A pathetic phallusy is our 'nod' to postmodernism, specifically to Lacanian phallocentrism and the 'parlez femme' of French postmodern feminism (Irigaray 1985). Lacan calls the phallus the signifier of sexual difference, a symbol of power and control in the symbolic order of patriarchy. Our 'linguistic turn' serves to call into question the power and potency of this symbol of patriarchy, and we hope we have exposed its shortcomings! We have also used the phrase in the sense whereby the living (consumer experience) is objectified or made inanimate by androcentric research assumptions.

Marketing is intuitive and consumer behaviour complex and often suffused with emotion. If market and marketing researchers are to be saved, if they are to truly begin to understand the consumer, they must confront their androcentric and anti-feminist roots and reinvent themselves to accommodate their suppressed feminine side. The sacredness associated with patriarchal principles must be obviated through recognition of those values which have previously been profaned. Only then will a more holistic and co-operative worldview be attained, one which is a human one as opposed to a masculine one. Eve, forever cast out and blamed for man's fall from grace, needs to be reinstated to her rightful place *at* Adam's side rather than *of(f)* his side.

> He created them male and female
> and blessed them and called them
> Mankind in the day they were created.
> Genesis 5: 2

REFERENCES

Anderson, P.F. (1983), 'Marketing, scientific progress and scientific method', *Journal of Marketing*, 47 (Fall), pp. 18–31.

Andreasen, A.R. (1983), 'Cost-conscious marketing research', *Harvard Business Review*, 83 (4), pp. 74–9.

Axelrod, M.D. (1975), 'Marketers get an eyeful when focus groups expose products, ideas, images, ad copy, etc. to consumers', *Marketing News*, 8 (28 February), pp. 6–7.

Belk, R.W., Wallendorf, M. and Sherry, J.F. (1989), 'The sacred and the profane in consumer behaviour: theodicy on the odyssey', *Journal of Consumer Research*, 16 (June), pp. 1–38.

Bloom, N. (1989), 'Have discussion groups had their day?', *Industrial Marketing Digest*, 14 (2), pp. 147–53.

Brady, J. and Davis, I. (1993), 'Marketing's mid-life crisis', *McKinsey Quarterly*, 2, pp. 17–28.

Bristor J.M. and Fischer, E. (1993), 'Feminist thought: implications for consumer research', *Journal of Consumer Research*, 19 (March), pp. 518–36.

Brown, S. (1995), 'Life begins at 40?', *Marketing Intelligence and Planning*, 13 (1), pp. 4–17.

Brownlie, D. and Saren, M. (1992), 'The four Ps of the marketing concept: prescriptive, polemical, permanent and problematical', *European Journal of Marketing*, 26 (4), pp. 34–47.

Buttle, F. (1994), Editorial, 'New paradigm research in marketing', *European Journal of Marketing*, 28, pp. 8–9.

Caruso, T. E. (1976), 'Moderators focus on groups: session yields 7 hypotheses covering technology trend, professionalism, training, techniques, reports, etc.', *Marketing News*, 10 (10 September), pp. 12–16.

Cooper, P. (1991), 'Comparison between the UK and the US: the qualitative dimension', *Journal of the Market Research Society*, 31 (4), pp. 509–20.

Cowan, D. (1994), 'Good information – Generals can't do without it. Why do CEOs think they can?', *Journal of the Market Research Society*, 36 (2).

Duelli Klein, R. (1983), 'How to do what we want to do: thoughts about feminist methodology', in G. Bowles and R. Duelli Klein (eds), *Theories of Women's Studies*, Routledge and Kegan Paul, London pp. 88–104.

Eisner, E.W. (1988), 'The primacy of experience and the politics of method', *Educational Researcher*, vol. 20 (June/July), pp. 15–20.

Fern, E.F. (1982), 'The use of focus groups for idea generation: the effects of group size, acquaintanceship, and moderator on response quantity and quality', *Journal of Marketing Research*, 19 (February), pp. 1–13.

Finch, J. (1984), 'It's great to have someone to talk to: ethics and politics of interviewing women', in C. Bell and H. Roberts (eds), *Social Researching: Politics, Problems, Practice*, Routledge, London, pp. 70–87.

Fleury, P. (1984), 'New qualitative studies', ESOMAR Congress Proceedings, Rome, September, pp. 629–47.

Fonow, M.M. and Cook, J.A. (1991), *Beyond Methodology: Feminist Scholarship as Lived Research*, Indiana University Press, Bloomington, IN.

Freeling, A. (1994), 'Marketing is in crisis – can market research help?', *Journal of the Market Research Society*, 36 (2), pp. 97–104.

Gatens, M. (1991), *Feminism and Philosophy: Perspectives on Differences and Equality*, Polity Press, Oxford.

Gordon, W. and Langmaid, R. (1988), *Qualitative Market Research: a practitioner's and buyer's guide,* Gower, London.

Greenbaum, T.L. (1987), *The Practical Handbook and Guide to Focus Group Research*, Lexington Books, Lexington, MA.

Haraway, D. (1991), *Simians, Cyborgs and Women: The Reinvention of Nature*, Routledge, New York.

Harding, S. (1991), *Whose Science, Whose Knowledge?,* Open University Press, Buckingham.

Hayward, W. and Rose, J. (1990), 'We'll meet again ... Repeat attendance at group discussions – does it matter?', *Journal of the Market Research Society*, 32 (3), pp. 377–407.

Henwood, K. and Pigeon, N. (1995), 'Remaking the link: qualitative research and feminist standpoint theory', *Feminism and Psychology*, 5 (1), pp. 7–30.

Hirschman, E.C. (1993), 'Ideology in consumer research, 1980 and 1990: A Marxist and feminist critique', *Journal of Consumer Research*, 19 (March), pp. 537–55.

Hodock, C.L. (1991), 'The decline and fall of marketing research in corporate America', *Marketing Research: A Magazine of Management and Application*, 3 (2), pp. 12–22.

Holland, N.J. (1990), *Is Women's Philosophy Possible?,* Rowman & Littlefield, Maryland.

Irigaray, L. (1985), *This Sex which is not One,* Cornell University Press, Ithaca, New York.

Jansen, G. and Peshkin, A. (1992), 'Subjectivity in qualitative research', in M.D. LeCompte, W.L. Millroy and J. Preissle (eds), *The Handbook of Qualitative Research in Education,* Academic Press Inc., San Diego, pp. 681–725.

Jay, N. (1981), 'Gender and dichotomy', *Feminist Studies*, 7 (1), pp. 38–56.

Joy, A. and Venkatesh, A. (1994), 'Postmodernism, feminism, and the body: the visible and the invisible in consumer research', *International Journal of Research in Marketing*, 11, pp. 333–57.

Kelly, L., Burton, S. and Regan, L. (1992), 'Defending the indefensible? Quantitative methods and feminist research', in H. Hinds, A. Pheonix and J. Stacey (eds), *Working Out: new directions in women's studies*, Falmer Press, London, pp. 149–59.

McQuarrie, C.F. and McIntyre, S.H. (1986), 'Focus groups and the development of new products by technologically driven companies: some guidelines', *Journal of Product Innovation*, 4 (1), pp. 40–4.

Morton-Williams, J. (1993), *Interviewer Approaches*, Dartmouth Publishing Company, Aldershot.

Oakley, A. (1981), 'Interviewing women: a contradiction in terms', in H. Roberts (ed.), *Doing Feminist Research*, Routledge and Kegan Paul, London, pp. 30–61.

Parasuraman, A. (1982), 'Is a Scientist versus technologist orientation conducive to marketing theory development?', in R.A. Bush and S.D. Hunt (eds) *Marketing Theories; Philosophy of Science Perspectives*, A.M.A., Chicago, IL.

Reinharz, S. (1979), *On Becoming a Social Scientist*, Jossey-Bass, San Francisco.

Robson, S. (1991), 'Ethics: informed consent or misinformed compliance?', *Journal of the Market Research Society*, 33 (1), pp. 19–28.

Robson, S. and Wardle, J. (1988), 'Who's watching whom? A study of the effects of observers on group discussions', *Journal of the Market Research Society*, 30 (3), pp. 333–59.

Sampson, P. (1985), 'Qualitative research in Europe: the state of the art and the art of the state', *European Research*, 13 (4), pp. 163–9.

Sargent, M. (1989), 'Uses and abuses of qualitative research from a marketing viewpoint', in S. Robson and A. Foster (eds), *Qualitative Research in Action*, Edward Arnold, London, pp. 114–24.

Satow, K. (1989), 'The changing state of qualitative research in the United States', *Journal of the Market Research Society*, 31 (4), pp. 521–5.

Schlackman, B. (1989), 'An historical perspective', in S. Robson and A. Foster, *Qualitative Research in Action*, Edward Arnold, London.

Schlackman, W. (1984), 'A discussion of the use of sensitivity panels in market research', *Journal of the Market Research Society*, 26 (3), pp. 191–208.

Stacey, J. (1988), 'Can there be a feminist ethnography?', *Women's Studies International Forum*, 11 (1), pp. 21–7.

Stanley, L. and Wise, S. (1993), *Breaking Out Again: feminist ontology and epistemology*, 2nd ed., Routledge, London.

Templeton, J.F. (1989), *Focus Groups: A guide for marketing and advertising professionals*, Probus Publishing Company, Chicago, IL.

Tuckel, P., Leppo, E. and Kaplan, B. (1993), 'A view from the other side of the mirror', *Marketing Management: A Magazine of Management and Applications*, 5 (4), pp. 24–7.

Twyman, W.A. (1973), 'Designing advertising research for marketing decisions', The Market Research Society Conference Proceedings.

Webster, F.E. (1988), 'The rediscovery of the marketing concept', *Business Horizons*, 31 (3), pp. 29–39.

Wells, W.D. (1974), 'Group interviewing', in R. Ferber (ed.), *Handbook of Marketing Research*, McGraw-Hill, New York.

13

ON ESCHATOLOGY, ONANIST SCATOLOGY, OR HONEST CATOLOGY?

Cats Swinging, Scat Singing, and Cat Slinging as Riffs, Rifts, and Writs in a Catalytic Catechism for the Cataclysm

Morris B. Holbrook

Old Irish Proverb: Beware of people who dislike cats

INTRODUCTION TO CATOLOGY

Key definitions

On eschatology. According to my *Webster's Dictionary* (1984), *eschatology* refers to 'a branch of theology concerned with the final events in the history of the world or of mankind' (p. 424). Some theologians entertain the apocalyptic vision that this end of the world will occur in a great Armageddon – that is, a battle between the forces of good and evil or a cataclysm involving 'a momentous and violent event marked by overwhelming upheaval and demolition' (p. 213).

Onanist scatology. According to the same source (Webster 1984), *scatology* refers to an 'interest in a treatment of obscene matters' (p. 1049) where 'obscene' means, among other things, 'disgusting to the senses' and 'abhorrent to morality or virtue' (p. 815). Not far removed in tone, *onanism* designates 'masturbation' or, more loosely, 'self-gratification' (p. 824) – from which it follows that *onanist* generally means 'perversely self-centred' or 'offensively self-indulgent'. So *onanist scatology* refers to the practice of branding someone with whom one happens to disagree as self-indulgently perverse.

Honest catology. Still according to the same source (Webster 1984), the word *cat* has at least three meanings: (1) 'a carnivorous mammal . . . long domesticated and kept by man as a pet or for catching rats and mice' – in other words, a feline animal; (2) 'a malicious woman'; and (3) slang for 'a guy' (p. 213). From this – to coin a phrase – it follows that *catology* refers to the study of feline creatures and that *honest catology* refers to a sincere attempt to find worthwhile characteristics of the feline temperament.

Confusion of terms

But – according to the views of traditional scholars in marketing, consumer research, and related disciplines – these *three terms* (eschatology, scatology, and catology) mean just about *the same thing*. Specifically, a conventional if insulting view of intellectual cats sees them as malicious and predatory, attaches to them strong tones of moral abhorrence, and darkly presages that – if allowed to roam free – they will somehow manage to precipitate the end of the world in the study of marketing as we know it. Needless to say, someone named Morris cannot help but find this attitude threatening. Hence, under the guise of 'Morris the Cat', I have frequently argued on behalf of certain catlike proclivities that I believe work toward the advance of marketing scholarship in general and of consumer research in particular. These catological claims are major themes in the present chapter.

More key terms

Cats swinging, scat singing, and cat slinging. In 'Bird Lives . . .' (Holbrook 1984), I proposed that 'Theory Development Is a Jazz Solo' – by which I wish to emphasise the suggestive analogies between the improvisatory performances (often called 'swinging') of jazz musicians (often called 'cats') and the creative process that leads toward the development of marketing or consumer-behaviour theory (referred to here as *Cats Swinging*). In 'Skylark . . .' (Holbrook 1990b), I suggested a role for lyricism in marketing and consumer research via the song-like expression of an author's feelings (as in the case of *Scat Singing*). And in 'Dogmatism and Catastrophe' (Holbrook 1989, 1993a), I contrasted the essentially canine dictates of managerial relevance as a goal for marketing research with the more feline virtues of freely and independently pursuing knowledge for its own sake (as stubbornly sought by individuals seeking '*cat*hexis' with their own life's work or '*cat*harsis' via self-actualisation). Unfortunately, those devoted to the more banausic or *dog*matic approaches (Webster 1988) have frequently branded the latter orientation *cat*astrophic and have maligned the more feline departures from the norms of traditional marketing research (in the form of what we might call *Cat Slinging*).

Riffs, rifts, and writs. I view the personal expressions by Morris the Cat just described as *riffs* – that is, short phrases used (as by jazz musicians) to support longer improvisatory solos or even to provide the musical foundation for whole pieces based on such musical material (Webster 1984: 1014). But, unfortunately, these riffs may also precipitate *rifts* – that is, breaks from conventional norms, cleavages from one's colleagues, or estrangement from one's intellectual companions (p. 1015). For example – regarding the various post-positivistic or interpretive approaches that have appeared as alternative routes to knowledge in marketing or consumer research (what the present volume calls 'escapology'), as in our study of consumption symbolism in the film 'Out of Africa' (Holbrook and Grayson 1986) – some commentators have attacked these innovations as unscientific and (recalling the eschatological preoccupation with onanist scatology) have accused the interpretivists of engaging in 'paroxysms of self-expression' (Calder and Tybout 1987: 139). Such critics have sought corrective means to restore their preferred approaches by means of prescriptive *writs* – that is, 'orders' or 'mandates' to 'perform or refrain from performing' various research practices sanctioned as required or defined as impermissible (p. 1362). For example, the prescriptions offered by those worried about the potential 'anarchy' of self-indulgence just mentioned appear as a guide to valid scientific conduct via the falsificationist approach to 'the confrontation of theory with data' (Calder and Tybout 1987: 138).

Summary of the crisis

Sadly enough, when one tells one's audience that doing marketing or consumer research is a lot like playing the saxophone (*cats swinging*) or rendering a jazz vocal (*scat singing*), one pretty much guarantees that such assertions (*riffs*) will encourage consternation (*rifts*) among those who will label them abhorrently self-indulgent (*onanist scatology*) and who will view them as leading directly to the end-of-the-world in marketing scholarship (*eschatology*). In other words, adventurous, irreverent, or escapist approaches (*honest catology*) will invariably evoke vicious attacks by the marketing establishment (*cat slinging*) accompanied by a recitation of accepted procedures (*writs*) deemed appropriate for doing research in the officially prescribed manner. With almost religious fervour, such traditionalists will invoke a *cat*alogue of atrocities associated with the feline temperament. According to the self-appointed critics and at the risk of *cat*achresis, if we let the intellectual cats roam free in our field of learning, they will *cat*apult our discipline into a state of *cat*aplexy or *cat*abolism, distracted by *cat*atonia, inflamed by *cat*arrh, and blinded by *cat*aracts.

But such *cat*calling or *cat*erwauling does great damage to progress in the study of marketing. During the Middle Ages, the sanctimonious persecution of cats led to an increase in the rodent population and thereby precipitated the Black Death that killed about three out of every four people in Europe. Speaking figuratively, I see no reason to hope that the contemporary persecution of intellectual cats in the field of marketing scholarship will produce happier results. As the old Irish proverb says, 'Beware of people who dislike cats.'

A catalytic catechism for the cataclysm

Toward the end of reversing the depressingly ailurophobic spirit just described, I wish to suggest a more feline-friendly set of precepts that may guide us and give us strength as we creep, with catlike tread, toward the coming millennium.

Specifically, I wish to prepare for the approaching Armageddon in marketing research (the *cataclysm*) by proposing a systematic questioning of the traditionally accepted answers (a new *catechism*) that I hope will prove helpful (*catalytic*) in encouraging an escape or provoking a change in the way we think about approaches to research on markets, consumers, and consumption (*a catalytic catechism for the cataclysm*).

If a person named Morris (clearly akin to the American corporate mascot Morris the Cat) is invited to Ireland (home of folks proverbially wary of people who dislike cats) to address the end of the world in our study of marketing (es-*chat*-ology with its clear evocation of the French 'chat' for cat), what choice has he but to resist the themes of eschatology and onanist scatology (cat slinging as rifts and writs) by developing an honest catology (cats swinging and scat singing as riffs) intended ultimately to provide a forward-looking, apocalypse-escaping, millennium-embracing catalytic catechism for the cataclysm? In short, therefore, I shall lump all these concerns together under one abbreviated term – namely, *honest catology* – to designate those articles of faith by which I propose to save the world.

Honest catology

In its broadest sense, *honest catology* illustrates the potential role of figurative language in general and of metaphor or irony in particular as forms of expression that may help to deepen our understanding of marketing or consumer research (cf. Holbrook 1990a, 1995a; Sherry 1991). Literal-minded traditionalists despise figurative language. They regard it as the end of the world in scientific discourse. Yet more recent views of rhetoric in science – those, say, of Feyerabend (1975, 1982), Rorty (1979), Booth (1974), or McCloskey (1985) – see knowledge as the outcome of persuasive conversations among participants in a scientific community. And persuasion hinges on rhetorical devices that deploy figures of speech.

In this sense, *catology* signals the manner in which controversial new styles of communication in marketing and consumer research spell the end of the world for the study of marketing as we have known it. The literal surrenders to the figurative. Directness succumbs to metaphor. Obviousness is snuffed out by irony. Matter-of-factness gives way to song. The old rhetoric dies. A new rhetoric emerges. And – in the best postmodern sense – the term 'catology' embodies its own meaning. By illustrating that which it itself defines, it becomes almost quintessentially reflexive.

Preview

The remainder of this chapter provides an example of honest catology in action by means of a brief account of where I think marketing research has travelled in the past and where – following this trajectory – I think it is headed in the future. This purpose forms the crucial thread for those seeking a connection between the preceding introductory remarks and the text that follows – that is, a link, a segue, or a con*cat*enation with the sequel. Specifically, the following narrative illustrates a perspective that the preceding paragraphs have preached.

CATOLOGY AND THE COURSE OF MARKETING AND CONSUMER RESEARCH

In what follows – self-indulgent as ever – I wish to provide a bit of a sales pitch for a book that I have just completed entitled *Consumer Research: Introspective Essays on the Study of Consumption* (Holbrook 1995a). This book presents a history of marketing research on consumers over the past twenty-five years in general as seen through the eyes of one consumer researcher in particular and as reported in a series of subjective personal introspective essays intended to capture the unfolding of key historical changes as they have occurred over time. Specifically, I attempt to present a picture of past trends, recent developments, and future directions in approaches to marketing research – with an emphasis on how my own evolving perspective on consumers has fitted into the changing field as a whole. I offer a narrative account aimed at conveying some sense of the evolution in our field as seen – rather idiosyncratically or even egocentrically – through my own eyes as a consumer researcher. Further, I construct this historical narrative according to a structure that we might regard as a catalytic catechism for the cataclysm.

Structure

The story to which I have just referred charts the progress over time of what I believe was the party line, received view, or conventional wisdom circa 1965. This traditional doctrine may be expressed in the following way:

[1. *SCIENTIFIC MARKETING RESEARCH IS NEOPOSITIVISTIC MANAGERIALLY RELEVANT STUDIES OF DECISIONS TO BUY GOODS & SERVICES.*]

Over the ensuing years, each part of this doctrine has been questioned and has fallen by the wayside, though usually not without a fight followed by attempts at revival. These changes – in rough chronological order – have affected the following aspects of the opening statement, as key parts of the conventional wisdom have been successively disputed, eliminated, and/or revised:

[8. SCIENTIFIC]
[2. MARKETING]
[9. RESEARCH IS]
[7. NEOPOSITIVISTIC]
[6. MANAGERIALLY RELEVANT studies of]

[5. DECISIONS]
[4. TO BUY]
[3. GOODS & SERVICES].

Alternatively, we may think of each chronologically numbered stage as the replacement of a traditional aspect with some newer view as follows:

[8. SCIENTIFIC ® HUMANISTIC]
[2. MARKETING ® CONSUMER]
[9. RESEARCH IS ® RESEARCH INCLUDES]
[7. NEOPOSITIVISTIC ® INTERPRETIVE]
[6. MANAGERIALLY RELEVANT ® INTRINSICALLY MOTIVATED studies of]
[5. DECISIONS ® EXPERIENCES]
[4. TO BUY ® IN THE CONSUMPTION OF]
[3. GOODS & SERVICES ® ARTWORKS & ENTERTAINMENT]

Thus, the opening statement has gradually given way to a broader perspective more pluralistic, more all-encompassing, and more inviting in its scope. Ultimately, as the progression through these various stages shows, very little of the traditional view remains. In other words, it has moved toward an embrace of catology in a manner that I shall now briefly chronicle.

1 In the beginning

Once upon a time – say, in the mid-1960s – most marketing academics believed in the conventional wisdom expressed by the self-confident claim contained in [1]. However, this modernistic faith in progress had arisen only after serious struggles that had set the stage for the received view circa 1965. Specifically, a far-reaching study sponsored by the Ford Foundation in the early 1960s had cast doubt on the academic credentials of business schools with respect to both their methodological refinement (rigour) and their usefulness to managerial practice (relevance). Business faculties were left with a troubled feeling of intellectual inferiority and now perceived the need to become more academically respectable, more scientific, and more helpful to managers.

This re-evaluation of business education inspired attempts to shake the ‘trade-school’ image, to improve the curriculum, and to revise standards for hiring and promoting. Increasingly, a professor could not hope to earn tenure without a doctorate and a long list of research publications in refereed journals. The standards for excellence in such research borrowed heavily from the ‘received view’ in the philosophy of science – that is, the ‘neopositivistic’ perspective associated with the conventional hypothetico-deductive approach to marketing research.

This neopositivistic orientation became the basis for MBA and PhD training in ways that continue to characterise such programmes at most schools in

America where the traditional view is still taught with great dedication, where the fundamentals of experimental design and survey methods are still honoured, and where students are still coached on the merits of meticulous model building and rigorous hypothesis testing. Yet, despite this lingering institutional allegiance to the scientific tradition, many marketing researchers have moved steadily in the direction of modified, extended, liberated, or even escapist views of their work as scientists or scholars. The remaining numbered points trace how that progress has unfolded since the 1960s.

2 *From MARKETING to CONSUMER research*

The first great change in the established credo involved replacing the single-minded emphasis on marketing *per se* with an emerging *awareness of the consumer*. The central impetus in this direction stemmed from the growing emphasis on *customer value* (Drucker 1954) and on the virtues of *customer orientation* (Levitt 1960), from which the importance of studying *buyer behaviour* follows immediately.

However exciting this discovery might have seemed to some, it was not news to the so-called 'Motivation Researchers' (Dichter 1960; Levy 1959; Martineau 1957) – who, for years, had drawn heavily on clinical and psychoanalytic approaches to studying consumer motivations but whose work had been criticised as both unscientific (Kassarjian 1974) and unethical (Packard 1957), thereby discouraging its acceptance in academic circles on both methodological and moral grounds. For these reasons, the growth of consumer-oriented studies awaited the appearance of an intellectual leader who could make peace with the forces of neopositivism. Such a figure emerged when Howard (1963) took the conventional wisdom in marketing theory strongly in the direction of applying a neopositivistic viewpoint to the study of buyer behaviour. This initial formulation of buyer-behaviour theory was followed rapidly by elaborations from Nicosia (1966); Engel, Kollat, and Blackwell (1968); Howard and Sheth (1969); and others – all of whom featured the boxes-and-arrows style of model building that Howard had originally borrowed from Herbert Simon and that now served as the backbone for a New Paradigm – that is, a new set of aims, concepts, and methods for the study of buyer behaviour (Laudan 1984).

3 *From GOODS & SERVICES to ARTS & ENTERTAINMENT*

The next 'casualty' in the Received View occurred when Kotler and Levy opened our eyes to the possibility that marketing and buyer behaviour involve a whole constellation of products not encompassed by the traditional definition of 'goods and services'. Thus, in broadening the concept of marketing, Kotler and Levy (1969; Kotler 1972) suggested that a 'product' can be literally *anything* of value that enters into an exchange – including not only conventional goods (coffee, toothpaste) and familiar services (restaurants, life insurance) but also various people (politicians), places (cities), things (works of art), ideas (social causes), and events (music festivals) not previously conceptualised as part of the marketing-exchange process.

This enlarged view of marketing opened possibilities for studying hitherto neglected kinds of products such as those found in commercial communication in general and in entertainment, the arts, advertising, and the media in particular (including music, visual art, movies, and television). For example, marketing studies now pursued such topics as preferences among popular singers, liking for jazz artists, radio listening, record buying, aesthetic appreciation, artistic perceptions, musical performance styles, the development of tastes over time, and other aspects of what I call 'consumer aesthetics' (Holbrook 1980). Though many consumer researchers have begun to subject these phenomena to increasingly sophisticated neopositivistic methods of empirical study, they remain endlessly complicated and elusive (Holbrook 1987c, 1987e) and continue to deserve our most dedicated investigation from a variety of methodological perspectives (Holbrook and Zirlin 1985). Further, these observations point the way to a broader focus on the nature of experiential consumption.

4 *From BUYING to CONSUMPTION*

As originally argued by Jacoby (1975, 1978) and Sheth (1979, 1982), consumer behaviour includes all activities involved in acquiring, using, and disposing of products (Holbrook 1987f). Yet, traditionally, the vast majority of our empirical research has focused on acquisition in general and on purchasing decisions in particular rather than on consumption (let alone disposition). In short, we have tended to study buying rather than *consuming*, brand selection rather than *product usage*, or choosing rather than *using* (Holbrook and Hirschman 1982). Given the desire of most marketing researchers to produce results of relevance to marketing managers, this state of affairs is hardly surprising. After all, Marketing Success = f(Sales) = f(Market Share) = f(Decisions to Buy). However, by the early 1980s, some consumer researchers had begun to emphasise that buying decisions tend to rest on what happens during consumption – that choosing depends on using.

As in so many other cases of apparent 'breakthroughs', this shift of attention from the purchase choice to the consumption experience was 'radical' only in the sense that it entailed a return to the 'roots' of marketing thought developed, years earlier, by Alderson (1957). Rediscovering Alderson's bedrock premise, a few consumer researchers began to insist on the importance of usage experiences as the basis for 'hedonic' consumption (Hirschman and Holbrook 1982) – that is, the role of what we have called 'fantasies, feelings, and fun' in the lives of consumers (Holbrook and Hirschman 1982). Such researchers began to look for ways to study consumption experiences independent of their effects on buying decisions or purchasing behaviour. From this perspective, many types of consumption deserve rigorous study. These include play (sports and games), leisure activities (hobbies and social events), and self-improvement programmes (dieting and working out). Further, this concern for consumption in general leads inevitably toward a focus on emotional experiences in particular.

5 *From reasoned DECISIONS to emotional EXPERIENCES*

The new emphasis on consumption as opposed to buying precipitated a shift in emphasis away from the prevailing focus on purchase decisions and brand choices toward a greater concern for the role of emotions, feelings, moods, and other affective aspects of consumer experiences. Though many marketing researchers continued to deal almost exclusively with information processing and buying decisions, the maturing work on consumption experiences during the late 1980s led others to look at the sorts of emotions experienced while consuming products or attending to advertisements. Increasingly, the respective roles of thoughts and feelings became a theme of great urgency in marketing and consumer research.

Work in this area has blossomed into a bibliography of names literally too numerous to mention. At the moment, I believe that the greatest gap in our studies of consumer emotions is that we have tended to focus predominantly on the affective aspects of advertising (e.g. Olney, Holbrook and Batra 1991) while neglecting the equally important feelings associated with consumption (e.g. Havlena and Holbrook 1986). For this reason, recent research has begun to devote increased attention to the emotional aspects of consumption experiences themselves (e.g. Holbrook and Gardner 1993).

6 *From MANAGERIAL RELEVANCE to INTRINSIC MOTIVATION*

By the time some of us had turned to an emphasis on the emotional aspects of consumption experiences, our work had departed fairly far from the traditional quest for discoveries useful to marketing managers. Indeed, a vocal group of management-oriented thinkers has long decried the lack of practical relevance characteristic of marketing academics in general (Myers, Massy and Greyser 1980; Webster 1988) and of consumer researchers in particular (Jacoby 1985a, 1985b). With a few lonely compatriot spirits – Bettman, Hirschman, Kassarjian, Levy, Wright – I have found myself fairly far toward the opposite extreme in this particular debate. Specifically, I advocate the pursuit of consumer research for its own sake *as an end in itself*. Obviously, this perspective argues against the privileged position of consulting or other strictly practical concerns (Holbrook 1985a, 1985b). Moreover, it supports essentially useless, impractical, a-relevant research prized for its intrinsic value (Holbrook 1986b). For these reasons, the perspective in question strikes many as at least controversial, probably heretical, clearly escapist, and maybe even un-American.

In such discussions, I distinguish between 'marketing' research and 'consumer' research on the basis of their guiding purposes. *Marketing research* is typically conducted for the sake of providing knowledge useful to practitioners. In other words, marketing research is generally utilitarian, instrumental, or 'banausic' (Holbrook 1987d). By contrast, *consumer research* is conducted for the sake of studying consumer behaviour where that type of knowledge may serve as an end in itself. In this sense, consumer research ought to be 'ludic' (playful) and 'autotelic' (self-justifying). This contrast between the banausic and the ludic or autotelic parallels the familiar distinction between extrinsic and intrinsic motivation. There is good reason to believe that *many activities thrive best when they are pursued for their own sake.* Many consumer researchers believe increasingly that – like sports, art, and sex – academic research is such an activity and that it tends to prosper when it is fun, pursued as an end in itself, and given freely rather than bartered for the sake of its potential relevance to managerial problems.

Further, this viewpoint carries implications for the study of marketing as a whole. Specifically, many marketing academics have tended increasingly to extend the call for intrinsically motivated enquiry past the boundaries of consumer research and into the broader area of research *in* marketing itself (Hirschman 1986; Levy 1976). Ultimately, some of us managed to smuggle this orientation into a report prepared by the AMA Task Force (1988). When the brains trust at the Marketing Science Institute (MSI) attacked our position as 'self-serving' (Webster 1988), I found myself defending what I called the 'feline' as opposed to the 'canine' side of the research enterprise (Holbrook 1989, 1993a) – with comments later added (Holbrook 1990a) on the subject of 'fishiness' (Pechmann 1990). To summarise, the essence of my argument is that – like individualistic cats but unlike obedient dogs – scholars in marketing should do the research that they value, unencumbered by distorting intrusions on academic freedom.

7 *From NEOPOSITIVISM to INTERPRETIVISM*

At about the same time that the controversy concerning managerial relevance began to heat up, changes had also begun to appear in the posture of some marketing and consumer researchers toward the 'received view' in the philosophy of science. Thus, questioning of the old neopositivistic premises had emerged (Anderson 1983; Deshpande 1983; Peter and Olson 1983). Essentially, the new critiques borrowed from such thinkers as Kuhn (1970, 1977), Feyerabend (1975, 1982), and Polanyi (1958) to propose the need for revising our devotion to the hypothetico-deductive method. This general line of thought has sometimes marched under the banner of 'postpositivism' or 'postmodernism'. However, some have objected to the inaccurate connotations of the former term (Hunt 1991), whereas others admit that very few people seem really to understand what the latter means (Sherry 1991). Hence, many have tended to prefer the term *interpretivism* or *interpretive approaches to knowledge* (Hirschman 1989; Hudson and Ozanne 1988).

Interpretive methods treat *consumer behaviour* as a *text* (Hirschman and Holbrook 1992) that requires explication by means of a semiological or hermeneutic enquiry (Ricoeur 1976, 1981). The hermeneutic approach views an interpreter as moving between a holistic view of the meaning in a text and the detailed scrutiny of its individual parts or elements in a way that establishes a self-correcting cycle that eventually converges on a valid interpretation via the celebrated *Hermeneutic Circle* (Gadamer 1975).

Marketing researchers have recently devoted increased effort to the interpretive, hermeneutic, or semiological side of consumer research – including work on the meaning of films, plays, novels, epic poems, music, television programmes, and so on – as examined via close readings of their symbolic consumption (Holbrook and Hirschman 1993). In this connection, some researchers have grown convinced that many of our biggest, most profound questions – What constitutes happiness? What role does consumption play in people's lives? What determines greatness in art? – cannot necessarily be resolved via neopositivistic studies of the type generally conducted by mainstream marketing researchers. Rather, we believe that progress on such questions often requires the application of a more interpretive approach.

8 *From SCIENCE to SCHOLARSHIP*

As suggested by consideration of the Hermeneutic Circle, interpretivists can defend themselves against the neopositivistic charge of not being scientific (Holbrook and O'Shaughnessy 1988). Yet, more fundamentally, it appears that perhaps the conventional devotion to science must itself fall. In this spirit, one way of replying to the neopositivists is to admit that interpretive work is basically humanistic and scholarly rather than scientific in their sense and then to agree with their implicit admission that, as a path toward generating knowledge, sound scholarship is often more useful than misplaced scientism (Holbrook, Bell and Grayson 1989). Here, one wonders if we have perhaps expended too much energy on trying to be scientists and not enough effort on trying to become scholars (Rotfeld 1985). In this connection, one senses that *some truths lie buried at a level of human experience too deep for science to penetrate.* Hence, in pursuit of such buried truths about the human condition, some of us attach growing interest to applications of the humanities in marketing and consumer research.

Lately, I have been persuaded that this second defence is potentially even more important than the first. A more humanistic research orientation has opened the door to insights from semiology, hermeneutics, literary criticism, cultural studies, critical theory, interpretive perspectives, phenomenology, existentialism, philosophy of art, aesthetics, axiology, ethics, law, and so on. This inherently escapist approach, recalling the fact that *an escapement* is a device that permits a watch or clock to tell the correct time, countenances the role of lyrical self-expression in marketing research and accepts the desirability of self-revelatory expressiveness in writing by consumer researchers (Holbrook 1990b) – impulses that horrify the aforementioned eschatologists preoccupied with onanist scatology (Calder and Tybout 1987) but that invoke the sage counsel found in the famous lyrics by Lorenz Hart: 'I'm wise, and I know what time it is now.'

9 *From IDENTITY to INCLUSIVENESS*

Finally, with all these changes occurring apace, it would seem highly presumptuous to make pronouncements on the subject of what 'research' really *is* (in terms of one identity). Rather, like other branches of the social sciences, the fields of marketing in general and consumer research in particular have entered a period of pluralism in which many approaches exist side-by-side. Such pluralism embraces perspectives drawn from a number of different disciplines and from a variety of methodological orientations. It recognises that competing points of view may shed light on the same issue (Lutz 1989).

This new pluralism spells a merciful end to pontifications on what constitutes good, worthwhile, or valuable research. Increasingly, many researchers believe that honest endeavour in the pursuit of knowledge can take innumerable forms and that it is futile to entrap ourselves by limiting the directions of our enquiries. *One such form* (among many alternative possibilities) might replace all nine facets of the initial credo from which we began with the following revised statement: *HUMANISTIC CONSUMER RESEARCH IN MARKETING INCLUDES INTERPRETIVE INTRINSICALLY MOTIVATED STUDIES OF EXPERIENCES IN THE CONSUMPTION OF ARTWORKS & ENTERTAINMENT.* This revised slogan simply reverses all the language in the conventional wisdom and thereby represents one possible view among many others that deserve attention. For example, it opens the way to an expanded focus on the usefulness of insights into consumption experiences to be gained from Subjective Personal Introspection.

As envisioned here, *Subjective Personal Introspection* or *SPI* delves into *observations on the nature of consumption drawn from one's own direct experience of the human condition.* In a sense, as a consumer, one can meaningfully conduct participant observation on one's own life. In general, participant observation involves the attempt to gain a fuller understanding of some phenomenon by becoming part of it. Analogously, SPI entails a form of participant observation in the world of everyday consumption experiences. Hence, an emphasis on the importance of introspection as a window on consumption assumes that all researchers enjoy a privileged role as participant observers in the consumption experiences of their own everyday lives. I believe that careful and systematic analyses of impressionistic private self-observations concerning one's own consumption behaviour can shed considerable light on the phenomena in question. This conviction has led me to explore phenomenological, autobiographical, and even psychoanalytic accounts of my own consumption activities – for example, in what I call my *ACR Trilogy* (Holbrook 1986a, 1987a, 1988a, 1988b). Such attempts at self-reflective analysis have proven quite distressing to some critics (Wallendorf and Brucks 1993), who have accused introspectionists of ego-centric eccentricity (reminiscent of our earlier remarks on onanist scatology, rifts, writs, and cat slinging). In part, the book mentioned earlier provides a defence of SPI against such criticisms (Holbrook 1995a), to which I would add: 'Lighten up!'

The current pluralistic view

Ultimately, then, we arrive at an escapementally enlightened pluralistic view that embraces a wide array of possible alternative approaches: *SCIENTIFIC & HUMANISTIC MARKETING & CONSUMER RESEARCH INCLUDES NEOPOSITIVISTIC & INTERPRETIVE MANAGERIALLY RELEVANT & INTRINSICALLY MOTIVATED STUDIES OF DECISIONS TO BUY GOODS & SERVICES AND EXPERIENCES IN THE CONSUMPTION OF ARTWORKS & ENTERTAINMENT.* Three aspects of this greatly revised credo warrant some emphasis.

First, the operative force of the word 'includes' means that the 'Current Pluralistic View' welcomes innumerable alternative approaches. Even in my own case, the fairly far-out perspective described under (*9*) applies only to *some* research and *not* to all the different types of studies that I would like to do. Some of my own work remains resolutely empirical, quantitative, and neopositivistic. For certain kinds of problems that lend themselves to empirical investigation within traditional paradigms, I would not have it any other way.

Second, I should warn those early in their careers that the pluralistic viewpoint advocated here can be quite dangerous as an employment strategy for those just starting out as marketing academics. It is often prudent to establish oneself via conventional approaches before engaging in more esoteric endeavours.

Third, like the proverbial cat, I believe passionately in the virtues of individuality. Here, I stress the need to avoid imposing restrictions on others, the goal of remaining tolerant of different approaches, the importance of embracing a diversity of ideas, the wisdom of encouraging all researchers to remain true to themselves, and the ultimate irreducible sanctity of academic freedom.

THE CATOLOGY OF TOMORROW

But what if we do manage to escape the eschatological crisis foretold by those preoccupied with onanist scatology and to enter the new age of honest catology toward which we have progressed over the course of the last quarter century? What then? I might prophesy the Shape of Catology to Come with reference to the three aspects of science distinguished by Laudan (1984): Aims, Concepts, and Methods.

Aims

I envision a continued movement of marketing scholars toward a more pure and basic style of research that insists on the intrinsically motivated and inherently feline pursuit of its own goals as ends in themselves rather than bowing to the canine temptations to serve business managers or other external constituencies. I sense this spirit of insistent individuality or refusal to sell out in recent anti-commercialistic books with titles like *Costs of Living: How Market Freedom Erodes the Best Things in Life* (Schwartz 1994); *A Nation of Salesmen: The Tyranny of the Market and the Subversion of Culture* (Shorris 1994); and *Marketing Madness: A Survival Guide for a Consumer Society* (Jacobson and Mazur 1995). In our own field, a comparable perspective implicitly characterises such projects as the present volume on *Marketing Eschatology*; the special issue of the *International Journal of Research in Marketing* on *Postmodernism* (Firat and Venkatesh 1993; Venkatesh, Sherry and Firat 1993); Douglas Brownlie and Mike Saren's issue of the *Journal of Marketing Management* devoted to *The Commodification of Marketing Knowledge* (Holbrook 1995c); or Stephen Brown's forthcoming issue of the *European Journal of Marketing* on *Postmodern Marketing* (see also Brown 1993, 1994, 1995). True, such implicit attitudes might be branded as 'elitist' by those quaintly anxious to preserve the old banausic flavour of marketing research. But the temper of the times has also begun to turn against the anti-elitist tyranny of political correctness (Bernstein 1994) and has moved toward actually celebrating the virtues of an elitism founded on the respect for high standards of excellence without regard to populist appeal or commercial payoffs (Fussell 1991; Hughes 1993; Henry 1994). In this connection, I envision a future world made safe for an elitist approach to the study of marketing (Holbrook 1995e).

Concepts

In terms of concepts in marketing or consumer research, we have by now transcended the traditional view of the buyer as a machine-like decision maker who cranks out purchasing choices in the manner of a well-engineered computer. In place of this mechanistic model, we increasingly recognise the consumer as a flesh-and-blood animal engaged in consumption experiences that produce emotional responses and other sorts of fantasies, feelings, and fun. In this connection, I believe that one important aspect of the uncharted territory that awaits discovery concerns the role of animals themselves as consumers – for example, as in the case of our household pets. Other consumer researchers have addressed issues related to the consumption *of* animals as pets (Hirschman 1994; Moore and Holbrook 1982; Sanders 1990). But here I propose a new focus on the important role of consumption *by* animals such as cats, dogs, ferrets, parrots, and gorillas (Holbrook 1987b). In this connection, needless to say, I especially favour studies of consumption by cats (Holbrook 1995e).

Methods

As noted by numerous commentators (Brown 1993, 1994, 1995; Firat and Venkatesh 1993; Hirschman and Holbrook 1992; Holbrook 1993b; Sherry 1991; Venkatesh, Sherry and Firat 1993), we have entered an age in which our methods and styles of research increasingly reflect the Ethos of Postmodernism. For example, one review characterises these trends as embodying what it calls 'The Nine P's of Postmodernism': *Paradox*, *Parody*, *Pastiche*, *Playfulness*, *Proliferation*, *Promiscuity*, *Polysemy*, *Panculturalism*, and *Pluralism* (Holbrook 1993b). One aspect of this postmodern ethos concerns an increased reliance on images and, indeed, the widely noticed displacement of conventional literal reality by a pictorial hyperreality in which signifiers float free from their underlying signifieds. These signifiers thereby surrender their logocentric meanings even while new importance attaches to their visual vividness. In this spirit, consistent with the ethos of postmodernism, I believe that some of the more traditional approaches to marketing research have devolved to a repetitive and obsessively literal-minded condition of inveterately dull blandness. As a remedy, I propose a need for greater imagination in what we think mentally, greater liveliness in what we write verbally, and greater vividness in what we represent visually.

An illustration: honest catology in action

I might illustrate my vision for the Catology of Tomorrow with a brief example torn from the pages of my ongoing investigation of consumption experiences in the lives of cats. When last I visited this topic (Holbrook 1995b), we had fondly bid adieu to our beloved eighteen-year-old and recently deceased Quarter the Cat. We may now begin to address the case of his successor – our wonderful new black Maine Coon kitten, whom we named Rocky Raccoon after the Beatles song and who is among the most ardently persistent consumers on this Planet Earth.

With respect to *aims*, I propose that the consumption experiences of Rocky the Cat deserve study *not* because of their possible relevance to marketing managers (say, the producers of pet-food products) but because they are in themselves *fascinating* (worth studying for their own sake). For example, consider Rocky's habits of turning somersaults in mid-air; of poking his paws under the door of Sally's waiting-room where her psychotherapy patients either freak out over this apparent attack by hairy black snakes or pat them politely; and of inventing games wherein he thinks of things for us to throw and then decides whether or not he wants to go and fetch them. These habits – and more – must be seen to be believed.

Figure 13.1a Stereo pairs showing consumption activities in the life of a cat

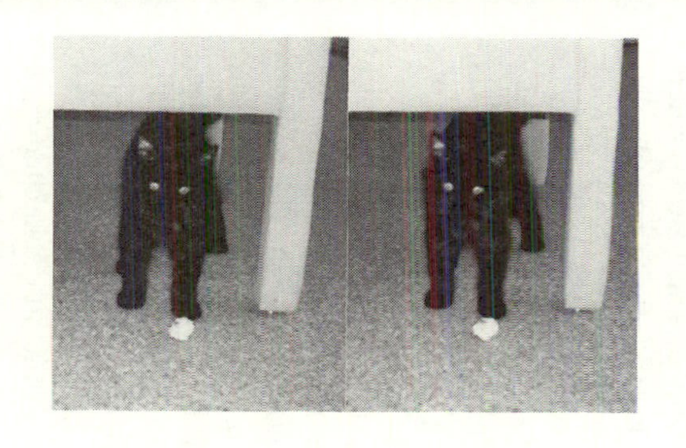

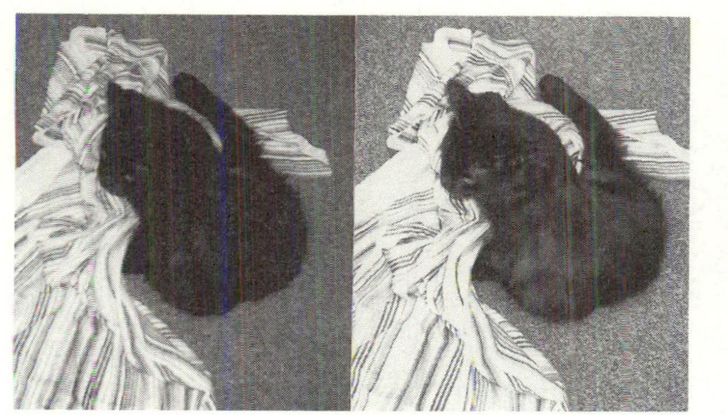

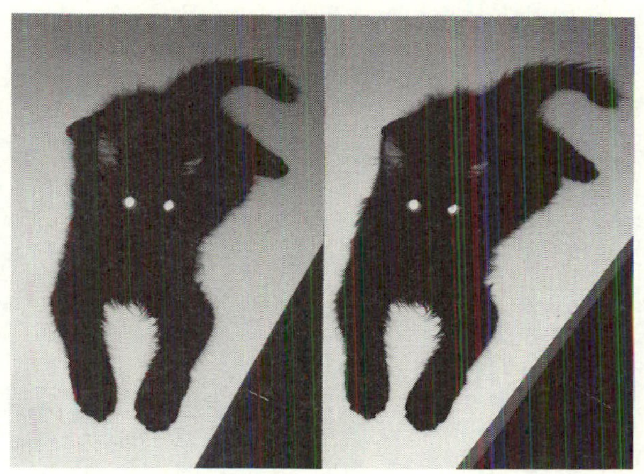

Figure 13.1b Stereo pairs showing consumption activities in the life of a cat

With respect to *concepts*, I suggest that the behaviour of small kittens offers insights into consumption experiences based on fantasies, feelings, and fun that corroborate our observations of consumers a little higher up on the phylogenetic chain – Rocky's manner of pretending that something or someone is chasing him (pure fantasy), his obvious sadness when we leave in the evening for our walk but his joy when we come back to him (pure feeling), and his reckless devotion to chasing just about anything that is attached to a piece of string (pure fun).

And with respect to *methods*, I close by illustrating what I take to be the power of three-dimensional photography to convey a deeper understanding of consumption experiences in the life of a kitten (Holbrook 1995d). The preceding pages, 252–3, contain eight stereo pairs (Figure 13.1) featuring Rocky in the midst of various consumption activities – toying with a helium balloon, sitting on the couch while contemplating his next move, squeezing himself into a snug spot for a nice nap, admiring some sexy covers from old jazz albums, striking a pose beside the sea coral, playing with his tin-foil ball, helping to rearrange the beach towel, and waiting patiently but firmly on the kitchen table with dinner in mind. If you look at either side of a given stereo pair, you will get a glimpse of Rocky's consumption style. But if you gaze between and past the members of a pair, relax your eyes, and let the two pictures float together until they fuse into a true stereoscopic image, you will experience a sense of three-dimensional depth that contributes greatly to the vividness, clarity, and impact of the visual impression.

In pursuing the aims, concepts, and methods just illustrated, one gains some premonition of the difference between the two-dimensionally flat world of marketing research to which we were once accustomed and the three-dimensionally deep world of sweet smells, ringing sounds, and bright glances that I envision as the hallmarks of the Honest Catology to Come. This Catology of the Future will replace the Old Received View by evading the stigmata of Onanist Scatology, by escaping the perils of the Eschatological End, and by breaking free with the joy of a tiny kitten blissfully at play into the sunshine of the Next Millennium.

Put into plain language, we therefore end – where we began – with a post-eschatological paraphrase of the Old Irish Proverb: *ONLY TRUST PEOPLE WHO LIKE CATS.*

ACKNOWLEDGEMENTS

The author has deeply appreciated the warm hospitality of his colleagues at the University of Ulster and of the sisters at St Clement's Retreat. He also gratefully acknowledges the support of the Columbia Business School's Faculty Research Fund.

REFERENCES

Alderson, Wroe (1957), *Marketing Behavior and Executive Action*, Richard D. Irwin, Homewood, IL.

AMA Task Force (1988), 'Developing, Disseminating, and Utilizing Marketing Knowledge', *Journal of Marketing*, 52 (October), pp. 1–25.

Anderson, Paul F. (1983), 'Marketing, Scientific Progress, and Scientific Method', *Journal of Marketing*, 47 (Fall), pp. 18–31.

Bernstein, Richard (1994), *Dictatorship of Virtue: Multiculturalism and the Battle for America's Future*, Alfred A. Knopf, New York, NY.

Booth, Wayne C. (1974), *Modern Dogma and the Rhetoric of Assent*, The University of Chicago Press, Chicago, IL.

Brown, Stephen (1993), 'Postmodern Marketing: Principles, Practice and Panaceas', *Irish Marketing Review*, 6, pp. 91–100.

Brown, Stephen (1994), 'Marketing as Multiplex: Screening Postmodernism', *European Journal of Marketing*, 28 (8/9), pp. 27–51.

Brown, Stephen (1995), *Postmodern Marketing*, Routledge, London, UK.

Calder, Bobby J. and Tybout, Alice M. (1987), 'What Consumer Research Is . . .', *Journal of Consumer Research*, 14 (June), pp. 136–40.

Deshpande, Rohit (1983), '"Paradigms Lost": On Theory and Method in Research in Marketing', *Journal of Marketing*, 47 (Fall), pp. 101–10.

Dichter, Ernest (1960), *The Strategy of Desire*, Doubleday & Company, New York, NY.

Drucker, Peter (1954), *The Practice of Management*, Harper, New York, NY.

Engel, James F., Kollat, David T. and Blackwell, Roger D. (1968), *Consumer Behavior*, Holt, Rinehart & Winston, New York, NY.

Featherstone, Mike (1991), *Consumer Culture and Postmodernism*, Sage Publications, London, UK.

Feyerabend, Paul (1975), *Against Method: Outline of an Anarchistic Theory of Knowledge*, Verso, London, UK.

Feyerabend, Paul (1982), *Science in a Free Society*, Verso, London, UK.

Firat, A. Fuat and Venkatesh, Alladi (1993), 'Postmodernity: The Age of Marketing', *International Journal of Research in Marketing*, 10 (August), pp. 227–49.

Fussell, Paul (1991), *BAD Or, The Dumbing of America*, Simon & Schuster, New York, NY.

Gadamer, Hans-Georg (1975), *Truth and Method*, ed. Garrett Barden and John Cumming, Crossroad, New York, NY.

Havlena, William J. and Holbrook, Morris B. (1986), 'The Varieties of Consumption Experience: Comparing Two Typologies of Emotion in Consumer Behavior', *Journal of Consumer Research*, 13 (December), pp. 394–404.

Henry, William A., III (1994), *In Defense of Elitism*, Doubleday, New York, NY.

Hirschman, Elizabeth C. (1986), 'Marketing, Intellectual Creativity, and Consumer Research', in R. J. Lutz (ed.), *Advances in Consumer Research*, vol. 13, Association for Consumer Research, Provo, UT, pp. 433–5.

Hirschman, Elizabeth C. (ed.) (1989), *Interpretive Consumer Research*, Association for Consumer Research, Provo, UT.

Hirschman, Elizabeth C. (1994), 'Consumers and Their Animal Companions', *Journal of Consumer Research*, 20 (March), pp. 616–32.

Hirschman, Elizabeth C. and Holbrook, Morris B. (1982), 'Hedonic Consumption: Emerging Concepts, Methods and Propositions', *Journal of Marketing*, 46 (Summer), pp. 92–101.

Hirschman, Elizabeth C. and Holbrook, Morris B. (1992), *Postmodern Consumer Research: The Study of Consumption As Text*, Sage Publications, Newbury Park, CA.

Holbrook, Morris B. (1980), 'Some Preliminary Notes on Research in Consumer Esthetics', in J. C. Olson (ed.), *Advances in Consumer Research*, vol. 7, Association for Consumer Research, Ann Arbor, MI, pp. 104–8.

Holbrook, Morris B. (1984), 'Theory Development Is a Jazz Solo: Bird Lives', in P. F. Anderson and M. J. Ryan (eds), *Proceedings*, 1984 AMA Winter Educators' Conference, American Marketing Association, Chicago, IL, pp. 48–52.

Holbrook, Morris B. (1985a), 'The Consumer Researcher Visits Radio City: Dancing in the Dark', in E. C. Hirschman and M. B. Holbrook (eds), *Advances in Consumer Research*, vol. 12, Association for Consumer Research, Provo, UT, pp. 28–31.

Holbrook, Morris B. (1985b), 'Why Business Is Bad for Consumer Research: The Three Bears Revisited', in E. C. Hirschman and M. B. Holbrook (eds), *Advances in Consumer Research*, vol. 12, Association for Consumer Research, Provo, UT, pp. 145–56.

Holbrook, Morris B. (1986a), 'I'm Hip: An Autobiographical Account of Some Musical Consumption Experiences', in R. J. Lutz (ed.), *Advances in Consumer Research*, vol. 13, Association for Consumer Research, Provo, UT, pp. 614–18.

Holbrook, Morris B. (1986b), 'Whither ACR? Some Pastoral Reflections on Bears, Baltimore, Baseball, and Resurrecting Consumer Research', in R. J. Lutz (ed.), *Advances in Consumer Research*, vol. 13, Association for Consumer Research, Provo, UT, pp. 436–41.

Holbrook, Morris B. (1987a), 'An Audiovisual Inventory of Some Fanatic Consumer Behavior: The 25-Cent Tour of a Jazz Collector's Home', in M. Wallendorf and P. F. Anderson (eds), *Advances in Consumer Research*, vol. 14, Association for Consumer Research, Provo, UT, pp. 144–9.

Holbrook, Morris B. (1987b), 'O, Consumer, How You've Changed: Some Radical Reflections on the Roots of Consumption', in F. Firat, N. Dholakia, and R. Bagozzi (eds), *Philosophical and Radical Thought in Marketing*, D. C. Heath, Lexington, MA, pp. 156–77.

Holbrook, Morris B. (1987c), 'Progress and Problems in Research on Consumer Esthetics', in D. V. Shaw, W. S. Hendon, and C. R. Waits (eds), *Artists and Cultural Consumers*, Association for Cultural Economics, Akron, OH, pp. 133–46.

Holbrook, Morris B. (1987d), 'Some Notes on the Banausic Interrelationships Among Marketing Academics and Practitioners', in R. W. Belk and G. Zaltman (eds), *Proceedings*, Winter Educators' Conference, American Marketing Association, Chicago, IL, pp. 342–3.

Holbrook, Morris B. (1987e), 'The Study of Signs in Consumer Esthetics: An Egocentric Review', in J. Umiker-Sebeok (ed.), *Marketing and Semiotics: New Directions in the Study of Signs for Sale*, Mouton de Gruyter, Berlin, pp. 73–121.

Holbrook, Morris B. (1987f), 'What Is Consumer Research?', *Journal of Consumer Research*, 14 (June), pp. 128–32.

Holbrook, Morris B. (1988a), 'The Psychoanalytic Interpretation of Consumer Research: I Am an Animal', *Research in Consumer Behavior*, 3, pp. 149–78.

Holbrook, Morris B. (1988b), 'Steps Toward a Psychoanalytic Interpretation of Consumption: A Meta-Meta-Meta-Analysis of Some Issues Raised by the Consumer Behavior Odyssey', in Michael J. Houston (ed.), *Advances in Consumer Research*, vol. 15, Association for Consumer Research, Provo, UT, pp. 537–42.

Holbrook, Morris B. (1989), 'Aftermath of the Task Force: Dogmatism and Catastrophe in the Development of Marketing Thought', *ACR Newsletter* (September), pp. 1–11.

Holbrook, Morris B. (1990a), 'Holbrook's Reply to Pechmann: Prelude and Poem', *ACR Newsletter* (September), p. 4.

Holbrook, Morris B. (1990b), 'The Role of Lyricism in Research on Consumer Emotions: Skylark, Have You Anything to Say to Me?', in M. Goldberg, G. Gorn, and R. Pollay (eds), *Advances in Consumer Research*, vol. 17, Association for Consumer Research, Provo, UT, pp. 1–18.

Holbrook, Morris B. (1993a), 'Comments on the Report of the AMA Task Force on the Development of Marketing Thought', in P. Rajan Varadarajan and A. Menon (eds), *Enhancing Knowledge Development in Marketing: Perspectives and Viewpoints*, American Marketing Association, Chicago, IL, pp. 19–23.

Holbrook, Morris B. (1993b), 'Postmodernism & Social Theory', *Journal of Macromarketing*, 13 (Fall), pp. 69–75.

Holbrook, Morris B. (1995a), *Consumer Research: Introspective Essays on the Study of Consumption*, Sage Publications, Thousand Oaks, CA.

Holbrook, Morris B. (1995b), 'Feline Consumption: Ethography, Felologies, and Unobtrusive Participation in the Life of a Cat', *European Journal of Marketing*, forthcoming.

Holbrook, Morris B. (1995c), 'The Four Faces of Commodification in the Development of Marketing Knowledge', *Journal of Marketing Management*, 11 (7), pp. 641–54.

Holbrook, Morris B. (1995d), 'The Power of Three-Dimensional Viewing: A Visual Aid for the Communication of Findings in Marketing Research', Working Paper, Columbia University.

Holbrook, Morris B. (1995e), 'The Three Faces of Elitism: Postmodernism, Political Correctness, and Popular Culture', *Journal of Macromarketing*, forthcoming.

Holbrook, Morris B. and Gardner, Meryl P. (1993), 'An Approach to Investigating the Emotional Determinants of Consumption Durations: Why Do People Consume What They Consume For As Long As They Consume It?', *Journal of Consumer Psychology*, 2 (2), pp. 123–42.

Holbrook, Morris B. and Grayson, Mark W. (1986), 'The Semiology of Cinematic Consumption: Symbolic Consumer Behavior in *Out of Africa*', *Journal of Consumer Research*, 13 (December), pp. 374–81.

Holbrook, Morris B. and Hirschman, Elizabeth C. (1982), 'The Experiential Aspects of Consumption: Consumer Fantasies, Feelings, and Fun', *Journal of Consumer Research*, 9 (September), pp. 132–40.

Holbrook, Morris B. and Hirschman, Elizabeth C. (1993), *The Semiotics of Consumption: Interpreting Symbolic Consumer Behavior in Popular Culture and Works of Art*, Mouton de Gruyter, Berlin.

Holbrook, Morris B., Bell, Stephen and Grayson, Mark W. (1989), 'The Role of the Humanities in Consumer Research: Close Encounters and Coastal Disturbances', in E. C. Hirschman (ed.), *Interpretive Consumer Research*, Association for Consumer Research, Provo, UT, pp. 29–47.

Holbrook, Morris B. and O'Shaughnessy, John (1988), 'On the Scientific Status of Consumer Research and the Need for an Interpretive Approach to Studying Consumption Behavior', *Journal of Consumer Research*, 15 (December), pp. 398–402.

Holbrook, Morris B. and Zirlin, Robert B. (1985), 'Artistic Creation, Artworks, and Esthetic Appreciation: Some Philosophical Contributions to Nonprofit Marketing', in R. W. Belk (ed.), *Advances in Nonprofit Marketing*, vol. 1, JAI Press, Greenwich, CT, pp. 1–54.

Howard, John A. (1963), *Marketing Management*, Richard D. Irwin, Homewood, IL.

Howard, John A. and Sheth, Jagdish N. (1969), *The Theory of Buyer Behavior*, John Wiley & Sons, New York, NY.

Hudson, Laurel Anderson and Ozanne, Julie L. (1988), 'Alternative Ways of Seeking Knowledge in Consumer Research', *Journal of Consumer Research*, 14 (March), pp. 508–21.

Hughes, Robert (1993), *Culture of Complaint: The Fraying of America*, Oxford University Press, New York, NY.

Hunt, Shelby D. (1991), 'Positivism and Paradigm Dominance in Consumer Research: Toward Critical Pluralism and Rapprochement', *Journal of Consumer Research*, 18 (June), pp. 32–44.

Jacobson, Michael F. and Mazur, Laurie Ann (1995), *Marketing Madness: A Survival Guide for a Consumer Society*, Westview Press, Boulder, CO.

Jacoby, Jacob (1975), 'Consumer Psychology as a Social Psychological Sphere of Action', *American Psychologist*, 30 (October), pp. 977–87.

Jacoby, Jacob (1978), 'Consumer Research: A State of the Art Review', *Journal of Marketing*, 42 (April), pp. 87–96.

Jacoby, Jacob (1985a), 'Serving Two Masters: Perspectives On Consulting', in E. C. Hirschman and M. B. Holbrook (eds), *Advances in Consumer Research*, vol. 12, Association for Consumer Research, Provo, UT, p. 144.

Jacoby, Jacob (1985b), 'The Vices and Virtues of Consulting: Responding to a Fairy Tale', in E. C. Hirschman and M. B. Holbrook (eds), *Advances in Consumer Research*, vol. 12, Association for Consumer Research, Provo, UT, pp. 157–63.

Kassarjian, Harold H. (1974), 'Projective Methods', in R. Ferber (ed.), *Handbook of Marketing Research*, McGraw-Hill Book Company, New York, NY, pp. 3:85–3:100.

Kotler, Philip J. (1972), 'A Generic Concept of Marketing', *Journal of Marketing*, 36 (April), pp. 46–54.

Kotler, Philip J. and Levy, Sidney J. (1969), 'Broadening the Concept of Marketing', *Journal of Marketing*, 33 (January), pp. 10–15.

Kuhn, Thomas S. (1970), *The Structure of Scientific Revolutions*, Second Edition, The University of Chicago Press, Chicago, IL.

Kuhn, Thomas S. (1977), *The Essential Tension: Selected Studies in Scientific Tradition and Change*, The University of Chicago Press, Chicago, IL.

Laudan, Larry (1984), *Science and Values: The Aims of Science and Their Role in Scientific Debate*, University of California Press, Berkeley, CA.

Levitt, Theodore (1960), 'Marketing Myopia', *Harvard Business Review*, 38 (July/August), pp. 45–56.

Levy, Sidney J. (1959), 'Symbols for Sale', *Harvard Business Review*, 37 (July–August), pp. 117–24.

Levy, Sidney J. (1976), 'Marcology 101 Or the Domain of Marketing', in K. L. Bernhardt (ed.), *Marketing: 1776–1976 and Beyond*, American Marketing Association, Chicago, IL, pp. 577–81.

Lutz, Richard J. (1989), 'Presidential Address, 1988 – Positivism, Naturalism and Pluralism in Consumer Research: Paradigms in Paradise', in T. K. Srull (ed.), *Advances in Consumer Research*, vol. 16, Association for Consumer Research, Provo, UT, pp. 1–8.

Martineau, Pierre (1957), *Motivation in Advertising*, McGraw-Hill Book Company, New York, NY.

McCloskey, Donald N. (1985), *The Rhetoric of Economics*, The University of Wisconsin Press, Madison, WI.

Moore, William L. and Holbrook, Morris B. (1982), 'On the Predictive Validity of Joint-Space Models in Consumer Evaluations of New Concepts', *Journal of Consumer Research*, 9 (September), pp. 206–10.

Myers, John G., Massy, William F. and Greyser, Stephen A. (1980), *Marketing Research and Knowledge Development: An Assessment for Marketing Managers*, Prentice Hall, Englewood Cliffs, NJ.

Nicosia, Franco M. (1966), *Consumer Decision Processes*, Prentice Hall, Englewood Cliffs, NJ.

Olney, Thomas J., Holbrook, Morris B. and Batra, Rajeev (1991), 'Consumer Responses to Advertising: The Effects of Ad Content, Emotions, and Attitude toward the Ad on Viewing Time', *Journal of Consumer Research*, 17 (March), pp. 440–53.

Packard, Vance (1957), *The Hidden Persuaders*, Pocket Books, New York, NY.

Pechmann, Cornelia (1990), 'Response to President's Column, September 1989', *ACR Newsletter* (June), pp. 5–7.

Peter, J. Paul and Olson, Jerry C. (1983), 'Is Science Marketing?', *Journal of Marketing*, 47 (Fall), pp. 111–25.
Polanyi, Michael (1958), *Personal Knowledge: Towards a Post-Critical Philosophy*, The University of Chicago Press, Chicago, IL.
Ricoeur, Paul (1976), *Interpretation Theory: Discourse and the Surplus of Meaning*, The Texas Christian University Press, Fort Worth, TX.
Ricoeur, Paul (1981), *Hermeneutics and the Human Sciences: Essays on Language, Action and Interpretation*, ed. and trans. John B. Thompson, Cambridge University Press, Cambridge, UK.
Rorty, Richard (1979), *Philosophy and the Mirror of Nature*, Princeton University Press, Princeton, NJ.
Rotfeld, Herbert (1985), 'Marketing Educators Must Become More "Scholarly"', *Marketing News* (July 19), pp. 35–6.
Sanders, Clinton R. (1990), 'The Animal "Other": Self Definition, Social Identity and Companion Animals', in M. E. Goldberg, G. Gorn and R. Pollay (eds), *Advances in Consumer Research*, vol. 17, Association for Consumer Research, Provo, UT, pp. 662–8.
Schwartz, Barry (1994), *Costs of Living: How Market Freedom Erodes the Best Things in Life*, W. W. Norton, New York, NY.
Sherry, John F., Jr. (1991), 'Postmodern Alternatives: The Interpretive Turn In Consumer Research', in T. S. Robertson and H. H. Kassarjian (eds), *Handbook of Consumer Behavior*, Prentice Hall, Englewood Cliffs, NJ, pp. 548–91.
Sheth, Jagdish N. (1979), 'The Surpluses and Shortages in Consumer Behavior Theory and Research', *Journal of the Academy of Marketing Science*, 7 (Fall), pp. 414–27.
Sheth, Jagdish N. (1982), 'Consumer Behavior: Surpluses and Shortages', in A. A. Mitchell (ed.), *Advances in Consumer Research*, vol. 9, Association for Consumer Research, Ann Arbor, MI, pp. 13–19.
Shorris, Earl (1994), *A Nation of Salesmen: The Tyranny of the Market and the Subversion of Culture*, W. W. Norton & Company, New York, NY.
Venkatesh, Alladi, Sherry, John F., Jr. and Firat, A. Fuat (1993), 'Postmodernism and the Marketing Imaginary', *International Journal of Research in Marketing*, 10 (August), pp. 215–23.
Wallendorf, Melanie and Brucks, Merrie (1993), 'Introspection in Consumer Research: Implementation and Implications', *Journal of Consumer Research*, 20 (December), pp. 339–59.
Webster, Frederick E., Jr. (1988), 'Comment', *Journal of Marketing*, 52 (October), pp. 48–51.
Webster's Ninth New Collegiate Dictionary (1984), Merriam-Webster, Springfield, MA.

14

THE FUTURE IS PAST

Marketing, apocalypse and the retreat from utopia

Stephen Brown and Pauline Maclaran

INTRODUCTION

Some years ago, a famous British marketing guru used to travel around the country entertaining the hitherto unenlightened with a presentation on the so-called oxymorons of marketing. After extracting a few cheap laughs with the familiar classics of the genre – 'military intelligence', 'postal service', 'airline food' or, doubtless if he were doing it today, 'royal family' – he would then explain to the audience that apparent contradictions in terms like 'marketing planning', 'marketing strategy' and 'marketing philosophy', were not only perfectly logical and ultimately attainable, but nothing less than the very secret of long-term success in business. True, he never addressed that most contradictory oxymoron of all – 'British marketing guru' – yet he did at least manage to persuade his listeners to reflect momentarily on the importance of adopting a marketing orientation.

At first glance, the title of this chapter might suggest some sort of oxymoronic imbroglio. Apart from the pretentious temporal transposition, almost every conceivable terminological combination – 'marketing apocalypse', 'utopia-apocalypse', 'marketing utopia' – is inherently contradictory. *Marketing apocalypse*, for example, carries connotations of mendacious tele-evangelists filling the heads and emptying the wallets of their credulous followers, an exercise in extortion that is the complete opposite of what marketing is widely believed to be about. *Apocalypse* and *utopia* are equally antithetical, in that the former term is tarred with death, destruction and dereliction, whereas the latter calls up pastoral images of peace, purity and Edenic perfection. However, just as the British marketing guru sought to demonstrate the relevance of his oxymorons, so too the first chapter of this book argued that, far from being charlatans, tele-evangelists are the very epitome of a marketing orientation. While not to everyone's taste, they invariably succeed in giving their customers exactly what they want – blood-curdling predictions of the end, the prospect of eternal salvation and, most importantly of all, the enormous pleasure that comes from imagining the fiery fate awaiting doubters, sinners and apostates. In a similar vein, the terms apocalypse and utopia are nothing less than two sides of the same coin. As Enzensberger (1978) emphasises, the eschatological idea of the end is never absolute or final, but merely a prelude to some sort of paradisaical thereafter. 'The idea of the apocalypse has accompanied utopian thought since its first beginnings, pursuing it like a shadow, like a reverse side that cannot be left behind: without catastrophe, no millennium, without apocalypse, no paradise' (Enzensberger 1978: 74).

If our first two prospective oxymorons are relatively easily explicated, the same cannot be said about 'marketing utopia'. Utopians, as everyone knows, are impractical, unrealistic, otherworldly dreamers, an accusation that has rarely, if ever, been levelled at marketing practitioners. Nor, for that matter, is the appellation applicable to the vast majority of marketing academics, who tend to pride themselves on being in touch with the 'real world' of practising managers (although few practitioners appear to appreciate the endeavours of their scholarly succubae[1]). What is more, the briefest acquaintance with the manifold literary utopias reveals that their authors, as a rule, are implacably opposed to the marketing system. Indeed, some of the most celebrated utopias of all time were directly inspired by iniquities perpetrated in marketing's name, or what would now be considered to be marketing's name. It would seem, then, that the terms 'marketing' and 'utopia' are completely contradictory, utterly opposed, the very mother of all oxymorons.

This chapter, however, will attempt to demonstrate that not only is marketing irredeemably utopian, but that this underpinning Arcadian urge provides a means of comprehending the copious alternative futures posited at the Marketing Eschatology Retreat, upon which this volume is based. In keeping with the time-honoured tripartite schema, our discussion commences with a potted history of Utopia; continues with a description of 'Marcadia', the utopian world that marketers inhabit; and concludes with a consideration of the Eschatology Retreat itself, which in many ways exemplified marketing's innate utopian propensity.

A SHORT HISTORY OF UTOPIA

If, as Nietzsche claims, only that which is without history can be defined, then Utopia lies far beyond definition, since it has a long, distinguished and disputatious history. Although the word was coined by Sir Thomas More in 1516, when he conflated the Greek terms *outopia* (no place) and *eutopia* (good place), the concept of a perfect world long predates the fictional island described by More's narrator, Raphael Hythloday. A paradisaical state is not only an essential element of the Judeo-Christian tradition, with its initial Garden of Eden and eventual City of God (not to mention the inter-regnum of earthly bliss that is the millennium), but it also forms part of our Greco-Roman heritage, be it Homer's Elysium, Plato's ideal city, Virgil's Arcadia or Hesiod's golden age (Manuel 1971a). Indeed, as Kumar (1991) makes clear, utopian-style milieux are a commonplace in most non-western cultures, though these tend to be religious or cosmological in character rather than codified in literary terms. Differences in forms of expression aside, and notwithstanding the risk of gross over-generalisation, it can be contended that just as the idea of the end of the world possesses universal appeal, so too the utopian predisposition is ubiquitous (Alexander and Gill 1984; Levitas 1990; Neville-Sington and Sington 1993; Levin 1994).

Regardless of their manifold forerunners, precursors and antecedents, it is generally accepted that Utopias, as distinctive literary genre, are a product of the Renaissance (Marin 1993). Stimulated in part by contemporaneous voyages of discovery – Columbus, Magellan, Vespucci, Drake, etc. – all manner of imaginary cities, valleys, islands, gardens and communities were explored in the wake of More's *Utopia* (Kumar 1987). Over the ensuing centuries, indeed, the realm of King Utopos expanded at an exponential rate, so to speak. According to the Manuels' magisterial compendium, utopianism flourished in the seventeenth and eighteenth centuries, reached its apex in the nineteenth, and has tended to decline somewhat in the twentieth. In all, they identify seven 'constellations' of utopian thought in the western tradition. These range from ancient and medieval wellsprings, of which the Joachimite age of the spirit is a prime example, through Christian and Enlightenment utopias, such as Bacon's *New Atlantis* and Campenella's *City of the Sun*, to the monumental endeavours of the great system builders of the industrial revolution like Comte, Saint-Simon and, above all, Marx (Manuel and Manuel 1979).

Clearly, the sheer number and staggering diversity of textual utopias, coupled with the very fluid boundaries of the genre, render any attempt at generalisation highly problematic. A host of typologies and classifications have been posited – soft utopias, hard utopias, sensate utopias, spiritual utopias, aristocratic utopias, plebeian utopias, collectivist utopias, individualist utopias and many more besides. Yet, despite the synoptic difficulties, it is arguable that three basic utopian forms, each of which is associated with a distinctive stage in the development of the literary corpus, can be discerned (see Manuel 1971b). The classical utopias of the Morean type tend to begin with a journey or departure, usually by sea, which is interrupted or diverted, often by a storm, and which enables the protagonist to stumble upon the utopia in question. Welcomed as a visitor, the narrator proceeds to describe the lineaments of the host society and the details of its day-to-day functioning. In complete contrast to the world that has been left behind, with all its sorrows, squabbles, discomforts, imperfections and unpleasantness, such societies are invariably happy, harmonious, congenial, content and perfect in almost every detail. Carefully planned, totally integrated and with every conceivable human need – food, shelter, social status, youth, beauty, sexual prowess, etc. – adequately catered for, the imagined society comprises a veritable heaven on earth, a place where time stands still, a haven from which the traveller has reluctantly returned to recount his tale, usually in the past narrative tense (Kumar 1991).

In addition to the travelogue variant of the utopian schema, as initiated by More, replicated by his innumerable imitators and modifications of which are still being written, the nineteenth century in particular witnessed the emergence of a second utopian form. Exemplified by the grand progressivist teleologies of Henri Saint-Simon, Auguste Comte and Karl Marx, with their respective reflections on 'industrial society', 'positive society' and 'communist society', these utopian visions share many of the characteristics of the archetypal first phase schema – harmony, integration, happiness, emancipation, communitarianism and an underpinning belief in the ultimate perfectibility of humankind. However, they also differ in several significant respects. In the first instance, detailed descriptions of the minutiae, the texture, the warp and weft of everyday life in the envisaged society are conspicuous by their absence. As Marx famously remarked on his contemptuous dismissal of such speculation, 'I write no recipes for the cookshops of the future.' Second, the societies being portrayed are not, in the main, confined to a limited geographical area, such as the blessed island or secret valley of the prototypical utopia. They tend, rather, to be much more ambitious – frequently universal or potentially universal – in their geographical scope. Third and most importantly, these depictions of the ideal society are not displaced in space (i.e. a hitherto undiscovered land, or isolated settlement, on the edge of the known world), but positioned at a future point in time.[2] Unlike the classic utopia, which deals with a perfect, albeit inaccessible, world *as it is*, the utopian theorists sketch a society as it *could*, *should* and, given the necessary commitment, *would* be (Bann 1993).

Although it has many antecedents, most notably Swift's *Gulliver's Travels* and Butler's *Erewhon*, the third category of utopia is primarily a product of the twentieth century. Variously described as dystopias, anti-utopias, counter-utopias, contra-topias, kakotopias and sub-topias, these comprise a complete inversion, a sort of grotesque mirror image, of the paradisaical original (Kumar 1987). Incarnated in celebrated works like Orwell's *1984*, Huxley's *Brave New World* and Zamyatin's *We*, not to mention the novels of J.G. Ballard or the cyberpunk strand of science fiction (Broderick 1995), such imagined societies are invariably nightmarish, desolate, terrifying, hostile, barbaric, totalitarian, regressive, anarchistic, pessimistic and utterly devoid of 'humanity', in its broadest sense. They offer, in short, 'a chilling vision of an alienated and enslaved world' (Kumar 1991: 27). So pervasive is this dystopic perspective indeed, that many commentators consider the twentieth century in general and the late-twentieth century in particular to be characterised by a wholesale retreat from utopia (Kumar 1995a). This capitulation is exemplified by the ignominious collapse of the great practical utopian experiments – principally those in the former Soviet empire – and the cynical posturing of postmodern intellectuals, who express nothing but absolute disdain for grand narratives, the Enlightenment project and the progressivist trajectory of modernity. In complete contrast to the optimistic, forward-looking, onward and upward ethos of the nineteenth-century utopians, a mood of dystopian negativity, entropy, ennui and ironic indifference now seems to prevail (Brown 1995; Kumar 1995b; Cahoone 1996).

Despite its latter-day buffeting and dramatic retreat from the intellectual high ground, the utopian predisposition remains very much alive. Contemporary utopias, however, tend to appeal to a *comparatively* limited constituency – feminism, ecology, drug culture, resurgent nationalism, new age religious and quasi-religious cults, etc. – or come in the form of the rose-tinted worlds of romantic fiction and television soap opera (Frankel 1987; Ayers 1993; Lebergott 1993; Relf 1993; Levin 1994). Even postmodernists offer a variation on the utopian theme with their 'vision of a neo-tribal paradise in which a set of spatially set forms of life carry on experiments, each in their own culture' (Lash and Friedman 1992: 1). By abandoning the high-modernist notion of a future paradise and, in effect, relocating utopia from a point in time to a place in space (e.g. cultures, movements, the body, local narratives), contemporary thinkers in many ways appear to be reverting to the older, pre-eighteenth-century, spatial forms of utopia, the type propounded by More and his countless disciples (Bann 1993).

MARCADIA POSTPONED

As a rule, commercial life rarely intrudes into literary utopias. Compared to the lengthy discussions of law, politics, religion, education, science, art, diet, customs, family affairs, social conditions and urban planning, utopian evocations of idealised marketing arrangements are few and far between. This reticence, it must be emphasised, is not simply another instance of the marketer's perennial complaint; the fact that everyone ignores, underrates or devalues the marketing system, despite its immense importance to the functioning of the economy as a whole. It tends, rather, to be overlooked in the utopian literature because commercial life in all its manifestations – buying, selling, borrowing, lending, forestalling, speculation, profiteering, cut-throat competition or whatever – is considered to be inimical to the good life. Marketing merely raises expectations, foments consumer desire, encourages frivolous or unwarranted expenditure and exploits pernicious human frailties like pride, sloth, cupidity, covetousness, greed, selfishness, concupiscence, fashion consciousness and so on (Campbell 1987; Berry 1994).

Marketing, in short, is considered to be part of the problem, not part of the utopian solution. Many literary utopias either circumvent the marketing system completely or assign its custodianship to the lowest orders of society. For example, in Cockaygne, the apocryphal poor man's heaven (akin to the 'Big Rock Candy Mountain' of the popular song), the rivers run with wine, a fountain of youth is permanently on tap and perfectly cooked morsels of food drop straight into the sybaritic inhabitants' mouths. In Aristotle's vision of the ideal city, trading-related activities are undertaken by 'those weakest in body and unfit for any other work'. In More's *Utopia*, such is the disdain for precious commodities and personal possessions that the principal use for gold, silver, jewels and suchlike is in the manufacture of spittoons and chamberpots. Similarly, the former travelling salesman, Charles Fourier – variously described as 'a madman' (Levin 1994: 26) and the 'greatest utopian after More' (Manuel 1971b:

132) – managed to find inspiration in the apparent iniquities of the marketing system. Struck by the exorbitant price of an apple in a Parisian shop, he concluded that existing socio-economic arrangements were hopelessly corrupt and thereafter devoted his life to the (ultimately unsuccessful) promulgation of an alternative utopian society known as the 'phalanstery' (Neville-Sington and Sington 1993).

Although, as Rooney (1985) has shown in his content analysis of ninety-one American utopias, the vast majority of authors either consider the marketing system to be a significant social problem or simply fail to discuss it in detail, there are at least two major exceptions to this general rule. Written at the end of the nineteenth century, Edward Bellamy's *Looking Backward* not only anticipates the modern credit card, champions the use of domestic servants and advocates unfettered competition (in the form of free trade), but it comprises an extended paean to the department store, then at the very height of its opulence and success. Bellamy's vision of a national store chain dispenses with the usual, substandard customer services provided by unsatisfactory sales personnel and replaces them with perfect clerks who process every order perfectly and thanks to whom satisfaction is invariably guaranteed. Equally detailed in its depiction of a marketing saturated society is Aldous Huxley's celebrated dystopia, *Brave New World.* Unbridled consumption, indeed, is deemed to be a vital social duty of its inhabitants, as is 'self-indulgence up to the very limits imposed by hygiene and economics. Otherwise the wheels stop turning.' Indoctrinated from birth by means of 'hypnopaedia', a process whereby slogans are repeated over and over again to infants as they sleep – and recalled during adulthood at moments of existential doubt concerning consumption – these aphorisms include 'we always throw away old clothes', 'ending is better than mending' and 'the more stitches, the less riches'.

While it is undeniable that Huxley's dystopian depiction of a society predicated on sex, drugs and naked hedonism is widely *read* as a utopia nowadays and Bellamy's prophetic novel, albeit today almost forgotten, proved to be one of the best-selling utopias of all time (a successful political movement, the Nationalists, sprang up in its wake and Bellamy himself was persuaded to stand for election), it is fair to conclude that utopian endorsements of the marketing system are conspicuous by their absence. For most utopians, and commentators on utopia, commercial life in all its forms comprises the complete antithesis of the good society, the perfect commonwealth, the utopian ideal. Thus, Marin famously described Disneyland as a 'degenerate utopia' (see Bann 1993); the McDonald's experience – McTopia – has been depicted in grotesque, nightmarish terms (O'Neill 1993); and Metrocentre, one of the largest shopping centres in Europe, damned as subtopia in Gateshead (Chaney 1990).

Disappointingly ubiquitous though it is, the utopians' manifest disdain for the marketing system is deeply ironic. The undeniable popularity and staggering commercial success of emblematic marketing institutions like Disneyland, McDonalds and Metrocentre, suggests that while they may not meet with the approval of the intellectual elite, they nonetheless perform an essentially utopian or quasi-utopian function for their countless satisfied customers. Such establishments, after all, comprise clean, safe, family-orientated fantasy environments which offer a momentary escape from the frustrations, imperfections and disappointments of everyday life. Granted, the brute reality of their crowds, queues and exorbitant prices is anything but utopian, yet the *image* they cultivate, circulate and rigidly control is nothing less than a contemporary Cockaygne, a latter-day Elysium, a Big Rock Candy Space Mountain. If, moreover, the very essence of marketing is the development, dissemination and manipulation of image, as many commentators maintain (Baudrillard 1988; York and Jennings 1995), then it follows that the *creation* of utopias, or utopian surrogates, is marketing's *raison d'être*. With its boundless ability to invent 'imaginary worlds of perfect appearances, perfect personal relationships, perfect families, perfect personalities, perfect careers, perfect holidays, perfect presents, perfect pizzas, perfectly pulled pints and perfect imperfections' (Brown 1995: 137), marketing more than any other contemporary cultural institution is arguably the keeper of the late-twentieth-century utopian flame.[3] The archetypal marketing utopias of fresh breath, clean clothing, shiny hair, safe sex and instant credit (aptly dubbed the 'never-never' by earlier generations of consumers) may be less grandiose than the visions of universal societal transformation propounded by the great nineteenth-century utopian prophets, but this too is very much in keeping with the low-key tenor of our chastened postmodern times (Kumar 1995b).

Just as the practices of marketing involve the creation, stimulation and exploitation of our utopian appetites – all the way from the impeccable 'dream world' of the department store, through the sale of products with a utopian pedigree (such as Oneida furniture or Kelloggs corn flakes), to the evanescent anal epiphany promised by advertisers of extra-soft toilet tissue – so too marketing theory and thought has a decidedly arcadian aspect. The very notion of a marketing orientation, with its ambition of perfectly satisfied, not to say delighted, customers, whose every conceivable want or need is anticipated, investigated and accommodated by perennially profitable companies, which are fully integrated around the marketing function and where careful analysis, planning, implementation and control are the orders of the day, is nothing less than a utopian hallucination that is utterly preposterous, some would say megalomaniac, in its ambition and scope. Call it what you will – Martopia, Maradise, Markeden, Marlennium, Marlysium, Markanadu, Marcanaan – but this Marcadian vision makes the world of *homo economicus* look positively naturalistic by comparison.

The utopian propensity within marketing thought is not of course confined to its overall ethos or orientation. On the contrary, marketing is suffused with utopianism at almost every level. It is apparent at the macro-level, in the form of the societal and generic marketing concepts (become a marketer and save the world or, if not, apply the metaphor to everything that moves); it is extant at the meso-level, as exemplified by the chimerical pursuit of a 'general theory' or the honorific appellation 'science' (the latter is doubly idealistic since science itself is irreparably utopian); it is discernible at the micro-level, in myriad pointless attempts to develop better, superior or more comprehensive marketing models (variations on the stages theory of internationalisation, product life cycle, strategic frameworks, hierarchy of advertising effects, etc.); and it is all too evident at the honey-I-shrunk-the-discipline level (almost anything written by Malcolm McDonald or Shelby Hunt).

Even marketing's inordinate fondness for importing concepts from adjacent disciplines is infused with utopian inclinations, whether it be Maslow's familiar hierarchy of needs, B.F. Skinner's (consumer) behaviourist paradigm, Kotler's three levels of marketing consciousness or the work of the renowned retailing theorist, Malcolm P. McNair. Maslow was a well-known eupsychic, Skinner wrote a best-selling utopia, *Walden Two*, Kotler's consciousness raising is clearly indebted to the likes of Teilhard de Chardin and McNair was profoundly affected by the work of fellow Bostonian-cum-retailing enthusiast, Edward Bellamy. Perhaps the most striking conceptual example of marketing utopianism, however, is found in those ubiquitous textbook diagrams of marketing functions or marketing's co-ordinating role within the firm (Figure 14.1). Circular, concentric and symmetrical, sometimes with radial elements, these are an almost exact replica of utopian representations of the ideal city, most notably Campenella's city of the sun. Of course, in their modern marketing equivalent, that which is most sacred – the customer – occupies the very centre of the circle and this holy-of-holies is surrounded by functionally sub-divided zones of steadily decreasing significance, over which control is less easily exercised or exercisable.

It almost goes without saying that this utopian inclination within marketing is largely attributable to American hegemony. The marketing academy is

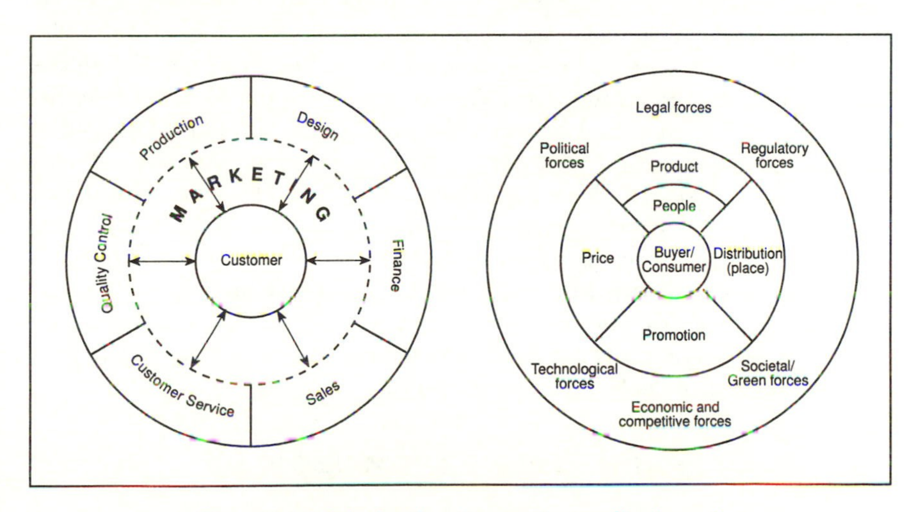

Figure 14.1 Marketing functions and co-ordinating role
Sources: Brown 1987; Dibb *et al.* 1994

completely dominated by North American scholarship, much to the annoyance of certain Europeans (Gummesson 1993), and as utopianism has had an enormously important influence upon America's self-image and worldview – Pilgrim fathers, Declaration of Independence, Mormon Trek, nineteenth-century model communities, light unto the nations, Land of the Free, etc. etc. etc. – it is perhaps not surprising that this penchant has insinuated itself deeply into marketing thought. Indeed, when the history of modern American marketing scholarship is examined, the three-stage developmental schema of utopianism, previously described, can be readily discerned.[4] It is blindly obvious, for example, that the earliest postwar explications of the marketing concept, such as those by Keith (1960) and McKitterick (1958), are absolute exemplars of the Morean blessed isle, traveller's tale, speaking picture, utopian tradition. They describe, usually in the past narrative tense, a single, isolated company that has miraculously found the secret of success in business, where customers are sated, profits illimitable and everything in the garden of marketing delights is rosy. The basic message, in effect, is that Marcadia *exists*, albeit somewhere over the rainbow.

In a similar vein, the universal, progressivist, 'someday my prince will come', second stage of marketing utopianism is apparent in the 'broadening' debate of the 1970s and the subsequent 'globalisation' hypothesis (Kotler and Levy 1969; Luck 1969; Kotler 1972; Levitt 1983). Here, the gates of Marcadia were thrown open to every sphere of activity – profit, not-for-profit, societal and so on – though the ultimate paradise of marketing orientation (or world domination!) was carefully positioned at a future point in time and only available to those who wish hard enough, *really*, *really* believe in it and are prepared to live by the all-important magic words, 'the customer is always right' (e.g. Figure 14.2). Of late, moreover, the third, dystopian, 'we're on the road to nowhere' stage of marketing development has come very much to the fore. Apart from the advent of 'shock-horror' advertising campaigns (e.g. Benetton) and the imperialistic, not to say totalitarian, propensity that undergirds concepts like 'internal marketing' (Whittington and Whipp 1992), the intellectual and philosophical premises of the discipline itself are being attacked on all fronts (e.g. Piercy 1992; Wensley 1990, 1995; Firat and Venkatesh 1993; Doyle 1995). Indeed, it is no exaggeration to state that the shiny second-phase vision of a marketing millennium – an eschaton of marketing orientation that will eventually come to pass – has been superseded by a somewhat retrospective inclination. We now look back on the late 1960s as a sort of golden age, a pre-lapidarian marketing paradise, a garden of markeden, from which today's academic backsliders have been forever and no doubt deservedly expelled.

THE RETREAT FROM UTOPIA

The trajectory of modern marketing thought may parallel the evolution of utopianism, from imagined other, through teleological consummation, to de-

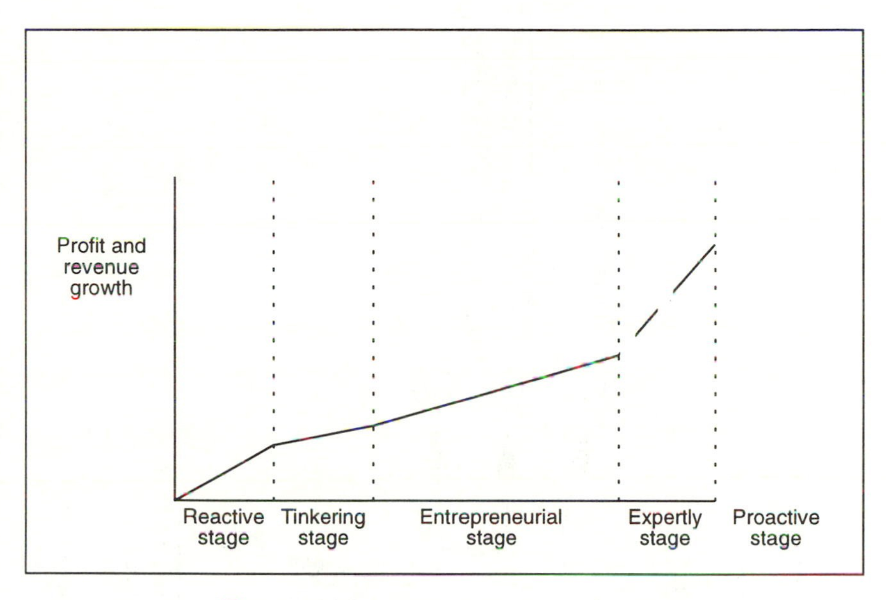

Figure 14.2 The growth of marketing in the firm
Source: Carson 1985

featist abandon, but the retreat from Marcadia is by no means complete. Just as the utopian proclivity still survives in the late-twentieth century, albeit in a fragmented, decentred, spatially circumscribed form, so too cornucopian visions of the land of marketing milk and honey continue to circulate. In keeping with contemporary conceptions of utopia, these tend to appeal to a *comparatively* limited constituency – critical theory, aesthetics, feminism, ecology and the like – and are essentially spatial rather than temporal in orientation. Perhaps the clearest example of this propensity is found in the relationship marketing paradigm, which, while far from universally espoused, is probably the most heavily-backed runner in today's Marcadian Derby. As Figure 14.3 indicates, the elements of the prototypical relationship marketing network are invariably placed in a distinctive spatial arrangement around the hub of the system, though the latter may be absent or decentred, as in the oft-cited case of so-called 'hollow' corporations. This spatial arrangement, what is more, carries clear paradisaical connotations since it patently resembles the radiating rays of numinous celestial light that have for centuries signified heaven, saints, angels and spiritual enlightenment in countless artistic representations of the godhead. It is, in short, a marchetype.

Although relationship marketing is worshipped by many marcadians at present, not least on account of its ostensibly communal, co-operative, egalitarian ethos of all-pervasive harmony, it is not the only serpent in the Garden of Markeden. A glance through the preceding chapters in this book reveals all manner of

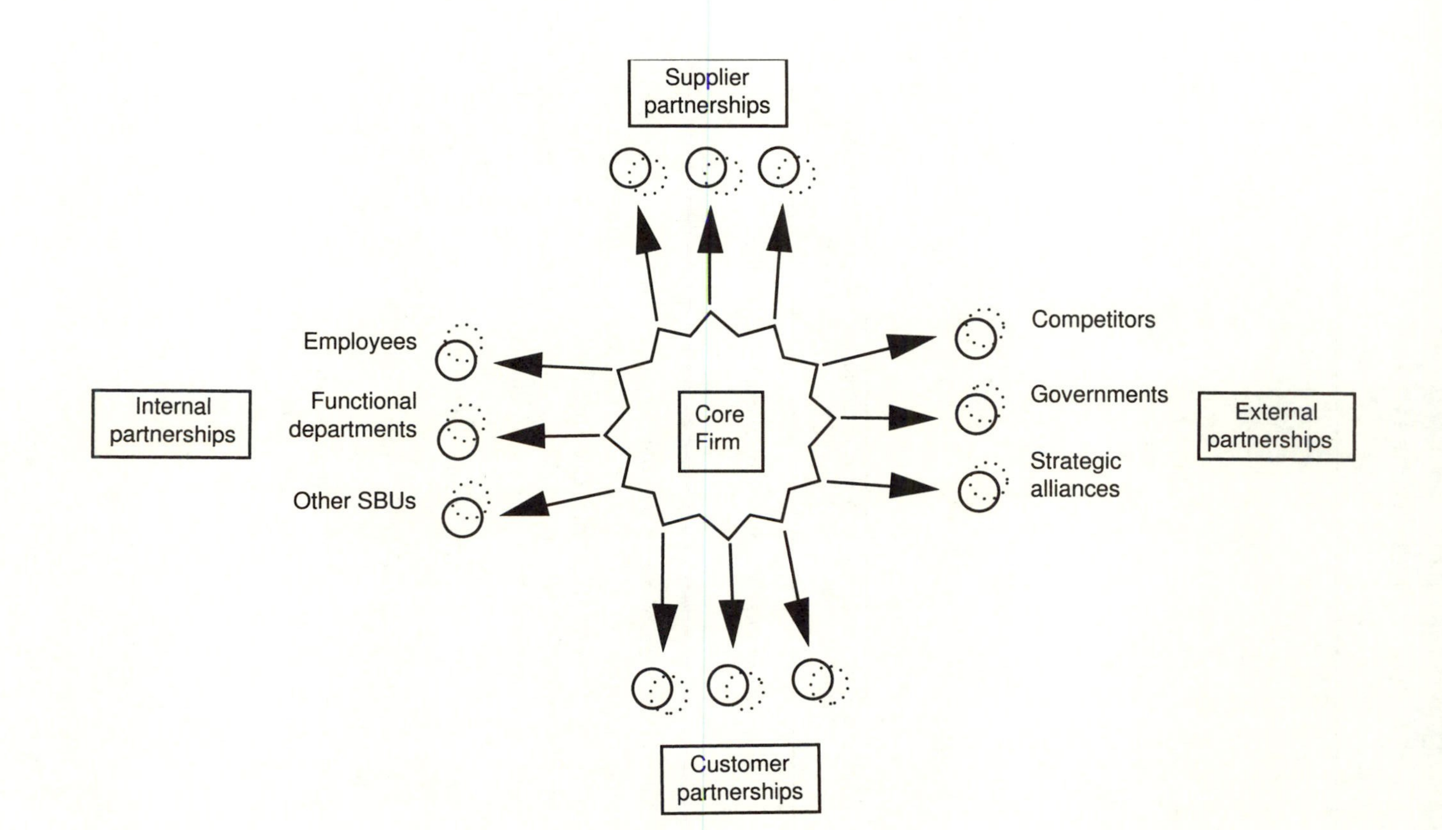

Figure 14.3 Relationship marketing
Source: Adapted from Doyle 1995

Martopian possibilities – Brown's postmodern Pandemonium, McDonagh and Prothero's eco-friendly resurrection, Belk's heavenly hope, Brownlie and Desmond's con-artist manifesto, Heilbrunn's narratological teleology, Kent's phenomenological paradise, Buttimer and Kavanagh's Elysium of the extreme, Teilhard de Hetzel's marnoösphere, Thomas's crusade for scientific respectability, O'Donohoe's ethnographic Erewhon, Catterall *et al.*'s feminist *fatwa*, Holbrook's catalogical cataclysm and, not least, Brown and Maclaran's hopelessly idealistic notion of Marcadia. This is not the place to criticise or deconstruct these utopian options, though an attempt to reveal the hidden truth about such attempts to reveal the hidden truth about the hidden truth of marketing – a sort of marketing tripocalypse – would be very much in keeping with the spirit of the present volume. Indeed, critics, cynics and casual readers may well conclude that for a book which set out to dance on the grave of marketing, this text has simply served to celebrate the discipline's continuing rude health.

Legitimate though it is, such an interpretation overlooks the essential point about terminal visions *per se*. The very act of exploring the ostensible final frontier permits us, in effect, to boldly go where no-one has gone before (and split the infinitive for good measure). It opens up hitherto occluded academic vistas, offers tantalising glimpses of scholarly oases, shimmering through the heat-haze on the intellectual horizon, and, by raising the exhilarating possibility of closure only to eclipse it with a new beginning, succeeds in temporarily elevating us from the quotidian round of routine research to the eternal realm of the transcendent. Granted, this suggestion of a metaphysical marketing moment may strike many readers as postmodern posturing at its most preposterous, but it was discernible during the Marketing Eschatology Retreat, from whence this volume derives. As anyone who attended the gathering will willingly testify, it comprised a three-day idyll of academic accomplishment and harmonious co-existence, interspersed with periodic visitations of awe-struck wonder, occasional flashes of rapture and fleeting episodes of communal communion. Much of this Arcadian atmosphere was doubtless attributable to the venue (Figure 14.4). Set high on a hill, in a seemingly isolated, otherworldly location, which is reached by a long and winding approach road through verdant, pastoral surroundings, St Clement's is a place dedicated to worship and contemplation, a cosmic off-cut, a slice from the sublime, a veritable piece of heaven on earth. Be that as it may, for many delegates the Marketing Eschatology Retreat was nothing less than a utopian experience where, according to one attendee, time stood still (Wright 1995). Another stated that it 'restored my faith in what I thought academic life was all about' (Rees 1995). And yet another, appropriately enough, was moved to adapt the ringing declaration of that great nineteenth-century utopian, Karl Marx, 'marketing academics of the world unite, you have nothing to lose but your chains' (Stevens 1995).

In retrospect, perhaps the most remarkable thing about the Retreat from Utopia was the total unanimity that the end of marketing was *not* nigh. Despite the conference theme and the apocalyptic 'call for papers', not a single speaker,

Figure 14.4 St Clement's Retreat House

out of twenty-six in total, concluded that marketing *had* attained its eschaton. On the contrary, the event was more akin to a eulogy than an elegy. Marketing was not only alive and well, it was kicking! Naturally, this atmosphere of utopian euphoria could simply be dismissed as sectarian self-interest – are marketing academics *really* prepared to pull the ontological rug from under their own feet? – but the attendant air of intellectual intoxication was so palpable that an alternative explanation must be sought. In this respect, it is worthwhile recalling a famous 1950s study of an apocalyptic sect that anticipated the imminent end of the world, *When Prophesy Fails*. Although Festinger *et al.*'s (1956) work has been severely criticised on ethical grounds – the researchers secretly infiltrated the cult and directly participated in the events as they unfolded – the exercise produced some compelling findings. The most intriguing of these was that when the prophesied cataclysm failed to occur on the expected day, the faith of the membership was *not* dented, disillusionment did *not* set in and, contrary to expectation, the disappointed believers did *not* disperse in disarray. Quite the reverse. Their belief in themselves and the imminence of the (inexplicably delayed) end was *reinforced*. So much so, that they redoubled their proselytising activities thereafter. Thus, in spite of the clear disconfirming evidence, the adepts responded with renewed vigour, with increased conviction and an overwhelming desire to convince the sceptics of the righteousness of their cause.

If these findings are accepted at face value – and several studies of end-times movements have come to much the same conclusions (Hamilton 1995) – the implications for marketing are clear. After Festinger, it can be contended that in spite of the ample, some would say overwhelming, evidence of the utter failure of marketing, of its intellectual bankruptcy, of its manifold inadequacies, of its incipient end, true believers will respond to the evidence of disconfirmation with optimism, with renewed vigour, with the absolute conviction that marketing – its miscalculations and errors of omission notwithstanding – is *still* a worthwhile pursuit. Thus, it is arguable that the enthusiasm expressed at the Eschatology Retreat is the clearest evidence yet that the end of marketing *has* occurred. Just as Shelby Hunt (1976) assumed he was celebrating marketing's coming of age when he was actually presiding over its Last Rights, so too the academic fanfares blown at the Eschatology Retreat were in fact marketing's Last Post – marketing's at long last post.[5]

CONCLUSION

Although it is easy to dismiss the entire corpus of utopian thought as mere works of fiction, as figments of overactive literary imaginations, as irrelevant to the everyday concerns of marketing academics and practitioners, it is nevertheless possible to extract some suitably apocalyptic conclusions from the marcadian retreat. When the unfolding historical drama of utopianism is examined, it is fair to say that marketing does not play a leading role. If anything, indeed, it is presented as the villain of the piece rather than the romantic hero. Although this antagonistic view of the marketing system is very much in keeping with the western intellectual tradition, such utopia myopia overlooks the positive side of marketing, the fact that despite the torrent of abuse heaped upon its head (often justifiably), it is a vitally necessary intermediary between production and consumption. In addition to this functional argument, however, it is apparent that utopianism pervades much of marketing practice and thought. Like it or not, our late-twentieth-century vision of the good life is either a marketing creation (Disneyland, Las Vegas) or mediated by marketing (the product as passport to an imagined world) or indeed both. What, after all, is the holiday 'promise' of Club 18–30 but a sexual utopia of the most lurid, licentious and lascivious kind? Marketing concepts and principles are no less paradisaical since they envisage perfect organisations with carefully co-ordinated marketing mixes, minutely detailed marketing plans, totally amicable inter-functional relationships, meticulously executed competitive strategies and absolutely unshakable customer orientated convictions. Mainstream marketing academics may not be prepared to admit it, but these portrayals are just as fantastic, fanciful and far-fetched as the marcadia, the martopia, the 'lovely-land' that is marketed to the masses (York and Jennings 1995).

If, in short, the vast majority of today's utopias are marketing inflected and the most active disseminators of contemporary visions of 'the perfect family', 'the ideal society' and, not least, 'the customer-orientated organisation' are marketing practitioners and theorists, then it follows that the utopians' longstanding disdain for the marketing system is somewhat misplaced, to put it mildly. It can quite legitimately be argued that utopia is no longer lost and found, it is bought and sold.

For many late-twentieth-century commentators, however, the rise of marketing-saturated consumer society is less an exemplar of the 'good place' version of utopia than the 'no place' *dystopian* propensity. In fact, it is fair to say that, for the current generation of intellectuals, the very concept of utopia is hopelessly compromised and irredeemably tainted. Thanks to the barbarities perpetrated in pursuit of the ideal society – Auschwitz, the Gulag, Tiananmen Square, ethnic cleansing, etc. – today's thinkers are increasingly inclined to stress the dark, dictatorial, totalitarian, fascistic side of the utopian impulse. Even Oscar Wilde's celebrated panegyric to utopia is readily interpretable in imperialistic terms – 'a map of the world that does not include utopia is not worth even glancing at, for it leaves out the country at which humanity is always landing. And when humanity lands there, it looks out, and, seeing a better country, sets sail. Progress is the realisation of utopias.'

Nevertheless, as Wilde also implies, it is arguable that the fundamental problem with utopia is not the vision itself. On the contrary, dreams of utopia are important and necessary. They are a call to metaphorical (and often literal) arms. According to Levitas (1990), indeed, utopianism is part of the collective unconscious and represents a deep-seated need within humankind to strive for perfection, for something better, for something above and beyond the sadly deficient all-too-imperfect present. It is, in effect, a primal urge that dates from the dawn of history and which is made manifest in many ways, shapes and forms ranging from the colony of hermaphrodite nudists envisaged by a seventeenth-century monk, Gabriel de Foigny, to the prospect of untold wealth and happiness currently obtainable for the paltry price of a National Lottery ticket. Most importantly of all perhaps, utopias perform a vital didactic function. They not only offer an arresting vision of future possibilities, but because they tend to be written in the past narrative tense, also imply that their depiction of the good life, an ideal world, is eminently attainable. It has already been achieved. The future is past. But – and this is a very big but – the history of utopianism clearly demonstrates that every attempt to enact, attain or realise a utopian vision has failed and failed ignominiously. Utopias, in fact, *can't* be achieved because a utopia achieved is no longer a utopia (Kumar 1993; Baudrillard 1994).

Despite the cavils of dyspeptic postmodern intellectuals, and the sorry history of utopianism, it can be contended that marketing and the marketing concept are compelling utopias, utopias that are truly astonishing in their attraction and power, utopias that dominate our lives both as commentators on and participants in the marketing system. *Marketing, indeed, can be defined as the production, distribution and consumption of utopias.* However, if the trajectory of utopian thought teaches us anything it is that a utopia realised is a recipe for disaster. It follows that the implementation of the marketing concept is the very worst thing that can happen to a firm. It is unrealistic; it is impracticable; it is unattainable; it is the kiss of death, a poisoned chalice, a suicide mission, a kind of

Kotler-kazi. Granted, this conclusion may strike many marketing academics as a gross heresy, yet it merely corroborates what numerous commentators are saying about the marketing concept (see Brownlie and Saren 1992; Carson *et al.* 1995). By all means let us adopt a marketing orientation, but an 'orientation' – in the sense of a general direction or heading – is all it should ever be. As none other than Peter Drucker (1994: 102–3) points out in an analogous conclusion, 'A theory of the business always becomes obsolete when an organisation attains its original objectives. Attaining one's objectives, then, is not cause for celebration; it is cause for new thinking.' It is, as they say, better to travel in hope than to arrive.

In these circumstances, perhaps it is time we stopped berating organisations for adopting the trappings rather than the substance of marketing. Perhaps companies succeed *despite* not because of marketing. Perhaps *marketing* is the cause of marketing's current sea of troubles. Perhaps, and this is the most disconcerting possibility of all, the real problem is not that marketing has never been properly implemented, as its apologists proclaim, but that it has been *too* successful. Marcadia *has* been attained, but it is no paradise. The hidden truth, then, about marketing is that it is not the truth. It is a dream, an escape, a mirage, an illusion, an ideology, a teleological end which when realised proves eschatological. Marketing apocalypse is neither imminent nor immanent; it is immaterial.

NOTES

1 One of the authors (SB) once heard a marketing practitioner describe himself as 'horny-handed and hairy-arsed'. Presumably, we can conclude that most academics are 'hairy-handed and horny-arsed'.

2 It should be pointed out that a number of first phase, Morean-style utopias are set in the future (the protagonist falls asleep and wakes up in a new world), but unlike second phase representations, which tend to be processual and dynamic in ethos, these future societies are essentially static and unchanging. They have already attained perfection.

3 A strong case could also be made for Hollywood movies, glossy magazines, popular music and certain television programmes, though the distinction between these imagined worlds and the ones created by marketing is not clear cut (product placement in films, etc.).

4 This three stage periodising schema should not be taken too literally. It seeks to describe the *dominant* or *representative* marcadian form during each era, not the only one. As with the utopian literature generally, variations on the 'blessed isle' schema continue to appear, the broadeners are still abroad and dystopian discussions of marketing crises have a very long ancestry. A potentially useful way of conceptualising this seemingly discontinuous continuity is in terms of Raymond Williams' (1980) suggestion that there are always three moments within a particular cultural form – 'dominant', 'emergent' and 'residual' – which change and mutate in keeping with evolving historical or environmental circumstances.

5 Of course, any apocalyptics foolish enough to contend that marketing *is* actually ending and that academic marketers' continuing enthusiasm is merely a dissonant response to failure and defeat, are themselves in danger of having *their* end of marketing prediction disconfirmed, with all the ensuing dissonance. It is ending, you know. It *is*. It is! IT IS!! Well, this book is anyway . . .

REFERENCES

Alexander, P. and Gill, R. (1984), *Utopias*, Duckworth, London.
Ayers, D. (1993), '"Politics here is death": William Borroughs's *Cities of the Red Night*', in K. Kumar and S. Bann (eds), *Utopias and the Millennium*, Reaktion, London, pp. 90–106.
Bann, S. (1993), 'Introduction', in K. Kumar, and S. Bann, (eds), *Utopias and the Millennium*, Reaktion, London, pp. 1–6.
Baudrillard, J. (1988), *Jean Baudrillard: Selected Writings*, ed. M. Poster, Blackwell, Oxford.
Baudrillard, J. (1994), *The Illusion of the End*, Polity, Cambridge.
Berry, C.J. (1994), *The Idea of Luxury*, Cambridge University Press, Cambridge.
Broderick, D. (1995), *Reading by Starlight: Postmodern Science Fiction*, Routledge, London.
Brown, R. (1987), 'Marketing – a function and a philosophy', *The Quarterly Review of Marketing*, 13 (Spring–Summer), pp. 25–30.
Brown, S. (1995), *Postmodern Marketing*, Routledge, London.
Brownlie, D. and Saren, M. (1992), 'The four Ps of the marketing concept: prescriptive, polemical, permanent and problematical', *European Journal of Marketing*, 26 (4), pp. 34–47.
Cahoone, L. (1996), *From Modernism to Postmodernism: An Anthology*, Blackwell, Oxford.
Campbell, C. (1987), *The Romantic Ethic and the Spirit of Modern Consumerism*, Blackwell, Oxford.
Carson, D.J. (1985), 'The evolution of marketing in small firms', *The European Journal of Marketing*, 19 (5), pp. 7–16.
Carson, D.J., Gilmore, A. and Maclaran, P. (1995), 'To Hell with the customer, where's the profit?', in S. Brown *et al.* (eds), *Proceedings of the Marketing Eschatology Retreat*, University of Ulster, Belfast, pp. 72–81.
Chaney, D. (1990), 'Dystopia in Gateshead: the Metrocentre as a cultural form', *Theory, Culture and Society*, 7 (4), pp. 49–68.
Dibb, S., Simpkin, L., Pride, W.M. and Ferrell, O.C. (1994), *Marketing: Concepts and Strategies*, Houghton Mifflin, Boston.
Doyle, P. (1995), 'Marketing in the new millennium', *The European Journal of Marketing*, 29 (13), pp. 23–41.
Enzensberger, H.M. (1978), 'Two notes on the end of the world', *New Left Review*, 110 (July–August), pp. 74–80.
Festinger, L., Reicken, H.W. and Schachter, S. (1956), *When Prophesy Fails: A Social and Psychological Study of a Modern Group that Predicted the Destruction of the World*, Harper and Row, New York.
Firat, A.F. and Venkatesh, A. (1993), 'Postmodernity – the age of marketing', *International Journal of Research in Marketing*, 10 (3), pp. 227–49.
Frankel, B. (1987), *The Post-industrial Utopians*, Polity, Cambridge.
Gummesson, E. (1993), 'Marketing according to textbooks: six objections', in D. Brownlie *et al.* (eds), *Rethinking Marketing: New Perspectives on the Discipline and Profession*, Warwick Business School Research Bureau, Coventry, pp. 248–58.
Hamilton, M.B. (1995), *The Sociology of Religion*, Routledge, London.
Hunt, S.D. (1976), 'The nature and scope of marketing', *Journal of Marketing*, 40 (July), pp. 17–28.
Keith, R.J. (1960), 'The marketing revolution', *Journal of Marketing*, 24 (January), pp. 35–8.
Kotler, P. (1972), 'A generic concept of marketing', *Journal of Marketing*, 36 (April), pp. 46–54.
Kotler, P. and Levy, S.J. (1969), 'Broadening the concept of marketing', *Journal of Marketing*, 33 (January), pp. 10–15.
Kumar, K. (1987), *Utopia and Anti-Utopia in Modern Times*, Blackwell, Oxford.

Kumar, K. (1991), *Utopianism*, Open University Press, Milton Keynes.
Kumar, K. (1993), 'The end of Socialism? The end of Utopia? The end of History?', in K. Kumar and S. Bann (eds), *Utopias and the Millennium*, Reaktion, London, pp. 63–80.
Kumar, K. (1995a), 'Apocalypse, millennium and utopia today', in M. Bull (ed.), *Apocalypse Theory and the Ends of the World*, Blackwell, Oxford, pp. 200–24.
Kumar, K. (1995b), *From Post-industrial to Post-modern Society*, Blackwell, Oxford.
Lash, S. and Friedman, J. (1992), *Modernity and Identity*, Blackwell, Oxford.
Lebergott, S. (1993), *Pursuing Happiness: American Consumers in the Twentieth Century*, Princeton University Press, Princeton.
Levin, B. (1994), *A World Elsewhere*, Jonathan Cape, London.
Levitas, R. (1990), *The Concept of Utopia*, Philip Allan, New York.
Levitt, T. (1983), 'The globalisation of markets', *Harvard Business Review*, 61 (May–June), reprinted in *Levitt on Marketing*, Harvard Business School Press, Boston, pp. 39–49.
Luck, D.J. (1969), 'Broadening the concept of marketing – too far', *Journal of Marketing*, 33 (July), pp. 53–5.
Manuel, F.E. (1971a), 'The golden age: a mythic prehistory for western utopia', in F.E. Manuel, *Freedom From History and Other Untimely Essays*, New York University Press, New York, pp. 69–88.
Manuel, F.E. (1971b), 'Toward a psychological history of utopias', in F.E. Manuel, *Freedom From History and Other Untimely Essays*, New York University Press, New York, pp. 115–48.
Manuel, F.E. and Manuel, F.P. (1979), *Utopian Thought in the Western World*, Belknap, Cambridge.
Marin, L. (1993), 'The frontiers of utopia', in K. Kumar and S. Bann (eds), *Utopias and the Millennium*, Reaktion, London, pp. 7–16.
McKitterick, J.B. (1957), 'What is the marketing management concept?', in F.M. Bass (ed.), *The Frontiers of Marketing Thought and Science*, American Marketing Association, Chicago, pp. 71–82.
Neville-Sington, P. and Sington, D. (1993), *Paradise Dreamed: How Utopian Thinkers Have Changed the Modern World*, Bloomsbury, London.
O'Neill, J. (1993), 'McTopia: eating time', in K. Kumar and S. Bann (eds), *Utopias and the Millennium*, Reaktion, London, pp. 129–37.
Piercy, N. (1992), *Market-led Strategic Change*, Butterworth-Heinemann, Oxford.
Rees, P. (1995), personal communication.
Relf, J. (1993), 'Utopia the good breast: coming home to mother', in K. Kumar and S. Bann (eds), *Utopias and the Millennium*, Reaktion, London, pp. 107–28.
Rooney, C.J. (1985), *Dreams and Visions: A Study of American Utopias, 1865–1917*, Greenwood Press, Westport.
Stevens, L. (1995), 'The witches of St. Clement's', unpublished manuscript.
Wensley, R. (1990), 'The voice of the consumer?: speculations on the limits of the marketing analogy', *The European Journal of Marketing*, 24 (7), pp. 49–60.
Wensley, R. (1995), 'A critical review of research in marketing', *British Journal of Management*, 6 (December), pp. S63–S82.
Whittington, R. and Whipp, R. (1992), 'Professional ideology and marketing implementation', *European Journal of Marketing*, 26 (1), pp. 52–63.
Williams, R. (1980), *Problems in Materialism and Culture*, Verso, London.
Wright, S. (1995), personal communication.
York, P. and Jennings, C. (1996), *Peter York's Eighties*, BBC Books, London.

NAME INDEX

Note: page numbers in italics refer to figures or illustrations

SUBJECT INDEX

Note: page numbers in italics refer to figures or illustrations